THE LAW OF RIVERS AND WATERCOURSES

THE LAW OF
RIVERS AND WATERCOURSES

by

A. S. WISDOM, Solicitor

FOURTH EDITION

LONDON:
Printed and Published by
SHAW & SONS LTD.
Shaway House,
Lower Sydenham, SE26 5AE
1979

B

First Published		...	May 1962
2nd Edition	...	...	October 1970
3rd Edition	...	...	February 1976
4th Edition	...	...	August 1979

SBN 7219 0082 8

Thames Water

Nugent House, Vastern Road,
Reading. Berks. RG1 8DB.

Telephone Direct Line: Reading (0734) 593
Switchboard: Reading (0734) 593333

STU

with compliments

PREFACE TO THE FOURTH EDITION

The object of this book is to summarise, within a reasonably confined but comprehensive compass, the law relating to rivers, water and watercourses.

Rivers are either tidal or non-tidal, navigable or not, give rise to the enjoyment of natural and acquired rights, and may in part flow underground or through artificial channels, and the arrangement of the earlier chapters has been influenced by these factors. Since any legal work on watercourses which ignored ferries, freshwater and sea fisheries, the sea and tidal environment, water resources, land drainage and pollution prevention would be incomplete, these subjects are dealt with in the succeeding chapters. Nor have lakes, ponds and percolating water been overlooked.

Water law entered upon a further phase once the Water Act 1973 wrought profound changes in water policy and management through the establishment of regional water authorities which replaced river authorities and water boards and took over the sewerage, sewage disposal and water supply services of local authorities.

Since then there has emerged a series of statutes codifying major sectors of functional law—the Salmon and Freshwater Fisheries Act 1975, the Land Drainage Act 1976, and shortly Part II of the Control of Pollution Act 1974 will in effect replace with improvements the provisions of the Rivers (Prevention of Pollution) Acts 1951 to 1961. These Acts are included in this edition and readers wishing to consult the Rivers (Prevention of Pollution) Acts 1951 to 1961 should refer to the third edition.

Other statutes and new case law affecting water have been included.

The law is that as stated on the 1st March 1979.

A.S.W.

COLEHILL,
DORSET.
1979.

CONTENTS

TABLE OF STATUTES

		PAGE
20 & 21 Geo.	Land Drainage Act, 1930	37, 211
5, c. 44.	s. 36 (1)	41
	s. 38...	10
22 & 23 Geo.	Thames Conservancy Act, 1932—	
5, c. xxxvii.	s. 77...	63
	s. 79...	60
	s. 97...	81
24 & 25 Geo.	Petroleum (Production) Act, 1934	18
5, c. 36.		
26 Geo. 5 &	Public Health Act, 1936—	
Edw. 8, c.	s. 14...	161
49.	s. 15...	233
	s. 16...	161
	s. 27...	346
	s. 30...	3, 349
	s. 31...	349
	s. 39...	346
	s. 48...	346
	s. 81...	346
	s. 82...	346
	s. 92...	346
	s. 108 (2)	346
	s. 140	344
	s. 141	346
	s. 231	28
	s. 259	98, 346
	(1)	50
	s. 260	50
	s. 261	50, 346
	s. 262	41, 50
	s. 263	51
	s. 264	41, 51
	s. 265	51
	s. 266	51
	s. 278	349
	s. 322	349
	s. 343 (1)	49
	Part XI	3, 49, 51
1 Edw. 8 & 1	Diseases of Fish Act, 1937	300
Geo. 6, c.	s. 1	300
33.	s. 2	301
	s. 3	301
	s. 4	301
	s. 8	302
	s. 10 (1)	281
	s. 13...	300
1 Edw. 8 & 1	Public Health (Drainage of Trade Premises) Act, 1937 ...	335
Geo. 6, c. 40.		346, 349
1 & 2 Geo. 6,	Administration of Justice (Miscellaneous Provisions)	
c. 63.	Act, 1938—	
	s. 9	150
2 & 3 Geo. 6,	Limitation Act, 1939—	
c. 21.	s. 2 (1) (d)	226
	s. 4 (1), (3)	25
	s. 27...	226
	(6)	226

TABLE OF CASES

A

[xxxiii]

PAGE

L

N

Q

TABLE OF CASES

S

TABLE OF STATUTORY INSTRUMENTS

The Law of
Rivers and Watercourses

CHAPTER 1

INTRODUCTION TO RIVERS AND WATERCOURSES

RIVERS AND WATERCOURSES DEFINED

Rivers in general

The difference between a river, tributary, watercourse, stream or ditch is largely one of degree measured by the size, length and breadth of the watercourse in question. In the legal sense also, there is no particular difference between any of these descriptive terms, since all are equally capable of giving rise to riparian and prescriptive rights, except in the case of temporary artificial watercourses and percolating water. Distinctions do abound, however, as will be related in succeeding chapters, between tidal and non-tidal rivers and navigable and non-navigable waterways.

A river or watercourse must have a natural source, such as a spring, lake or initial tributaries, and then flow in a certain direction along a more or less defined channel consisting of the bed and banks or shores, until it terminates in tidal waters or joins another river.

The primary essentials of a river are its bed, the banks and the water flowing therein, and it is also necessary to consider:—

(1) The catchment area of the river which comprises the total extent of its natural drainage basin within which lie the tributaries and feeder streams discharging into the parent river or river system.

(2) The uses and functions of the river and its tributaries for the various purposes of agriculture, fisheries, industry, water supply, transport, navigation, drainage, milling, ballast, boating, recreation, public health and amenities, etc. It is neither useful nor practicable to classify these purposes, but they all involve either

[1]

(a) the user or application of the water when within the confines of the river channel, i.e. for fishing, navigation, boating, etc.; (b) the employment of water abstracted or diverted from the river for agriculture, domestic uses, water supplies or industry (for cooling or processing purposes); or (c) the discharge of trade or sewage effluents or surface water into the river.

(3) Since the passing of the Water Resources Act, 1963, water contained in underground strata must be taken into account, particularly from the point of view of its abstraction, its prevention of pollution (and purity), and the contribution it may afford in providing water to meet future demands. Surface and underground water sources are linked to the extent that rivers obtain underground water through their banks and bed, and, conversely, a proportion of river flow may be lost to underground strata by percolation through the bed or banks. The presence of water bearing strata by no means coincides with the extent of a river catchment basin.

Legal writers in former times had no difficulty in defining rivers and watercourses. *Woolrych*[1] referred to a river as a running stream pent in on either side with walls and banks, and bearing that name where the waters flow and reflow, as where they have their current one way. *Angell*[2] defined a watercourse as a body of water issuing *ex jure* from the earth, and by the same law pursuing a certain direction in a defined channel, until it found a confluence with tidal water.

Statutory definitions of a river and watercourse

From the point of view of various statutes relating to rivers and water, there is no particular distinction to be drawn between the expressions " river ", " stream ", " watercourse " and kindred terms.

Section 116 (1) of the Land Drainage Act, 1976, defines " watercourse " as including " all rivers, streams, ditches, drains, cuts, culverts, dikes, sluices, sewers (other than public

---

[1] *Woolrych* on Waters, 31.
[2] *Angell* on Watercourses, 2.

sewers within the meaning of the Public Health Act, 1936) and passages through which water flows ". A similar interpretation is contained in the Water Act, 1945, section 59 (1) and Schedule 3, section 1. Section 41 of the Land Drainage Act, 1976, contains a restricted definition of " ditch " as including a culverted and piped ditch but not including a watercouse vested in or under the control of a drainage body.

Section 30 of the Public Health Act, 1936, refers to " any natural or artificial stream, watercourse, canal, pond or lake " and Part XI of the same Act variously employs the terms " ditch ", " watercourse " and " stream " without specifically defining them. Under section 56(1) of the Control of Pollution Act, 1974, " stream " includes any river, stream, watercourse or inland water (whether natural or artificial), excluding (1) any lake or pond not discharging to a stream, (2) any sewer vested in a water authority, and (3) any tidal waters.

The River Boards Act, 1948 (now repealed), spoke of "rivers, streams and inland waters " without defining them, but section 135 (1) of the Water Resources Act, 1963, gives a comprehensive meaning to " inland water " (*see* footnote [5] on p. 177) and the same section also defines " watercourse " in terms somewhat similar to that given in the Land Drainage Act, 1976. The definition of " inland water " referred to in section 41 (1) of the Salmon and Freshwater Fisheries Act, 1975, follows the same definition as that given in the Water Resources Act, 1963. And, similarly, section 38 (1) of the Water Act, 1973, adopts the same definitions for " inland water " and " watercourse " as those used in the Water Resources Act, 1963.

Rivers and watercourses at common law

The word " watercourse " has been construed in cases dealing with the interpretation of legal documents explaining that term. In *Taylor v. St. Helens Corporation*,[1] the word " watercourse " in a grant was held to mean either (1) an easement or right to the running of water, or (2) the channel through which the water ran, or (3) the land over which the water flowed; the meaning, in each case, had to be determined by the context. *Doe d. Egremont (Earl) v. Williams*[2] decided

---

[1] (1877), 6 Ch. D. 264.
[2] (1848), 11 Q.B. 688.

that a watercourse reserved in a lease had to be taken to be
the stream and flow of the water, and not the channel through
which it flowed.   A watercourse includes a tidal river.[1] Where
the question at a trial is whether there is a watercourse or not,
the judge ought, before he leaves the question for the jury,
to instruct them as to what constitutes a watercourse at law.[2]

(1) Water flowing in a channel

The main criterion of a river at common law is that it
should consist of water flowing in a channel with banks more
or less defined, although it is not necessary that water should
flow continuously in the channel which may occasionally be
dry.[3] From the moment water issues from the ground and
runs in a defined channel it constitutes a watercourse.[4] In
Stollmeyer v. Trinidad Lake Petroleum Co.,[5] a stream flowed
in a permanently defined channel and was fed exclusively by
rainwater running off the surface of the land and the stream
ceased to flow for a considerable time each year; held that
this was a watercourse, since a river which naturally runs
dry a good portion of the year does not cease to be a river
merely because at times it is accustomed to become dry.   In
*West Riding of Yorkshire Rivers Board v. Reuben Grant & Sons
Ltd.*,[6] it was held that the fact that a watercourse was covered
in was not material, unless done by a local authority in order
to turn it into a sewer.

The word " stream " in its more usual application implies
water running between defined banks, but it is not confined
to that meaning; in essence it is water in motion as distinguished
from stagnant water.[7] The following two Commonwealth
cases may be used as illustrations.   In order to constitute a
watercourse, such as creates riparian rights, there must be a
stream of water flowing in a defined channel or between
something in the nature of banks; the stream may be very
small and need not always run, nor need the banks be clearly
or sharply defined, but there must be a course marked on the

---

1 *Somerset Drainage Comrs. v. Bridgewater Corpn.* (1899), 81 L.T. 729.
2 *Briscoe v. Drought* (1860), Ir. R. 11 C. L. 264.
3 *R. v. Oxfordshire* (1830), 1 B. & Ad. 301.
4 *Dudden v. Clutton Union* (1857), 11 Ex. 627.
5 [1918] A.C. 491.
6 (1903), 67 J.P. 183.
7 *M'Nab v. Robertson*, [1897] A.C. 129 H.L. Sc.

earth by visible signs along which the water flows.[1] A river may for part of its length, leave or depart from its normal defined channel without necessarily ceasing to be regarded as a river, and where a well defined natural stream empties into a swamp and all definite channel is lost, but emerges again into a well defined channel below, it is a question of fact whether it is the same stream.[2]

Bourne flows of underground water in a chalk area, which run periodically in times of flood across the surface of the ground in a channel, do not constitute a watercourse,[3] but water, which after flowing in a defined natural channel, comes lower down to a chalk bed, where the water gradually filters into and is absorbed in the chalk, is none the less a watercourse.[4]

(2) Waste surface water

In order to constitute a natural stream of water, the water must flow between something in the nature of banks, or in a defined channel,[5] and water which percolates discontinuously through or along strata, e.g. percolating water from marshy ground, cannot be described as a stream.[6] No claim can be made either as a natural right or as an easement by prescription to water which does not flow in a definite course, but which should be regarded as surface water or surface drainage.[7] In *Phillimore v. Watford R.D.C.*,[8] an agricultural channel constructed by a landowner on his land to carry off surface water but in which there was no constant flow of water was held not to be a natural stream or watercourse within the meaning of section 17 of the Public Health Act, 1875. Waste water which is allowed to flow from a canal is not a watercourse, since the water in the canal is not flowing water.[9] Water which squanders itself over an undefined area, such as

---

[1] *Lyons v. Winter* (1899), 25 V.L.R. 464—an Australian case.
[2] *Mansford v. Ross & Glendenning* (1886), 5 N.Z.L.R.C.A. 33.
[3] *Pearce v. Croydon R.D.C.* (1910), 74 J.P. 429.
[4] *Maxwell Willshire v. Bromley R.D.C.* (1917), 87 L.J. Ch. 241.
[5] *Daws v. M'Donald* (1887), 13 V.L.R. 689—an Australian case.
[6] *M'Nab v. Robertson, supra.*
[7] *Kena Mahomed v. Bohatoo Sircar* (1863), Marsh 506; *Adinarayana v. Ramudu* (1914), I.L.R. 37 Mad. 304.
[8] [1913] 2 Ch. 434.
[9] *Staffordshire Canal Co. v. Birmingham Canal Co.* (1866), L.R. 1 H.L. 254.

surface water the supply of which is casual and its flow
following no regular or definite course, is not a watercourse.[1]
But a right may be acquired by long user to the natural flow
of water from surface springs although the water does not flow
in a defined channel.[2]

(3) Underground water

So far, only water flowing on the surface has been considered. Can water which flows under the earth be dealt
with in the same light as a stream on the surface? The
position has been stated in a series of legal decisions.

In *Chasemore v. Richards*,[3] it was said that—

> " It appears that the principles which apply to
> flowing water in streams and rivers on the surface
> apply equally to water in a defined and known under-
> ground channel, but such principles do not relate to
> underground water which merely percolates through
> the strata in no known channels ".

The court decided in *Bradford Corporation v. Ferrand*[4] that
there could be no riparian rights in respect of underground
water flowing in a defined channel, where the existence and
course of the channel was not known and could not be
ascertained except by excavation. Again, Lord Watson in
M'Nab v. Robertson[5] stated—

> " I see no reason to doubt that a subterranean flow
> of water may in some circumstances possess the very
> same characteristics as a body of water running on the
> surface; but in my opinion, water, whether falling from
> the sky or escaping from a spring which does not flow
> onward with any continuity of parts, but becomes
> dissipated in the earth's strata, until it issues from them
> at a lower level, through dislocation of the strata or
> otherwise, cannot with any propriety be described as
> a stream ".

---

[1] *Rawstron v. Taylor* (1855), 11 Ex. 369.
[2] *Ennor v. Barwell* (1860), 3 L.T. 170.
[3] (1859), 7 H.L.C. 374.
[4] [1902] 2 Ch. 655.
[5] [1897] A.C. 129 H.L. Sc.

A watercourse which sinks underground, pursues a subterranean course for a short space and then emerges again, does not cease to be a stream.[1]

(4) Artificial watercourses

In the case of a natural stream, the riparian owner on the banks can exercise riparian rights and *prima facie* is the owner of the river bed to the centre line of the river. But whether a person through whose land an artificial watercourse passes possesses the same rights which he would have had had the watercourse actually been a natural one, depends upon the character of the watercourse, whether it is of a permanent or temporary nature, upon the circumstances under which it was created, and the mode in which it has in fact been used and enjoyed.[2]

Artificial watercourses are discussed in greater detail in Chapter 7, but, generally speaking, if an artificially constructed watercourse is of a permanent character and its origin is unknown, the inference from the user may be that the channel was originally constructed so that all the riparian owners should have the same rights as they would have had if the watercourse had been a natural one.[2] On the other hand, riparian rights will not arise, where from the nature of the case, it is obvious that the enjoyment of an artificial watercourse depends on temporary circumstances, and is not of a permanent character.[3]

Formerly, in the legal sense it was possible for a natural stream to become an artificial one, *i.e.* a stream could be held to be a sewer by reason of the discharge of sewage thereto. But it was established in *George Legge & Son Ltd. v. Wenlock*,[4] that the status of a natural stream cannot be altered to that of a sewer within the meaning of the Public Health Acts by

---

[1] *Dickinson v. Grand Junction Canal* (1852), 7 Ex. 300.
[2] *Baily & Co. v. Clark Son & Morland*, [1902] 1 Ch. 649.
[3] *Wood v. Waud* (1849), 3 Ex. 748.
[4] [1936] 2 All E.R. 1367.

the discharge of sewage into it since the coming into operation of the Rivers Pollution Prevention Act, 1876.[1]

CONSTITUENTS OF A RIVER

It has been said[2] that a river or watercourse consists of (1) the bed or *alveus;* (2) the bank or shore; and (3) the water flowing therein.

(1) The river bed

In ordinary language, the bed is the channel of the river between its banks which accommodates the flow of water when the river is neither dry nor overflowing. There are several decisions dealing with the bed of a river. In *Menzies v. Breadalbane*,[3] the bed was stated to comprise all the soil below the high water mark either of the ordinary daily tides or of the ordinary floods. This definition is applicable to both tidal and non-tidal rivers, but subsequent case law distinguishes between the bed of a non-tidal river and the bed of a tidal river.

In *Goolden v. Thames Conservators*,[4] the bed of the non-tidal Thames was taken to mean the soil underneath the waters of the river between banks. But possibly the best definition of the bed of a non-tidal river is that stated in an American case, *State of Alabama v. State of Georgia*,[5] which was cited in *Hindson v. Ashby*[6] and in *Thames Conservators v. Smeed, Dean & Co.*,[7] viz.:—

" The bed of a river is that portion of its soil which is alternatively covered and left bare as there may be

---

1 *See* now the Control of Pollution Act, 1974.
2 *Angell* on Watercourses, 3.
3 (1828), 32 R.R. 103.
4 (1891), [1897] 2 Q.B. 338.
5 (1859), 54 U.S. 427.
6 [1896] 2 Ch. 1.
7 [1897] 2 Q.B. 334.

an increase or diminution in the supply of water, and which is adequate to contain at its average and mean stage during the entire year without reference to the extraordinary freshets of the winter or spring, or the extreme droughts of the summer or autumn ".

On turning to consider the bed of a tidal river, an immediate complication ensues, since at low water the bed of a tidal estuary consists of land water discharging to the sea and the foreshore of the river bounded by the bank above ordinary high water mark, whereas at high water both the bed and the foreshore are submerged.[1] Here there is a choice of case law to consider.

Pearce v. Bunting[2] distinguished between " bed " and " shore " and held that the " bed " was the river between low water mark. In *Miller v. Little*[3] the river in an estuary was dealt with as a river at the low water state of the tide. Conversely, *Thames Conservators v. Smeed, Dean & Co.*, *supra* (which disapproved of *Pearce v. Bunting*), decided that the bed of a tidal river referred to the soil between high water mark on either side.[4]

(2) The river bank

The most detailed reference to what is meant by a river bank is to be found in an American case, *Howard v. Ingersoll*[5]:—

" The banks are the elevations of land which confine the waters in their natural channel when they rise the

---

1 *See Stuart Moore's* " History and Law of Fisheries " (1903), p. 122.

2 [1896] 2 Q.B. 360.

3 (1878), 4 L.R. Ir. 302.

4 *See Coulson & Forbes* on " Water ", 6th Ed., p. 97, Note (c).

5 (1851), 17 Ala. 781.

highest and do not overflow the banks; and in that condition of the water the banks and the soil which is permanently submerged form the bed of the river. The banks are part of the river bed, but the river does not include lands beyond the banks ".

Until recently, the English courts have had little to say about river banks. *Newcastle (Duke) v. Clark*[1] distinguished between river banks and walls, and another case—*Monmouth Canal & Railway Co. v. Hill*[2]—spoke of the banks of a canal as meaning the substantial soil which confines the water on either side of the canal, and also that the banks of the canal include the towpath.

However, the court of appeal in *Jones v. Mersey River Board*[3] has examined the meaning of " bank " in more detail. There, Jenkins, L.J., in considering the powers of a river board under section 38 of the former Land Drainage Act, 1930, to deposit spoil on the banks of a watercourse, said he adopted in substance the definitions given in *Howard v. Ingersoll*, *supra*, and in the Monmouth case, and held that " banks " meant so much of the land adjoining or near to the river as performed or contributed to the function of containing the river. The application of this definition (he went on to say) to any particular case must depend to a great extent on the particular facts of each case, including the character of the river and its surroundings. The word " bank " was not to be limited to the actual slope or vertical face where those banks actually met the river, but included the land adjoining or near to the river to the extent to which it served the river. In *Oakes v. Mersey River Board*,[4] the Lands Tribunal held that an artificially constructed bank comes within the expression " banks " in section 38 of the Land Drainage Act, 1930.

---

1 (1818), 8 Taunt. 627.
2 (1859), 28 L.J. Ex. 283.
3 [1957] 3 All E.R. 375.
4 (1957), J.P.L. 824.

(3) The flowing water

Generally speaking, there can be no ownership or right of property in the running water of a stream, except that by the general law applicable to running streams each riparian owner is entitled to the ordinary use of the water flowing past his land.[1] Flowing water is *publici juris* in the sense that all may reasonably use it who have a right of access to it, and that none can have any property in the water itself, except in the particular portion he may choose to abstract from the stream and take into his possession, and that during the time of his possession only.[2] If the abstraction or appropriation is abandoned, the water again becomes *publici juris*.[3] An easement to take or use water from a stream may be acquired by grant, prescription or statute, or a claim may be established by custom to the flow of water from a well or spring for domestic purposes by the inhabitants of a district.[4] A landowner has a right to appropriate surface water which flows over his land in no defined channel although the water is thereby prevented from reaching a watercourse which it previously supplied.[5] An owner may appropriate water in an artificial channel, unless riparian rights have been acquired by the other owners.[6]

Apart from appropriation, a proprietary interest in flowing water may arise by statute,[7] or where a stream rises and remains in one particular property and no one is entitled to share the user of the water with the owner of the property.[8] Also, water supplied by a water undertaking to a consumer and standing in his pipes may be the subject of larceny.[9]

---

[1] *White (John) & Sons v. White*, [1906] A.C. 72.

[2] *Embrey v. Owen* (1851), 6 Ex. 353; *Mason v. Hill* (1833), 5 B. & Ad. 1; *Williams v. Morland* (1824), 2 B. & C. 910.

[3] *Liggins v. Inge* (1831), 7 Bing. 682.

[4] *Harrop v. Hirst* (1868), 19 L.T. 426.

[5] *Broadbent v. Ramsbotham* (1856), 11 Ex. 602; *Chasemore v. Richards* (1859), 7 H.L. Cas. 349.

[6] *Ennor v. Barwell* (1860), 2 Giff. 410.

[7] *Medway Co. v. Romney (Earl)* (1861), 9 C.B. 575.

[8] *Holker v. Porritt* (1875), 33 L.T. 125.

[9] *Ferens v. O'Brien* (1883), 11 Q.B.D. 21.

There is no property in water percolating through the subsoil until it has been appropriated.[1]   Water has been held to be an article for the purposes of the Factories Acts.[2]

---

[1] *Ballard v. Tomlinson* (1885), 29 Ch. D. 115.

[2] *Longhurst v. Guildford, Godalming and District Water Co.*, [1961] 3 All E.R. 545, H.L.

CHAPTER 2

THE SEA AND FORESHORE

In considering the water surrounding the shores, a number of terms and expressions used in that connection are encountered, such as tidal waters, the sea, the high seas, territorial waters, the continental shelf, fishery limits and the foreshore.

The expression " tidal waters " has been defined by statute for various purposes,[1] but does not appear to have been concisely defined at common law, although its meaning has been discussed in cases concerned with the line of demarcation between the tidal and non-tidal portions of a river as to which *see* LIMITS OF TIDAL PART OF A RIVER, pp. 259, 260.

Under statute the term " sea " has been held to include an estuary or arm of the sea[2]; the coast up to the high water mark[3]; and the waters of any channel, creek, bay or estuary and of any river so far up that river as the tide flows.[4] The coast is, properly speaking, not the sea, but the land which bounds the sea.[5]

It is proposed to consider the waters which are subject to the tidal influence under the following heads:—(1) the high seas, (2) territorial waters, (3) the continental shelf, (4) fishery limits, (5) the foreshore, and (6) tidal rivers.

---

[1] *See, e.g.,* s. 3 of the Railways Clauses Act, 1863, s. 108 of the Explosives Act, 1875, s. 742 of the Merchant Shipping Act, 1894, s. 27 (4) of the Land Drainage Act, 1976, and s. 56 (1) of the Control of Pollution Act, 1974.

[2] Prevention of Oil Pollution Act, 1971, s. 29 (1).

[3] Sea Fisheries Regulation Act, 1966, s. 20 (1).

[4] Coast Protection Act, 1949. s. 49 (1), but *see also* s. 49 (2) and Sch. 4.

[5] *R. v. Forty-nine Casks of Brandy* (1836), 3 Hag. Adm. 257.

THE HIGH SEAS

By English law the high seas commence at low water mark[1] and comprise everything beyond, although under international law the general opinion appears to be that the high seas commence outside the limits of territorial waters, which are appropriated to the adjacent state, and the definition assigned to the high seas is that it means all parts of the sea that are not included in the territorial sea or in the territorial waters of a state.[2]

The high seas are open to all for navigation,[3] commerce and fishery,[4] and also for flying and laying submarine cables and pipe-lines,[5] and the soil of the bed of the sea beyond territorial waters does not belong to the Crown or to any individual or state, but this general statement is subject to certain qualifications. By treaty one state may obtain exclusive rights of navigation and fishing over the sea against another state, and the uninterrupted possession of part of the sea bed over a period by one state may give that state a prescriptive or other right to that part to the exclusion of other nations. The Crown may exercise certain rights over areas of the sea bed and subsoil outside territorial waters as designated by Order in Council made pursuant to the Continental Shelf Act, 1964. Ships whilst navigating the high seas are subject to the laws of their own countries.

TERRITORIAL WATERS

Under international law no uniform breadth for the territorial or coastal waters of a state within which limits the state is deemed to exercise exclusive territorial sovereignty has been established, and many states have *ex parte* laid down limits for their territorial waters of between three to twelve or more miles beyond the land boundary, and they have also prescribed zones of the high seas contiguous to their territorial waters in order to control and prevent infringements of their regulations

---

[1] *R. v. Keyn* (1876), 2 Ex. D. 63.
[2] *See* the Report of the First United Nations Conference on the Law of the Sea (1958) (Cmnd. 584), Convention on the High Seas, art. 1.
[3] *See* THE RIGHT OF NAVIGATION, pp. 58-60.
[4] *See* FISHING ON THE HIGH SEAS, p. 255.
[5] *See* the Report on the Law of the Sea (1958) (Cmnd. 584), Convention on the High Seas, art. 2.

regarding fishing, customs, immigration and so forth within territorial waters.[1]

Under English law as regards territorial waters, the jurisdiction of the Crown extends " over the open seas adjacent to the coasts of the United Kingdom and of all other parts of Her Majesty's dominions to such a distance as is necessary for the defence and security of such dominions ". So reads the preamble to the Territorial Waters Jurisdiction Act, 1878, which enacts that an offence committed by a person, whether a subject or not, within territorial waters is an offence within the jurisdiction of the admiral although it may have been committed on board or by means of a foreign ship.[2] This Act was passed to give effect to the minority decision of the judges in *R. v. Keyn*.[3] " Territorial waters " are defined under the Act as meaning such part of the sea adjacent to the coast of the United Kingdom or any other part of Her Majesty's dominions as is deemed by international law to be within the territorial sovereignty of Her Majesty, and for the purposes of the Act any part of the open sea within one marine league of the coast measured from low water mark is deemed to be open sea within the territorial waters of Her Majesty's dominions.[4] But in the *Anglo-Norwegian Fisheries Case*[5] the view that territorial waters should be measured from low-water mark by following the coast line was not accepted.

It appears that at present the three-mile limit applies to the territorial waters of the United Kingdom,[6] except as regards sea-fishing where the British fishery limits are those prescribed by the Fishery Limits Act, 1976. The court will treat as conclusive a statement by the appropriate officer of the Crown as to the extent of territorial waters.[7]

To what extent has the Crown any right or property in the sea bed below low water mark ? In *R. v. Keyn, supra*, a

---

[1] *See* the Report of the First United Nations Conference on the Law of the Sea (1958) (Cmnd. 584), Convention on Territorial Sea and Contiguous Zone.

[2] Territorial Waters Jurisdiction Act, 1878, s. 2.

[3] (1876), 2 Ex. D. 63.

[4] Territorial Waters Jurisdiction Act, 1878, s. 7. *See also* s. 9 of the North Sea Fisheries Act, 1893.

[5] [1951] International Court of Justice Reports 116.

[6] *Post Office v. Estuary Radio Ltd.* [1968], 2 Q.B. 740; [1967] 5 All E.R. 663, C.A.; *R. v. Kent Justices, Ex parte Lye*, [1967] 2 Q.B. 153; [1967] 1 All E.R. 560.

[7] *The Fagerness* (1927), P. 311, C.A.

minority of the court held that the sea within three miles of the coast of England was part of the territory of that country, but the majority of the judges did not agree with that. This issue did not appear to be affected by the passing of the Territorial Waters Jurisdiction Act, 1878.

In two cases prior to *R. v. Keyn*, namely, *Gammel v. Comrs. of Woods and Forests*[1] and *Gann v. Free Fishers of Whitstable*,[2] and in a later decision affecting Scotland, *Lord Advocate v. Wemyss*,[3] some of the judges expressed the opinion that the soil of the sea within three miles of low water mark was vested in the Crown. It was also stated in *A.-G. for British Columbia v. A.-G. for Canada*,[4] that the question whether the shore below low water mark within three miles of the coast formed part of the territory of the Crown, or was merely subject to special powers for protective and police purposes, was not one which belonged to municipal law alone and that it was not desirable at present that any municipal court should pronounce upon it.

It seems, therefore, that at the present time the majority decision in *R. v. Keyn* holds the field, *i.e.* that the Crown has no right on the seacoast to the soil below low water mark. It was held in *Stephens v. Snell*[5] that land below low water mark is not any part of the Kingdom, although in a later case[6] Phillimore, L.J., stated that the Crown claimed property in the soil of the sea under the territorial waters within one marine league of the coast measured from low water mark and also the mines and minerals under the soil. However, the Crown can obtain a title to the sea bed below low water mark against a subject[7]; so also may a subject.[8] Islands which raise from the sea within the limits of territorial waters are presumed to be the property of the Crown and the onus of establishing a title by adverse possession lies upon the person asserting such possession.[9]

---

[1] (1859), 3 Macq. 419, H.L.   [2] (1864), 11 H.L.C. 192.

[3] [1900] A.C. 66.   [4] [1914] A.C. 153.

[5] (1954), "Times", June 5th.

[6] *The Putbus, Owners, etc. of Ship Zenatia v. Owners of Ship Putbus* [1969] 2 All E.R. 676 at p. 683.

[7] *See* the Cornwall Submarine Mines Act, 1858.

[8] *E.g.*, as regards oyster beds extending below low water mark: *Gann v. Free Fishers of Whitstable* (1865), 11 H.L.C. 192; *Foreman v. Free Fishers of Whitstable* (1869), L.R. 4 H.L. 266; *Loose v. Castleton* (1978) The Times, 21st June, 1978.

[9] *Secretary of State for India v. Chelikani Rama Rao* (1916), L.R. 43 Ind. App. 192.

By the Protection of Wrecks Act, 1973, the Secretary of State may make an order designating an area around the site of a wreck in United Kingdom waters[1] as a restricted area, provided he is first satisfied that it is, or may prove to be, the site of a vessel lying wrecked on or in the sea bed, and that on account of the historical, archaeological or artistic importance of the vessel, or of any objects contained or formerly contained in it which may be laying on the sea bed in or near the wreck, the site ought to be protected from unauthorised interference.[2]

It is an offence for a person in a restricted area to tamper with, damage or remove any part of a wrecked vessel or any object formerly contained in it, or to carry out diving or salvage operations directed to the exploration of the wreck or remove objects from it or from the sea bed.[3] The Secretary of State may grant a licence subject to any conditions or restrictions to a competent and properly equipped person to carry out salvage operations in a restricted area.[4]

The Secretary of State may also make an order designating an area around a vessel lying wrecked in United Kingdom waters as a prohibited area, if satisfied that the vessel is a potential danger to life or property because of anything contained in it, and on that account it ought to be protected from unauthorised interference. It is an offence for a person, without written authority granted by the Secretary of State, to enter a prohibited area whether on the surface or under the water.[5]

A person guilty of an offence as above is liable on summary conviction to a fine of not more than £400, or on conviction on indictment to a fine.[6] Action taken for the sole purpose of dealing with an emergency, or by a body exercising statutory powers, or out of necessity due to stress of weather or navigational hazards, does not constitute an offence under the Act.[7]

---

[1] " United Kingdom waters " means any part of the sea within the seaward limits of the United Kingdom, and includes any part of a river within the ebb and flow of ordinary spring tides. " The sea " includes any estuary or arm of the sea. (Protection of Wrecks Act, 1973, s. 3 (1).)
[2] *Ibid.*, s. 1 (1). [3] *Ibid.*, s. 1 (3).
[4] *Ibid.*, s. 1 (5). [5] *Ibid.*, s. 2.
[6] *Ibid.*, s. 3 (4). [7] *Ibid.*, s. 3 (3).

THE CONTINENTAL SHELF

The Continental Shelf Act, 1964, was passed to give effect to the Convention on the High Seas (Cmnd. 584) which contains provision for coastal states to exercise sovereign rights over the continental shelf (which is defined as being the sea bed and subsoil of the submarine areas adjacent to the coast but outside the area of territorial waters to a prescribed depth) for the purpose of exploring and exploiting its natural resources.

The Act enables Orders in Council to be made[1] designating areas of the sea within which any rights exercisable by the United Kingdom outside territorial waters with respect to the sea bed and subsoil and their natural resources become vested in the Crown, except in relation to coal where such rights become exercisable by the National Coal Board. The licensing and other provisions of the Petroleum (Production) Act, 1934, are applied in relation to petroleum.[2]

The Act also provides in respect of designated areas for the protection of installations by prohibiting ships from entering specified parts of such areas, the application of the criminal and civil law as regards acts or omissions, the safety of navigation, the discharge of oil, wireless telegraphy, radioactive substances, submarine cables and pipe-lines and as to the use and supply of natural gas.[3]

The Mineral Workings (Offshore Installations) Act, 1971, empowers the Secretary of State to make regulations[4] for the registration of offshore installations[5] and their construction and survey,[6] and for the safety, health and welfare of persons

---

[1] Certain Orders in Council have been made, but they are outside the ambit of this book.

[2] Continental Shelf Act, 1964, s. 1.

[3] *See ibid.*, ss. 2-9.

[4] Regulations are not included in this book.

[5] " Offshore installation " means any installation which is maintained, or is to be established, for underwater exploitation or exploration; " exploration " means exploration with a view to exploitation; " Underwater exploitation " or " underwater exploration " means exploitation or exploration from or by means of any floating or other installation which is maintained in the water, or on the foreshore or other land intermittently covered with water, and is not connected with dry land by a permanent structure providing access at all times and for all purposes. (Mineral Workings (Offshore Installations) Act, 1971, s. 1 (3).)

[6] *Ibid.*, ss. 2, 3, 7.

on offshore installations in waters to which the Act applies.[1] [2]
There are also provisions regarding the appointment and duties
of managers of such installations,[3] and for the application of
the criminal law and civil law to installations in territorial
waters and designated areas.[4]

FISHERY LIMITS

British fishery limits[5] extend to 200 miles[6] from the baselines[7] from which the breadth of the territorial sea adjacent
to the United Kingdom, the Channel Islands and the Isle of
Man is measured, although Her Majesty may by Order in
Council for the purpose of implementing an international
agreement or the arbitral award of an international body or
otherwise declare that British fishery limits extend to another
specified line. Where the median line[8] is less than 200 miles
from the baselines mentioned above and no other line is
specified by Order in Council, British fishery limits extend to
the median line.[9]

The Ministers[10] may by order[11] designate any country outside
the United Kingdom, the Channel Islands and the Isle of Man,

---

1 " Waters to which the Act applies " means the waters in or adjacent to the
United Kingdom up to the seaward limits of territorial waters, and the waters
in any designated area within the meaning of the Continental Shelf Act, 1964.
(Mineral Workings (Offshore Installations) Act, 1971, s. 1 (2) (a).)

2 Ibid., ss. 6, 7.

3 Ibid., ss. 4, 5.

4 Ibid., s. 8.

5 Subject to s. 10 (2) (b) of the Fishery Limits Act, 1976, references to British
fishery limits in any enactment relating to sea fishing or whaling are to the limits
set by or under s. 1 of that Act (Fishery Limits Act, 1976, s. 1 (5)).

6 " Miles " means international nautical miles of 1,852 metres (ibid., s. 8).

7 As to the promulgation of base lines, see the Territorial Waters Order in
Council, September, 1964. In Anglo-Norwegian Fisheries Case, [1952] 1 T.L.R.
181, the International Court of Justice did not accept the view that territorial
waters should always be measured from low-water mark by following the
coast line.

8 The median line is a line every point of which is equidistant from the nearest
points of, on the one hand, the baselines mentioned above and, on the other
hand, the corresponding baselines of other countries (Fishery Limits Act, 1976,
s. 1 (4)).

9 Ibid., s. 1.

10 " The Ministers " means the Minister of Agriculture, Fisheries and Food
and the Secretaries of State concerned with sea fishing in Scotland and Northern
Ireland respectively (Fishery Limits Act, 1976, s. 8).

11 Such orders are subject to annulment pursuant to a resolution of either
House of Parliament (ibid., s. 2 (7)) and orders are made by statutory instrument
(ibid., s. 6 (1)).

and in relation to it, areas within British fishery limits in which, and descriptions of sea fish[1] for which, fishing boats[2] registered in that country may fish.

A foreign fishing boat[3] not registered in a country for the time being designated under the Fishery Limits Act, 1976, must not enter British fishery limits except for a purpose recognised by international law or by any convention for the time being in force between Her Majesty's Government in the United Kingdom and the government of the country to which the boat belongs. Any such boat entering those limits for such a purpose must return outside the limits as soon as the purpose has been fulfilled and must not fish or attempt to fish while within the limits. A foreign fishing boat so registered must not fish or attempt to fish within British fishery limits except in an area and for descriptions of fish for the time being designated in relation to that country.

At any time when a foreign fishing boat is in an area within British fishery limits and either it is prohibited from fishing in that area at all or it is permitted to fish only for certain descriptions of fish, then, its fishing gear, or so much thereof as is not required for permitted fishing, must be stowed in accordance with an order made by the Ministers.

If the above provisions are contravened in the case of a fishing boat the master of the boat is liable on summary con viction to a fine not exceeding £50,000 or on conviction on indictment to a fine, and the court on conviction may order the forfeiture of any fish or fishing gear found in the boat or taken or used by any person from the boat.

---

1 " Sea fish " includes shellfish, salmon and migratory trout, and " sea fishing " has a corresponding meaning (*ibid.*, s. 8).

2 " Fishing boat " means any vessel employed in fishing operations or any operations ancillary thereto (*ibid.*, s. 8).

3 " Foreign fishing boat " means a fishing boat which is not (*a*) registered in the United Kingdom, the Channel Islands or the Isle of Man; or (*b*) exempted from registration by regulations under s. 373 of the Merchant Shipping Act, 1894; or (*c*) owned wholly by a person who is (within the meaning of the Merchant Shipping Act, 1894) qualified to own a British ship (Fishery Limits Act, 1976, s. 8).

These provisions do not prohibit or restrict fishing by fishing boats registered in a country outside the United Kingdom in an area with respect to which special provision is made by arrangement between Her Majesty's Government in the United Kingdom and the Government of that country for fishing by such boats for the purpose of scientific research.[1] The Ministers may by order license fishing by British or foreign fishing boats in any specified area within British fishery limits.[2]

THE FORESHORE

Limits and Ownership

The foreshore or seashore—the two words mean the same in the strict legal sense[3]—is the portion of land which lies between high and low water mark at ordinary tides,[4] or more particularly the land between the high and low water mark between the ordinary flux and reflux of the sea.[5] Ordinary high tide is taken at the point of the line of the medium high tide between the springs and neaps, ascertained by the average of the medium tides during the year,[6] that is to say, the point on the shore which is about four days in each week for the most part of the year reached and covered by the tides.[7]

Nor is there any distinction in law between " sea shore " and " sea beach ". " Beach " or " shore " in the ordinary sense include not only the land lying between the lines of medium high and low tide; they cover also land which is washed by the ordinary spring tides and often land which is only washed, if at all, by exceptionally high tides but which, nevertheless, is in character more akin to the " foreshore " than to the " hinterland ".[8]

---

[1] Fishery Limits Act, 1976, s. 2.
[2] Sea Fish (Conservation) Act, 1967, s. 4, as substituted by s. 3 of the Fishery Limits Act, 1976.
[3] *Mellor v. Walmesley*, [1905] 2 Ch. 164; Note definition given to " seashore" by s. 49 (1) of the Coast Protection Act, 1949.
[4] *A.-G. v. Chambers* (1854), 23 L.T.O.S. 238; *Scratton v. Brown* (1825), 4 B. & S. 485.
[5] *Blundell v. Catterall* (1821), 5 B. & Ald. 268.
[6] *Tracey Elliot v. Morley (Earl)* (1907), 51 S.J. 625.
[7] *A.-G. v. Chambers, supra.*
[8] *Government of the State of Penang v. Beng Hong Oon* [1971] 3 All E.R. 1163.

The soil of the foreshore and the bed of arms and estuaries of the sea, and of tidal navigable rivers, so far as the tide ebbs and flows, lies *prima facie* in the ownership of the Crown,[1] unless excluded by a stronger title,[2] or the Crown has parted with the ownership.[3] The ownership of the Crown in tidal waters is subject to the public rights of fishery and navigation and rights ancillary thereto.[4] Land above the foreshore is presumed to belong to the adjoining owner,[5] but there is no legal presumption that the foreshore between high and low water mark belongs to the owner of adjacent property.[6] Any encroachment on the soil of the foreshore is a purpresture against the Crown if vested in the Crown and is in the nature of a public nuisance to the king's subjects either as their right of navigation or right of way.[7] An unauthorised erection on the bed of the foreshore by a person who is not the owner may be restrained by injunction at the suit of the Attorney-General whether it amounts to a nuisance or not and may also be abated by a private owner.[8]

In many cases the foreshore is owned by the lord of the manor,[9] or a local authority[10] or a private individual,[11] and may be parcel of an adjoining manor,[12] town[13] or land.[14] Title to the foreshore may be held in gross[15] and may be freehold

---

[1] *Malcomson v. O'Dea* (1863), 27 J.P. 820; *Bulstrode v. Hall* (1663), 1 Sid. 148; *Kirby v. Gibbs* (1667), 2 Keble 274; *Dickens and Kemp v. Shaw* (1823), 1 L.J.O.S.K.B. 122; *A.-G. v. Emerson*, [1891] A.C. 649; *A.-G. v. Richards* (1795), 2 Anst. 603; *A.-G. v. Storey* (1912), 109 L.T. 430.
[2] *A.-G. v. London Corpn.* (1849), 13 Jur. 372.
[3] *Le Strange v. Rowe* (1866), 4 F. & F. 1048.
[4] *Fitzhardinge (Lord) v. Purcell* (1908), 72 J.P. 276.
[5] *Lowe v. Govett* (1832), 1 L.J.K.B. 224.
[6] *Webber v. Richards* (1844), 2 L.T.O.S. 420.
[7] *R. v. Betts* (1850), 16 Q.B. 1022; *R. v. Randall* (1842), Car. & M. 496; *R. v. Russell* (1827), 6 B. & C. 566.
[8] *R. v. Grosvenor* (1819), 2 Stark. 511; *A.-G. v. Johnston* (1819), 2 Wils. Ch. 87; *Orr Ewing v. Colquhoun* (1877), 2 A.C. 839.
[9] *A.-G. v. Hanmer* (1858), 22 J.P. 543.
[10] *A.-G. v. Burridge* (1822), 10 Price 350.
[11] *Bristow v. Cormican* (1878), 3 A.C. 641.
[12] *Re Walton-cum-Trimley, ex p. Tomline* (1873), 28 L.T. 12; *Beaufort (Duke) v. Swansea* (1849), 3 Ex. 413; *Kirby v. Gibbs* (1667), 2 Keble 294.
[13] *Foster v. Warblington U.D.C.*, [1906] 1 K.B. 648.
[14] *Brew v. Haren* (1877), Ir. R. 11 C.L. 198.
[15] *Mulholland v. Killen* (1874), Ir. R. 9 Eq. 471; *Healy v. Thorne* (1870), Ir. R. 4 C.L. 495.

or leasehold,[1] and can pass to a subject by (a) express grant; (b) prescription; (c) possessory title.

(1) Express grant

A subject may be the owner of part of the foreshore by express grant from the Crown and the grant will be construed strictly in favour of the Crown *pro publico bono* and against the grantee.[2] The foreshore will pass from the Crown if the grant contains a sufficient description of the soil between high and low water mark.[3] Thus, a grant of " lands within the flux and reflux of the sea " is a clear recognition that the foreshore between the land boundary of a manor and low water mark was vested in the lord.[4] Whether the grant of a manor by the seacoast includes the foreshore depends on the language of the grant, *i.e.* whether it can be presumed from the grant that the boundary is formed by high water mark, in which case the foreshore is excluded from the grant, or whether the boundary extends to low water mark, when the foreshore is within the grant.[5] If it is doubtful whether a grant includes the foreshore, as where under an ancient grant of a manor, its limits are not sufficiently defined, evidence of modern acts of ownership are admissible to show that the foreshore is parcel of the manor.[6] Evidence of acts of user antecedent to the grant may be given to explain what was granted.[7]

Such acts of continuous ownership include rights of anchorage, groundage and taking wreck, royal fish and seaweed, constructing jetties, licences to take shingle, sand and gravel.[8] It appears that in such cases the question for the jury is

---

1 *Mercer v. Denne*, [1904] 2 Ch. 534.
2 *A.-G. v. Parmeter, Re Portsmouth Harbour* (1811), 10 Price 378.
3 *A.-G. v. Hanmer* (1858), 22 J.P. 543.
4 *A.-G. v. Emerson*, [1891] A.C. 649; *Hindson v. Ashby*, [1896] 2 Ch. 1.
5 *Hastings Corpn. v. Ivall* (1874), L.R. 19 Eq. 558.
6 *Beaufort (Duke) v. Swansea Corpn., supra.*
7 *Van Diemens' Land Co. v. Table Cape Marine Board*, [1906] A.C. 92.
8 *Chad v. Tilsed* (1821), 5 Moore 185; *Le Strange v. Rowe* (1866), 4 F. & F. 1048; *Brew v. Haren* (1877), Ir. R. 11 C.L. 198; *Lord Advocate v. Blantyre* (1879), 4 A.C. 770.

whether the grant, coupled with the evidence of acts of ownership, satisfy the jury that the shore in question passed by the grant.[1]

(2) Grant by prescription

In the absence of an express grant, evidence of acts of ownership by the claimant may be regarded as acts of possession, taken into account along with other acts and circumstances, in determining whether the claimant and his predecessors in title have been in prescriptive proprietary possession of the foreshore.[2] In an action against a mere trespasser, a sufficient possessory title can be established by persons claiming the foreshore, without producing evidence sufficient to displace the title of the Crown.[3]

Evidence of long user, coupled with a grant, may be given to satisfy the court as to the claimant's title to a portion of foreshore.[4] It is necessary to put forward a very strong case of prescription to induce the court to think that there has been a grant of part of the foreshore[5] and it is practically impossible to lay down precise rules in regard to the character and amount of possession necessary in order to give a riparian proprietor a prescriptive right to the foreshore.[5] Each case must depend upon its own circumstances.[6] Proof by the lord of an adjoining manor of the ownership of a several fishery over part of the foreshore raises a presumption against the Crown that the freehold of that part of the foreshore is vested in the owner of the several fishery.[7] Evidence of a custom to take " wreck of the sea, flotsam and jetsam ",[8] building a retaining wall on the foreshore and taking sand, stone and seaweed from the shore,[9] have been held admissible in proving title to the seashore.

---

[1] A.-G. v. Jones (1862), 2 H. & C. 347.
[2] Lord Advocate v. Wemyss, [1900] A.C. 48.
[3] Hastings Corpn. v. Ivall (1874), L.R. 19 Eq. 558.
[4] Beaufort (Duke) v. Swansea Corpn. (1849), 3 Ex. 413; A.-G. for Ireland v. Vandeleur, [1907] A.C. 369.
[5] Dickens & Kemp v. Shaw (1823), 1 L.J.O.S.K.B. 122.
[6] Lord Advocate v. Young (1887), 12 A.C. 544.
[7] A.-G. v. Emerson, [1891] A.C. 649; Somerset (Duke) v. Fogwell (1826) 5 B. & C. 875.
[8] Hamilton v. A.-G. for Ireland (1880), 5 L.R. Ir. Ch. 555.
[9] Lord Advocate v. Young, supra; Calmady v. Rowe (1844), 6 C.B. 861; Linnane v. Nestor and McNamara, [1943] I.R. 208.

(3) *Possessory title*

A person obtains title to the foreshore where he has held it against the Crown for more than sixty years, or twelve years where a subject is the owner of the foreshore.[1]

Accretion and encroachment

Land which is added slowly, gradually and imperceptibly to the foreshore, whether by accretion (otherwise alluvium, or land washed up by the sea) or dereliction (land left dry by the sea) belongs by general immemorial custom to the owner of the land above high water mark, and not to the Crown, if the land so added is above high water mark. Land which becomes added to the foreshore above low water mark belongs to the owner of the foreshore.[2] Conversely, where there is a gradual and imperceptible encroachment by the action of the tides, the land which was formerly above high water mark becomes the property of the owner of the foreshore to the detriment of the owners of the land,[3] and the foreshore between high and low water mark which is encroached upon passes to the owner of the soil of the tidal water,[4] or becomes part of the sea. The public rights of navigation and fishing over the foreshore follow the foreshore, as it alters by accretion or dereliction for the time being.[5] " Imperceptible ", in this issue, as considered with the words " slow and gradual ", must be understood as expressive only of the manner of the accretion, and as meaning imperceptible in its progress and not imperceptible after a long lapse of time.[2] The recognition of title by alluvial means is largely governed by the fact that the accretion is due to the nominal action of physical forces; in that it must be " gradual, slow and imperceptible ", the last two words are only qualifications of the word " gradual ", and that word with its qualifications only defines the test relative to the conditions to which it is applied.[6]

---

[1] Limitation Act, 1939, s. 4 (1), (3). *See A.-G. of Southern Nigeria v. Holt & Co. Ltd.*, [1915] A.C. 599; *Philpot v. Bath* (1905), 21 T.L.R. 634.

[2] *Gifford v. Lord Yarborough* (1828), 5 Bing. 163; *Doe d. Seebkristo v. East India Co.* (1856), 10 Moo. P.C.C. 140.

[3] *Re Hull and Selby Rly. Co.* (1839), 5 M. & W. 327; *Mahoney v. Neenan and Neenan (No. 2)* (1966), 100 I.L.T.R. 205.

[4] *Scratton v. Brown* (1825), 4 B. & C. 485.

[5] *Mercer v. Denne*, [1904] 2 Ch. 534, [1905] 2 Ch. 538.

[6] *Secretary of State for India v. Vizianagaram* (1921), L.R. 49 Ind. App. 67.

The doctrine of accretion is based on the theory that from day to day, week to week, and month to month a man cannot see where his old line of boundary was by reason of the gradual and imperceptible accretion of alluvium to his land.[1] Thus, where there is an acquisition of land from the sea or a river by gradual, slow and imperceptible means, there from the supposed necessity of the case and the difficulty of having to determine year by year to whom an inch or a foot or a yard belongs, the accretion by alluvium is held to belong to the owner of the adjoining soil.[2] The title by accretion to a new formation of alluvion land is not generally founded on equity of compensation, but on a gradual accretion by adherence to some particular land, and the land so gained follows the title of that to which it adheres.[3]

The rule as to accretion is limited to the seashore and land abutting on rivers of running water, and does not extend to canals, lakes or ponds[4]; it applies to the sea and to tidal and non-tidal waters, whether navigable or not.[5] It has no application to a non-tidal sheet of more or less stagnant water such as one of the Norfolk Broads.[4]

At one time it was considered doubtful whether the law of accretion took effect where the original boundary line was clear and fixed so that it was easy to ascertain whether the accretions, as they became perceptible, were on one side of the boundary or on the other.[6] But it was decided in *Brighton & Hove General Gas Co. v. Hove Bungalow Ltd.*,[7] that the general law of accretion also applied where a natural accretion, gradual and imperceptible, abuts on land of which the former boundary was already well known and readily ascertainable.

---

[1] *Hindson v. Ashby* (1896), 60 J.P. 454; *Foster v. Wright* (1878), 44 J.P. 7.

[2] *Lopez v. Muddun Mohun Thokoor* (1870), 13 Moo. Ind. App. 467.

[3] *Sree Eckowrie Sing v. Heeraloll Seal* (1868), 12 Moo. Ind. App. 136.

[4] *Trafford v. Thrower* (1929), 45 T.L.R. 502.

[5] *Foster v. Wright, supra.*

[6] This doubt was expressed in *Ford v. Lacy* (1861), 30 L.J. Ex. 351, and in *Hindson v. Ashby, supra.*

[7] [1924] 1 Ch. 372; see also *A.-G. v. M'Carthy*, [1911] 2 I.R. 260; *Secretary of State for India v. Foucar* (1933), 61 L.R. Ind. App. 18.

On a conveyance of land which includes a portion of foreshore any accretions subsequent to the conveyance become
the property of those claiming under the grantee,[1] and a
conveyance of land bounded by the seashore passes the land
from time to time added by accretion.[2] Land added by
accretion in consequence of gradual and imperceptible recession
of the sea assumes the legal characteristics of the land to which
it accretes and may become freehold or leasehold or subject to
customary rights.[3]

Where accretions of land on the seashore are shown to
have been perceptible by marks and measures as they took
place, e.g. where accretions of land are due to the erection of
harbour works and to the removal of shingle under licence,
the land so gained belongs to the Crown and not to the
adjacent owner.[4] So, also, the property on the original
foreshore which is suddenly altered by artificial reclamatory
work upon it remains as before.[5] Where land is suddenly
overrun by the sea and marks remain by which its limit may
be recognised, or where there is a temporary encroachment,
the property remains in the owner of the land encroached
upon.[6]

The operation of the rule of accretion is not affected by the
fact that the riparian land is scheduled or measured in the title
deeds.[7] Where there is an action on accretion involving the
Crown and the claimant admits the Crown's title to the foreshore, the onus is upon the Crown to prove the former line
of the foreshore.[8] Islands which arise within the three mile
territorial limit have been held to be the property of the
Crown and that the onus of establishing a title by adverse
possession lies upon the person asserting such possession.[9]

As to the accretion of land resulting from drainage works,
see section 36 of the Land Drainage Act, 1976.

---

[1] *Mellor v. Walmesley* (1905), 93 L.T. 574.
[2] *Scratton v. Brown* (1825), 4 B. & C. 485; *Nesbitt v. Mablethorpe U.D.C.*
(1917), 81 J.P. 289.
[3] *Mercer v. Denne*, [1904] 2 Ch. 538.
[4] *A.-G. v. Reeve* (1885), 1 T.L.R. 675.
[5] *A.-G. of Southern Nigeria v. Holt*, [1915] A.C. 599.
[6] *Hayes v. Hayes* (1897), 31 I.L.T. 392.
[7] *A.-G. of Southern Nigeria v. Holt & Co. (Liverpool) Ltd., supra.*
[8] *A.-G. v. Chamberlaine* (1858), 4 K. & J. 292.
[9] *Secretary of State for India v. Chelikani Rama Rao* (1916), 85 L.J.P.C.
222.

Rights over the foreshore

There exist at common law certain rights which can be exercised with respect to the sea and seashore. First, there are the public rights of navigation[1] and fishery.[2] Then there are other rights some of which the public may enjoy, and some which are proprietary rights exercisable only by the owner of the foreshore or by his licensee; these rights include the right of access to and passage over the foreshore, bathing, taking shells, seaweed, sand, gravel and shingle. Lastly, there are the prerogative rights of the Crown relating to wreck and royal fish.

(1) *Access over the foreshore*

The public rights at common law over the foreshore are limited to fishing, navigation and ancillary rights, and walking, bathing and beachcombing, though tolerated by the Crown, give no legal rights in the public. " It is notorious that many things are done on the foreshore by the public which they have no right to do "[3]; strictly speaking they are not entitled to cross the shore even for bathing, whether on foot or with bathing machines, or amusement, or to hold public or religious meetings there, without the consent of the owner. But the right to use the foreshore for bathing may be claimed by custom or prescription.[4] Where bathing is permitted it must be carried out in a decent manner and it is an offence to bathe uncovered at places where persons should not bathe without indecent exposure.[5] A right to place chairs on the seashore for hire cannot be claimed by prescription under the Prescription Act, 1832, since it is a right in gross.[6] A local authority may make byelaws regulating bathing in the sea under section 231 of the Public Health Act, 1936, or by means of a private Act. There is no general right for the public to shoot over

---

[1] *See* THE RIGHT OF NAVIGATION, pp. 58-66.

[2] *See* FISHERY ON THE FORESHORE, pp. 256-258.

[3] *Alfred A. Beckett v. Lyons*, [1966] 2 W.L.R. 421.

[4] *Llandudno U.D.C. v. Woods*, [1899] 2 Ch. 705; *Brighton Corpn. v. Packham* (1908) 72 J.P. 318; *Brinckman v. Matley*, [1904] 2 Ch. 313; *Blundell v. Catterall* 1821), 5 B. & Ald. 268.

[5] *R. v. Reed* (1871), 12 Cox C.C. 1.

[6] *Ramsgate Corpn. v. Debling* (1906), 70 J.P. 132.

the foreshore, although the owner of the foreshore may do so.[1] Access over the foreshore is permissible in the following cases:—(1) by the public in case of peril or necessity[2]; (2) an owner of land adjoining the sea by virtue of his tenement has the same right of access to the sea as a riparian owner has in respect of a tidal river,[3] and this access is from every part of the frontage over every part of the foreshore and includes a right of access to the sea across the foreshore left bare by the receding tide[4]; (3) under Part V of the National Parks and Access to the Countryside Act, 1949, the public may enjoy access for open air recreation to open country, which includes foreshore; (4) the inhabitants of a parish or local fisherman may by immemorial custom acquire a right over the foreshore[5]; (5) in many instances the public are admitted on portions of the seashore vested in local authorities subject to any local regulations or byelaws in force.

Where a district council own the foreshore, byelaws can be made under section 164 of the Public Health Act, 1875, or section 15 of the Open Spaces Act, 1906. It is also possible for a local authority to make byelaws for the prevention of danger, obstruction or annoyance to persons using the seashore and esplanades or promenades under sections 82 and 83 of the Public Health Acts Amendment Act, 1907. Byelaws to regulate the speed and use as regards navigation of pleasure boats and requiring the use of effective silencers on pleasure boats propelled by internal combustion engines to a distance seaward not exceeding 1,000 metres from low water mark can be made under section 76 of the Public Health Act, 1961 as amended by section 17 of the Local Government (Miscellaneous Provisions) Act, 1976. Under local Acts some seaside local authorities are empowered to make byelaws, and regulations for sea beaches and foreshore vested in them.[6] An

---

1 *Fitzhardinge (Lord) v. Purcell*, [1908] 2 Ch. 139.
2 *Blundell v. Catterall, supra; Brinckman v. Matley, supra; see also* s. 513 of the Merchant Shipping Act, 1894.
3 *A.-G. of Straits Settlement v. Wemyss* (1888), 13 A.C. 192.
4 *Coppinger v. Shean*, [1906] 1 Ir. R. 519.
5 *Mercer v. Denne*, [1904] 2 Ch. 534; *Aiton v. Stephen* (1876), 1 A.C. 456.
6 *See Gray v. Sylvester* (1897), 61 J.P. 807; *Parker v. Bournemouth Corpn.* (1902), 66 J.P. 440; *Moorman v. Tordoff* (1908), 72 J.P. 142; *Glee v. Meadows* (1911), 75 J.P. 142.

owner of the foreshore may bring an action for injunction to restrain trespass thereon.[1]

(2) *Right to take seaweed, shells, sand and shingle*

The general rule is that natural products found on the seashore between high and low water mark, such as seaweed deposited or growing there, and shells, sand, shingle and gravel, belong to the owner of the foreshore and can only be removed by him or his licensee, and not by the general public, since the public have no general right to enter on the seashore for such purposes.[2] But a right to take sand, shells, shingle and seaweed may exist under statute,[3] or be claimed by prescription.[4]

Seaweed cast or growing on the foreshore is the property of the foreshore owner,[5] who may bring an action in trespass or trover for the wrongful taking of seaweed cast by the sea on the shore.[6] The owner of land adjoining the foreshore is entitled to seaweed deposited there by the tides above high water mark on his property.[7] The public are entitled to take floating seaweed as an incident of the right to navigate or fish,[8] but the lord of the manor cannot claim an exclusive right to cut seaweed below low water mark except by grant or prescription.[9] The owner of land on which there lies decomposed seaweed which has become a nuisance may be liable to remove it.[10]

A claim to take shingle and sand by the inhabitants of a town cannot be founded on custom, since the claim relates to a profit *a prendre* in the soil of another person, which may

---

[1] *Behrens v. Richards*, [1905] 2 Ch. 614.
[2] *Howe v. Stawell* (1833), Alc. & N. 348; *Brew v. Haren* (1877), I.R. 11 C.L. 198.
[3] *E.g.*, 7 Jac. 1, c. 18 (1609).
[4] *Hamilton v. A.-G.* (1880), 9 L.R. Ir. 271; *A.-G. v. Hanmer* (1858), 22 J.P. 543.
[5] *Howe v. Stawell, supra; Lowe v. Govett* (1832), 3 B. & Ad. 863; *Hamilton v. A.-G., supra.*
[6] *Brew v. Haren. supra; Calmady v. Rowe* (1844), 6 C.B. 681; *Hastings Corpn. v. Ivall* (1874), L.R. 19 Eq. 558; *Stoney v. Keane* (1903), 37 I.L.T. 212; *Linnane v. Nestor & McNamara*, [1943] I.R. 208.
[7] *Mahoney v. Neenan and Neenan (No. 2)* (1966), 100 I.L.T.R. 205.
[8] *Baird v. Fortune* (1861), 5 L.T. 2.
[9] *Benest v. Pipon* (1829), 1 Knapp 60.
[10] *Margate L.B. v. Margate Harbour Co.* (1869), 33 J.P. 437.

arise only by grant or prescription.[1] But in *Lynn Regis v. Taylor*,[2] a custom for the freemen of an ancient borough and for ship owners to dig ballast was held good, and the taking of stones from waste land, whether adjoining the foreshore or otherwise, for the purpose of repairing highways may be pleaded as a prescriptive right by the inhabitants of a parish.[3] However, a special custom to take shingle above high water mark for highway repairs is bad as to parts of the beach which are private property.[4] Such a claim does not extend to removing shingle so as to cause injury to adjoining property or to expose land to the inroads of the sea,[5] and an injunction may be obtained against taking valuable stones found on the foreshore.[6] So also, a custom for the inhabitants of a parish who are landowners to take sand which has drifted from the shore to adjoining closes is bad, since the deposited sand becomes part of the soil of the close and belongs to the owner thereof.[7] The inhabitants of a county have no right to take sea-washed coal from the foreshore, because a fluctuating body such as that cannot acquire a prescriptive right of that nature.[8]

There are a number of recent statutes which affect the winning of materials from the foreshore. A highway authority are empowered to dig and carry away gravel, sand, stone and other material from waste or common land, and may gather and carry away stones, but in doing so must not remove such quantity of stones or other materials from the sea beach so as to cause damage by inundation or increased danger of encroachment by the sea.[9] Section 18 of the Coast Protection Act, 1949, makes it an offence to excavate any materials (including minerals and turf) on, under or forming part of the seashore to which that section applies, except under

---

[1] *Constable v. Nicholson* (1863), 14 C.B.N.S. 230; *Pitts v. Kingsbridge Highway Board* (1871), 25 L.T. 195; *MacNamara v. Higgins* (1854), 4 I.C.L. 326.
[2] (1684), 3 Lev. 160.
[3] *Padwick v. Knight* (1852), 7 Ex. 854; *Clowes v. Beck* (1851), 13 Beav. 347.
[4] *Pitts v. Kingsbridge Highway Board* (1871), 25 L.T. 195.
[5] *A.-G. v. Tomline* (1880), 14 Ch. D. 58 ; *Cowper (Earl) v. Baker* (1810), 17 Ves. 128; *Chalk v. Wyatt* (1810), 3 Mer. 688; *Canvey Island Comrs. v. Preedy*, [1922] 1 Ch. 179.
[6] *Cowper (Earl) v. Baker, supra.*
[7] *Blewett v. Tregonning* (1835), 3 Ad. & El. 554.
[8] *Alfred A. Beckett Ltd. v. Lyons*, [1966] 2 W.L.R. 421; *Goodman v. Saltash Corpn.* (1882), 7 A.C. 633; *Blewitt v. Tregonning* (1835), 3 Ad. & El. 554.
[9] Highways Act, 1959, s. 48; *see also* s. 55.

licence from a coast protection authority. It has been held[1] that planning permission is not required for operations for getting sand or gravel from the sea bed taking place below low water mark in areas outside the limits of the jurisdiction of the county, but that the provisions of the Town and Country Planning Acts apply in respect of operations in areas beyond low water mark which fall within the administrative boundaries of a local planning authority, *i.e.* in a tidal estuary falling *inter fauces terrae.*

Wreck

Wreck is a royal franchise belonging to the Crown, unless the right has been granted to a subject, who may only obtain a title to wreck by charter or prescription. In many parts of England wreck belongs to the lords of the manors, and it may also be claimed as part or parcel of a hundred or town.[2] The right of the subject to wreck may be presumed by long user, unless there is sufficient evidence to the contrary to rebut this.[3] The right to wreck will not pass under the general terms of a grant.[4] Nor will it pass by a grant of the seashore by itself, and whilst a royal grant of wreck to the lord of a manor gives him, as an incident, the right to pass over the foreshore to take wreck, it does not pass the right to the soil of the shore.[5] But where there is a grant of a manor with rights of anchorage, groundage, wreck, etc., this is a strong presumption that the soil of the seashore was intended to pass.[6] In order to constitute a legal wreck, the goods must come to land; if they continue at sea the law distinguishes them as jetsam, flotsam or lagan.[7]

By the statute De Prerogativa Regis (1324) the King was entitled to wreck of the sea throughout the realm, and the rights relating to wreck and salvage are now contained in Part IX of the Merchant Shipping Act, 1894; the Crown being

---

[1] (1949), J.P.L. 421.
[2] *Palmer v. Rouse* (1858), 3 H. & N. 505; *Calmady v. Rowe* (1844), 6 C.B. 861.
[3] *Biddulph v. Arthur* (1755), 2 Wils. 23.
[4] *Alcock v. Cooke* (1829), 2 M. & P. 625.
[5] *Dickens & Kemp v. Shaw* (1823), 1 L.J.O.K.S.B. 122.
[6] *Le Strange v. Rowe* (1866), 4 F. & F. 1048; *Chad v. Tilsed* (1821), 2 Brod. & Bing. 403.
[7] *Palmer v. Rouse, supra.*

entitled to all unclaimed wreck found in any part of Her Majesty's dominions, except where this right has been granted to another person.[1] " Wreck " includes jetsam, flotsam, lagan and derelict found in or on the shores of the sea or any tidal water,[2] and also fishing boats or fishing gear lost or abandoned at sea and found or taken possession of within territorial waters of the United Kingdom or found or taken possession of beyond such waters and brought within such waters.[3] The provisions of the Merchant Shipping Act, 1894, and of various other statutes relating to wreck and salvage have been applied (with the necessary exceptions, adaptations and modifications) to aircraft as they apply to vessels.[4]

In accordance with *Constable's Case*,[5] " flotsam " is when a ship is sunk or otherwise perished and the goods float on the sea; "jetsam" is when the ship is in danger of being sunk and, to lighten the ship, the goods are cast into the sea, and afterwards, notwithstanding, the ship perishes; " lagan " is when the goods which are so cast into the sea, and afterwards the ship perishes, and the goods are so heavy that they sink to the bottom, and the mariners, to the intent to have them again, tie them to a buoy or cork or such other thing that will not sink, so that they may find them again. None of these goods which are called jetsam, flotsam or lagan, are called wreck so long as they remain in or upon the sea, but if any of them by the sea be put upon the land, then they shall be said wreck. " Derelict " is a term applied to a ship abandoned or deserted at sea[6] without any hope of recovery.[7]

To constitute wreck, goods must have touched the ground, though they need not have been left dry.[8] It is not necessary that a vessel must be lost with all hands to constitute wreck.[9] Floating timber found without an apparent owner at sea,

---

[1] Merchant Shipping Act, 1894, s. 523.
[2] *Ibid.*, s. 510.
[3] Sea Fisheries Act, 1968, s. 17.
[4] Civil Aviation Act, 1949, s. 51; Aircraft (Wreck and Salvage) Order, 1938 (S.R. & O. 1938, No. 136).
[5] (1601), 5 Co. Rep. 106a.
[6] *Crossman v. West* (1887), 13 A.C. 160.
[7] *The Aquila* (1798), 1 Ch. Rb. 37.
[8] *R. v. Forty-nine Casks of Brandy* (1836), 3 Hag. Adm. 257.
[9] *Dunwich Corpn. v. Sterry* (1831), 1 B. & Ad. 831.

having drifted from the shore is not wreck.[1] Things floating between high and low water mark, not having touched the ground, are not wreck; if fixed to the land between high and low water mark, with some water around them, they are *wreccum maris*. If having once touched the land between high and low water mark, the goods are again afloat, they are not necessarily wreck and their legal character will depend upon their state at the time they are seized and secured with possession and whether, for instance, the person who seized them as salvor, was in a boat, wading or swimming. Property which comes ashore is wreck and belongs to the Crown or to a grantee of wreck; whilst at sea it belongs to the King in his office of Admiralty as derelict, flotsam, jetsam or lagan. Above high water mark the property belongs to the lord of the manor as Crown grantee, but below low water mark he has no claim, since it is on the high seas and belongs to the Admiralty. The position between high and low water mark is this; when the tide covers this space it is sea, and when it recedes it is again land and within the jurisdiction of the lord of the manor. If the property is not claimed by the true owner within a year it belongs to the Crown, so long as it is afloat or surrounded by water.[2] If the property in goods can be proved, the lord of the manor is not entitled to them as wreck.[3]

Royal fish and fowl

The statute De Prerogativa Regis[4] enacted that the King is entitled to whales and sturgeons taken in the sea or elsewhere within the realm, except in certain places privileged by the King. The statute applies to royal fish found on the shore or caught near the coasts (presumably within territorial waters), but such fish found and taken within the precincts or jurisdiction of the Cinque Ports belong to the Lord Warden. Claims by the Crown of the right to take dolphin, grampuses and other fish of a great size have not been recognised.[5]

---

[1] *Palmer v. Rouse* (1858), 22 J.P. 773.
[2] *R. v. Two Casks of Tallow* (1837), 6 L.T. 558.
[3] *Hamilton & Smyth v. Davis* (1771), 5 Burr 2732.
[4] 17 Ed. 2 st. 2, c. 11; *see also Royal Fishery of Banne Case* (1619), Dav. Ir. 35; *Warren v. Matthews* (1703), 1 Salk. 357.
[5] *Cinque Ports (Lord Warden) v. R.* (1831), 2 Hag. Ad. 484.

Sir Matthew Hale in his work " De Jure Maris " referred to three types of royal fish, namely:—sturgeon, porpoise and whale, but not salmon or lamprey, and he stated that whales " taken in the wide sea or out of the precincts of the sea belonging to the Crown " belong to the taker. In Scotland salmon and mussel fisheries are royal fish.[1]

White swans are " fowl royal " and those which are wild and unmarked and found swimming in an open and common river belong to the Crown under the royal prerogative. A subject may have property in white swans not marked and in his private waters, and if they escape out of his waters into an open and common river, he is entitled to claim them back.[2]

It is interesting to note that swans on the Thames belong either to the Crown or to the Dyers and Vintners Companies, which guilds have enjoyed the privilege from time immemorial to own and mark swans there. The ceremony of " swan-upping " on the Thames, when the cygnets claimed by the two companies are marked or nicked on the mandibles, is carried out each year. Royal birds are not marked.

Jurisdiction over the foreshore

Formerly, in the absence of evidence to the contrary, the foreshore below high water mark was treated as being excluded from the limits of the adjoining parish or township[3] and, accordingly the occupiers of a pier were only liable for rates in respect of that part of the pier covering land above high water mark.[4] Now, by section 72 of the Local Government Act, 1972, every accretion from the sea, whether natural or artificial, and any part of the seashore to low water mark, which did not on the 26th October, 1972, form part of a parish, is annexed to and incorporated with in England the parish or parishes which such accretion or seashore adjoins, and in Wales the community or communities which such accretion or sea-shore adjoins in proportion to the extent of the common boundary, and is accordingly annexed to and incorporated

---

[1] *Lord Advocate v. Sinclair* (1867), L.R. 1 H.L. Sc. 176; *Parker v. Lord Advocate*, [1904] A.C. 364.
[2] *Case of Swans* (1592), 7 Coke 15b.
[3] *Bridgewater Trustees v. Bootle-cum-Linacre* (1866), 7 B. & S. 348.
[4] *R. v. Musson* (1858), 22 J.P. 609.

with the district and county in which that parish or community is situate. The part of the seashore comprised between high and low water mark forms part of the body of the adjoining county the justices of which, and not the Admiralty, have jurisdiction to take cognizance of offences committed there, whether or not committed when the shore is covered with water.[1] The foreshore belonging to the Crown and under the management of the Minister of Transport immediately before the 1st April, 1950, is now managed by the Crown Estate Commissioners.[2]

COAST PROTECTION AND SEA DEFENCE

It is part of the prerogative and duty of the Crown to preserve the realm from the inroads of the sea and to protect the land from the inundation of the water for the benefit, not of an individual, but of the whole commonwealth.[3] Commissioners of sewers were established for that purpose in 1427,[4] and later in more permanent form under the Bill of Sewers of 1531.[5] That Act provided for the appointment of commissioners of sewers with powers to make surveys of sea defences and obstructions to rivers, to maintain and repair existing walls and sewers, to remedy nuisances and to levy rates for payment of the expenses so incurred. The Sewers Act, 1833, empowered commissioners to erect new works and restricted their jurisdiction to the coast and navigable rivers.

Under the Land Drainage Act, 1861,[6] new commissions of sewers could be issued by the Crown on the recommendation of the Inclosure Commissioners and commissioners were to continue until they were superseded by the Crown, *i.e.* they were made permanent instead of having to be renewed every ten years. The functions of the commissioners were more clearly defined by the division of their acts and duties into

---

[1] *Embleton v. Brown* (1860), 3 E. & E. 234.
[2] Coast Protection Act, 1949, Part III (now repealed) ; *see* the Crown Estate Acts, 1956 and 1961.
[3] *Per* Fry, J., in *A.-G. v. Tomline* (1880), 14 Ch. D. 58; *see also Hudson v. Tabor* (1877), 2 Q.B.D. 290.
[4] Under 6 Hen. 6, c. 5.
[5] 23 Hen. 8, c. 5, as amended by later statutes, including 3 & 4 Edw. 6, c. 8. and 13 Eliz. 1. c. 9.
[6] *See also* the Land Drainage Acts of 1914, 1918 and 1926.

the maintenance and improvement of existing works and the construction of new works. In addition, new elective drainage boards, vested with all the powers of commissioners of sewers, could be established by provisional order for drainage districts. Apart from the Act of 1861, drainage authorities were created for particular districts under special Acts.

The general statutes relating to drainage districts and commissioners of sewers were repealed by the Land Drainage Act, 1930 (since replaced by the Land Drainage Act, 1976), which although originally concerned mainly with the drainage of inland waters, does permit drainage works to be carried out in defence against sea water,[1] and it appears that the main objectives of water authorities under that Act are to control the flow of inland waters and to keep out sea water from farm lands[2]; however, in view of recent serious flooding both from the sea and inland rivers, the objectives of water authorities must also include the protection of urban areas and property generally. The powers of an internal drainage board or water authority under the Land Drainage Act, 1976, are permissive only and not imperative and a water authority cannot be required or directed to repair a sea wall,[3] although a duty to maintain sea banks may be imposed by a local Act.[4]

See, further, Chapter 12—LAND DRAINAGE.

The Coast Protection Act, 1949, constituted maritime district councils as coast protection authorities for their areas to carry out works of construction, repair, maintenance, improvement, etc., for protecting land against erosion and encroachment by the sea. Provision is made for establishing coast protection boards or joint committees of coast protection authorities.

Coast protection authorities are concerned with protecting against destruction parts of the coast, including built-up areas,

---

[1] Land Drainage Act, 1976, s. 17 (2).
[2] *Per* Scott, L.J., in *Symes v. Essex Rivers Catchment Board* (1937), 101 J.P. 179.
[3] *Smith v. Cawdle Fen Comrs.* (1938), 82 S.J. 890; *Gillett v. Kent Rivers Catchment Board*, [1938] 4 All E.R. 810; *East Suffolk Rivers Catchment Board v. Kent* (1940), 105 J.P. 129.
[4] *Sephton v. Lancashire River Board*, [1962] 1 All E.R. 183.

and preventing erosion caused by wave and tidal action, whereas water authorities may carry out drainage works for the purpose of defence against sea water or tidal water anywhere in water authority areas, irrespective of whether such works are undertaken in connection with their " main river ".[1]

In addition to water authorities and coast protection authorities, various dock, port, harbour and navigation authorities possess statutory powers in relation to sea defence within their particular areas.

Sea walls and embankments

Since it is the duty of the Crown to protect the realm from the inroads of the sea by maintaining the natural barriers and erecting artificial barriers, a subject who owns the foreshore will be restrained by injunction from removing a natural barrier of shingle, although removed for sale in the ordinary and legitimate way, if by such removal the neighbouring land is thereby exposed to the inroads of the sea.[2] So also, a person responsible for a sea wall is entitled to an injunction to restrain others from removing shingle from the foreshore so as to expose the wall and the lands protected thereby to a greater risk of inundation of the sea.[3] The Attorney-General may maintain an action on behalf of the public to restrain the commission of such an act,[4] and a coast protection authority may by order prohibit the excavation or removal of materials on, under or forming part of the seashore.[5] An owner of land outside a sea wall (originally erected to prevent the excursion of the sea into the land beyond the wall) has no right to send sea water through the wall on to the land behind, or to make a breach in the wall, which would expose the land within to the risk of such an event happening.[6]

---

[1] Land Drainage Act, 1976, s. 17 (2).
[2] *A.-G. v. Tomline, supra; Isle of Ely Case* (1609), 10 Co. Rep. 141a; *Maldon Corpn. v. Laurie* (1933), 97 J.P. Jo. 132.
[3] *Canvey Island Comrs. v. Preedy*, [1922] 1 Ch. 179; *Holien v. Tipping*, [1915] 1 I.R. 210.
[4] *A.-G. v. Shrewsbury Bridge Co.* (1882), 46 L.T. 687.
[5] Coast Protection Act, 1949, s. 18; *see also Anderson v. Jacobs* (1905), 93 L.T. 17; *Burton v. Hudson*, [1909] 2 K.B. 564.
[6] *Symes v. Essex Rivers Catchment Board, supra.*

Persons occupying land adjoining the sea may erect such defences as are necessary for the preservation of their own land although such erections may render it necessary for their neighbours to do the same,[1] but the consent of the coast protection authority is required for coast protection works, other than that of maintenance or repair.[2] A person who, in order to protect his house from the sea, places rocks and piles on the foreshore belonging to his neighbour, may acquire an easement over his neighbour's land for protecting his house from the sea by means of the rocks and piles placed on the land.[3]

There is nothing inconsistent with the purposes of a sea wall or embankment erected to protect the neighbouring lands, in a public right of way along the surface, and where the public have had uninterrupted and open user of the right of way a dedication of a public highway may be presumed by the owner of the soil.[4] The authority responsible for the repair of a sea wall (but not in occupation thereof) with a public footpath along the top are required to repair the wall so as to restrain the sea water, but are not under a duty to keep the footpath in repair, nor liable to members of the public injured by using the wall which collapses.[5]

Repair of sea walls and river banks

At common law, it appears that there is no duty, in the absence of some specific legal obligation to the contrary, upon a riparian owner to keep his portion of the bank in repair: *Hudson v. Tabor*.[6] That case decided that a landowner was not under any common law liability to repair his sea wall for the protection of his neighbours, and in view of that decision and the other cases hereafter mentioned, it seems this principle extends to the bank of a river, tidal or non-tidal. In most cases, where a river frontager repairs his bank he

---

[1] *R. v. Pagham Sewers Comrs.* (1828), 8 B. & C. 355.
[2] Coast Protection Act, 1949, s. 16.
[3] *Philpot v. Bath* (1905), 21 T.L.R. 634.
[4] *Greenwich Board of Works v. Maudsley* (1870), 35 J.P. 8.
[5] *Hunwick v. Essex Rivers Catchment Board* (1952), 116 J.P. 217.
[6] (1877), 2 Q.B.D. 290; *A.-G. v. Tomline, supra; Thomas & Evans Ltd. v. Mid-Rhondda Co-operative Society*, [1940] 4 All E.R. 357.

does so at his own volition to preserve his property against erosion.

But a legal obligation to maintain or repair a bank may arise by prescription, custom, tenure, covenant or under statute.[1] Most of the cases in point are concerned with sea walls.

An example of prescriptive liability is to be found in *R. v. Leigh*,[2] where it was said that a landowner might by prescription be obliged to maintain a sea wall not only against ordinary weather and tides, but also against extraordinary tempest.[3] Where a corporation are liable to repair sea walls, *e.g.* under the terms of a grant from the Crown, a person who suffers damage by the decay of the walls may sue the corporation for damages.[4]

Cases dealing with liability *de ratione tenurae* include *R. v. Baker*[5] and *London & N.W. Rly. v. Fobbing Sewers Comrs.* (here it was held that where a farm has been subject *rationae tenmae* to repair a sea wall, such liability attaches to every part of the farm, though the farm has been sold and has become vested in several different purchasers),[6] and *see Morland v. Cook*[7] on covenant.

A liability to repair may arise where the want of repair of a bank has caused adjoining land to become a public nuisance,[8] or an owner may be required to abate a statutory nuisance due to the flooding of his land by a breach in the bank.[9] A right to go on to another riparian owner's land to repair the

---

[1] Before *Hudson . v. Tabor*, the grounds for an obligation to repair also included frontage, ownership and *per usum rei* (*Callis* on " the Law of Sewers " (1622), pp. 115-122).
[2] (1839), 10 Ad. & El. 398.
[3] *See also Keighley's Case* (1609), 10 Co. Rep. 139a; *Fobbing Sewers Comrs. v. R.* (1886), 51 J.P. 227; *R. v. Essex Sewers Comrs.* (1823), 1 B. & C. 477; *Griffith's Case* (1564), Moore Rep. 69.
[4] *Lyme Regis Corpn. v. Henley* (1834), 1 Scott 29.
[5] (1867), L.R. 2. Q.B. 621.
[6] (1896), 75 L.T. 629.
[7] (1868), 18 L.T. 496; *see also Smith v. River Douglas Catchment Board* (1949), 113 J.P. 388.
[8] *A.-G. v. Tod Heatley*, [1897] 1 Ch. 560; *Thames Conservators v. London Port Sanitary Authority* [1894], 1 Q.B. 647.
[9] *Clayton v. Sale U.D.C.* (1926), 90 J.P. 5.

banks of a river to make it available for working a mill may be claimed as an easement.[1]

The common law position regarding obligations to repair has been affected by statute, *vide* sections 262, 264 of the Public Health Act, 1936 (where landowners may be required to culvert watercourses)[2] and section 26 of the Land Drainage Act, 1976 (which requires water authorities to commute obligations imposed on persons by reason of tenure, custom, prescription or otherwise to do works . . . by way of repairing banks of certain watercourses).[3]

The Land Drainage Act, 1930 (now replaced by the Land Drainage Act, 1976), did not affect any existing obligations to repair banks, etc., which arose by reason of tenure, custom, prescription or otherwise,[4] and *North Level Comrs. v. River Welland Catchment Board*[5] decided that the general wording of the Act or any scheme made under it did not transfer an obligation to repair an artificial bank from the plaintiffs to the catchment board set up under the Act.

In *Harrison v. Great Northern Rly.*,[6] a company who undertook to maintain a channel for conveying water, neglected to do so and was held responsible for the injury arising from the banks of the channel giving way in a period of extraordinary rainfall, in consequence of the outlet of the channel not being sufficiently widened by other persons whose duty it was to keep the outlet of a certain width. In *Vyner v. North Eastern Rly.*,[7] a company which was responsible by statute for maintaining a river navigation, was held not to be liable to maintain flood banks behind the natural river banks, since these banks were not constructed to keep the water within the *alveus* of the river.

Navigation commissioners who are under a statutory duty to maintain sea walls will be liable for damage caused by an overflow not only to land reclaimed by them, but also for

---

[1] *Roberts v. Fellowes* (1906), 94 L.T. 279; *Liford's Case* (1614), 77 E.R. 1206.
[2] *See* p. 50.
[3] *See* p. 231.
[4] Land Drainage Act, 1930, s. 36 (1).
[5] (1938), 102 J.P. 82.
[6] (1864), 3 H. & C. 231.
[7] (1898), 14 T.L.R. 554.

property adjoining such land.[1] Where there is a statutory obligation that a river wall must be maintained at a certain height, failure to do so will render those responsible to an action for negligence, and an act of God, such as an extraordinary high tide, will not excuse them from liability.[2]

A parish council cannot be convicted for not rebuilding a sea wall washed away by the sea, over the top of which an alleged highway used to pass,[3] nor for failing to repair part of a highway washed away by the sea.[4] But a highway authority under an obligation to keep up a road is chargeable with the cost of works necessary for the preservation of the road, even though they may not actually form part of it, such as a sea wall and groynes necessary to prevent a road running along the seashore from being periodically injured by the inroads of the sea. The fact that a footpath along the top of a sea wall is besides being part of the highway, used as a promenade for purposes of pleasure, does not affect the liability to repair.[5]

---

[1] *Bramlett v. Tees Conservancy* (1885), 49 J.P. 214; *Collins v. Middle Level Comrs.* (1869), 20 L.T. 442.

[2] *Nitro-Phosphate Co. v. London Docks Co.* (1878), 9 Ch. D. 503; *Wear River Comrs. v. Adamson* (1877), 2 A.C. 750.

[3] *R. v. Inhabitants of Paul* (1840), 2 Moo. & R. 307.

[4] *R. v. Hornsea* (1854), 2 C.L.R. 596; *R. v. Landulph (Inhabitants)* (1834), 1 Moo. & R. 393.

[5] *Sandgate U.D.C. v. Kent C.C.* (1898), 79 L.T. 425; *R. v. Lordsmere (Inhabitants)* (1886), 51 J.P. 86.

CHAPTER 3

RIVERS AND LAKES

TIDAL RIVERS

A tidal river is one in which the tide ebbs and flows, where the bed *prima facie* belongs to the Crown, and the public have the right to use it for purposes of navigation and fishing.

A river is a tidal river in such parts only as are within the regular ebb and flow of the highest tides,[1] and the flow of the tide is strong *prima facie* evidence of a public navigable river, but whether a particular water is or is not of that character depends upon the situation and nature of the channel. Not every ditch or cutting forms part of the public navigable river, even though it is large enough to admit the passage of a boat; the question is one of degree and is for the jury to determine having regard to all the facts.[2] "Tidal waters" include those waters not merely where there is a horizontal ebb and flow, but also where there is a vertical rise and fall caused by the ordinary sea tide[3]—*see also* Limits of Tidal Part of a River, pp. 259, 260.

Ownership of soil of bed

The right to the soil of a tidal navigable river is not by presumption of law vested in the owners of the adjoining lands,[4] but lies *prima facie* in the Crown so far as the tide

---

[1] *Reece v. Miller* (1882), 8 Q.B.D. 626; *Lynn Corpn. v. Turner* (1774), 1 Cowp. 86; *Horne v. Mackenzie* (1839), 6 Cl. & Fin. 628; *see also* definition given in s. 3 of the Railways Clauses Act, 1863.

[2] *Sim E Bak v. Ang Yong Huat*, [1923] A.C. 429; *Ilchester (Earl) v. Rashleigh* (1889), 61 L.T. 477; *Miles v. Rose* (1814), 5 Taunt. 705.

[3] *West Riding of Yorkshire Rivers Board v. Tadcaster R.D.C.* (1907), 97 L.T. 436.

[4] *R. v. Smith* (1780), 2 Doug. K.B. 441.

flows and reflows,[1] unless another person can sustain a stronger title.[2] In earlier cases it was held that the Crown was the owner of the soil of " public navigable rivers ",[3] " navigable rivers ",[4] and " tidal navigable rivers ",[5] but it was eventually established in *Murphy v. Ryan*[6] that the Crown had no rights, and the public had no right to fish, in a navigable river beyond the point where the tide ebbed and flowed. The ownership of the Crown is for the benefit of the subjects who have the public right of fishing and navigation with its ancillary rights, and the Crown can only grant the bed of the sea or a tidal river subject to such rights.[7] The right of the Crown to the bed of a tidal river is limited to the ordinary high water mark along the shore and as far up the river as the tide flows.[8]

There is some doubt whether the *medium filum aquae* or middle line of a tidal river should be drawn in the middle of the channel at ordinary low tide or is represented by the centre line of the river between ordinary high water mark on each side of the river, but probably the boundary line is the centre of the channel at low water.[9]

Navigation on tidal waters

See pp. 58 to 66.

Alteration in channel

Where a tidal river shifts its channel gradually and imperceptibly the ownership of the bed remains in the Crown,[10]

---

[1] *Fitzhardinge (Lord) v. Purcell*, [1908] 2 Ch. 139; *Gann v. Free Fishers of Whitstable* (1865), 11 H.L.C. 192; *Malcomson v. O'Dea* (1863), 10 H.L.C. 593; *Lord Advocate for Scotland v. Hamilton* (1852), 1 Macq. 46 H.L.; *Bulstrode v. Hall* (1663), 1 Sid. 148; *R. v. Trinity House* (1662), 1 Sid. 86.

[2] *Re Alston's Estate* (1856), 21 J.P. 163; *A.-G. v. London Corpn.* (1849), 12 Beav. 8.

[3] *Lord Advocate for Scotland v. Hamilton* (1852), 1 Macq. 46, H.L.

[4] *R. v. Smith* (1780), 2 Doug. K.B. 441.

[5] *R. v. Trinity House* (1662), 1 Sid. 86; *Bulstrode v. Hall* (1663), 1 Sid. 148.

[6] (1868), I.R. 2 C.L. 143.

[7] *Fitzhardinge (Lord) v. Purcell, supra; Malcomson v. O'Dea, supra.*

[8] Crown Lands Act, 1866, s. 7.

[9] *Hale's* " De Jure Maris ", First Treatise, p. 354; *Stuart Moore's* " Law of Fisheries ", pp. 118-123; *Pearce v. Bunting* (1896), 60 J.P. 695; *Thames Conservators v. Smeed*, [1897] 2 Q.B. 334; *Miller v. Little* (1878), 4 L.R. Ir. 302; *A.-G. v. Newcastle Corpn.* (1903), 67 J.P. 155.

[10] *Scratton v. Brown* (1825), 4 B. & C. 485; *Re Hull & Selby Rly. Co.* (1839), 5 M. & W. 527.

but if the change in the course of the river is sudden and perceptible and the original boundary is reasonably ascertainable, the right to the soil remains as before.[1] On this question there is no difference between tidal and non-tidal or navigable and non-navigable rivers.[2] If by the irruption of the waters of a tidal river, a new channel is formed in the land of a subject, although the rights of the Crown and of the public may come into existence and be exercised in what has become a portion of the tidal river, the right of the soil remains in the owner, so that if at any time thereafter the waters should recede and the river again changes its course, leaving the river channel dry, the soil becomes again the exclusive property of the owner free from all rights of the Crown and the public.[3]

See also ACCRETION AND ENCROACHMENT, pp. 25 to 27.

CHANGE IN COURSE OF RIVER, p. 48.

Jurisdiction

Tidal navigable rivers, where they are *intra fauces terrae*, form part of the adjoining county for both civil and criminal jurisdiction.

See also JURISDICTION OVER THE FORESHORE, pp. 35, 36.

NON-TIDAL RIVERS

A non-tidal river differs from its tidal counterpart in that usually neither the Crown nor the public have any rights or privileges therein or thereover, although many of the more important non-tidal rivers are subject to a public right of navigation. The bed of a non-tidal river is *prima facie* in private ownership and the public have no right to fish therein, and riparian owners on tidal navigable rivers possess similar rights and natural easements to those which belong to riparian owners above the flow of the tide, subject to the public right of navigation.

---

[1] *Ford v. Lacy* (1861), 30 L.J. Ex. 351; *Thakurin Ritraj Koer v. Thakurin Sarfaraz Koer* (1905), 21 T.L.R. 637.

[2] *Foster v. Wright* (1878), 44 J.P. 7; *Hindson v. Ashby*, [1896] 2 Ch. 1.

[3] *Carlisle Corpn. v. Graham* (1869), 21 L.T. 333.

Ownership in soil of bed

The Crown is not of common right entitled to the soil or bed of non-tidal inland waters,[1] and in the ordinary case, *prima facie*, the proprietors on each side of a non-tidal river are respectively entitled to the soil *usque ad medium aquae*.[2] In *Blount v. Layard*,[3] it was stated that the natural presumption is that a man whose land abuts on a river owns the bed of the river up to the middle of the stream, and if he owns the land on both sides, the presumption is that the whole bed of the river belongs to him, unless it is a tidal river. This presumption applies to land of any tenure, whether freehold, leasehold or former copyhold,[4] and whether the river is navigable or non-navigable.[5] *See also* PRESUMPTIONS AS TO OWNERSHIP OF FISHERIES on pp. 268-270. But the right to the bed of a stream is not inseparably bound up for ever with the right to the bank, since an owner of both may retain one and part with the other.[6]

Title to the bed of a non-tidal river is established similar to that for dry land. The general rule of conveyancing is that where a piece of land is conveyed, which is bounded by a non-navigable river, the conveyance passes the moiety of the soil of the river unless there is something in the language of the deed, or in the nature of the subject-matter of the grant, or in the surrounding circumstances, sufficient to rebut this presumption. This rule applies although the measurement of the property can be satisfied without including the half of the bed of the river, and although the land is described as bounded by a river, and notwithstanding that the map which is referred to in the grant does not include the bed of the river.[7] The rule also applies where land is conveyed by Act of Parliament.[8]

---

[1] *Johnston v. O'Neill*, [1911] A.C. 552; *Smith v. Andrews*, [1891] 2 Ch. 678; *Bristow v. Cormican* (1878), 3 A.C. 641.
[2] *R. v. Wharton* (1701), Holt K.B. 499; *Wishart v. Wyllie* (1835), 1 Macq. 389, H.L.; *Bickett v. Morris* (1866), 30 J.P. 532; *Edleston v. Crossley & Sons Ltd.* (1868), 18 L.T. 15; *Bristow v. Cormican, supra.*
[3] (1888), [1891] 2 Ch. 681.
[4] *Tilbury v. Silva* (1890), 45 Ch. D. 98.
[5] *Foster v. Wright* (1878), 44 J.P. 7; *Hindson v. Ashby*, [1896] 2 Ch. 71.
[6] *Smith v. Andrews*, [1891] 2 Ch. 678.
[7] *Micklethwait v. Newlay Bridge Co.* (1886), 51 J.P. 132; *Tilbury v. Silva* (1890), 45 Ch. D. 98; *Thames Conservators v. Kent*, [1918] 2 K.B. 272; *Hesketh v. Willis Cruisers* (1968), 19 P. & C.R. 573, C.A.
[8] *R. v. Strand Board of Works* (1863), 4 B. & S. 526.

Acts of ownership exercised on the bed and banks of a river sufficient to prove possession by a claimant are admissible in evidence.[1] The fact that a river is of more than ordinary breadth does not prevent a conveyance of premises bounded by the river from operating to convey the portion of the bed and soil of the river abutting thereon up to midstream.[2]

The presumption of law that a conveyance of land adjoining a river passes half the soil of the river without special mention does not apply unless the bed is in the disposition of the grantor, and an award under an Inclosure Act of waste bordering on a river does not carry with it the river bed *ad medium filum*.[3] Nor does the rule apply in the case of canals[4] or tidal waters.[5] Conveyances of riparian land fronting a river will not be construed as passing any portion of the bed of the river if the fishing in such waters is vested in another ownership.[6]

The rule that where a stream flows between two manors or properties, in the absence of evidence to the contrary, the boundary is to be taken to be the *medium filum aquae*, is applied where there is an island by drawing a *medium filum* as the boundary through each arm of the stream.[7] However, in a Scottish decision,[8] it was decided that when the bed of a river is divided by an island into a main and subsidiary channels, the latter being dry at times, the *medium filum* of the river is the centre of the bed from bank to bank, and not the centre line of the main channel.[8] A shifting sand-bank in the bed of a river has been held to be a portion of the bed and not to

---

[1] *Costard & Wingfield's Case* (1586), 2 Leon. 44; *Hollis v. Goldfinch* (1823), 1 B. & C. 208; *Jones v. Williams* (1837), 2 M. & W. 326; *Hanbury v. Jenkins*, [1901] 2 Ch. 401.

[2] *Dwyer v. Rich* (1870), I.R. 4 C.L. 424.

[3] *Ecroyd v. Coulthard*, [1898] 2 Ch. 358; *Hough v. Clark* (1907), 23 T.L.R. 682.

[4] *Chamber Colliery Co. v. Rochdale Canal Co.*, [1895] A.C. 564.

[5] *R. v. Trinity House* (1662), 1 Sid. 86.

[6] *Devonshire (Duke) v. Pattinson* (1887), 20 Q.B.D. 263; *Waterford Conservators v. Connolly* (1889), 24 I.L.T. 7.

[7] *Great Torrington Commons Conservators v. Moore Stevens*, [1904] 1 Ch. 347.

[8] *Menzies v. Breadalbane* (1901), 4 F. (Ct. of Sess.) 55.

affect the rights of the riparian owners, which extend from the shore to the *medium filum*.[1]

It seems that for the purposes of riparian boundaries and fishery limits, the position of the *medium filum aquae* in a non-tidal river is represented by a line running down the middle of the bed at the ordinary state of the river, *i.e.* the midline of the usual flow of the river without regard to periods of flood water or drought.[2] It does not appear to have been established how the boundaries of land abutting on the banks of a river are to be prolonged into the river to the middle line thereof, particularly if a boundary lies at an obtuse angle to the bank. It was, however, decided in *Crook v. Seaford Corpn.*[3] that the boundaries of the sea-beach above high water mark fronting on to the defendant's field comprised two lines drawn from the extremities of such field perpendicular to the sea-coast towards the sea and continued until they reached high water mark.

Where two parishes are separated by a river, the *medium filum* is the presumptive boundary between them,[4] and where a parish comes down as far as the banks of a river, there is a *prima facie* presumption that the parish extends as far as the middle of the river.[5] In the case of two counties separated by a river, in the absence of any words in an Act determining the boundary, the ordinary rule of *medium filum aquae* applies and the middle of the river continuously forms the boundary line between the two counties.[6]

Change in course of river

Where a river changes its course suddenly and perceptibly and if the former marks remain and the extent can be reasonably ascertained, the soil remains in the former owners and the *medium filum* remains as the boundary between the riparian properties. But where the change is gradual and imperceptible over a period of years the gradual accretions of land

---

[1] *Zetland (Earl) v. Glover Incorporation of Perth* (1870), 8 Macph. (Ct. of Sess.) 144.

[2] *Hindson v. Ashby*, [1896] 2 Ch. 71, and *see Stuart Moore's* " History and Law of Fisheries ", pp. 114-118.

[2] 1871), 6 Ch. App. 551.

[4] *R. v. Landulph (Inhabitants)* (1834), 1 Mood. & R. 393 N.P.

[5] *MacCannon v. Sinclair* (1859), 23 J.P. 757.

[6] *R. v. Brecon (Inhabitants)*, *Re Glastonbury Bridge* (1850), 14 J.P. 655.

from water belong to the owner of the land added to and the land gradually encroached upon by water ceases to belong to the former owner[1] and the *medium filum* will alter accordingly. These principles apply to tidal and non-tidal rivers alike.[2] Whether a strip of land has ceased to be part of a river is a question to be determined not by any hard and fast rule but by regard to all the material circumstances of the case, including the fluctuations of the river, the nature of the land, and its growth and user.[3]

See also ACCRETION on pp. 25-27 and ALTERATION IN CHANNEL at pp. 45, 46.

Watercourses and local authorities

The powers of local authorities in relation to rivers, streams and watercourses within their districts are usually confined to the enforcement of the provisions of Part XI of the Public Health Act, 1936, and the exercise of certain miscellaneous functions conferred under a variety of Acts of Parliament.

(1) *Public Health Act, 1936, Part XI*

The following matters are statutory nuisances for the purposes of Part III of the Public Health Act, 1936, namely:—

(*a*) Any pond, pool, ditch, gutter or watercourse which is so foul or in such a state as to be prejudicial to health[4] or a nuisance;

(*b*) Any part of a watercourse, not being ordinarily navigated by vessels employed in the carriage of goods by water, which is so choked or silted up as to obstruct or impede the proper flow of water and thereby to cause a nuisance or give rise to conditions prejudicial to health.

---

[1] *Ford v. Lacy* (1861), 7 H. & N. 151; *Carlisle Corpn. v. Graham* (1869), 21 L.T. 333; *Thakurin Ritraj Koer v. Thakurin Sarfaraz Koer* (1905), 21 T.L.R. 637; *Mursumat Imam Bandi v. Hurgovind Ghose* (1848), 4 Moo. Ind. App. 403.

[2] *Foster v. Wright* (1878), 44 J.P. 7; *Hindson v. Ashby*, [1896] 2 Ch. 1.

[3] *Hindson v. Ashby, supra.*

[4] " Prejudicial to health " means injurious, or likely to cause injury, to health (Public Health Act, 1936, s. 343 (1)).

In the case of an alleged nuisance under paragraph (b) above nothing in that provision is deemed to impose any liability on any person other than the person by whose act or default the nuisance arises or continues.[1]

A local authority may deal with any pond, pool, ditch, gutter or place containing or used for the collection of drainage, filth, stagnant water or matter likely to be prejudicial to health, by draining, cleansing or covering it, or otherwise preventing it from being prejudicial to health, but not so as to interfere with any private right or with public drainage, sewerage or sewage disposal works. The council may also execute any works of maintenance or improvement incidental to or consequential on the exercise of the above power and contribute towards the expenses incurred by any other person in doing anything mentioned above.[2]

Upon a complaint by a local authority against the local authority of an adjoining district that a watercourse or ditch which forms the boundary between their districts, or which lies in the adjoining district but near to the boundary, is so foul and offensive as injuriously to affect the district of the complainants, the magistrates court having jurisdiction in the place where the watercourse or ditch is situate may make an order for the cleansing of the watercourse or ditch and for the execution of such work as may be necessary.[3]

A local authority may require the owner of land laid out for building to fill up, pipe or culvert any watercourse or ditch on such land or abutting thereon, before the building operations are begun or whilst in progress.[4] In boroughs, urban districts and certain rural districts, streams and watercourses cannot be culverted except in accordance with plans

---

[1] Public Health Act, 1936, s. 259 (1); and see *Neath R.D.C. v. Williams* [1951] 1 K.B. 115.

[2] Public Health Act, 1936, s. 260.

[3] *Ibid.*, s. 261.

[4] *Ibid.*, s. 262.

and sections submitted to and approved by the local authority,[1] and the owner or occupier of land within such districts may be required by the local authority to repair, maintain and cleanse any culvert in, on or under his land.[2]

A local authority is empowered to contribute towards the expenses of the execution of works for any of the purposes mentioned in the foregoing provisions of Part XI of the Public Health Act, 1936, or may by agreement with the owner or occupier themselves execute any works required.[3] The powers contained under Part XI (save in relation to proceedings taken in respect of a statutory nuisance) are not exercisable with respect to streams and watercourses under the jurisdiction of a land drainage authority, except after consultation with that authority.[4]

The consent of the drainage authority is required where the erection or alteration of a culvert would be likely to affect the flow of a non-main river watercourse.[5]

(2) Miscellaneous powers of local authorities

(a) Regulation of vessels.

A local authority may licence the proprietors of pleasure boats and vessels, and the boatmen or other persons in charge thereof, and make byelaws for regulating the numbering and naming of such boats and vessels, the number of persons to be carried therein, mooring places, fixing rates of hire, the qualifications of boatmen and other persons in charge, and for securing their good and orderly conduct whilst in charge.[6]

---

1 Public Health Act, 1936, s. 263.
2 Ibid., s. 264.
3 Ibid., s. 265.
4 Ibid., s. 266.
5 Land Drainage Act, 1976, s. 28 (1).
6 Public Health Act, 1875, s. 172; see also the Public Health Acts Amendment Act, 1890, s. 44 (2); Public Health Acts Amendment Act, 1907, s. 94; Public Health Act, 1961, ss. 54 (6), 76; Local Government (Miscellaneous Provisions) Act, 1976, ss. 17, 18, 81 (1), Sch. 2.

(b) Waterways in a national park, country park, etc.

A local planning authority, or any other authority as directed
by the Secretary of State for the Environment after consultation, may as respects a waterway[1] in a national park and
within the area of the authority, carry out such work and do
such other things as appear necessary or expedient for facilitating the use of the waterway by the public for sailing, boating,
bathing or fishing.[2] Similarly, a local planning authority
whose area consists of or includes a national park which is
bounded by the sea or by a waterway, may, on land in or in
the neighbourhood of the national park, carry out such works
(including the construction of jetties and other works) and do
such other things as appear necessary or expedient for facilitating the use of the waters adjoining the national park by the
public for sailing, boating, bathing, fishing and other forms of
recreation.[3] The local planning authority may make byelaws
regulating the use of works carried out by them in the waters
bounding a national park and of any facilities or services
provided in connection with the works.[4] Where there is a
lake[5] in a national park, the local planning authority may make
byelaws for prohibiting or restricting traffic on the lake,
including the regulation of all forms of sport or recreation
involving the use of boats or vessels, prescribing rules of navigation and imposing speed limits,[6] requiring the use of effectual
silencers on boats or vessels propelled by internal combustion
engines, requiring the registration of boats or vessels and
making reasonable charges for such registration.[6]

Where a country park provided by a local authority comprises a waterway the kinds of open-air recreation for which
the local authority may provide facilities and services includes
sailing, boating, bathing and fishing, and if a country park is
bounded by the sea, or by a waterway which is not part of the

---

[1] " Waterway " means any lake, river, canal or other waters being (in any
case) waters suitable, or which can reasonably be rendered suitable, for sailing,
boating, bathing or fishing (National Parks, etc., Act, 1949, s. 114 (1)).
[2] *Ibid.*, s. 13. *See also ibid.*, ss. 74, 75 and Sch. 2.
[3] Countryside Act, 1968, s. 12 (3), (4).
[4] *Ibid.*, s. 12 (5).
[5] " Lake " includes any expanse of water other than a river or canal (*ibid.*,
s. 13 (13)).
[6] *Ibid.*, s. 13 (1)-(3).

sea, the local authority may carry out such work and do such things as appear to them necessary or expedient for facilitating the use of the waters so adjoining the country park by the public for sailing, boating, bathing, fishing and other forms of recreation. These powers include power to erect buildings or carry out works on land adjoining the sea or other waters but outside the country park, and to construct jetties or other works wholly or partly in the sea or other waters. Before taking action under these provisions, the local authority must consult with, and seek the consent of, any water authority having functions relating to the sea or other waters in question.[1]

The definition of " open country " in section 59 (2) of the National Parks and Access to the Countryside Act, 1949, for the purposes of Part V of that Act (which enable the public to have access for open-air recreation to open country as regards which access agreements or orders can be made or land can be acquired by local planning authorities) has been extended, if in the countryside, to include (*a*) a river[2] or canal, and (*b*) any expanse of water through which a river, or some part of its flow, runs, and (*c*) a strip of the adjacent land on both sides of a river or canal, or of any such expanse of water, of reasonable width, and where a highway crosses or comes close to the river, canal or other water, so much of any land connecting the highway with the strip of land as would, if included together with the strip in an access agreement or order, afford access from the highway to some convenient launching place for small boats. Heads (*b*) and (*c*) above do not apply as respects, or as respects land held with (1) a reservoir owned or managed by statutory undertakers or by a water authority, or (2) a canal owned or managed by the British Waterways Board. The strip of adjacent land comprised in an access order must be wide enough to allow passage on foot along the water and also to allow the public to picnic at convenient places and, where practicable, to embark or disembark, and must include the banks, walls or embankments along the water and any tow-path or other way or track beside the water. Local planning

---

[1] Countryside Act, 1968, s. 8 (1)-(4).
[2] " River " includes a stream and the tidal part of a river or stream (*Ibid.*, s. 16 (9)).

authorities are required to exercise their powers under Part V of the Act of 1949 over any such strip of land with special regard to the interests of persons using small boats who must circumvent obstacles or obstructions on the water by passing round on foot with their boats, and in the interest of persons wishing to obtain access from a highway to convenient launching places for small boats.[1]

For the purposes of section 20 (1) of the Water Act, 1973 (relating to recreation), statutory water undertakers may set apart any land held by them and provide, improve, alter, renew and maintain such buildings and other works and do such other things as may be necessary or expedient. The undertakers may make reasonable charges for these purposes and may also make byelaws with respect to a waterway which they own or manage, and any land held therewith, for (*inter alia*) regulating sailing, boating, bathing, fishing and other forms of recreation, prohibiting the use of the waterway by boats not currently registered with the undertakers as provided by the byelaws, and requiring the provision of sanitary appliances for preventing pollution.[2]

    (c)   *Ferries—see* Chapter 9.

    (d)   *Land Drainage—see* pp. 251 to 253.

    (e)   *Water rights—see* p. 118.

    (f)   *Coast protection—see* p. 37.

    (g)   *Byelaws for seashore—see* p. 29,

    (h)   *Sewage disposal—see* pp. 370 to 372.

    (i)   *Highway purposes.*

The highway authority for a highway may, for the purpose of draining it or of otherwise preventing surface water from flowing on to it, construct or lay and scour, cleanse and keep open ditches, gutters, drains, watercourses, bridges, culverts,

---

[1] Countryside Act 1968, s. 16 (1)-(4).

[2] Countryside Act, 1968, s. 22; Water Act, 1973, s. 40, Sch. 8, para. 92, Sch. 9; Control of Pollution Act, 1974, s. 108 (2), Sch. 4.

tunnels or pipes in the highway or in land adjoining or lying near to the highway.[1]

A highway authority may be authorised by order to divert part of a navigable watercourse[2] (including a towpath) if necessary or desirable in connection with the construction, improvement or alteration of a highway or for providing a new means of access to premises from a highway. An order may be made providing for the construction as part of a highway of a bridge over, or tunnel under, any navigable waters,[2] and a highway authority may also divert any part of a non-navigable watercourse in connection with highway purposes.[3]

LAKES AND PONDS

In general, the law relating to flowing water appears to apply equally in the case of standing water in lakes and ponds. There is, however, at least one point of difference, namely, that the law of accretion does not apply to non-flowing water in lakes and ponds.[4] A lake in a national park for the purposes of section 13 of the Countryside Act, 1968, is defined as including any expanse of water other than a river or canal.

There are but a few cases dealing with lakes, and they are concerned mainly with the ownership of lake beds. *Marshall v. Ulleswater Steam Navigation Co.*,[5] decided that the plaintiff was the owner of the bed and soil of the Lake of Ulleswater upon proof that he held a grant of a several and exclusive right of fishery in the lake; but the court was in doubt whether the soil of lakes, like that of fresh-water rivers, *prima facie* belonged to the riparian owners on either side *ad medium filum aquae*, or whether the soil belonged to the Crown by virtue of the royal prerogative.

---

[1] Highways Act, 1959, s. 103; *see also ibid.*, s. 308 (saving for works of land drainage authorities, and s. 6 of the Highways (Miscellaneous Provisions) Act, 1961 (power to fill in roadside ditches).

[2] " Navigable waters " or " navigable watercourse " means waters or a watercourse over which a public right of navigation exists. (Highways Act, 1971, s. 12 (5).)

[3] *Ibid.*, ss. 10-13.

[4] *Trafford v. Thrower* (1929), 45 T.L.R. 502.

[5] (1863), 3 B. & S. 732.

In a slightly later case,[1] it was held that a grant from James I, the owner of a non-tidal Irish lake, of land adjacent to that lake, did not pass the soil of the lake *ad medium filum*. But the doubt expressed in the Ulleswater case was resolved in two later decisions. In *Bristow v. Cormican*,[2] it was held that the Crown had no *de jure* right to the soil or fisheries of an inland non-tidal lake, and *Johnston v. O'Neill*[3] decided that the Crown was not of common right entitled to the soil or waters of an inland non-tidal lake and that this principle applied irrespective of the size of the lake. These decisions lead to the conclusion that, since the Crown has no *prima facie* interest in the soil of a non-tidal lake (unless, presumably, the Crown actually owns the bed or adjoining land), the soil and bed of such lakes belong to the owner or owners of the adjacent banks *ad medium filum*. As to the rights of joint owners of a lake, *see Menzies v. Macdonald*.[4] Two lakes joined by a narrow and shallow channel, which is not a river and is divided by a causeway, may be regarded as separate and distinct lakes.[5]

As the Crown has no right to the fisheries of inland non-tidal lakes,[6] and since the public have no common law right to fish therein,[7] irrespective of the size of the lake, it seems clear that in non-tidal lakes and pools the right of fishery belongs *prima facie* to the riparian owners *ad medium filum aquae*.

See also FISHERIES IN LAKES AND PONDS, pp. 271, 272.

If the waters of a lake or pond are polluted, an owner has the same remedies as are available to a riparian owner on the banks of a river or stream,[8] but the Control of Pollution

---

[1] *Bloomfield v. Johnston* (1868), Ir. 8 C.L. 89.

[2] (1878), 3 A.C. 641, H.L.

[3] [1911] A.C. 552.

[4] (1856), 2 Macq. 463.

[5] *MacKenzie v. Bankes* (1878), 3 A.C. 1324; *Cochrane v. Earl of Minto* (1815), 6 Pat. App. 139.

[6] *Bristow v. Cormican, supra.*

[7] *Johnston v. O'Neill*, [1911] A.C. 552; *Toome Eel Fishery (N.I.) v. Cardwell*, [1963] N.I. 92.

[8] *See* p. 103.

Act, 1974, is not applicable to lakes and ponds which do not discharge to a stream.[1]

As in the case of non-tidal rivers, the public do not have as of right the liberty to navigate on non-tidal lakes, but a right to navigate thereon may be acquired by dedication, immemorial user or by statute.[2] In *Bourke v. Davis*,[3] it was held that no authority could be produced for saying that a lake in private grounds, touched at one point only by a public road, could be subjected to a right for persons to launch boats from the road and boat on the lake for pleasure. The privilege of washing and watering cattle at a pond and taking and using the water for culinary and other domestic purposes is an easement.[4]

---

[1] Control of Pollution Act, 1974, s. 56 (1).

[2] *Marshall v. Ulleswater Steam Navigation Co., supra; Micklethwait v. Vincent* (1892), 67 L.T. 225; *Blower v. Ellis* (1886), 50 J.P. 326.

[3] (1889), 62 L.T. 34.

[4] *Manning v. Wasdale* (1836), 5 Ad. & El. 758; *Smith v. Archibald* (1880), 5 A.C. 489.

CHAPTER 4

NAVIGATION ON RIVERS

THE RIGHT OF NAVIGATION
Navigation on tidal rivers

The right of navigation exists as a right of way in all tidal waters and in such inland waters as are subject to the right to navigate. The right of navigation in tidal waters is a right of way thereover for all the public for all purposes of navigation, trade and intercourse,[1] and at common law the public have always had a right paramount to the rights of property of the Crown and its grantees to navigate over every part of a common navigable river.[2] Therefore, if the Crown grants a portion of the bed and soil of an estuary or tidal river, the grantee takes subject to the public right and cannot as owner of the soil in any way interfere with the enjoyment of the public right.[3] That the public have a right to the free use of the sea for the purposes of navigation has been unchallenged law from the earliest times. It has frequently been enunciated in the form that the sea is a public highway and that ships have the right *eundi redeundi et morandi* over every part of it, no matter to whom the soil lying thereunder may belong.[4]

A tidal navigable river means a river which is subject to the vertical flow and reflow of the ordinary tides and navigable as such. It includes the navigable parts of the river where fresh water is arrested by the horizontal flow of the tide. Parts of a river which are affected only by extraordinary tides are not part of the navigable river.[5] The mouth of a river

---

[1] *Blundell v. Catterall* (1821), 5 B. & Ald. 268.
[2] *Williams v. Wilcox* (1838), 8 Ad. & El. 314.
[3] *Gann v. Free Fishers of Whitstable* (1864), 11 H.L.C. 192.
[4] *Denaby & Cadeby Main Collieries v. Anson*, [1911] 1 K.B. 171.
[5] *Reece v. Miller* (1882), 8 Q.B.D. 626; *West Riding of Yorkshire Rivers Board v. Tadcaster R.D.C.* (1907), 97 L.T. 436.

comprehends the whole space between the lowest ebb and the highest flood mark.[1] The word "navigable" in the legal sense, as applied to a river in which the soil *prima facie* belongs to the Crown and fishing to the public, imports that the river is one in which the tide ebbs and flows.[2]

The right of navigation is simply a right of way and the public have a mere right to use a river for the purposes of navigation similar to the right which the public have to pass along a public road or footpath through a private estate,[3] and a navigable river is a public highway navigable by all Her Majesty's subjects in a reasonable manner and for a reasonable purpose.[4]

The right to navigate extends *prima facie* over the entire space over which the tide flows and is not suspended when the tide is out or too low for vessels to float.[5] Whilst the flow of the ordinary tides is strong *prima facie* evidence of the existence of a public navigable river, and the actual user of the river for navigation is the strongest evidence of its navigability[6]; whether a river is navigable or not is a question for a jury.[7]

In *Sim E Bak v. Ang Yong Huat*,[8] it was held that whether a particular water is navigable depends upon the character and nature of the channel and that not every ditch or cutting forms part of a public navigable river, although large enough to admit the passage of a boat. Every creek or river into which the tide flows is not on that account necessarily a public navigable channel, although sufficiently large for that purpose.[9] If there is a broad and deep channel, calculated to serve for the purposes of commerce, it will be natural to conclude that it

---

[1] *Horne v. MacKenzie* (1839), 6 Cl. & Fin. 628.
[2] *Murphy v. Ryan* (1868), Ir. R. 2 C.L. 143.
[3] *Orr Ewing v. Colquhoun* (1877), 2 A.C. 839.
[4] *Original Hartlepool Collieries Co. v. Gibb* (1877), 5 Ch. D. 713.
[5] *Colchester Corpn. v. Brooke* (1845), 7 Q.B.D. 338.
[6] *Rose v. Miles* (1815), 5 Taunt. 705; *Ilchester v. Rashleigh* (1889), 61 L.T. 477; *Lynn Corpn. v. Turner* (1774), 1 Cowp. 86.
[7] *Vooght v. Winch* (1819), 2 B. & Ald. 662.
[8] [1923] A.C. 429.
[9] *R. v. Montague* (1825), 4 B. & C. 598.

has been a public navigation, but a small stream intermittently navigated by very small boats is not necessarily navigable.[1]

Navigation on non-tidal rivers

The public have no right at common law to navigate on non-tidal inland waters,[2] but a right to do so may be acquired by immemorial usage by the public,[3] by dedication of riparian owners[4] or under statute.[5] A claim to establish a public right of navigation over a non-tidal stream must be treated as if it were a claim for a right of way on dry land,[6] and the right thus acquired is simply a right of way; the public who have acquired by user the right to navigate on an inland water have no right of property.[7]

The principles of navigation which apply to tidal rivers differ from those pertaining to non-tidal navigable rivers. First, the right of navigation on tidal rivers is unlimited, in that all vessels are entitled to use the whole of the channel at all times,[8] whereas the right on non-tidal waters is confined to the extent of the user or grant in question and may extend to the whole of the watercourse or be restricted to a particular portion.[9] Secondly, the banks of a non-tidal river belong *prima facie* to the riparian owners, and the right of navigation thereon does not extend, presumably, to landing or mooring on the banks,[10] save by custom, grant or statute, or at places on the bank which are known to be public landing-places.[11] It was decided in *Leith-Buchanan v. Hogg*,[12] that a right of navigation in a non-tidal loch on the part of the public did not include a right to beach or moor boats on private ground for carrying on the business of a boat-hirer, and that a right on the part of the public to embark and disembark on private

---

[1] *Ilchester v. Rashleigh, supra; see also Bower v. Hill* (1835), 2 Scott 535.
[2] *Bourke v. Davis* (1889) 44 Ch. D. 110; *Johnston v. O'Neill,* [1911] A.C. 552.
[3] *Bower v. Hill, supra.*
[4] *Simpson v. A.-G.,* [1904] A.C. 476.
[5] *See, e.g.,* s. 79 of the Thames Conservancy Act, 1932.
[6] *Bourke v. Davis, supra.*
[7] *Orr Ewing v. Colquhoun* (1877), 2 A.C. 839.
[8] *R. v. Randall* (1842), Car. & M. 496.
[9] *Williams v. Wilcox* (1838), 8 A. & E. 314.
[10] But *see Campbell's Trustees v. Sweeney,* [1911] S.C. 1319.
[11] *Drinkwater v. Porter* (1835), 7 C. & P. 181.
[12] [1931] S.C. 204; *see also Iveagh (Earl) v. Martin,* [1960] 2 All E.R. 668.

ground could not be acquired by prescription. A public right of navigation on inland waters does not include a right to fish by the public[1] or to shoot wild-fowl.[2]

The riparian owners of a non-tidal stream might perhaps be able to establish a private right of way, or a right of boating for recreation for themselves and their friends by custom, but the existence of such a right or custom would not entitle the public to boat on the river or support the claim that it was a highway.[3]

See also NON-TIDAL RIVERS, pp. 45 to 49.

Incidents of the Right of Navigation

(1) *Passage and Grounding*

The public right to navigate includes all such rights upon the waterway as, with relation to the circumstances of each river, are necessary for the full and convenient passage of vessels along its channel; a boat may remain aground till the tide serves, if she cannot reach her destination in a single tide, and no toll can be demanded by the owner of the soil (except in a harbour).[4] It seems that a vessel is entitled to remain temporarily in one place until the wind or weather, or possibly also the season, permits it to leave, or until it has obtained a cargo, or completed repairs, but a vessel cannot remain permanently moored, *e.g.* for the purpose of supplying commodities required by ships for use whilst being navigated, because such permanent occupation by one person to the exclusion of the public is a violation of their right of free passage.[5] It should be noted that the rights of all vessels on a navigable river are not co-extensive, since whilst a small boat may be entitled to go up to the furthest point she can reach so as to give the public the benefit of the public way, the same right does not exist as regards a large vessel, which is not entitled under extraordinary circumstances to proceed to a place where large vessels are not accustomed to go and where there is no accommodation for loading or unloading them.[6]

---

1 *Smith v. Andrews*, [1891] 2 Ch. 678.
2 *Micklethwait v. Vincent* (1892), 67 L.T. 225.
3 *Bourke v. Davis* (1889), 44 Ch. D. 110.
4 *Colchester Corpn. v. Brooke* (1845), 7 Q.B. 339.
5 *Denaby & Cadeby Main Collieries Ltd. v. Anson*, [1911] 1 K.B. 171; *Iveagh (Earl) v. Martin*, [1960] 2 All E.R. 668.
6 *The Swift*, [1901] P. 168.

(2) *Anchoring, Mooring and Landing*

The right to anchor either by means of a mooring or anchor is a necessary part of the right to navigate in tidal waters.[1] The right to drop anchor or moor may be one of the incidents of the right to navigate a public river, but it can only be exercised as a reasonable incident in the course of such navigation,[2] or it may exist by grant, custom or statute. But there is no common law right to lay or maintain permanent moorings on another person's land without his permission and it is not an ordinary incident of navigation, although such a right may arise by custom or statute.[3] " Mooring " has shades of meaning according to those who use it and the circumstances in which it is used, and the meaning given to it is primarily a matter of fact for the magistrates, such as whether they hold that dropping an anchor for a specified period of time amounts to mooring.[4]

Where the public right of navigation in tidal waters includes the right to use a quay on payment of a fee, this extends only to the use in the course of embarking or disembarking, loading or unloading a vessel, or in the course of carrying out repairs to a vessel as is necessary or desirable before she can resume her voyage, and the public right does not extend to using the quay as a place of business for repairing vessels.[5]

There is no general right to land or embark either passengers or goods on the foreshore or the land adjoining thereto, other than at places appropriated by usage, grant or statute for such purposes,[6] or with the consent of the owner. Since the banks of a non-tidal navigable river are privately owned, the consent of the riparian owner is necessary to land or moor a vessel to the bank, except at a public landing-stage,[7] and a right for the public to embark or disembark on private ground, or to beach or moor vessels there for carrying on the business of a boat-hirer cannot be acquired by prescription.[8] The existence of a

[1] *Gann v. Free Fishers of Whitstable* (1865), 11 H.L.C. 192.
[2] *Campbells' Trustees v. Sweeney*, [1911] S.C. 1319.
[3] *Fowey Marine (Emsworth) Ltd. v. Gafford*, [1967] 2 All E.R. 472.
[4] *Evans v. Godber* [1974] 1 W.L.R. 1317. *See also The Alletta and The England* [1925] 2 Lloyd's Rep. 479; *Liverpool and N. Wales Steamship Co. Ltd. v. Mersey Trading Co. Ltd.* [1908] 2 Ch. 460.
[5] *Iveagh (Earl) v. Martin*, [1960] 2 All E.R. 668.
[6] *Blundell v. Catterall* (1821), 5 B. & Ald. 268.
[7] *Drinkwater v. Porter* (1835), 7 C. & P. 181.
[8] *Leith-Buchanan v. Hogg*, [1931] S.C. 204.

towpath along a navigable river would not appear to permit vessels to moor or land there, unless the vessel is engaged in towing.

The right of owners of fishing vessels to fix moorings in the soil of the foreshore in tidal and navigable waters for the purpose of attaching their boats to them may be claimed either as an ordinary incident of the navigation in such waters, or on the presumption of a legal origin by grant from the Crown of the foreshore subject to such user, or by concession from the former owner of the foreshore.[1]

(3) Towing

The banks of navigable rivers are in private ownership and are not subject to a common law right for the public to tow, but a right of towing may exist thereon by custom,[2] usage or prescription,[3] dedication or statute.[4]

A towpath may be either a private path by a canal, or a public right of way subject to a right of towing[5] or a highway restricted to be used only by horses employed in towing barges.[6] The soil of a towpath may be vested by statute in the navigation authority,[7] but in other cases, a navigation authority may have only a statutory use or easement of the soil sufficient for the purposes of navigation.[8] Although conservators may have no ownership of property in the soil of the towpath, they will be entitled to restrain by injunction an adjoining landowner from using the towpath so as to obstruct its free use for navigation.[9] Where the freehold

---

[1] A.-G. v. Wright, [1897] 2 Q.B. 318; Wyatt v. Thompson (1794), 1 Esp. 252.

[2] Wyatt v. Thompson, supra.

[3] Ball v. Herbert (1789), 3 Term Rep. 253; Pierce v. Lord Fauconberg (1757), 1 Burr. 292; Vernon v. Prior (1747), 3 Term. Rep. 254; Kinloch v. Neville (1840), 6 M. & W. 795.

[4] See s. 77 of the Thames Conservancy Act, 1932.

[5] Vide s. 27 (6), (7) of the National Parks, etc., Act, 1949.

[6] Winch v. Thames Conservators (1874), 36 J.P. 646; R. v. Severn & Wye Rly. (1819), 2 B. & Ald. 648.

[7] Bruce v. Willis (1840), 11 A. & E. 463.

[8] Badger v. S. Yorks Rly. (1858), 7 W.R. 130; Hollis v. Goldfinch (1823), 1 B. & C. 205.

[9] Lea Conservancy Board v. Button (1879), 45 L.T. 385; A.-G. v. Wilcox 1938), 82 S.J. 566.

interest in a towpath is vested in the riparian owners subject to the right of towing, they may use the towpath as they wish, provided no interference, injury or obstruction is caused thereto,[1] and an owner of land adjoining the towpath may erect a wharf on his own land and take goods across the towpath to the wharf.[2]

In *Winch v. Thames Conservators*,[3] the conservators who kept open the towpath and took an aggregate toll for the use of the whole navigation, were held to be under a duty to those using the towpath to take reasonable care that the whole towpath was kept in such a state as not to expose the users to undue danger, and to be liable in damages to any person who sustained loss as a result of a portion of towpath being out of repair, unless the defective condition was a latent one, the existence of which the conservators were ignorant although using reasonable care.

The banks of a canal have been held to include the towpath,[4] and a towpath is not confined to the mere beaten track but includes so much of the bank as may be ordinarily used by horses towing barges.[5] As to whether a navigation authority can dedicate portions of a towpath as a public right of way, *see Thames Conservators v. Kent*[6] and *Grand Junction Canal v. Petty*.[7] A prescriptive right to a public towpath on the banks of a navigable river is not destroyed in consequence of part of the river adjoining the towpath becoming converted into a floating harbour under statute, although the towpath is thereby subject to use at all times of the tide, whereas before it was only used when the tide was sufficiently high for purposes of navigation.[8] As to whether a towpath comes under the jurisdiction of inclosure commissioners, *see Simpson v. Scales*.[9]

---

[1] *Thames Conservators v. Kent* (1918) 83 J.P. 85.
[2] *Monmouthshire Canal & Rly. Co. v. Hill* (1859), 23 J.P. 679.
[3] (1874), 36 J.P. 646.
[4] *Monmouthshire Canal & Rly. Co. v. Hill, supra.*
[5] *Winch v. Thames. Conservators, supra.*
[6] (1918), 83 J.P. 85.
[7] (1888), 52 J.P. 692.
[8] *R. v. Tippett* (1819), 3 B. & Ald. 193.
[9] (1801), 2 Bos. & P. 496.

Extinguishment of right of navigation

A public right of navigation in a river or creek may be extinguished either by Act of Parliament,[1] or writ of *ad quod damnum* and inquisition thereon (this procedure is now otiose), or under certain circumstances by commissioners of sewers— *see* now river authorities[2]—or by natural causes such as the recess of the sea or an accumulation of mud. In such cases the river ceases to be navigable, at least until such causes are counteracted.[3] If a river is choked with mud that does not give the public a right to cut another passage through the adjoining lands.[4] Should a navigable river gradually shift its course and follow an entirely new channel distinguishable from the old one, it seems that the right of navigation will follow to the new channel, although the bed of the soil and the right of fishing may be vested in the owner of the adjoining land, so as to bar the right of the Crown to the bed and of the public to the fishery.[5] If navigation commissioners restore a silted up channel, the right of navigation is restored to the new channel.[6]

Navigation versus fishing

In general, the right of navigation takes precedence over the right of fishery in tidal waters and navigable rivers; thus, in *Gann v. Free Fishers of Whitstable*,[7] the grant of an oyster-bed in the sea below low water mark was held to have been taken by the grantee subject to the public right of navigation, so that he could not in respect of his ownership of the soil make any demand which in any way interfered with the enjoyment of the public right of navigation. But this rule is subject to qualification; since the right of navigation must be exercised reasonably, and where it conflicts with a right of fishing the right must not be abused so as to work an injury to the fishing.[8] If a vessel grounds on an oyster-bed and does

---

[1] *See*, for instance, s. 112 of the Transport Act, 1968.
[2] *See* s. 27 of the Land Drainage Act, 1976.
[3] *R. v. Montague* (1825), 4 B. & C. 598.
[4] *Ball v. Herbert* (1789), 3 T.R. 253.
[5] *Carlisle Corpn. v. Graham* (1869), L.R. 4 Ex. 366; *Williams v. Wilcox* (1838), 8 Ad. & El. 314.
[6] *R. v. Betts* (1850), 16 Q.B. 1022; *Vooght v. Winch* (1819), 2 B. & Ald. 662.
[7] (1864), 11 H.L. 192; *Whitstable Free Fishers v. Foreman* (1868), 32 J.P. 596.
[8] *Original Hartlepool Collieries Co. v. Gibb* (1877), 41 J.P. 660.

damage, the master will be held liable if he was aware of the existence of the bed or if the grounding was due to improper navigation, or if after grounding and receiving notice of the existence of the bed he fails to take reasonable means to remove his vessel as speedily as possible.[1]

OBSTRUCTIONS TO NAVIGATION

The obstruction of a public navigable river is a public nuisance at common law and may be the subject of indictment,[2] or an information filed by the Attorney-General against the person responsible,[3] or an application to the court for *mandamus* where applicable,[4] or the nuisance may be abated by decree of the court.[5] An obstruction which is a private nuisance may be abated in a reasonable manner, provided the least injurious means are employed,[6] but a private person cannot abate an obstruction in a navigable channel amounting to a public nuisance unless he suffers some special injury beyond that suffered by the rest of the public[7]; in such circumstances he is entitled to bring an action on proof of special damage.[8] An obstruction which interferes with a right of access is an injury to private property and is actionable without proof of special damage.[9] Under section 31 of the Malicious Damage Act, 1861, it is an offence to do any injury or mischief so as to obstruct the navigation of a navigable river or canal.

Obstructions in navigable rivers may be classified as (1) Erections on the river bed; (2) Works on the foreshore; (3) Wreck; (4) Bridges; (5) Locks, weirs and dams; (6) Miscellaneous obstructions.

---

[1] *Colchester Corpn. v. Brooke* (1845), 7 Q.B. 339; *The Octavia Stella* (1887), 57 L.T. 632; *The Swift*, [1901] P. 168; *The Bien*, [1911] P. 40.
[2] *R. v. Watts* (1798), 2 Esp. 675; *R. v. Russell* (1827), 6 B. & C. 566; *R. v. Ward* (1836), 4 Ad. & El. 384; *R. v. Tindall* (1837), 6 Ad. & El. 143.
[3] *R. v. Clark* (1702), 12 Mod. Rep. 615; *A.-G. v. Richards* (1795), 2 Anst. 603; *A.-G. v. Johnson* (1819), 2 Wils. Ch. 87; *A.-G. v. Lonsdale* (1868), 20 L.T. 64; *A.-G. v. Terry* (1874), 30 L.T. 215; *A.-G. v. Wright*, [1897] 2 Q.B. 318.
[4] *R. v. Bristol Dock Co.* (1839), 1 Ry. & Can. Cas. 548.
[5] *A.-G. v. Parmeter* (1811), 10 Price 412.
[6] *Hill v. Cock* (1872), 36 J.P. 552.
[7] *Colchester Corpn. v. Brooke*, *supra*; *Dimes v. Petley* (1850), 15 Q.B. 276; *A.-G. v. Thames Conservators* (1862), 1 Hem. & H. 1.
[8] *Rose v. Miles* (1815), 4 M. & S. 101.
[9] *Rose v. Groves* (1843), 5 Man. & G. 613.

(1) Erections on River Bed

A riparian owner is entitled to build an erection on his land though covered with water, provided that it does not interfere with the rights of navigation or with the rights of other riparian owners.[1] But, on the other hand, any structure on the bed of a navigable river may amount to an obstruction of the navigation, as in *A.-G. v. Terry*,[2] where a wharf extending three feet into the river, which had a navigable width of sixty feet, was held to be a tangible and substantial interference with the navigation.

Whether an obstruction in a navigable river amounts to a nuisance is a question of fact; an encroachment is not necessarily a nuisance and it is for the jury on the facts of the case to say whether the public have been in any way inconvenienced.[3] An obstruction must be a nuisance at the time of erection,[4] and whilst an anticipated injury is generally not sufficient to support an action,[5] an erection which was not an obstruction at the time it was erected may become such owing to the river silting up or otherwise.[6] If the encroachment is of a trifling nature the courts will not interfere, *e.g.* if the erection is in a reasonable situation and a reasonable space is left for the passage of vessels on the river,[7] or where the consequences of the encroachment are slight.[8]

To constitute a nuisance there must be some actual obstruction of a navigable river[9] which produces inconvenience to the public in the use of the river for the purposes of the navigation.[10] Where there is an obstruction the question is whether it occasions any hindrance to the navigation of the river by vessels of any description and not whether the

---

[1] *Orr Ewing v. Colquhoun* (1877), 2 A.C. 839; *see also* p. 94.
[2] (1874), 30 L.T. 315.
[3] *R. v. Shepard* (1822), 1 L.J.O.S.K.B. 45.
[4] *R. v. Bell*, (1822) 1 L.J.O.S.K.B. 42.
[5] *Orr-Ewing v. Colquhoun, supra;* but *see A.-G. v. Lonsdale, supra.*
[6] *Williams v. Wilcox* (1838), 8 Ad. & El. 314.
[7] *R. v. Russell* (1827), 6 B. & C. 566.
[8] *R. v. Tindall* (1837), 6 Ad. & El. 143.
[9] *R. v. Betts* (1850), 16 Q.B. 1022.
[10] *R. v. Shepard, supra; R. v. Grosvenor* (1819), 2 Stark. 511.

obstruction causes a benefit to the navigation in general,[1] and it is no defence that the inconvenience occasioned is counterbalanced by some benefit to the public.[2] Where the person causing the obstruction does so for the purposes of his own trade, this is too remote a benefit to the public generally and will not be justified.[3]

The owners of a wharf on a navigable river who are granted a licence under the authority of an Act of Parliament by the river conservators to construct a jetty are not liable to an action by adjoining owners on the grounds that the jetty obstructs their free navigation in common with the rest of the public, since the effect of the Act was to contemplate some interference with the navigation.[4] But though a statutory licence may be the licensee's justification so far as the public right of navigation is concerned, it does not authorise a licensee thereby to affect injuriously another riparian owner's land.[5]

A right to obstruct a navigable river cannot be acquired by length of time,[6] but this may be authorised by statute, e.g. where a railway company are authorised to construct a railway on the bed of a navigable river.[7] If a statute permits the navigation to be obstructed, no action will lie for damage caused by the execution of the authorised works,[8] unless the works are carried out negligently or are outside the statutory powers.[9]

See also OBSTRUCTION, pp. 94 to 99.

(2) Works on the foreshore

Part II of the Coast Protection Act, 1949, contains provisions designed to restrict certain types of works detrimental

---

[1] *R. v. Randall* (1842), Car. & M. 496.
[2] *R. v. Ward* (1836), 4 Ad. & El. 395; *R. v. Tindall* (1837), 6 Ad. & El. 143; *A.-G. v. Terry* (1874), 30 L.T. 315 (over-ruling *R. v. Russell* (1827), 6 B. & C. 566).
[3] *A.-G. v. Terry* (1874), 30 L.T. 315.
[4] *Kearns v. Cordwainers' Co.* (1859), 6 C.B.N.S. 388; *A.-G. v. Thames Conservators* (1862), 8 L.T. 9.
[5] *Lyon v. Fishmongers' Co.* (1876), 1 A.C. 662; *Lawes v. Turner & Frere* (1892), 8 T.L.R. 584; *Joliffe v. Wallasey L.B.* (1873), L.R. 9 C.P. 62; *Burley Ltd. v. Lloyd Ltd.* (1929), 45 T.L.R. 626.
[6] *Vooght v. Winch* (1819), 2 B. & Ald. 662.
[7] *Abraham v. Great Northern Ry. Co.* (1851), 16 Q.B. 586.
[8] *Cracknell v. Thetford Corpn.* (1869), L.R. 4 C.P. 629.
[9] *Geddis v. Bann Reservoir* (1878), 3 A.C. 430; *Brownlow v. Metropolitan Board of Works* (1864), 16 C.B.N.S. 546; *Joliffe v. Wallasey L.B., supra.*

to navigation. The previous written consent of the Secretary of State for Trade and Industry is required where any of the following operations will cause or is likely to result in obstruction or danger to navigation, namely:—

(1) the construction, alteration or improvement of any works on, under or over any part of the seashore[1] lying below high water mark of ordinary spring tides,

(2) the deposit of any object or materials[2] on any such part of the seashore lying below high water mark of ordinary spring tides, or

(3) the removal of any object or materials from any part of the seashore lying below low water mark of ordinary spring tides.

The consent of the Secretary of State to the operations under heads (1) and (3) above applies in relation to any part of the sea bed in a designated area under the Continental Shelf Act, 1964.[3]

The Secretary of State can refuse consent or give it subject to such conditions as they think fit, having regard to the nature and extent of the obstruction or danger which it appears to them would otherwise be caused or be likely to result.[4]

Certain operations are exempt from the above restrictions, such as the carrying out of approved coast protection work, dredging operations (including the deposit of dredged materials) authorised by a local Act, the removal of sunken vessels or obstructions or dangers to navigation by a conservancy, harbour or navigation authority.[5] Any person who carries out any operation in contravention of the above restrictions or who fails to comply with conditions subject to which the Secretary of State have given their consent is guilty of an offence under the Act.[6]

---

[1] " Seashore " means the bed and shore of the sea, and of every channel creek, bay or estuary, and of every river as far up that river as the tide flows and any cliff, bank, barrier, dune, beach, flat or other land adjacent to the shore (Coast Protection Act, 1949, s. 49 (1)).

[2] " Materials " includes minerals and turf but not seaweed (Coast Protection Act, 1949, s. 49 (1)).

[3] Continental Shelf Act, 1964, s. 4.

[4] Coast Protection Act, 1949, s. 34.

[5] See more particularly s. 35 of the Coast Protection Act, 1949.

[6] Coast Protection Act, 1949, ss. 36, 43.

(3) Wreck

The owner of a vessel sunk in the fairway of a navigable river is under a duty, so long as he retains possession, management and control of her, to take reasonable precautions to prevent other vessels from striking the wreck and to warn other vessels of its position; he is liable for damage to another vessel if the damage could have been prevented by reasonable skill and care on his part.[1] This duty may be transferred with the transfer of the possession and control of the wreck to another person.[2]

Where a vessel is sunk in a navigable river by misfortune or accident an indictment cannot be maintained against the owner for not removing it.[3] If a vessel sinks in a navigable channel owing to the negligence of the owners of the vessel and thereby obstructs the navigation and blocks the approaches to a wharf, the owners are liable at common law for the damage caused by the obstruction to the navigation and the wharf and cannot escape liability by abandoning the wreck. The damages recoverable are the reasonable cost of removing the wreck.[4] Under statute conservancy and harbour authorities have power to remove or destroy vessels sunk, stranded or abandoned in waters under their jurisdiction and to sell the wreck and reimburse their expenses from the proceeds of sale.[5]

(4) Locks, Weirs and Dams

In early cases dealing with the Thames it was held that hindering the course of a navigable river by causing locks to be built thereon was contrary to Magna Charta[6]; as also was

---

[1] *The Douglas* (1882), 46 L.T. 488; *The Snark*, [1900] P. 105; *Brown v. Mallett* (1848), 5 C.B. 599; *Harmond v. Pearson* (1808), 1 Camp. 515.
[2] *White v. Crisp* (1854), 10 Ex. 312; *Uptopia (Owners) v. Primula (Owners), The Uptopia*, [1893] A.C. 492.
[3] *R. v. Watts* (1798), 2 Esp. 675.
[4] *Dee Conservancy Board v. McConnell*, [1928] 2 K.B. 159; for other cases on recovery of expenses, *see The Harrington* (1888), 59 L.T. 72; *The Sea Spray* (1907), 96 L.T. 792; *The Wallsend* (1907), 96 L.T. 851; *The Ella*, [1915] P. 111; *Boston Corpn. v. Fenwick* (1923), 129 L.T. 766; *Barraclough v. Brown*, [1897] A.C. 615; *Wilson v. Cator* (1863), 1 New Rep. 314; *Jinman v. East Coast Insurance Co.* (1878), 42 J.P. 809; *The Emerald, The Greta Holme*, [1896] P. 192.
[5] *E.g.*, Merchant Shipping Act, 1894, ss. 530, 531, 534; Harbour, Docks and Piers Clauses Act, 1847, s. 56.
[6] *R. v. Clark* (1702), 12 Mod. Rep. 615.

diverting part of the Thames so as to weaken the current for carrying barges, which could not be done without an *ad quod damnum* or by statute.[1]

Weirs on navigable rivers which impede the navigation have long been declared by statute to be a nuisance. Magna Charta (1215) stated that all weirs except on the coast should be put down, and a later statute[2] ordered the destruction of all weirs, mills and other fixed engines for fishing which had been set up during the reign of Edward I. A weir appurtenant to a fishery which obstructs the whole or part of a navigable river is legal, therefore, if granted by the Crown before that reign.[3] In an Irish case,[4] it was held that the erection of weirs in a tidal river was a nuisance to the navigation and an indictable offence at common law, but a claim to a weir in a non-navigable river is within the Prescription Act, 1832.[5] Today many locks and weirs are erected under statutory authority.

See also OBSTRUCTIONS IN WATERCOURSES, pp. 232, 234.

OBSTRUCTIONS TO PASSAGE OF FISH, pp. 285 to 290.

WEIRS OBSTRUCTING FISHERIES, p. 273.

(5) Bridges

A bridge across a navigable river, the erection of which is not authorised, is not necessarily an obstruction,[6] although unnecessary delay in opening a swing bridge carrying a public highway across a dock may amount to an obstruction.[7]

A railway company who are required by statute to carry a bridge across a canal at a certain height will be held responsible for an obstruction to canal traffic caused by the bridge being at a lower elevation due to ground subsiding from causes beyond the control of either the railway company

---

[1] *Hind v. Manfield* (1614), Noy. 103.
[2] 25 Edward III st. 4, c. 4 (1350).
[3] *Williams v. Wilcox* (1838), 8 Ad. & El. 314; *Rolle v. Whyte* (1868), 8 B. & S. 116.
[4] *R. v. Ryan* (1845), 8 I.L.R. 119.
[5] *Rolle v. Whyte, supra; Leconfield v. Lonsdale* (1870), L.R. 5 C.P. 657.
[6] *R. v. Betts* (1850), 16 Q.B. 1022.
[7] *Wiggins v. Boddington* (1828), 3 C. & P. 544.

or the canal company.[1] For other cases on railway bridges
across a navigation, *see London & Birmingham Ry. Co. v.
Grand Junction Canal Co.*[2]; *Priestley v. Manchester & Leeds
Ry. Co.*[3]; *Manser v. Northern & Eastern Counties Ry. Co.*[4];
Ferrand v. Midland Ry. Co.[5]; *Abraham v. Great Northern Ry.
Co.*[6] *See also* section 20 of the Highways Act, 1959, section
3 of the Highways (Miscellaneous Provisions) Act, 1961 and
sections 10 to 13 of the Highways Act, 1971.

See also STRUCTURES OVER WATERCOURSES, pp. 233, 234.

(6) Miscellaneous obstructions

The removal of a mooring anchor fixed in a known part of
a navigable river to another part of that river covered by the
ordinary tides, so that a vessel sailing in part of the river
ordinarily used by ships runs foul of and hits the anchor, may
amount to an obstruction.[7] The continued mooring of a
boat across a public navigable creek which prevents a person
from navigating his barges and makes him convey his goods
longer by land is special damage for which an action lies.[8]
Mooring several vessels in a river in breach of a local byelaw
so as to prevent other vessels passing is also an obstruction.[9]
Stacking colliery refuse so that it falls into a navigable river
and causes an obstruction is an indictable offence,[10] as is also
the casting of ballast from a ship into navigable water to the
prejudice of the navigation.[11]

THE RIGHTS OF RIPARIAN OWNERS ON NAVI-GABLE RIVERS

The rights of proprietors on the banks of a stream are
founded on the right of access which they have to the water,

---

[1] *Rhymney Ry. Co. v. Glamorganshire Canal Co.* (1904), 91 L.T. 113; *see
also North Staffordshire Ry. Co. v. Hanley Corpn.* (1909), 73 J.P. 477.

[2] (1835), 1 Ry. & Can. Cas. 224.

[3] (1840), 4 Y. & C. Ex. 63.

[4] (1841), 2 Ry. & Can. Cas. 380.

[5] (1901), 17 T.L.R. 27.

[6] (1851), 16 Q.B. 586.

[7] *Hancock v. York, Newcastle Ry. Co.* (1850), 10 C.B. 348; *Joliffe v. Wallasey
Local Board* (1873), 38 J.P. 40.

[8] *Rose v. Groves* (1843), 5 Man. & G. 613; *Dobson v. Blackmore* (1847),
9 Q.B. 991.

[9] *Stubbs v. Hilditch* (1887), 51 J.P. 758.

[10] *R. v. Stephens* (1866), 14 L.T. 593.

[11] *Michell v. Brown* (1858), 23 J.P. 548; *see also United Alkali Co. v. Simpson,*
[1894] 2 Q.B. 116; *Wheal Remfrey China Clay Co. v. Truro Corpn.,* [1923]
2 K.B. 594; *Colbran v. Barnes* (1861), 11 C.B.N.S. 246.

and a riparian owner on the banks of a tidal navigable river has rights and natural easements similar to those which belong to a riparian owner above the flow of the tide, subject to the public right of navigation.[1] *See also* RIPARIAN RIGHTS. pp. 83 to 89.

The rights which are of particular importance to a riparian owner on the banks of a navigable river are those concerned (1) with his access to the river for purposes of navigation, (2) for mooring boats, and (3) building erections on the bank and bed.

(1) Right of Access

A public navigable river is a public highway, and where there is a highway the owners of land on the banks are entitled to go on the river from any spot on their own land.[2] The same principle applies whether access is required by a landowner to or from the sea, tidal or non-tidal rivers or lakes.[3] The owner of a wharf on the bank of a public navigable river has, like other subjects of the realm, the right of navigating the river as one of the public. This is not a right which he enjoys as a riparian owner, but one which he enjoys in common with the rest of the public. But where the right of navigation is connected with an exclusive right of access to and from a particular wharf, it ceases to be a right held in common with the rest of the public and becomes a form of enjoyment of the land, and of the river in connection with the land, the disturbance of which may be vindicated in damages or restrained by an injunction.[4] Any interference with a right of access to a navigable river is actionable without proof of special damage,[5] but whether an obstruction amounts to an interference with a

---

[1] *Lyon v. Fishmongers' Co.* (1876), 1 A.C. 683; *North Shore Ry. Co. v. Pion* (1889), 14 A.C. 612.

[2] *Marshall v. Ulleswater Navigation Co.* (1871), L.R. 7 Q.B. 166.

[3] *Hindson v. Ashby,* [1896] 2 Ch. 1; *A.-G. of Straits Settlements v. Wemyss* (1888) 13 A.C. 192.

[4] *Lyon v. Fishmongers' Co., supra.*

[5] *Rose v. Groves* (1843), 6 Scott N.R. 645; *Dobson v. Blackmore* (1847), 9 Q.B. 991.

riparian owner's access to his frontage which is a private right is a question of fact to be determined by the circumstances of each particular case.[1]

A riparian owner's right of access is not necessarily affected by the fact that a highway[2] or sea wall[3] intervenes between his land and the river. Where due to accretion or works of reclamation, the water has receded from the bank or foreshore, a riparian owner is entitled to have access over the land so added.[4] The right of access includes a right for the riparian owner to land and cross any intervening shore at all states of the tide even where private property is involved.[5] If the right of access is removed or injuriously affected in the exercise of compulsory powers, it is an interest in land for which compensation is payable under the Lands Clauses Acts.[6]

(2) Right to Moor

A riparian owner may moor vessels of ordinary size alongside his wharf for purposes of loading and unloading at reasonable times and for a reasonable time and the owner of adjoining premises will be restrained by injunction from interfering with the access of the vessel although it overlaps his premises.[7] But the vessel will not be allowed to interfere with the proper access to the neighbouring premises if used as a wharf, nor to the free entrance to or exit from such premises if used as a dock by other vessels.[8] If a vessel is

---

[1] *Bell v. Quebec Corpn.* (1879), 5 A.C. 84; *A.-G. v. Thames Conservators* (1862), 1 Hem. & M. 1; *A.-G. of Straits Settlements v. Wemyss* (1888), 13 A.C. 192.

[2] *Tetreault v. Montreal Harbour Comrs.*, [1926] A.C. 299.

[3] *Port of London Authority v. Canvey Island Comrs.*, [1932] 1 Ch. 446.

[4] *Hindson v. Ashby*, [1896] 2 Ch. 1; *A.-G. of Southern Nigeria v. John Holt & Co. (Liverpool) Ltd.*, [1915] A.C. 599.

[5] *Metropolitan Board of Works v. McCarthy* (1874), L.R. 7 H.L. 243; *Macey v. Metropolitan Board of Works* (1864), 10 L.T. 66.

[6] *Mellor v. Walmesley*, [1905] 2 Ch. 164; *Marshall v. Ulleswater Steam Navigation Co.* (1871), L.R. 7 Q.B. 166; *A.-G. for Straits Settlements v. Wemyss, supra; Duke of Buccleuch v. Metropolitan Board of Works* (1872), L.R. 5 H.L. 418.

[7] *A.-G. v. Thames Conservators, supra; Dalton v. Denton* (1857), 6 L.T. 228; *Temple Pier Co. v. Metropolitan Board of Works* (1865), 11 Jur. N.S. 337.

[8] *Original Hartlepool Collieries v. Gibb* (1877), 5 Ch. D. 713; *Land Securities Co. Ltd. v. Commercial Gas Co.* (1902), 18 L.T. 405.

moored alongside a wharf, and access is required to a neighbouring wharf, the vessel must be moved to give that access
at once[1]; if the vessel is fixed a person entitled to access may
pass over the vessel.[2]

A riparian owner may also moor a floating wharf and
boathouse alongside his premises, provided the navigation is
not thereby obstructed.[3] The question of whether planning
permission is required for the mooring of a vessel or floating
structure in a navigable channel depends upon the particular
circumstances. If a vessel is moored or anchored to the bank
or shore for a purpose which is incidental to the ordinary
course of navigation, planning consent is not normally necessary. But consent is needed for the construction of a landing-
stage, pile or jetty for mooring purposes, since this is an
operation in, on or over land covered by water. The mooring
of a houseboat for residential purposes, or of a structure, *e.g.*
for a helicopter station, is something not in the ordinary
course of navigation, and amounts to a material change in the
use of the mooring, and probably of the bank, for which
consent is required. One has to take into account the type of
vessel or structure, its navigability, the user proposed and
whether the mooring is permanent or temporary. These
matters emerge on Ministry decisions arising out of planning
appeals.

(3) Right to erect Navigation Works

A riparian owner can build erections on the bed and banks
of a natural stream much in the same way as he may on any
part of his land not covered by water, provided that he does
not interfere with any rights of navigation or with the other
riparian owners above or below him.[4] However, a riparian
owner who is also owner of the soil of a navigable river has
no greater right to use the *alveus* of a tidal river than of a
non-tidal river.[5] The erection of works, such as wharves,

---

1 *Land Securities Co. v. Commercial Gas Co.* (1902), 18 T.L.R. 405.
2 *Eastern Counties Ry. Co. v. Dorling* (1859), 5 C.B.N.S. 821.
3 *Booth v. Ratté* (1889), 62 L.T. 198.
4 *Orr Ewing v. Colquhoun* (1877), 2 A.C. 839.
5 *A.-G. v. Lonsdale* (1868), L.R. 7 Eq. 377.

jetties, piles, etc., on the bed of a navigable river are, generally speaking, permissible unless there is some actual interference with the navigation, in which event the obstruction will be treated as a nuisance,[1] but an erection which at the present moment is not a nuisance, may become so by a change in circumstances.[2] An unauthorised erection on the bed or foreshore of tidal waters by a person who is not the owner is a purpresture and liable to abatement by the Crown or the owner of the soil.

The owner of a structure on the shore of a navigable river which, either from its original defective construction or from want of repair, presents a dangerous hidden obstruction to the river, is responsible for any injury thereby occasioned, such as to a barge coming to the structure, without any default on the part of the person in charge of the barge; the remedy of the owner of the structure is either to keep it in repair or to give notice of the danger.[3] A wharf must be kept in a fit and proper condition to receive a vessel,[4] and a wharfinger must take reasonable care to ascertain that the bottom of the river adjoining his jetty is in such a condition as not to cause injury to a vessel using the jetty[5]; but a wharfinger will not be liable in negligence if the river bed is in its normal state and the nature of the river is known to those in charge of the ship.[6]

CONSERVANCY AND NAVIGATION AUTHORITIES

The King as Lord High Admiral is conservator of all ports, havens, rivers, creeks and arms of the sea and protector of the navigation thereof, and the Crown under the royal prerogative exercised a degree of jurisdiction over the " royal rivers ". In the course of time, the conservancy in many rivers has devolved upon various public bodies, whether they

---

[1] *See also* ERECTIONS ON RIVER BED, pp. 67, 68.

[2] *A.-G. v. Terry* (1874), 30 L.T. 215.

[3] *White v. Phillips* (1863), 9 L.T. 388; *Brownlow v. Metropolitan Board of Works* (1864), 16 C.B.N.S. 546; *Curling v. Wood* (1847), 16 M. & W. 628; *The Grit* (1924), 132 L.T. 638.

[4] *The Ville de St. Nazaire* (1903), 51 W.R. 590.

[5] *The Moorcock* (1889), 14 P.D. 64.

[6] *Tredegar Iron & Coal Co. v. Calliope (Owners), The Calliope*, [1891] A.C. 11; *The Humorist*, [1944] P. 28.

be commissioners, conservators, municipal corporations, navigation authorities and companies, port or harbour boards or other bodies corporate.

The precise rights, powers and duties of a conservancy or navigation authority can only be defined and interpreted in each case by reference to their particular statutes, and, generally speaking, such statutes contain provisions for the maintenance and improvement (or restoration) of a navigable river by means of locks and weirs, dredging and clearing the channel of obstructions, for regulating the navigation by means of byelaws, for charging tolls on traffic, and, sometimes, for licensing erections and works on the river bed.

Some indication of the rights and obligations of conservancy authorities can be gleaned from the common law.

Property in Rivers

Where a river is placed under the jurisdiction of trustees or a board of conservators by statute for purposes of navigation, the ownership of the bed and banks does not normally vest in them, unless specifically vested in them by statute.[1] If the language of the statute is in doubt as to whether the soil of the river should vest in a navigation company, the court may infer that the company have only a use of the soil or easement necessary for the purposes of navigation.[2] In *Hollis v. Goldfinch*,[3] it was held that the proprietors of a navigation did not necessarily acquire an interest in the soil of the river bank to maintain an action for trespass. However, the wording of an Act of Parliament may amount to a statutory transfer of land which has the effect of vesting the land in a navigation authority without a deed of conveyance.[4] A navigation company do not as a rule have a proprietary interest in the water of a river, by virtue of their statutes,[5]

---

[1] *R. v. River Weaver Navigation Trustees* (1827), Pratt 28; *Lea Conservancy Board v. Button* (1879), 12 Ch. D. 383.

[2] *Badger v. S. Yorks Rly. Co.* (1858), 1 E. & E. 359; *R. v. Aire & Calder Navigation Co.* (1829), 9 B. & C. 820.

[3] (1823), 1 B. & C. 205.

[4] *Bruce v. Willis* (1840), 11 A. & E. 463.

[5] *A.-G. v. Great Northern Ry. Co.*, [1909] 1 Ch. 775.

but a proprietary interest in the river water may be created by statute.[1] The public who have acquired by use the right to navigate on an inland water have no right of property.[2]

In *A.-G. v. Great Eastern Ry. Co.*[3] a railway company was restrained from taking a large quantity of water for the use of their station from a river under the control of conservators, credit being given to the evidence on their part that taking such water would impede the navigation, against the evidence on the part of the company that taking such water would produce no appreciable effect. An information lies for cutting down the banks of a public river and thereby diverting the course of the water, although that part of it is by statute vested in private persons, and an action given them for damages done to it.[4]

The Conservators of the River Thames, who have no proprietary interest at large in the bed and soil of the non-tidal river, have been held to be the guardians of the navigation of the Thames, and the protector of the bed and soil of the river for navigation purposes, and to have certain conservancy rights in connection with the maintenance and improvement of the navigation—they may dredge and grant licences for landing-places, wharves and jetties irrespective of the ownership of the soil.[5]

Maintenance of Navigation

At common law the owner of the bed of a navigable river is not obliged to clear the channel of natural obstructions, such as weed and silt, and is not liable for any damage, *e.g.* by overflow of the river, which thereby results to adjoining owners.[6] Likewise, a navigation authority, empowered by statute to protect the navigation and to take tolls for the use of the navigation, are not under a duty to cut weeds and

---

1 *Medway Co. v. Romney* (1861), 25 J.P. 550.

2 *Orr Ewing v. Colquhoun* (1877), 2 A.C. 839.

8 (1871), 35 J.P. 788; *see also Medway Co. v. Romney, supra.*

4 *R. v. Stanton* (1678), 2 Show. 30.

5 *Cory v. Bristow* (1877), 2 A.C. 262; *Thames Conservators v. Port of London Sanitary Authority* (1894), 58 J.P. 335.

6 *Hodgson v. York Corpn.* (1873), 28 L.T. 836; *Bridge's Repair Case* (1609), 3 Co. Rep. 33.

dredge silt, unless required for the benefit of the navigation.[1] In *Forbes v. Lee Conservancy Board*,[2] the court decided that unpaid trustees appointed for public purposes in aid of the common law right of navigating an ancient navigable river were not liable to remove obstructing piles, since the duty of removing obstructions imposed by the statute was discretionary and not compulsory. A landowner, who is authorised by Act of Parliament to improve the navigation of a river running through his land, was held not bound to maintain or repair the locks; there was no evidence that the locks had been dedicated to the public as a highway, and if the tolls are not sufficient to defray the cost of navigation, the owner is justified in closing them down altogether.[3] A person who is empowered to make navigable a river is entitled to take tolls for the carriage of goods in barges over the river made navigable.[4] Some navigation Acts provide for the payment of compensation in case of damage sustained by reason of the navigation.[5]

However, where a navigation authority choose to keep the navigation open to the public and take tolls for its use, they are under a common law duty to take reasonable care that the public may navigate without danger to their lives or property,[6] and this may include a duty to regulate traffic.[7] This principle has been held to apply whether the tolls are taken for the profit of the authority or are applied to the maintenance of navigation works.[8] In *Winch v. Thames Conservators*,[9] which was concerned with injury arising from a defective towpath, the defendants were held to be liable on the ground that so long as they kept open the towpath and took tolls for its use they were under an obligation to those who used it to take reasonable care to see that it was in such a state as not to expose persons using it to undue danger, but the defendants

---

[1] *Parrett Navigation Co. v. Robins* (1842), 10 M. & W. 593; *Cracknell v. Thetford Corpn.* (1869), 38 L.J.C.P. 353.
[2] (1879), 4 Ex D. 116.
[3] *Simpson v. A.-G.*, [1904] A.C. 476.
[4] *Tamar Marine Navigation Co. v. Wagstaffe* (1863), 4 B. & S. 288; *Juxon v. Thornhill* (1628), Cro. Car. 132.
[5] *R. v. Delamere* (1865), 13 W.R. 757.
[6] *Parnaby v. Lancaster Canal Co.* (1839), 11 A. & E. 223.
[7] *Boxes v. British Waterways Board*, [1971] 2 Lloyd's Rep. 183, C.A.
[8] *Mersey Docks v. Gibbs* (1864), 14 L.T. 677.
[9] (1874), 31 L.T. 128.

would not have been liable if the defective state of the towpath was a latent one, the existence of which the defendants might be ignorant though using reasonable care, or if they had given notice of it to those who paid tolls or had informed them that they must take the towpath as they found it. It is clear that the duty to take reasonable care does not extend so as to render a conservancy authority responsible for damage caused by hazardous obstructions in a navigable river where there is no evidence that they knew or ought to have known of a possible danger and there is no negligence on their part.[1]

The issue of information and charts by a conservancy board indicating the minimum depth of water in a navigable channel does not give rise to a warranty that such minimum depth would be found on any given date in the bed of a river which was constantly changing, and this does not amount to a breach of duty to exercise reasonable care in the performance of their navigation functions.[2]   A port authority who provide moorings in a river for vessels are not under an absolute duty to keep the mooring buoys fit for the purposes for which they are used but only under a duty to take all reasonable steps to see that the buoys are so fit.[3]

Regulation of navigation

Many of the authorities concerned with rivers, harbours and other inland navigations are empowered under their private Acts to make byelaws or rules for regulating the navigation of vessels using the waters under their jurisdiction. Where such rules are not and cannot be made, Her Majesty in Council on the application of any person having authority in such waters, or, if there is no such person, any person interested in the navigation thereof, may make such rules, and those rules as regards vessels navigating such waters

---

[1] *Gridley v. Thames Conservators* (1886), 3 T.L.R. 108; *Queens of the River S.S. Co. v. Eastern Gibb & Co. and Thames Conservators* (1907), 96 L.T. 901; *Stevens v. Thames Conservators*, [1958] 1 Lloyds Rep. 401.

[2] *The Neptun*, [1938] P. 21.

[3] *Williams & Sons Ltd. v. Port of London Authority* (1933), 39 Com. Cas. 77.

have the same force as if they were part of the collision regulations.[1]

This reference to collision regulations means the regulations for preventing collisions at sea[2] made pursuant to section 418 of the Merchant Shipping Act, 1894, which must be observed by all vessels (and seaplanes and hovercraft) upon the high seas and in all waters connected therewith navigable by seagoing vessels, but which do not apply where local rules have been made for the navigation of a harbour, river, lake or inland water.

It is the duty of a person in charge of a vessel to take reasonable care and to use reasonable skill to prevent the vessel from doing injury,[3] and negligence in exercising this duty amounts to a breach of good seamanship, or a breach of the international or local regulations for preventing collisions.

In some instances a " speed limit " is imposed by statute or under byelaw in respect of vessels navigating inland waters; e.g., " persons must not navigate steam vessels at a greater rate than five miles per hour ".[4] But on other waters the position as regards speed may be dealt with by a provision making it an offence to fail to navigate a vessel with care and caution and at such a speed and in such a manner as not to endanger life or cause injury to persons or to property.[5]

As to the offence of taking a vessel without the consent of the owner or other lawful authority, see section 12 of the Theft Act, 1968.

Byelaws can be made by water authorities for prohibiting or regulating the use of inland waters for boating, swimming or other recreational purposes and for registering boats and

---

1 Merchant Shipping Act, 1894, s. 421 (1).

2 See the Collision Regulations and Distress Signals Order, 1977 (S.I. 1977 No. 982) as amended by S.I. 1977 No. 1301; the Hovercraft (Application of Enactments) (Amendment) Order, 1977 (S.I. 1977 No. 1257).

3 The Vianna (1858), Sw. 405; The Voorwaats and The Khedive (1880), 5 A.C. 876.

4 Tisdell v. Combe (1838), 7 Ad. & El. 788.

5 E.g., s. 97 of the Thames Conservancy Act, 1932.

charging for registration.[1] The Secretary of State may by order confer on certain bodies who own or manage an inland waterway, such as navigation authorities, local authorities, water authorities, power to make byelaws, subject to confirmation by the Secretary of State, in relation to the waterway.[2]

---

[1] *See* s. 79 of the Water Resources Act, 1963.
[2] Transport Act, 1968, s. 113.

CHAPTER 5

NATURAL RIGHTS OF WATER

RIPARIAN RIGHTS

Nature of riparian rights

The proprietor of land on the banks of a natural stream is entitled to the enjoyment of what are commonly known as " riparian rights ". Lord Wensleydale in *Chasemore v. Richards*[1] said:—

> " The subject of rights to streams of water flowing on the surface has been of late years fully discussed, and, by a series of carefully considered judgments,[2] placed upon a clear and satisfactory footing. It has been settled that the right to the enjoyment of a natural stream of water on the surface *ex jure naturae* belongs to the proprietor of the adjoining lands as a natural incident to the right to the soil itself; and that he is entitled to the benefit of it, as he is to all the other advantages belonging to the land of which he is the owner. He has the right to have it come to him in its natural state, in flow, quantity and quality, and to go from him without obstruction, upon the same principle that he is entitled to the support of his neighbour's soil for his own in its natural state. His right in no way depends on prescription or the presumed grant of his neighbour, nor from the presumed acquiescence of the proprietors above and below ".

---

[1] (1859), 7 H.L. Cas. 349.

[2] *E.g.*, Parke, B., in *Embrey v. Owen* (1851), 6 Ex. 353, 369; Lord Kingsdown in *Miner v. Gilmour* (1859), 12 Moo. P.C.C. 131. Later cases in point include *Swindon Waterworks Co. v. Wilts. & Berks. Canal Co.* (1875), 33 L.T. 513; *McCartney v. Londonderry Rly.*, [1904] A.C. 301; *Nuttall v. Bracewell* (1866), 4 H. & C. 714; *White (John) & Sons v. White*, [1906] A.C. 72; *Stollmeyer v. Trinidad Lake Petroleum Co.*, [1918] A.C. 485.

The rights of a riparian owner to the enjoyment of the quantity of the flowing water in an inland water as regards its abstraction or impounding are now subject to control by means of a licensing system operated by water authorities under Part IV of the Water Resources Act, 1963. The purpose of this chapter is to set out the common law principles applicable to riparian rights as these principles existed prior to the Act of 1963, and the common law rights of riparian owners to abstract water from, and to construct or alter impounding works in, an inland water referred to hereafter in this chapter must be construed in the light of the statutory controls dealt with in Chapter 11, which (subject to specified exceptions) require that a person after 1st July, 1965, may only abstract water from a source of supply, or construct or alter impounding works in an inland water, in pursuance of a licence granted by the water authority.

The right of using flowing water does not necessarily depend upon the ownership of the soil covered by such water,[1] and " the right to have a stream flow in its natural state, without diminution or alteration is an incident of property in the land through which it passes; but flowing water is *publici juris*, not in the sense that it is *bonum vacans*, to which the first occupant may acquire an exclusive right, but that it is public and common in this sense only, that all may reasonably use it who have a right of access to it, and that none can have any property in the water itself, except in the particular portion which he may choose to abstract from the stream and take into his possession, and that during the time of his possession only ".[2] The right to resist interference with a natural flow of water, or a flow legally established, is independent of the actual user of the water.[3]

Riparian rights are founded on the right of access to the stream and a riparian tenement must be in reasonable proximity to the water. A site some distance from a river but connected to it by a strip of land may be too far from the river bank to

---

[1] *Lord v. Sydney Comrs.* (1859), 12 Moo. P.C. 473.

[2] *Per* Parke, B., in *Embrey v. Owen* (1851), 6 Ex. 353.

[3] *Frechette v. Compagnie Manufacturie de St. Hyacinthe* (1883), 9 A.C. 170.

sustain the character of a riparian tenement. The expression " riparian tenement " connotes, in addition to contact with the river, a reasonable proximity to the river bank, " and nobody could reasonably suggest that the site of Paddington Station is a riparian tenement although it is connected to the River Thames by a strip of land many miles long, nor could it be reasonably suggested that the whole of a large estate was a riparian tenement, because a small portion was bounded by a stream ". Whether a particular piece of land sustains the character of a riparian tenement is a question of fact, and must be determined according to the special circumstances.[1] For riparian rights properly so named to arise, the land must be in actual contact with the stream, but lateral contact is as good *jure naturae* as vertical, that is to say, a man has as much right to water flowing past his land as he has to water flowing over his land. In the case of a tidal river, where the foreshore is left bare at low water, although the bank is not always in contact with the flow of the stream, it is in such contact for a great part of every day in the regular course of nature, which is sufficient foundation for a natural riparian right.[2] Whilst the right of a riparian owner on the banks of a tidal navigable river exists *jure naturae*, it is essential to its existence that his land should be in contact with the flow of the stream, at least at the times of ordinary high tides.[3] Land which is separated from a river by a strip of land in separate ownership does not abut on the river.[4] The right of a riparian owner to the lateral tributaries or feeders of a main stream applies to water flowing, in a defined and natural channel or watercourse, and does not extend to water flowing over or through land previous to its arrival at such watercourse.[5] If a person wishes to exercise or assert riparian rights, *e.g.* to stop pollution of a river, it is only necessary for him to purchase a small portion of the bank of the stream.[6]

---

[1] *Attwood v. Llay Main Collieries*, [1926] Ch. 444.
[2] *North Shore Rly. v. Pion* (1889), 14 A.C. 621; *Stockport Waterworks Co. v. Potter* (1864), 10 L.T. 748.
[3] *Dawood Hashim Esoof v. Tuck Sein* (1931), 58 Ind. App. 80, P.C.
[4] *A.-G. v. Rowley Bros. and Oxley* (1910), 75 J.P. 81.
[5] *Broadbent v. Ramsbotham* (1856), 11 Ex. 602.
[6] *Crossley v. Lightowler* (1867), 16 L.T. 438.

Riparian owners

The rights of a riparian owner do not depend on his owner-ship of the soil of the stream,[1] and are derived entirely from the possession of land abutting on the river and if the owner grants any portion of his land so abutting the grantee becomes a riparian owner and has similar rights. If the owner grants away part of his estate not abutting on the river, the grantee has no water rights by virtue merely of his occupation. Nor can he have them by express grant, except as against the grantor so as to sue other persons in his own name for an infringement of them.[2] Riparian rights are not easements to be granted or reserved as appurtenant to what is respectively sold or retained, but are parts of the fee simple and inheritance of the land sold or retained. If such rights are not granted or reserved the vendor remains, and the purchaser becomes, a riparian owner.[3] A riparian owner cannot, except as against himself, confer on one whom is not a riparian owner any right to use the water of the stream, and any user by a non-riparian owner, even under a grant from a riparian owner, is wrongful if it sensibly affects the flow of the water by the lands of other riparian owners.[4]

In *Kensit v. G.E. Ry. Co.*,[5] the owner of land not abutting on a river with the licence of a higher riparian owner took water from the river and after using it for cooling certain apparatus returned it to the river unpolluted and undiminished; held: a lower riparian owner could not obtain an injunction against the landowner so taking water, or against the riparian owner through whose land it was taken.

Where there are riparian proprietors on each side of a non-tidal river, in the ordinary case, *prima facie*, they are entitled to the soil of the bed *usque ad medium aquae*,[6] but occasionally the same person owns the banks on both sides and he is entitled to change the channel as he pleases, provided he restores the

---

[1] *Lyon v. Fishmongers' Co.* (1876), 1 A.C. 673.
[2] *Stockport Waterworks Co. v. Potter, supra.*
[3] *Portsmouth Waterworks Co. v. L.B. & S.C. Ry.* (1906), 26 T.L.R. 175.
[4] *Ormerod v. Todmorden Joint Stock Mill* (1883), 11 Q.B.D. 155.
[5] (1884), 27 Ch. D. 122.
[6] *Wishart v. Wyllie* (1853), 1 Macq. 389, H.L.

water to the old channel before it leaves his land and provided it flows out of his land into the lands below as it was want to do, neither increased nor diminished in quantity, quality or direction.[1]

Rights and duties of riparian owners

The rights and duties of a riparian proprietor are clearly stated by Lord Denman in *Mason v. Hill*,[2] *viz.*:—

" the possessor of land through which a natural stream runs, has a right to the advantage of that stream flowing in its natural course, and to use it when he pleases for any purpose of his own not inconsistent with the similar rights in the proprietors of the land above and below. A proprietor above cannot diminish the quantity or injure the quality of water which would otherwise descend, nor can a proprietor below throw back the water without his licence or consent ".

Riparian proprietors are entitled, except so far as their rights are varied by statute or special circumstances, to require that nothing shall be done to affect to their prejudice either the quality or the quantity of the stream as it flows in a natural state. When an Act of Parliament authorises interference with the natural flow, the original rights of the riparian proprietors are impaired only so far as the reasonable exercise of the statutory rights impairs them.[3]

Persons on the banks of a flowing stream have by nature certain rights to use the water on the stream, whether they exercise those rights or not, and they may begin to exercise such rights when they will.[4] A riparian owner who has acquired a right to divert water from a stream is not bound to continue the exercise of that right, but if he abandons the right and restores the water to its original channel, he may

---

[1] *Nuttall v. Bracewell* (1866), 15 L.T. 313; *Holker v. Porritt* (1875), 39 J.P. 196.

[2] (1853), 5 B. & A. 1.

[3] *Edinburgh Water Trustees v. Sommerville & Son*, (1906) 95 L.T. 217; *see also Medway Co. v. Romney (Earl)* (1861), 4 L.T. 87.

[4] *Sampson v. Hoddinott* (1857), 1 C.B.N.S. 590.

be bound to do so in such a manner as not to expose the servient tenement to injury.[1]

The flow of a natural stream creates natural rights and liabilities between all the riparian proprietors along the whole of its course, and subject to reasonable use by himself, each proprietor is bound to allow the water to flow on without altering the quantity or quality.[2] Apart from a use authorised by statute, grant or prescription, any unreasonable and unauthorised interference with the use of the water, to the prejudice of one entitled to its use, may be the subject of an action for damages,[3] and may be restrained by injunction,[4] even though there may be no actual damage to the plaintiff.[5] It is not necessary to show damage to the plaintiff's reversionary interest, it is enough to show obstruction of his right from which the law will infer damage.[5] In *Ingram v. Morecroft*[6] the defendant sold part of his land to the plaintiff and covenanted for quiet enjoyment and afterwards the defendant raised the level by three inches of a brook running past the plaintiff's grounds through the defendant's property; held that this was not a proper subject for the interference of the court.

The natural rights of riparian owners apply to watercourses flowing in known and defined natural channels, whether upon or below the surface of the ground, and have no application (a) where a flow of surface water squanders itself over an undefined area[7]; (b) in the case of underground water which merely percolates through the strata in no known channels[8]; or (c) as regards an artificial watercourse, unless, taking into account its character (whether it be temporary or permanent), the circumstances under which it was presumably created and the mode in which it has been used and enjoyed, the conclusion can be reached that the watercourse has acquired the status

---

[1] *Bridges v. Saltaun* (1873), 45 Sc. Jur. 372.
[2] *Gaved v. Martyn* (1865), 19 C.B.N.S. 732.
[3] *Dickinson v. Grand Junction Canal* (1852), 21 L.J. Ex. 241.
[4] *Robinson v. Byron (Lord)* (1785), 1 Bro. C.C. 588.
[5] *Sampson v. Hoddinott, supra; Sharp v. Wilson, Rotheray & Co.* (1905), 93 L.T. 155.
[6] (1863) 33 Beav. 49.
[7] *Rawstron v. Taylor* (1855), 11 Ex. 369.
[8] *Chasemore v. Richards* (1859), 7 H.L.C. 374.

of a natural watercourse.[1] In addition to riparian rights in respect of a stream, there may exist acquired rights or easements of water, which are discussed in Chapter 6.

A riparian owner on the banks of a navigable or tidal river has similar rights and natural easements to those which belong to a riparian owner on the banks of a non-tidal or non-navigable river and there is not distinction in principle except that in the former case, there must be no interference with the public right of navigation.[2]

Classification of riparian rights

In considering the natural rights of riparian owners in detail it is convenient to divide them into:—

(1) rights as to the natural quantity of the water, such as its abstraction, diversion, obstruction and overflow, which are discussed hereafter in this Chapter;

(2) rights dealing with the natural quality of the water, namely its purity and pollution—also referred to in this Chapter.

(3) rights of riparian owners on the banks of a navigable river, as to which *see* pp. 72 to 76.

ABSTRACTION AND DIVERSION AT COMMON LAW

Ordinary use of water

A proprietor on the banks of a natural stream has a right to the ordinary use of the water flowing past his land, namely to the reasonable use of the water for his domestic purposes and for his cattle, without regard to the effect which such use may have, in case of deficiency upon proprietors lower down the stream.[3] In the ordinary or primary use of flowing water a riparian proprietor is under no restriction, and if in the exercise of his ordinary rights he exhausts the water altogether, a lower riparian owner cannot complain.[4] " Domestic

---

[1] *Baily & Co. v. Clark Son & Morland*, [1902] 1 Ch. 649.

[2] *North Shore Ry. Co. v. Pion* (1889), 61 L.T. 525; *Lyon v. Fishmongers' Co.* (1876), 35 L.T. 569; *A.-G. v. Lonsdale* (1868), 20 L.T. 64.

[3] *Miner v. Gilmour* (1859), 12 Moo. P.C.C. 131; *Norbury (Lord) v. Kitchin* (1863), 7 L.T. 685; *White & Sons v. White*, [1906] A.C. 72.

[4] *McCartney v. Londonderry Ry. Co.*, [1904] A.C. 301.

purposes "[1] have been held to include " drinking and culinary purposes, cleansing and washing, feeding and supplying the ordinary quantity of cattle and so on ", and if a riparian owner does not use the water for such purposes, he is not entitled to appropriate to other purposes the amount which he would be entitled to take for domestic purposes.[2]

The common law rights of a riparian owner to abstract water from an inland water for ordinary or primary purposes, *i.e.* domestic household purposes or agricultural purposes other than spray irrigation, as they existed before 1st July, 1965, continue in force after that date without the requirement of a licence to abstract in so far as such rights fall within the exemption from the requirement of a licence conferred by section 24 (2) of the Water Resources Act, 1963 (*see* p. 187), but otherwise subject to the provisions of that Act.

Extraordinary use of water

In addition to the ordinary use of flowing water, a riparian proprietor has the right to the use of the water for any other purpose, provided he does not thereby interfere with the rights of other proprietors either above or below him. Subject to this condition, a riparian proprietor may dam up the stream for the purposes of a mill, or divert the water for irrigation, but he has no right to interrupt the regular flow of the stream, if he thereby interferes with the lawful use of the water by other proprietors and inflicts upon them a sensible injury.[3] In the exercise of extraordinary rights, the limit of which has never been accurately defined, and probably is incapable of exact definition, a riparian proprietor is under considerable restrictions:—(1) the use must be reasonable; (2) the purposes for which the water is taken must be connected with his tenement; (3) he is bound to restore the water which he has taken and uses for these purposes substantially undiminished in volume and unaltered in character.[4]

---

[1] *See also* cases referred to under s. 35 of the Waterworks Clauses Act, 1847, as to definition of " domestic purposes " in relation to water supply.
[2] *A.-G. v. Great Eastern Ry.* (1871), 23 L.T. 344.
[3] *Miner v. Gilmour, supra.*
[4] *Swindon Waterworks Co. v. Wilts. & Berks. Canal* (1875), 33 L.T. 513; *Stollmeyer v. Trinidad Lake Petroleum Co.,* [1918] A.C. 485; *Attwood v. Llay Main Collieries,* [1926] Ch. 444.

An extraordinary use extends to (a) purposes of manufacture[1]; (b) irrigation, so long as the running stream is not exhausted[2]; (c) damming a river for milling.[3] But the term does not include uses such as supplying a town with water,[4] nor supplying a lunatic asylum and jail.[5]

In *Swindon Waterworks Co. v. Wilts. & Berks. Canal*,[6] waterworks undertakers became riparian owners by buying a mill and collected the water into a permanent reservoir to supply an adjoining town with water; held that this was not a reasonable use of the water which could be justifiably made by an upper riparian owner, and that the canal company as lower riparian owners were entitled to an injunction to restrain such use. Whether the use of a stream is reasonable under the circumstances is a question for the jury.[7]

In *McCartney v. Londonderry Ry. Co.*,[8] a railway company wanted to abstract water from a stream which was crossed by the railway (which was the only point where their property adjoined the stream), and to use the water for working their engines along the whole of their line. The court held that the company could not do so, since the purpose was unconnected with the land where it crossed the stream.

In *Attwood v. Llay Main Collieries*,[9] where the defendants drew on river water for their colliery, the taking of water for such extraordinary purposes without returning it to the river was held to be an unauthorised user, and since it amounted to a complete diversion of part of the river and a confiscation of the rights of the plaintiff as lower riparian owner, it was not necessary for the plaintiff, in order to secure relief, to prove damage or the future possible acquisition of prescriptive rights by the defendants.

---

1 *Dakin v. Cornish* (1845), 6 Ex. 360.
2 *Embrey v. Owen* (1851), 6 Ex. 353.
3 *Belfast Ropeworks v. Boyd* (1887), 21 L.R. Ir. 560.
4 *Swindon Waterworks Co. v. Wilts. & Berks. Canal, supra.*
5 *Medway Co. v. Romney (Earl)* (1861), 9 C.B.N.S. 575.
6 (1875), 33 L.T. 513.
7 *Norbury (Lord) v. Kitchin* (1863), 7 L.T. 685.
8 [1904] A.C. 503 (overruling *Sandwich (Earl) v. Great Northern Ry.* (1878). 10 Ch. D. 707). See also *Owen v. Davies*, [1874] W.N. 175; *Roberts v. Gwyrfai District Council*, [1899] 2 Ch. 608.
9 [1926] Ch. 444.

Irrigation

A riparian owner may use the water of a stream for purposes of irrigation, provided the diversion is not continuous and he returns the water again to the stream with no other diminution than that caused by the evaporation and absorption attendant on irrigation.[1] But if he diverts water for irrigation and delays the passage of the water so as to injure the natural rights of a lower riparian owner, that owner has a ground of action against him.[2] Where there is a right to irrigate it is immaterial what means are taken to turn the water on to the land, provided that no more than the lawful quantity of water is diverted,[3] but the common law does not recognise ordinary or extraordinary rights to take water for spray irrigation, since the water is not returned to the river.[4] What quantity of water may be taken for irrigation depends on the circumstances of each case.[5]

The rights of a riparian owner to abstract water from an inland water for extraordinary or secondary purposes which exist at common law, and similar rights which may be acquired by contract, under statute, or as an easement, can only be exercised after 1st July, 1965, by the holder of a licence to abstract granted by the water authority, unless he is exempt from the requirement of a licence (see p. 187).

Diversion in general

A person diverting a stream into a new and artificial channel for his own convenience must make it capable of carrying off all the water which may reasonably be expected to flow into it, irrespective of the capacity of the old and natural channel.[6] It is the duty of anyone who interferes with the course of a stream to see that the works which he substitutes for the natural channel are adequate to carry off the water brought down even by extraordinary rainfall, and if damage results

---

[1] *Embrey v. Owen* (1851), 6 Ex. 353.
[2] *Sampson v. Hoddinott* (1857), 21 J.P. 375.
[3] *Greenslade v. Halliday* (1830), 6 Bing. 379.
[4] *Rugby Joint Water Board v. Walters*, [1966] 3 All E.R. 497.
[5] *Attwood v. Llay Main Collieries*, [1926] Ch. 444.
[6] *Fletcher v. Smith* (1877), 2 A.C. 781 ; *Hanley v. Edinburgh Corpn.*, [1913] A.C. 488.

from the deficiency of the substitute which he has provided for the natural channel he will be liable.[1]

An upper riparian owner who has the right to take water by a channel of a certain size cannot enlarge the channel so as to divert more water to the prejudice of a lower owner,[2] and where a riparian owner is entitled to abstract water from a stream for a particular purpose, he cannot use it for other purposes.[3] A person who diverts water from a stream in large quantities so as to leave insufficient for other users may be restrained without the plaintiffs having to prove actual damage or inconvenience, because the defendant's act if repeated often enough might ripen into an adverse right.[4]

If a riparian owner makes up for the deficiency of water which he abstracts from a river by turning into the river before it leaves his land water from other sources, although he gives the lower riparian owner the quantity of water he is entitled to, it is no defence to an action by the lower owner, because he is entitled to the natural water of the river and is not bound to receive foreign water of a character and quality different from that of the natural river.[5]   In *Shears v. Wood*,[6] it was alleged that the defendant placed a dam across a stream and prevented the water from running along its usual course to the plaintiff's mill.   Held: that such allegation was supported by proof that in consequence of the dam, the water was prevented from being regularly supplied to the mill, although the stream was not diverted, as the dam was erected above the mill and the water returned to its regular course long before it reached the mill and there was no waste of water.

A lower riparian owner must not divert the flow of water in a river to such an extent as to interfere with the free passage

---

[1] *Greenock Corpn. v. Caledonian Ry. Co.*, [1917] A.C. 556; *R. v. Southern Canada Power Co.*, [1937] 3 All E.R. 923; *see also Pemberton v. Bright*, [1960] 1 All E.R. 792.

[2] *Bealey v. Shaw* (1805), 6 East 208.

[3] *A.-G. v. Great Eastern Ry. Co.* (1871), 6 Ch. App. 572.

[4] *Harrop v. Hirst* (1868), 19 L.T. 426.

[5] *Young & Co. v. Bankier Distillery Co.*, [1893] A.C. 691.

[6] (1822), 7 Moore C.P. 345.

of fish up the river, and an upper riparian owner has a remedy if the diversion materially obstructs the passage of fish.[1]

If a public body are empowered by statute to divert or interfere with the course of a stream and fail to obtain the consent of a riparian owner in the manner prescribed by the statute, they will be restrained from altering the stream without any proof of sensible injury to the riparian owner.[2]

For cases on the abstraction and diversion of percolating and underground water, *see* Chapter 8—UNDERGROUND AND PERCOLATING WATER.

As to restrictions on the abstraction of water from navigable rivers, *see* PROPERTY IN RIVERS, pp. 77, 78.

OBSTRUCTION AT COMMON LAW

The rights and obligations of a riparian owner with respect to the obstruction of the natural flow of water in a stream may be considered under the following heads:—(1) placing erections on the river bed; (2) use of water for milling purposes; (3) clearing the channel; (4) diverting flood water. But before dealing with these topics, it should be noted (*a*) that the construction or alteration of impounding works, such as a dam or weir, in an inland water requires a licence from the water authority under section 36 of the Water Resources Act, 1963 (*see* p. 198), and (*b*) that the erection, alteration or repair of a structure in, over or under a main river watercourse needs the consent of the water authority under section 29 of the Land Drainage Act, 1976 (*see* p. 233).

(1) Placing erections on the river bed

In the case of a non-tidal river, each riparian proprietor *prima facie* has the property in the soil of the bed or *alveus*

---

[1] *Pirie & Sons Ltd. v. Kintore (Earl)*, [1906] A.C. 478; *Fraser v. Fear* (1912), 107 L.T. 423.

[2] *Roberts v. Gwyrfai R.D.C.*, [1899] 2 Ch. 608; *A.-G. v. Bristol Waterworks Co.* (1855), 10 Ex. 884.

from his own side to the *medium filum flumen*, but he is not entitled to use the *alveus* in such a manner as to interfere with the natural flow of the watercourse or abridge the width of the stream, or to interfere with its natural course, but anything done *in alveo* which produces no sensible effect on the stream is allowable.[1] Thus, an embankment which narrows a stream but does not obstruct it, will not give rise to an action at law without proof of damage.[2] A riparian owner may build an erection on his land though covered with water, so long as it does not interfere with any rights of navigation, or with the rights of other riparian owners[3]; thus, an obstruction cannot be erected in a stream so as to throw back the water on to an upper riparian owner's land and thereby flood his land or injure his mill.[4] But such a right could be acquired as an easement.[5] The erection of piers in the bed of a river to support a building, which results in the flooding of adjoining banks without causing actual damage constitutes an unlawful obstruction and diversion of the water of the river for which an injunction will be granted.[6] Subject to his right to catch fish, a riparian owner is not entitled to erect obstructions which interfere with the free passage of fish which prevent fish from reaching the upper portions of the river to the detriment of the upper owners.[7]

In an action for obstruction it is not necessary for the plaintiff to prove either that damage has been sustained or that it is likely to be sustained.[8] When abating an obstruction the least injurious means must be employed in interfering with the wrongdoer's property, and injury must not be caused to an innocent third party or to the public.[9]

---

[1] *Bickett v. Morris* (1866), 30 J.P. 532; *Massereene & Ferrard v. Murphy* (1931), N.I. 192; *Edleston v. Crossley & Sons Ltd.* (1868), 18 L.T. 15.

[2] *Thompson v. Horner*, [1927] N.I. 191.

[3] *Orr Ewing v. Colquhoun* (1877), 2 A.C. 839, H.L.

[4] *Saunders v. Newman* (1818), 1 B. & Ald. 258.

[5] *Alder v. Savill* (1814), 5 Taunt. 454; *Wright v. Howard* (1823), 1 Sim. & St. 190.

[6] *Massereene & Ferrard v. Murphy, supra.*

[7] *Hamilton v. Donegal (Marquis)* (1795), 3 Ridg. P.R. 267.

[8] *Edleston v. Crossley & Sons Ltd., supra; Norbury (Earl) v. Kitchen* (1866), 15 L.T. 501; *Williams v. Morland* (1824), 2 B. & C. 910.

[9] *Hill v. Cock* (1872), 26 L.T. 185; *Roberts v. Rose* (1865), 4 H. & C. 103.

A riparian owner may place stakes and wattles on the soil of a river to prevent erosion by floods and make pens to prevent cattle from straying.[1]

See also OBSTRUCTIONS TO NAVIGATION, pp. 66 to 72.

OBSTRUCTIONS IN WATERCOURSES, pp. 232, 234.

OBSTRUCTIONS TO PASSAGE OF FISH, pp. 286 to 290.

WEIRS OBSTRUCTING FISHERIES, p. 273.

(2) Use of water for milling purposes

The reasonable uses which a riparian owner may lawfully make of the water passing his land include turning its natural gravitation into water power, by weirs or other kinds of contrivances, erected in *alveo fluminis*, although their effect, if not carefully and reasonably used, might be to cause sensible injury to lower proprietors.[2] Thus, a riparian proprietor may erect a mill on the banks of a running stream and take the water from the stream to work the mill, so long as he does not pen back the water upon his neighbour above, nor injuriously affect the volume and flow of the water to his neighbour below, unless he has acquired a prescriptive right to do so.[3] Likewise, he may dam up the stream within his own property and divert the water for the purpose of the mill without the consent of the other riparian owners above him, provided he builds the dam at a place so much below the lands of such owners as not to obstruct the water from flowing away as freely as before, and without asking leave of the owner below him, if he takes care to restore the water to its natural channel.[4] Notwithstanding that a river is navigable, a riparian owner can acquire an interest in its water power and sell the same along with and as appurtenant to his land.[5] Ownership of an artificial dam does not turn the running stream into a pond so as to give the owner of the dam an exclusive right to use the whole

---

[1] *Hanbury v. Jenkins*, [1901] 2 Ch. 401.

[2] *Belfast Ropeworks Co. Ltd. v. Boyd* (1888), 21 L.R. Ir. 560; *Loud v. Murray* (1851), 17 L.T.O.S. 248; *Palme v. Persse* (1877), 11 I.R. Eq. 616.

[3] *Nuttall v. Bracewell* (1866), L.R. 2 Ex. 1.

[4] *Orr Ewing v. Colquhoun* (1877), 2 A.C. 839, H.L.

[5] *Hamelin v. Bannerman*, [1895] A.C. 237.

of the running water.[1] A licence to erect a dam at a particular place does not warrant the licensee erecting it on another spot.[2]

A mill owner may bring an action for an infringement of his water rights, although he has not enjoyed them precisely for twenty years in the same state,[3] but an action for diverting water from a mill will not lie if there is no sensible diminution of water by reason of the diversion.[4] The court may require the defendant to give an undertaking not to work his land in such a manner as to obstruct or interfere with the passage and flow of the water to the plaintiff's mill.[5] The onus lies on the plaintiff to prove damage to his mill.[6] The court may also grant an injunction to restrain the defendant from preventing water flowing to a mill in regular quantities.[7]

(3) Clearing the channel

A riparian owner is under no liability at common law to clear the channel where the stream becomes silted up or choked with weeds due to natural causes or to compensate adjoining owners whose land is consequently flooded.[8] The accustomed course of a natural stream which a riparian owner is entitled to have preserved is the natural and apparently permanent course existing when the right is asserted or called in question, and a riparian owner cannot remove a long continued natural accretion of gravel or a shoal on the river bed so as to restore the flow of the water to its former state as to velocity, direction and height[9]; nor is he entitled to alter the level of a river by removing obstructions which by lapse of time have become embedded and consolidated in and form part of the river bed, if thereby he diminishes or increases the flow of water which a millowner lower down has been enjoying owing to the diversion of the stream or the alteration in its

---

[1] *White & Sons v. White*, [1906] A.C. 72.
[2] *Mason v. Hill* (1833), 5 B. & Ad. 1.
[3] *Saunders v. Newman* (1818), 1 B. & Ald. 258.
[4] *Embrey v. Owen* (1851), 15 Jur. 633.
[5] *Elwell v. Crowther* (1862), 31 Beav. 163.
[6] *Morgan v. Last* (1886), 2 T.L.R. 262.
[7] *Robinson v. Byron (Lord)* (1785), 1 Bro. C.C. 588.
[8] *Bridges Repair Case* (1609), 12 Co. Rep. 33; *Parrett Navigation Co. v. Robins* (1842), 10 M. & W. 593; *Cracknell v. Thetford Corpn.* (1869), L.R. 4 C.P. 629; *Hodgson v. York Corpn.* (1873), 37 J.P. 725; *Normile v. Ruddle* (1912), 47 I.L.T. 179.
[9] *Withers v. Purchase* (1889), 60 L.T. 819.

level by the obstructions.[1] But possible remedies are available under the Land Drainage Act, 1976,[2] or under section 259 of the Public Health Act, 1936.[3]

(4) Protection against flooding

At common law a riparian owner on the banks of a non-tidal river has the right to raise the river banks from time to time as it becomes necessary so as to confine the flood water within the banks and prevent it from overflowing his land, provided that he can do so without injury to others,[4] that is to say, without actual injury to the property on the opposite side of the river, or above or below him.[5] In *Menzies v. Breadalbane*,[6] it was decided that a proprietor on the banks of a river has no right to build a mound which would, if completed, in times of ordinary flood throw the river water on to the ground of an owner on the opposite bank so as to overflow and injure them. Whilst a riparian owner is entitled to protect his property from flooding, he cannot for that purpose execute works of alteration to the bed of the stream which also have the effect of increasing its normal flow and diminishing that past a nearby mill.[7] This right as regards inland waters, whether tidal or non-tidal, should be compared with the broader rights of an owner on the seashore, who is entitled to protect himself against the inroads of the sea by erecting appropriate works in a *bona fide* manner, without regard to any damage thereby caused to his neighbours.[8] The word " flood " is difficult to define, but means a large and sudden movement of water and in essence is some abnormal violent situation; seepage of water was not caused by flood.[9]

On the other hand, in the case of an extraordinary flood, a riparian owner may fence off his land and turn the flood

---

[1] *Fear v. Vickers* (1911), 27 T.L.R. 558; *McGlone v. Smith* (1888), 22 L.R. Ir. 554.
[2] *See* Chap. 12.
[3] *See* p. 49.
[4] *Trafford v. The King* (1832), 8 Bing. 204; *Ridge v. Midland Ry.* (1888), 53 J.P. 55.
[5] *Bickett v. Morris* (1866), 30 J.P. 532.
[6] (1828), 3 Bli. N.S. 414.
[7] *Provinder Millers (Winchester) Ltd. v. Southampton County Council*, [1939] 4 All E.R. 157.
[8] *R. v. Comrs. of Pagham Level* (1828), 8 B. & C. 355.
[9] *Young v. Sun Alliance and London Insurance Ltd.* [1976] 3 All E.R. 561.

away without regard to the consequences of whether his neighbour is injured by it or not,[1] and if a flood embankment is placed some distance from the river, the person erecting it is not liable if during heavy floods water flows in front of the embankment and on to his neighbour's land.[2] In these cases, the action taken by the riparian owner must be in respect of warding off a common danger and not merely to transfer to some other person's land a danger which exists on his own land.[3] Further, a riparian owner may erect a bank on his land to prevent the old course of the river being gradually altered, if the bank was built on old foundations and it is shown to be a local custom for owners to embank under such circumstances.[4]

In a New Zealand case,[5] where the defendant erected a stop-bank to prevent water from a drain overflowing and flooding his land, the overflow from the drain was held not to be water which the defendant was bound to allow to flow over his land and that such overflow was not floodwater running in a defined channel, and the action failed.

A right to discharge flood water on to another person's lands, e.g. by opening sluice gates and to prevent damage to one's own land may be acquired as an easement.[6]

Where a riparian owner for the protection of his own land erects a wall along the side of the river to prevent flooding and many years after pulls down part of the wall in connection with building operations, with the result that a neighbour's property is damaged by flood, the neighbour has no right to the protection of the wall and cannot maintain an action for damages on the ground of negligence, or nuisance, or on the principle of *Rylands v. Fletcher*.[7]

See also COAST PROTECTION AND SEA DEFENCE, pp. 36 to 42.

---

[1] *Nield v. London & N.W. Ry.* (1874), 44 L.J. Ex. 15; *Lagon Navigation Co v. Lambeg Bleaching Co.*, [1927] A.C. 226.
[2] *Gerrard v. Crowe*, [1921] 1 A.C. 395.
[3] *Whalley v. Lancashire & Yorks Rly.* (1884), 50 L.T. 472; *Thomas v. Birmingham Canal Co.* (1879), 43 L.T. 435; *Maxey Drainage Board v. Great Northern Rly.* (1912), 106 L.T. 429.
[4] *Farquharson v. Farquharson* (1741), 3 Bli. N.S. 421.
[5] (1956), N.Z.L.R. 948.
[6] *Simpson v. Godmanchester Corpn.*, [1897] A.C. 696.
[7] *Thomas & Evans Ltd. v. Mid-Rhondda Co-operative Socy.*, [1940] 4 All E.R. 357.

ESCAPE, OVERFLOW AND DISCHARGE OF WATER

Position of Landowners

There is no liability for the action of water naturally on land; thus, where an excavated gravel pit filled with water which eroded the adjoining land and deprived it of natural support, the owner of the pit was held not to be liable.[1] Nor will the court restrain the draining of gravel pits into a stream to the injury of watercress beds supplied by the stream.[2]

The owner of land, who uses his land in the natural manner and without negligence or wilfulness, is not responsible for an escape of water which comes on to and damages a neighbour's land,[3] and the proprietor of higher ground has a natural right to have the water which falls on his own land discharged to the contiguous lower land of another proprietor,[4] even though by an improved system of drainage or other means, the higher proprietor brings about an increase in the flow of water to the lower land.[5] But this right does not permit an owner to deliberately drain his land on to lands of adjoining occupiers.[6]

In a Canadian case[7] it was held that the defendant, being the owner of vacant higher land, was not under a duty to take positive steps to ensure that surface water on his land did not run off to the possible injury of the plaintiff (who occupied adjoining lower land) and was not liable in negligence for failing to keep catch basins and drains clear. The defendant was, however, liable for diverting flood waters by removing a stone barrier bounding the defendant's land so that substantial quantities of water which would not otherwise have overflowed the boundary wall, flowed onto the plaintiff's land and caused damage. The plaintiff might have acquired an easement by prescription in the wall in order that water might be diverted from his land.

---

1 *Rouse v. Gravelworks Ltd.*, [1940] 1 K.B. 489.
2 *Weeks v. Heward* (1862), 10 W.R. 557.
3 *West Cumberland Iron & Steel Co. v. Kenyon* (1879), 11 Ch. D. 782; *Bartlett v. Tottenham*, [1932] 1 Ch. 114.
4 *Gibbons v. Lenfestey* (1915), 84 L.J.P.C. 158.
5 *Jordeson v. Sutton, Southcotes & Drypool Gas Co.*, [1899] 2 Ch. 217.
6 *Thomas v. Gower R.D.C.*, [1922] 2 K.B. 76.
7 *Loring v. Bridgewood Golf and Country Club Ltd.* (1974) 44 D.L.R. (3rd) 161.

A riparian owner has no remedy if the stream overflows and damages his own land, unless he can show that the injury is due to some unlawful act of another riparian owner above or below him,[1] or that some other person or body is responsible for maintaining the channel and has neglected to do so.[2]

An owner of land has an unqualified right to drain his land for agricultural purposes in order to get rid of mere surface water, the supply of which is casual and follows no regular or definite course, and a neighbour cannot complain that he is thereby deprived of such water which otherwise would have come to his land,[3] and it is lawful for persons to drain their land and let the water run into a stream though the result is to swell the water more, particularly at times, than it would have been swollen but for that drainage.[4] As to the right of water authorities to discharge treated sewage effluent to watercourses, and statutory restrictions on discharges of trade and sewage effluents to streams, see Chapter 15.

An owner who, for his own purposes, brings on his land and collects and keeps there anything likely to do mischief if it escapes, i.e. water collected in a reservoir, must keep it at his peril, and if he does not do so is prima facie answerable for all the damage which is the natural consequence of its escape.[5] But a person who stores water on his own land and uses all reasonable care to keep it safely there, is not liable to an action for an escape of the water which injures a neighbour, if the escape is caused by an agent beyond his control, such as a storm which amounts to vis major, or the act of God, in the sense that it is practically, though not physically, impossible to resist it.[6] Nor is a person liable for consequences brought about by the collecting and impounding on his land by another person of water, or any other dangerous element, not for the

---

[1] *Mason v. Shrewsbury & Hereford Rl. Co.* (1871), 25 L.T. 239.
[2] *Harrison v. Great Northern Ry. Co.* (1864), 3 H. & C. 231; *Smith v. River Douglas Catchment Board* (1949), 113 J.P. 388.
[3] *Rawstron v. Taylor* (1855), 11 Ex. 369; *Greatrex v. Hayward* (1853), 8 Ex. 291; *Broadbent v. Ramsbotham* (1856), 11 Ex. 602; *Weeks v. Heward* (1862), 10 W.R. 557; *Bartlett v. Tottenham, supra.*
[4] *Durrant v. Branksome U.D.C.* (1897), 76 L.T. 739.
[5] *Rylands v. Fletcher* (1868), 19 L.T. 220.
[6] *Nichols v. Marsland* (1875), 33 L.T. 265.

owner's purposes, but for the purposes of the other person.[1] Similarly, the owner of land is not liable under the *Rylands v. Fletcher* principle if it is shown that he had no control over the reservoir or knowledge of the circumstances which caused the overflow.[2] Again, the owner is not liable if a trespasser is responsible for allowing the escape of water collected in an artificial pond on the owner's land.[3]

Discharge of Water from Mines

Much of the law under the heading of escape and overflow is concerned with the discharge of water from a mine to an adjoining mine. The owner of a mine at a higher level than an adjoining mine is entitled to work the whole of his mine in the usual and proper manner for the purposes of mineral working, and he is not liable for any water which in consequence of his works flows by gravitation or natural means into an adjoining mine,[4] provided that his works are carried on with skill.[5]

On this principle, a mine owner will not be liable if in the ordinary course of working he taps a spring from which the water by gravitation rises to the surface and floods an adjoining mine.[6] Also since the right to work mines is a right of property, which when duly exercised begets no responsibility, where mineral workings have caused a subsidence of the surface and a consequent flow of rainfall into an adjacent lower coal-field, the injuries being entirely from gravitation and percolation, are not valid ground for a claim in damages.[7] In *Smith v. Kenrick*,[8] the owner of a mine on a higher surface, in the ordinary course of working removed a barrier of coal between his mine and a mine on a lower level, so that water percolated into the higher mine and inundated the lower

---

[1] *Whitmores (Edenbridge) Ltd. v. Stanford*, [1909] 1 Ch. 427; *Saxby v. Manchester & Sheffield Ry. Co.* (1869), L.R. 4 C.P. 198.
[2] *Box v. Jubb* (1879), 3 Ex. D. 76; *Nield v. London & N. W. Ry. Co.* (1874), L.R. 10 Ex. 4.
[3] *Barker v. Herbert*, [1911] 2 K.B. 633; *Rickards v. Lothian*, [1913] A.C. 263.
[4] *Baird v. Williamson* (1863), 15 C.B.N.S. 376.
[5] *Hurdman v. North Eastern Ry.* (1878), 38 L.T. 339.
[6] *Young & Co. v. Bankier Distillery Co.*, [1893] A.C. 691.
[7] *Wilson v. Waddell* (1876), 35 L.T. 639.
[8] (1849), 7 C.B. 515.

mine; held that the owner of the higher mine was not responsible for the injury so occasioned.

But if a mine owner does not merely suffer the water to flow through his mine, but employs some active agent, such as pumping,[1] or sinking or boring,[2] or tapping a river bed,[3] or diverting the course of a stream,[4] to throw on an adjacent mine water which would not naturally come there, or which might only do so more gradually and slowly and in much smaller volume, he will be liable for any resultant damage, though this is done in the ordinary course of working and without negligence.[5]

POLLUTION AT COMMON LAW

Rights of riparian owners as to quality of water

A riparian proprietor has a right to the natural stream of water flowing through his land in its natural state, and if the water is polluted by a proprietor higher up the stream, so as to occasion damage in law, though not in fact, to the first riparian proprietor, he has a good cause of action against the upper proprietor, unless the latter has gained a right to pollute by long enjoyment or grant.[6] Anyone who fouls the water of a natural stream infringes a right of property of the riparian owner, who can maintain an action against the infringer without proving actual damage, and obtain an injunction to prevent the continuation of the injury.[7] If from a particular place, there is sent into a river a quantity of polluting matter which exceeds the minimum of which the law will not take account, the plaintiff is entitled to an order.[8] The position of non-riparian proprietors in relation to pollution is dealt with on pp. 132 to 134.

---

[1] *Lomax v. Stott* (1870), 39 L.J. Ch. 834.
[2] *Scots Mines Co. v. Leadhills Mines Co.* (1859), 34 L.T.O.S. 34.
[3] *Crompton v. Lea* (1874), 31 L.T. 469.
[4] *Fletcher v. Smith* (1877), 2 A.C. 781.
[5] *Young & Co. v. Bankier Distillery Co.*, [1893] A.C. 691.
[6] *Wood v. Waud* (1849), 3 Ex. 748; *Mason v. Hill* (1833), 5 B. & Ald. 1; *Embrey v. Owen* (1851), 6 Ex. 353; *Young v. Bankier Distillery Co.*, [1893] A.C. 691; *Haigh v. Deudraeth R.D.C.*, [1945] 2 All E.R. 661; *Pride of Derby Angling Assocn. v. British Celanese Ltd.*, [1953] 1 All E.R. 179.
[7] *Jones v. Llanrwst U.D.C.*, [1911] 1 Ch. 393; *Crossley & Sons v. Lightowler* (1867), 16 L.T. 438; *Chesham (Lord) v. Chesham U.D.C.* (1935), 79 S.J. 453.
[8] *Staffordshire County Council v. Seisdon R.D.C.* (1907), 96 L.T. 328.

In an action for pollution the plaintiff may claim an injunction and damages for nuisance and trespass,[1] or he may proceed on the principle of *Rylands v. Fletcher*, whereby the polluter is absolutely responsible for an escape of deleterious matter as a trespass.[2] For an action alleging negligence, *see Esso Petroleum Co. Ltd. v. Southport Corpn.*[3] Persons other than riparian owners can bring an action for pollution, such as the owner of a fishery in tidal or non-tidal waters,[4] or a person whose well is polluted.[5]

The principle that the waters of a natural stream must not be polluted applies also to:—

(1) Tidal waters[6];

(2) Water which percolates discontinuously either on the surface or through underground strata[7]; *see further* POLLUTION OF PERCOLATING WATER on p. 142;

(3) Artificial watercourses of a permanent character which by the circumstances of their origin and user are deemed to be natural, but not artificial watercourses the enjoyment of which depends on temporary circumstances and are not of a permanent character and which do not give rise to riparian rights[8]; *see further* POLLUTION OF ARTIFICIAL WATERCOURSES, on pp. 132 to 134;

(4) Wells supplied by water percolating through the earth and not flowing in any defined channel[9];

(5) Ponds and inland lakes (*see* p. 56).

---

1 *Pride of Derby Angling Assocn. v. British Celanese Ltd., supra.*
2 *Jones v. Llanrwst U.D.C., supra.*
3 [1956] A.C. 218.
4 *Nicholls v. Ely Beet Sugar Factory Ltd.*, [1931] 2 Ch. 84; *Owen v. Faversham Corpn.* (1908), 73 J.P. 33.
5 *Ballard v. Tomlinson* (1885), 29 Ch. D. 115.
6 *Lyon v. Fishmongers' Co.* (1876), 1 A.C. 677.
7 *Ballard v. Tomlinson* (1885), 29 Ch. D. 115; *Hodgkinson v. Ennor* (1863), 4 B. & S. 229.
8 *Sutcliffe v. Booth* (1863), 27 J.P. 613; *Baily v. Clark, Son & Morland*, [1902] 1 Ch. 649.
9 *Womersley v. Church* (1867), 17 L.T. 190; *Ballard v. Tomlinson, supra.*

The meaning of pollution

Whilst a riparian owner can maintain an action to restrain the fouling of the water of the river without having to show that the fouling is actually injurious to him,[1] it must be proved that he has sustained some actual damage.[2] No action will lie if the damage is temporary, or too minute, or too trivial to support a case,[3] and a waste discharge which merely makes water temporarily muddy is not actionable.[4]

Raising the temperature of river water by the discharge of heated water will cause pollution,[5] as will also the addition of hard water to a soft water stream,[6] or if water is rendered unsuitable for the purposes of another riparian owner, such as sheep washing[7] or cattle drinking.[8]

Pollution is the result of something which changes the natural quality of the water.[9] It is not necessary to show deterioration of the stream in general, and it is sufficient to prove that something has been added to the water which deteriorates the quality and purity of the water at the point where the offending matter enters the stream.[10]

Where pollution may be permissible or lawful

Pollution may occur in such circumstances as to preclude the possibility or likelihood of legal action, or the person responsible may claim that he does so in the exercise of a lawful right. Thus, if pollution is confined to a person's own property and the stream is free from noxious matter where it leaves his land,[11] or if the pollution affects only the land of

---

[1] *Crossley & Sons Ltd.* v. *Lightowler* (1867), 16 L.T. 438.
[2] *Elmhirst* v. *Spencer* (1849), 2 Mac. & G. 45.
[3] *Lillywhite* v. *Trimmer* (1867), 16 L.T. 318; *A.-G.* v. *Gee* (1870), 23 L.T. 299;
Lee Conservancy Board v. *Bishop's Stortford U.D.C.* (1906), 70 J.P. 244.
[4] *Taylor* v. *Bennett* (1836), 7 C. & P. 329.
[5] *Tipping* v. *Eckersley* (1855), 2 K. & J. 264.
[6] *Young* v. *Bankier Distillery Co.*, [1893] A.C. 691.
[7] *A.-G.* v. *Luton L.B.* (1856), 20 J.P. 163.
[8] *Oldaker* v. *Hunt* (1855), 3 W.R. 297.
[9] *John Young & Co.* v. *Bankier Distillery Co.*, [1893] A.C. 691, H.L.
[10] *A.-G.* v. *Birmingham, Tame & Rea District Drainage Board*, [1908] 2 Ch.
551.
[11] *Elmhirst* v. *Spencer* (1849), 14 L.T.O.S. 433.

someone who is not entitled to complain of the nuisance,[1] then in such cases an action cannot be supported.

A legal right to pollute a watercourse may be acquired by—

(a) Proof of a claim to an immemorial custom, e.g. to win minerals from a mine and to wash impurities in the minerals in an adjacent stream, provided that the claim is not indefinite and unreasonable and the user is confined to the necessary working of the mine.[2] But a custom cannot authorise an act the effect of which is to create an evil which must be illegal, such as collecting a mass of sewage matter and pouring it into a river at one point in such a quantity that the river cannot dilute it.[3]

(b) Under an Act of Parliament which has the effect of superseding common law rights,[4] or of preserving existing rights to pollute.[5]

(c) By means of a grant express or implied.[6]

(d) By prescription; see EASEMENT TO POLLUTE WATER, on pp. 119 to 121.

Pollution of fisheries

A person who is entitled to a fishery has a right of action for an injunction and damages against anyone who unlawfully does any act which disturbs the enjoyment of the fishery, e.g. by discharging matter into the water of a stream which drives away the fish and injures the breeding.[7] Where evidence is given that large masses of crude sewage are discharged into a river and immediately afterwards fish died in large numbers, the proper inference, in the absence of an alternative cause for the death of the fish having been proved, is that the fish died from deoxygenation of the water by

---

[1] *Ormerod v. Todmorden Mill Co.* (1883), 11 Q.B.D. 155; *Stockport Waterworks Co. v. Potter* (1864), 3 H. & C. 300; *Fergusson v. Malvern U.D.C.* (1908), 72 J.P. 101.
[2] *Carlyon v. Lovering* (1857), 1 H. & N. 784; *Wright v. Williams* (1836), 1 M. & W. 77.
[3] *A.-G. v. Richmond* (1866), 14 L.T. 398.
[4] *Lee Conservancy Board v. Hertford Corpn.* (1884), 48 J.P. 628.
[5] *Somerset Drainage Comrs. v. Bridgwater Corpn.* (1899), 81 L.T. 729.
[6] *Hall v. Lund* (1863), 1 H. & C. 676.
[7] *Fitzgerald v. Firbank*, [1897] 2 Ch. 96; *Bidder v. Croydon L.B.* (1862), 6 L.T. 778; *Child v. Greenhill* (1639), Cro. Car. 553.

sewage, and the owner of the fishery is entitled to damages,[1] and an injunction.[2] Interference with a several fishery is the invasion of a legal right and an action may be maintained without proof of special damage.[3]

An indictment will lie against a gas company for a nuisance in conveying gas refuse into a river whereby fish are destroyed and the water is rendered unfit for drinking,[4] but a remedy for pollution by indictment may be taken away by statute.[5]

Statutory provisions prohibiting the pollution of fish and fisheries are set out on p. 344.

Remedies for pollution

(a) Damages

Where an injury has been done to the private rights of a person, whether landlord or tenant, he is entitled to damages, although only nominal, and where in such a case an injury is apprehended an injunction will be granted against the party in default.[6] A party merely licensed by a riparian owner to use the water may maintain an action for fouling the water,[7] but a person who is not a riparian owner and has no easement or right to use the water, cannot maintain an action for pollution.[8] The damages recoverable represent the loss suffered by the plaintiff as the natural result of the wrong done to him by the acts of the defendant[9]; thus, damages may be recovered for injury to the plaintiff's house and fishing and for procuring a new water supply and engine; but not usually for loss of amenities.[10]

(b) Injunction

Where a man has a right to the use of a watercourse flowing through his land and polluting matter is discharged into it

---

1 *Dulverton R.D.C. v. Tracy* (1921), 85 J.P. 217.
2 *A.-G. v. Birmingham Corpn.* (1858), 22 J.P. 561; *Bidder v. Croydon L.B., supra; Oldaker v. Hunt* (1855), 19 J.P. 179.
3 *Nicholls v. Ely Beet Sugar Factory Ltd.* (1936), 154 L.T. 531.
4 *R. v. Medley* (1834), 6 C. & P. 292.
5 *R. v. Bristol Dock Co.* (1810), 12 East 429.
6 *Nixon v. Tynemouth Union* (1888) 52 J.P. 504.
7 *Whaley v. Laing* (1857), 2 H. & N. 476.
8 *Ormerod v. Todmorden Mill Co.* (1883), 47 J.P. 532; *Dickinson v. Shepley Sewerage Board* (1904), 68 J.P. 363.
9 *Granby (Marquis) v. Bakewell U.D.C.* (1923), 87 J.P. 105.
10 *Harrington (Earl) v. Derby Corpn.,* [1905] 1 Ch. 205.

so as to cause him either present permanent injury, or such injury is likely to continue and increase so as to become serious and permanent, the court will grant an injunction to restrain the discharge. In determining whether the injury is serious or not, the court will regard all the circumstances that may arise from it, and particularly the effect of the nuisance upon the value of the estate and the prospect of dealing with it to advantage.[1]

A person having established his right at law is not, as a matter of course, entitled to an injunction, particularly where the injunction would not restore the plaintiff to the right he has established and where the act complained of may be compensated by pecuniary damages.[2] The court will not grant an injunction if the nuisance has been to a great extent abated since the institution of proceedings,[3] nor where the defendants have since the commencement of the action taken steps to remedy the injury.[4] An injunction will be refused if the injury is too trivial[5] or if the pollution is unlikely to recur.[6]

An injunction restraining a local authority from polluting a river by sewage will not apply to another authority to whom the functions of the former authority are transferred.[7] If a local authority do no act themselves to cause a nuisance, but neglect to perform their duty of providing a satisfactory and healthy drainage system, this is no ground of action by an individual for damages or an injunction, and the remedy lies by way of prerogative writ of *mandamus*.[8] When granting an injunction to restrain pollution from sewage matter, it is the usual practice to grant an immediate injunction restraining any new connections with the river and to suspend the operation of the order for a period in respect of existing

---

1 *Goldsmid v. Tunbridge Wells* (1866), 14 L.T. 154.
2 *Wood v. Sutcliffe* (1851), 21 L.J. Ch. 253.
3 *Lillywhite v. Trimmer* (1867), 16 L.T. 318.
4 *L.C.C. v. Price's Candle Co. Ltd.* (1911), 75 J.P. 329.
5 *A.-G. v. Preston Corpn.* (1896), 13 T.L.R. 14; *A.-G. v. Gee* (1870), 23 L.T. 299.
6 *Chapman, Morsons & Co. v. Aukland Union* (1889), 23 Q.B.D. 294.
7 *A.-G. v. Birmingham Corpn.* (1880), 15 Ch. D. 423.
8 *Glossop v. Heston & Isleworth L.B.* (1879), 12 Ch. D. 102.

sewers to enable the defendants to alter their sewage works so as to comply with the order.[1]

In an action to restrain the discharge of polluting matter into a stream, where the defendants ask that damages, in lieu of an injunction, might be given, an injunction may be granted,[2] and in *Chapman, Morsons & Co. v. Aukland Union*,[3] where a *bona fide* action was brought for an injunction to prevent the sanitary authority from continuing to discharge sewage into a stream, the judge refused an injunction because the discharge was unlikely to recur but gave damages.[4]

An injunction will be granted to prevent the inconvenience of repeated actions in the case of continued pollution.[5] Once the plaintiff has proved his right to an injunction, it is no part of the court's duty to enquire how the defendant can best remove the nuisance. The plaintiff is entitled to an injunction immediately, unless the removal of the nuisance is physically impossible, and the defendant must find his way out of the difficulty, whatever the inconvenience or cost may be.[6] During wartime an injunction will be suspended until the end of the war.[7]

When the difficulty of removing the injury is great, the court will suspend the operation of the injunction for a period, with liberty to the defendant to apply for an extension of time.[8] Where important public interests are involved, such as improving the drainage of a town, the court will protect the private rights of the individual if affected in any material degree, but will at the same time have regard to the nature and extent of the alleged injury and to the balance of inconvenience.[9] An injunction once granted may be discharged by the court if the circumstances which existed at the date of the judgment have been changed.[10]

---

[1] *A.-G. v. Birmingham Corpn.* (1858), 4 K. & J. 528; *Pride of Derby Angling Assocn. v. British Celanese Ltd.*, [1953] 1 All E.R. 179.
[2] *Pennington v. Brinksop Hall Coal Co.* (1877), 37 L.T. 149.
[3] (1889), 23 Q.B.D. 294.
[4] (1889), 23 Q.B.D. 294.
[5] *Pennington v. Brinksop Hall Coal Co., supra.*
[6] *Goldsmid v. Tunbridge Wells* (1866), 14 L.T. 154.
[7] *Dexter v. Aldershot U.D.C.* (1915), 79 J.P. 580.
[8] *A.-G. v. Colney Hatch Lunatic Asylum* (1868), 19 L.T. 708.
[9] *Lillywhite v. Trimmer* (1867), 16 L.T. 318.
[10] *A.-G. v. Birmingham Drainage Board*, [1912] A.C. 788.

The fact that a person has submitted to an injury by pollution for some time trusting to the assurance of a local authority that they were carrying out works which would eventually remove the evil, does not preclude him on the grounds of *laches* from applying for an injunction,[1] but he may be guilty of such an amount of acquiescence as would disentitle him to an injunction.[2]

A *quia timet* action may be maintained to restrain imminent danger of a substantial kind, or where the apprehended injury, if it comes about, will be irreparable.[3] There must be evidence of an actual present danger or the immediate probability of a nuisance.[4] An injunction will not be granted whereby it is merely shown that if, at some future time and in altered circumstances, the defendant does or fails to do some act, a case for an injunction will be established.[5]

If a decree of the court is made, restraining a local authority from pouring their sewage into a river to the injury of the plaintiff, it is no excuse for a breach of the injunction that they have attempted to deodorise the sewage so as to make it innocuous and have failed; it is their duty, if they can obey the order by no other means, not to discharge the sewage into the river at all, and the court may order a sequestration of their property.[6] On a motion by the plaintiffs for sequestration in breach of an undertaking given by the defendants against further pollution, the court instead of making a sequestration order may grant an injunction in the terms of the undertaking and penalise the defendants by ordering them to pay all the costs of the application.[7] A writ of sequestration against a local authority for its failure to comply with an undertaking not to pollute a river will not lie for an accidental breach of the undertaking.[8]

In an action for pollution where an injunction is claimed, it is no defence for the defendant to show that the water was

---

1 *A.-G. v. Birmingham Corpn.* (1858), 4 K. & J. 528.
2 *Wood v. Sutcliffe* (1851), 21 L.J. Ch. 253.
3 *Fletcher v. Bealey* (1885), 28 Ch. D. 688.
4 *A.-G. v. Kingston-on-Thames Corpn.* (1865), 12 L.T. 665.
5 *Bank View Mills Ltd. v. Nelson Corpn.*, [1943] 1 K.B. 337.
6 *Spokes v. Banbury* (1865), 13 L.T. 428.
7 *Marsden & Sons Ltd. v. Old Silkstone Collieries Ltd.* (1914), 13 L.G.R. 342.
8 *Monckton v. Wolverhampton Corpn., The Times,* November 26, 1960.

also fouled by other manufacturers[1]; or that the share he contributed to the nuisance is infinitesimal and unappreciable,[2] or that the injunction if granted would result in unemployment[3] or inconvenience a large body of the public.[4]

(c) Public nuisance

If pollution is caused to such an extent as to constitute a public nuisance, the Attorney-General may institute proceedings on behalf of the public by indictment,[5] or he may commence civil proceedings on his own motion by an information,[6] but more commonly an aggrieved party, as relator, will apply for the sanction of the Attorney-General.[7] Where the Attorney-General proceeds on his own behalf, the court may grant an injunction to restrain the continuance of the nuisance,[8] and in a relator action, where the relator may be a private individual[9] or a corporation,[10] his claim for damages may be joined with the claim for an injunction.[11] A private person may maintain an action in respect of a public nuisance, without the Attorney-General, if he can show that he has sustained a particular damage other than and beyond that suffered by the public and that the damage is direct and substantial.[12] The Attorney-General is entitled to apply for an injunction in respect of an anticipated offence, *e.g.* where a public authority proposes to breach a statute without excuse.[13]

---

1 *St. Helens Smelting Co. v. Tipping* (1865), 12 L.T. 776; *Crossley v. Lightowler* (1867), 2 Ch. App. 478.
2 *Blair & Sumner v. Deakin* (1887), 57 L.T. 522.
3 *Pennington v. Brinsop Hall Coal Co.* (1877), 5 Ch. D. 769.
4 *A.-G. v. Leeds Corpn.* (1870), 5 Ch. App. 583.
5 *R. v. Medley* (1834), 6 C. & P. 292; *R. v. Bradford Navigation Co.* (1865), 6 B. & S. 631.
6 *Ware v. Regent Canal Co.* (1858), 23 J.P. 3.
7 *A.-G. v. Basingstoke* (1876), 45 L.J. Ch. 726.
8 *A.-G. v. Shrewsbury Bridge Co.* (1882), 21 Ch. D. 752; *A.-G. v. Birmingham Drainage Board* (1910), 26 T.L.R. 95.
9 *A.-G. v. Lonsdale* (1868), 33 J.P. 534.
10 *A.-G. v. Logan* (1891), 55 J.P. 615.
11 *A.-G. v. Cockermouth L.B.* (1874), 30 L.T. 590.
12 *Benjamin v. Storr* (1874). 30 L.T. 362; *Rose v. Miles* (1815) 4 M. & S. 101.
13 *A.-G. v. Wellingborough U.D.C.* (1974) *The Times*, 29th March.

CHAPTER 6

ACQUIRED RIGHTS OR EASEMENTS OF WATER

NATURE AND CHARACTERISTICS OF WATER EASEMENTS

In addition to the enjoyment of natural riparian rights to which the owner or occupier of land abutting on a river is entitled, which are founded on his right of access to the river, a riparian owner may also acquire rights in the nature of easements. He may acquire a right to use the water in a manner not justified by his natural rights, but an acquired right has no operation against the natural rights of a landowner higher up the stream, unless the user by which it was acquired affects the use which the landowner has made of the stream, or his power to use it, so as to raise the presumption of a grant, so that the tenement above (or below) becomes a servient tenement and the tenement in respect of which the acquired right is used becomes a dominant tenement.[1] An easement must be connected with the enjoyment of the dominant tenement and cannot exist in gross.[2]

The general rule of law is that, independent of any particular enjoyment used to be had by another, every man has the right to have the advantage of a flow of water in his own land, without diminution or alteration; but an adverse right may exist founded on the occupation of another, and though the stream is either diminished in quantity, or even corrupted in quality, as by means of the existence of certain trades, yet if the occupation of the party so taking or using it have existed for so long a time as may raise the presumption of a grant, the other party whose land is below must take the stream subject to such adverse right.[3]

---

[1] *Sampson v. Hoddinott* (1857), 1 C.B.N.S. 570.

[2] *Ackroyd v. Smith* (1850), 10 C.B. 164; *Stockport Waterworks Co. v. Potter* (1864), 3 H. & C. 300.

[3] *Bealey v. Shaw* (1805), 6 East 208.

Every owner of land on the banks of a river has *prima facie* an equal right to use the water and cannot acquire a right to throw the water back on the proprietor above or to divert it from the proprietor below without a grant or twenty years' enjoyment which is evidence of a grant.[1]

An easement must be distinguished from what may be a restrictive covenant,[2] or a mere licence or covenant for a person to do a particular thing[3]; and an easement cannot be acquired in respect of a temporary watercourse constructed for a specific purpose.[4]

An easement exercised for the benefit of the dominant estate is not invalid merely because from the very nature of its exercise it confers some benefit on other persons. Thus, a corporation, as owners of land, had for more than 200 years opened, as of right, the gates of certain locks belonging to another person upon a river in times of flood in order to prevent damage to those lands; held that the easement was good and was none the worse because it benefited land belonging to other persons.[5]

An easement cannot be acquired if it is not within the power of the presumed grantor to grant it,[6] as in *National Guaranteed Manure Co. v. Donald*,[7] where the right of a company to the flow of water in a canal ceased upon the stopping up and conversion of the canal into a railway. In *Rochdale Canal Co. v. Radcliffe*,[8] it was held that the defendant's claim to draw off surface water from the canal was bad since the canal company did not have any statutory power to grant water for such purpose.[9]

---

[1] *Wright v. Howard* (1823), 1 Sim. & St. 190.

[2] *Keppell v. Bailey* (1834), 2 My. & K. 517.

[3] *Hill v. Tupper* (1863), 2 H. & C. 121.

[4] *Burrows v. Lang*, [1901] 2 Ch. 502; *Beeston v. Weate* (1856), 20 J.P. 452; *Arkwright v. Gell* (1839), 5 M. & W. 203.

[5] *Simpson v. Godmanchester Corpn.*, [1897] A.C. 696.

[6] *Preston Corpn. v. Fullwood L.B.* (1885), 53 L.T. 718.

[7] (1859), 4 H. & N. 8.

[8] (1852), 18 Q.B. 287.

[9] *See also McEvoy v. Great Northern Rly.*, [1900] 2 Ir. R. 325; *Staffordshire Canal Co. v. Birmingham Canal Co.* (1866), L.R. 1 H.L. 254.

ACQUISITION OF EASEMENTS OF WATER

An easement in respect of water or a watercourse may arise either by (1) grant; (2) prescription; (3) custom; or (4) statute.

(1) Grant

A legal easement of water as an incorporeal hereditament may only be created or transferred by deed,[1] and a verbal licence is not sufficient to confer such an easement.[2] But despite the lack of a formal agreement, the court acting on the equitable doctrine of acquiescence, in cases where the owner of the servient tenement has granted permission to the enjoyment of an easement or has not objected thereto, and the dominant owner or others have incurred expense in executing works, may decide that the dominant owner has acquired a right of user over a watercourse and will restrain the servient owner by injunction from interfering with the flow of water.[3]

An easement created by express deed of grant must be construed according to the wording of the grant,[4] and a grant of a watercourse may mean either the right to the running of water, or the land over which the water runs, or the channel through which the water flows.[5]   Where rights of water are created by deed, the court cannot take into consideration the rights which the parties would have had as riparian owners or otherwise, and the nature and extent of their interest must be regulated wholly by the deed.[6]   Whether a grant has been executed is a question for the jury to presume.[7]

Where part of a property is sold, all continuous and apparent easements over the other part of the property which

---

[1] *Hewlins v. Shippam* (1826), 5 B. & C. 221; *Fentiman v. Smith* (1805), 4 East 107; *Nuttall v. Bracewell* (1866), 15 L.T. 313.

[2] *Cocker v. Cowper* (1834), 5 Tyr. 103.

[3] *Devonshire (Duke) v. Eglin* (1851), 14 Beav. 530; *Liggins v. Inge* (1831), 7 Bing. 682; *Bankart v. Tennant* (1870), 23 L.T. 137.

[4] *New Windsor Corpn. v. Stovell* (1884), 51 L.T. 626.

[5] *Taylor v. St. Helens Corpn.* (1877), 6 Ch. D. 264; *Brain v. Marfell* (1879), 41 L.T. 457.

[6] *Northam v. Hurley* (1853), 1 E. & B. 665; *Chadwick v. Marsden* (1867), 16 L.T. 666; *Rawstron v. Taylor* (1855), 11 Ex. 369.

[7] *Dewhirst v. Wrigley* (1834), 47 E.R. 529.

are necessary to the enjoyment of the part sold will pass to the purchaser. Therefore, where the owner of two or more adjoining houses sells one of them, that house is entitled to the benefit of and is subject to the burden of all existing drains communicating with the other house, without any express reservation or grant for that purpose.[1] As to what is meant by a continuous easement, *see Suffield v. Brown.*[2]

(2) Prescription

On the principle that a right to an incorporeal hereditament may be acquired by lapse of time, a prescriptive grant to a particular right to a watercourse may be claimed on proof of long user without interruption and as of right.[3] Where there has been a long continued enjoyment of an exclusive character of a right of property, the courts will be apt to presume that such enjoyment is rightful if the right or property is such that it can have a legal origin.[4] For example, after long enjoyment of a watercourse running to a house and garden through the ground of another, it is presumed that the owner of the house has a right to the watercourse, and an injunction will be granted unless the party can show a special licence or an agreement to restrain it in point of time.[5] By common law, the user of such a right must be shown to have continued since time immemorial—an expression which for reasons originally connected with the imposition of time limits for actions on the recovery of land[6]—was held to commence from the reign of Richard I or 1189. The undoubted difficulties of proving the enjoyment of a right since 1189 lead to the courts holding that evidence of enjoyment for as long as anyone could remember raised a presumption that enjoyment had existed for the requisite period.[7]

---

[1] *Pyer v. Carter* (1857), 1 H. & N. 916; *Ewart v. Cochrane* (1861), 5 L.T. 1; *Watts v. Kelson* (1871), 24 L.T. 209; *Bunting v. Hicks* (1894), 70 L.T. 455.

[2] (1864), 9 L.T. 627.

[3] *Goodman v. Saltash Corpn.* (1882), 48 L.T. 239.

[4] *Foster v. Warblington U.D.C.*, [1906] 1 K.B. 648; *Hammerton v. Dysart (Duke)*, [1916] 1 A.C. 57.

[5] *Callaghan v. Callaghan* (1897), 31 I.L.T. 418; *Wilson v. Stewart* (1748), 2 How. E.E. 532; *Finch v. Resbridger* (1700), 2 Vern. 390.

[6] *See Gale* on Easements (13th Ed.), pp. 116-120.

[7] *Jenkins v. Harvey* (1835), 1 Cr. M. & R. 894.

This presumption could, however, be defeated by proof that the actual origin of the enjoyment was of more recent date than the prescription,[1] and accordingly the courts introduced a new doctrine, namely, the presumption of the lost modern grant. On evidence of enjoyment of a right for a period of between twenty to sixty years, the jury could presume that an actual grant of the easement had been made at some time since 1189 but before the period of years of enjoyment supporting the claim, and that the grant had been lost in modern times.[2] Thus, twenty years exclusive enjoyment of water in any particular manner affords a conclusive presumption of right in a party enjoying it.[3] The doctrine has been applied to presume a grant, e.g. for a corporation to discharge sewage into a tidal river,[4] for a franchise ferry,[5] and for water to irrigate a mill meadow.[6]

The Prescription Act, 1832, provides a third alternative of establishing a right to an easement by long user. Under section 2, a claim lawfully made at common law, by custom, prescription or grant to any watercourse[7] or the use of any water[8] which has been actually enjoyed by the claimant without interruption for a full period of twenty years can only be defeated or destroyed by proof that such right was first enjoyed at any time prior to such period of twenty years. Where such a right has been so enjoyed for a full period of forty years, the right is deemed absolute and indefeasible unless enjoyed by some consent or agreement given or made for that purpose by deed or writing. The Act does not replace the other methods of prescriptive claims at common law or under the doctrine of the modern lost grant and all these methods are sometimes pleaded alternatively.

---

[1] *Bury v. Pope* (1586), Cro. Eliz. 118.

[2] *Dalton v. Angus* (1881), 6 A.C. 740; *Baily v. Clark*, [1902] 1 Ch. 649; *Rolle v. Whyte* (1868), L.R. 3 Q.B. 303.

[3] *Bealey v. Shaw* (1805), 6 East 208; *Hanna v. Pollock*, [1900] 2 I.R. 664.

[4] *Somerset Drainage Comrs. v. Bridgewater Corpn.* (1899), 81 L.T. 729.

[5] *Dysart v. Hammerton*, [1914] 1 Ch. 822.

[6] *Scott v. Hanson* (1829), 1 Russ. & M. 128.

[7] *Wright v. Williams* (1836), 1 M. & W. 77; *Ward v. Robins* (1846), 15 M. & W. 237.

[8] *Race v. Ward* (1855), 4 E. & B. 702; *Manning v. Wasdale* (1836), 5 Ad. & El. 758; *Macnaghten v. Baird*, [1903] 2 Ir. R. 731; *Leconfield v. Lonsdale* (1870), L.R. 5 C.P. 657; *Drewitt v. Sheard* (1836), 7 C. & P. 465.

A prescriptive right must be limited and defined by the user and where the user is unlimited and water is taken without stint and without regard to the needs of the servient owner, a prescriptive right cannot be obtained.[1]

The enjoyment of an easement to be recognised at law must not be secret, unknown and unsuspected by the servient owner. In *Liverpool Corporation v. Coghill*,[2] a noxious discharge from a factory into the plaintiff's sewers made intermittently and mainly by night was unknown to the plaintiffs and was held to be of such a character as not to establish a prescriptive right. The enjoyment of an easement must be shown to be uninterrupted and as of right.[3]

(3) Custom

An easement may be claimed as a particular custom by the inhabitants of a district, *e.g.* for the flow of water from a spring, well or pond for domestic or culinary purposes or for washing or watering cattle,[4] and the inhabitants can maintain an action without having suffered individual damage for any infringement of the right.[5] Such a claim will be bad if it is too wide to be the subject of a custom, as where a claim is made on behalf of the public at large or is not confined to any particular class of persons.[6] A claim by tin miners to use a natural stream for washing ore and carrying away river washings was held to be a good custom since it was definite and reasonable and the user was limited to the necessary working of the mine.[7]

(4) Statute

Easements relating to water may arise in the exercise of powers conferred upon a body by a general or private statute.

---

[1] *A.-G. v. Great Northern Rly.*, [1909] 1 Ch. 775.

[2] [1918] 1 Ch. 307.

[3] *Eaton v. Swansea Waterworks Co.* (1851), 17 Q.B. 267.

[4] *Race v. Ward* (1855), 4 E. & B. 702; *Manning v. Wasdale* (1836), 5 Ad. & El. 758.

[5] *Harrop v. Hirst* (1868), 19 L.T. 426.

[6] *Dungarven Guardians v. Mansfield*, [1897] 1 I.R. 420.

[7] *Carlyon v. Lovering* (1857), 1 H. & N. 784; *Ivimey v. Stocker* (1866), 1 Ch. App. 396; *Gaved v. Martyn* (1865), 13 L.T. 74.

Statutory water undertakers may acquire by agreement or compulsorily rights to take water from a stream or other source,[1] and a local authority or county council may be authorised to abstract water from a river, stream or lake in order to afford a water supply for houses provided by them.[2]

SPECIFIC EASEMENTS OF WATER

Easement of Abstraction, Diversion and Obstruction

The right of diverting water which in its natural course would pass over or along the land of a riparian owner and of conveying it to the land of the party diverting it is an easement well known at law. Ordinarily such an easement can be created only by grant or by long continued enjoyment from which the existence of a former grant may be reasonably presumed.[3]   But such a right may also be created by statute.[4] Where a prescriptive right to discharge surface water across adjacent property by a specific channel has been acquired, the obstruction of the channel on the servient tenement, by the tenant of the latter, is an invasion of a legal right for which an action is maintainable without proof of actual perceptible damage.[5]

Subject to specified exceptions, after 1st July, 1965, a person may only abstract water from an inland water or underground strata, or construct or alter impounding works in an inland water, in pursuance of a licence granted by the water authority under Part IV of the Water Resources Act, 1963 (see Chapter 11).

Once an easement to divert or obstruct a watercourse has been obtained, the diversion or obstruction cannot subsequently be altered or increased so as to increase the burden on the servient tenement and to affect injuriously the column

---

1 Water Act, 1945, s. 26.
2 Housing Act, 1957, s.103.
3 *Beeston v. Weate* (1856), 5 E. & B. 986.
4 *Mason v. Shrewsbury Ry. Co.* (1871), 25 L.T. 239.
5 *Claxton v. Claxton* (1875), I.R. 7 C.L. 23.

and flow of water to the neighbour below. In *Bealey v. Shaw*,[1] the court held that a mill owner who had acquired a prescriptive right to divert water from a stream to his mill, was unable to alter his sluices so as to divert more water.[2] An alteration to the dimensions of a mill wheel will not destroy the easement,[3] nor will a change in the character or property to which a prescriptive right is annexed necessarily affect the prescription, *e.g.* a change from a fulling mill to a mill for grinding corn which causes no injury to the servient tenement.[4]

A slight alteration in the course of a stream does not destroy any right annexed to it,[5] and a prescription to have a watercourse to an ancient mill is not destroyed by the old mill being pulled down and a new mill being built on the same stream.[6]

If the owner of a water mill worked by a ground-shot wheel at a low head of water, alters the wheel to a brest-shot wheel, which requires a high head of water, and after that, for twenty years and more, discontinues the use of the brest-shot wheel and resumes the use of the ground-shot wheel, his discontinuance will cause the mill owner to lose his right to the higher head of water.[7]

Easement to pollute water

A riparian owner has a right to the natural stream of water flowing through his land in its natural state and if the water is polluted by a riparian owner higher up the stream so as to occasion damage in law, though not in fact, to the first-mentioned owner, he has a good cause of action against the upper owner, unless the latter has gained a right to pollute by long enjoyment or otherwise.[8] The privilege of washing away sand, stone and rubble dislodged in the necessary working of

---

1 (1805), 6 East 208.
2 *See also Brown v. Best* (1747), 1 Wils. 174.
3 *Saunders v. Newman* (1818), 1 B. & A. 258.
4 *Luttrell's Case* (1601), 4 Co. Rep. 86.
5 *Hall v. Swift* (1838), 6 Scott 167.
6 *Palmis v. Hebblethwaite* (1688), 2 Show. 249.
7 *Drewett v. Sheard* (1836), 7 C. & P. 465.
8 *Wood v. Waud* (1849), 3 Ex. 748.

a tin mine and sending the same down a natural stream running through another's land may be claimed as a local custom or pleaded as a prescriptive right under the Prescription Act, 1832.[1] So also, a claim to empty and discharge water from a copper mine, which has been impregnated with metallic substances, into a neighbour's watercourse is a claim to a watercourse within the Prescription Act, 1832.[2] Such rights can only be acquired by continual perceptible injury to the servient tenement over a period of twenty years.[3]

Where a prescriptive right to foul a stream has been acquired, the fouling must not be considerably enlarged to the prejudice of other people. The fact that the stream is fouled by others is no defence to an action to restrain pollution by one person.[4] Even assuming that a prescriptive right to foul a stream can be acquired, such right must be restricted to the limits of it when the period of prescription commenced, and if the pollution is substantially increased, whether gradually or suddenly, the court will interfere by injunction to prevent the wrongful excess. If it is impossible to separate the illegal excess from the legal user, the wrongdoer must bear the consequences of any restriction necessary to prevent the excess, even if it unavoidably extends to a total prohibition of the user.[5] A riparian owner who has a prescriptive right to take, in a particular way and at a particular place, water from a river and to return the water in a polluted condition, is not entitled to take the water in any other way or place; nor to use his common law right of taking it in such a manner as to add to the pollution of the river.[6] If the enjoyment of an alleged easement to pollute has been secret and unknown and unsuspected by the plaintiffs or their predecessors, the easement is not of such a character as would establish a prescriptive right.[7]

---

[1] *Carlyon v. Lovering* (1857), 1 H. & N. 784.
[2] *Wright v. Williams* (1836), 1 M. & W. 77.
[3] *Goldsmid v. Tunbridge Wells Comrs.* (1866), 1 Ch. App. 349; *Murgatroyd v. Robinson* (1857), 7 E. & B. 391.
[4] *Crossley v. Lightowler* (1867), 16 L.T. 438.
[5] *Blackburne v. Somers* (1879), 5 L.R. Ir. 1.
[6] *McIntyre Bros. v. McGavin*, [1893] A.C. 268.
[7] *Liverpool Corpn. v. Coghill*, [1918] 1 Ch. 307.

A prescriptive right to foul a well will be defeated by variation and excess in the degree of fouling during the prescriptive period.[1] A mere change in the nature of the polluting matter which does not increase the pollution as against the servient tenement to any substantial or tangible extent does not necessarily destroy an easement.[2] But a complete change of business to that originally carried on by a person having a prescriptive right to foul a river, even though the alteration of user lessens the pollution, is not permissible.[3] Where a prescriptive right is claimed to pollute a river, the question before the court is whether the claim is for an immemorial or prescriptive right to pollute not limited to the purposes of the business, or for the more limited right to do so for the purposes of the business as carried on for more than twenty years.[4]

Prescription may only be claimed for something which can have a lawful origin at common law,[5] and an easement cannot be claimed in respect of anything which would be injurious to public health,[6] or which would cause a nuisance, e.g. the discharge of untreated sewage into tidal waters so as to pollute oyster beds.[7] Nor can a prescription be claimed to pollute waters which under statute are forbidden to be polluted, i.e. see sections 3, 4 of the (former) Rivers Pollution Prevention Act, 1876,[8] the Salmon and Freshwater Fisheries Act, 1923.

Easements regarding underground and percolating water

Prescriptive rights may be acquired in respect of water flowing in an underground stream through a known and defined channel since the principles which regulate the rights

---

[1] Millington v. Griffiths (1874), 30 L.T. 65.

[2] Baxendale v. McMurray (1867), 31 J.P. 821; Somerset Drainage Comrs. v. Bridgewater Corpn. (1899), 81 L.T. 729.

[3] Clarke v. Somerset Drainage Comrs. (1888), 59 L.T. 670.

[4] Moore v. Webb (1857), 1 C.B.N.S. 673.

[5] Goodman v. Saltash Corpn. (1882), 48 L.T. 239.

[6] Blackburne v. Somers, supra.

[7] Foster v. Warblington U.D.C., [1906] 1 K.B. 648; Hobart v. Southend Corpn. (1906), 94 L.T. 337.

[8] Owen v. Faversham Corpn. (1908), 73 J.P. 33; Butterworth v. West Riding of Yorkshire Rivers Board, [1909] A.C. 45; Hulley v. Silversprings Bleaching Co., [1922] 2 Ch. 268; Green v. Matthews (1930), 46 T.L.R. 206.

of landowners are applicable to all water flowing in a certain and defined course, whether in an open channel or in a known subterranean channel.[1] But there can be no express grant or reservation of water which percolates through underground strata, having no defined course and no defined limits, because the above principles do not apply to percolating underground water.[2]

Underground water which does not flow in a channel cannot be the subject of property or capable of being conveyed.[3] Similarly, an easement cannot be created in respect of mere surface water, the supply of which is casual, and its flow following no regular or definite course.[4] A claim to have water percolate through the banks of a river cannot be acquired by prescription,[5] although a prescriptive right can be acquired in water issuing from a spring or well above ground.[6] Nor can a claim be established under the Prescription Act, 1832, to waste water from a canal.[7]

See also Chapter 8—UNDERGROUND AND PERCOLATING WATER.

Easements of artificial watercourse

See Chapter 7—ARTIFICIAL WATERCOURSES.

Easement to discharge or receive water

A claim to empty and discharge polluted water from a mine into the watercourse of a neighbour may be made under the Prescription Act, 1832.[8] In *Cawkell v. Russell*,[9] the court held that the plaintiff had a right to discharge ordinary refuse

---

[1] *Chasemore v. Richards* (1859), 7 H.L.C. 349.

[2] *Dickinson v. Grand Junction Canal* (1852), 7 Ex. 300.

[3] *Ewart v. Belfast Poor Law Comrs.* (1881), 9 L.R. Ir. 172.

[4] *Rawstron v. Taylor* (1855), 11 Ex. 369; *Greatrex v. Hayward* (1853), 18 Ex. 291.

[5] *Roberts v. Fellowes* (1906), 94 L.T. 281.

[6] *Balston v. Bensted* (1808), 1 Camp. 463; *Race v. Ward* (1855), 19 J.P. 563.

[7] *Staffordshire Canal Co. v. Birmingham Canal Co.* (1866), L.R. 1 H.L. 254.

[8] *Wright v. Williams* (1836), 1 M. & W. 77; *Carlyon v. Lovering* (1857), 1 H. & N. 784.

[9] (1856), 26 L.J. Ex. 34; *Charles v. Finchley L.B.* (1883), 47 J.P. 791.

water into another person's drain. A prescriptive right may be acquired to send sewage from one sanitary district into the sewers of another district,[1] or for a highway authority to discharge surface water from a highway on to adjoining land.[2] But the right of a corporation to discharge effluent into a river does not create an easement or grant in favour of the riparian owners which would require the corporation to continue forever the discharge.[3]

A right to receive the flow of water from another man's land may also be acquired as an easement. In *Ivimey v. Stocker*,[4] tin-bounders had from before the time of living memory used the water of an artificial watercourse arising in the land of another person. The tin-bounders abandoned the mine, which came into the possession of the plaintiffs, and the owner of the land on which the watercourse rose sought to divert the watercourse. Held: that the plaintiffs had either by prescription or custom acquired a right to use the water.

A right to go upon another person's land and take water from a pump,[5] pond,[6] spring or well[7] may be acquired as an easement.

Secondary easements

When an easement is granted, it includes all such secondary easements as are necessary for its proper enjoyment. Thus, where there is a prescriptive right to lay pipes across another person's property, a right will be implied for the purpose of entering the land and mending pipes.[8] Similarly, a prescriptive

---

[1] *A.-G. v. Acton L.B.* (1882), 22 Ch. D. 221; but see *Phillimore v. Watford R.D.C.,* [1913] 2 Ch. 434.

[2] *A.-G. v. Copeland,* [1902] 1 K.B. 694.

[3] *Deeds (John S.) & Sons Ltd. v. British Electricity Authority and Croydon Corporation* (1950), 114 J.P. 533.

[4] (1866), 14 L.T. 427; *Gaved v. Martyn* (1865), 13 L.T. 74; *Powell v. Butler* (1871), I.R. 5 C.L. 309.

[5] *Polden v. Bastard* (1865), L.R. 1 Q.B. 156.

[6] *Manning v. Wasdale* (1836), 4 Ad. & El. 758.

[7] *Race v. Ward* (1855), 4 E. & B. 702; *Smith v. Archibald* (1880), 5 A.C. 489.

[8] *Pomfret v. Ricroft* (1669), 1 Sid. 429; *Goodhart v. Hyett* (1883), 25 Ch. D. 182; *Thurrock Grays, etc., Sewerage Board v. Goldsmith* (1914), 79 J.P. 17; *Brown v. Best* (1747), 1 Wils. 174.

right to a watercourse includes the right to enter on the land of the servient tenement for the purpose of cleansing and scouring the watercourse,[1] or to repair the banks.[2] But a privilege granted by deed to make a goit across another person's land does not include the subsequent right to enter on the land to widen the goit, since the power to make the goit was extinguished.[3] If the principal easement ceases, secondary easements will also be extinguished.[4]

EXTINGUISHMENT OF WATER EASEMENTS

An easement of water may be extinguished by operation of law or by release.

Operation of Law

Where an easement is granted for a specific purpose, it will cease when the purpose is accomplished. Thus, an easement to take water to fill a canal ceases when the canal is converted into a railway and no longer exists.[5] If the dominant and servient tenements become vested in one and the same person the easement is extinguished if there is unity of ownership, but only suspended if there is unity of possession.[6]

Release

Release may be express or implied. An easement of water may be expressly released by deed, but in equity an easement may become extinguished by consent or acquiescence.[7] An implied release may arise in three different ways:—

(a) Licence given to servient owner

A parol or written licence may have the effect of extinguishing an existing easement, as where the owner of the dominant

---

[1] *Peter v. Daniel* (1848), 5 C.B. 586; *Lidford's Case* (1614), 11 Co. Rep. 46b.
[2] *Roberts v. Fellowes* (1906), 94 L.T. 279; *Hodgson v. Field* (1806), 7 East 613.
[3] *Bostock v. Sidebottom* (1852), 18 Q.B. 813.
[4] *Beeston v. Weate* (1856), 5 E. & B. 986.
[5] *National Manure Co. v. Donald* (1859), 4 H. & N. 8.
[6] *Canham v. Fisk* (1831), 1 Tyr. 155; *Thomas v. Thomas* (1835), 1 Gale 61; *James v. Plant* (1836), 4 Ad. & El. 761.
[7] *Davies v. Marshall* (1861), 4 L.T. 581.

tenement gives permission to the servient owner to use his land in a way which is incompatible with the future enjoyment of the easement.[1]

(b) *Abandonment by Non-user*

Once a prescriptive right has been acquired it cannot be lost by any subsequent act not amounting to a surrender, even though such act would have, previous to the acquisition of the right, rendered the user precarious.[2] The mere suspension of the exercise of a prescriptive right is not sufficient to destroy the right without some evidence of an intention to abandon it, *e.g.* where a factory has not been used for more than twenty years and has gone to ruin. But a long continued suspension may render it necessary for the person claiming the right to show that some indication was given during the period that he ceased to use the right of his intention to preserve it. The question of abandonment of a right is one of intention to be decided on the facts of each particular case.[3] Mere non-user of a right to water over ten years,[4] or the obstruction by weeds of a navigable drain for sixteen years,[5] will not be taken by themselves as presumptions of abandonment. Where a corporation has the right to discharge sewage effluent to a watercourse, this does not create a right in the riparian owners to any continuance of the discharge if the corporation wish to abandon it.[6]

(c) *Alteration in user of dominant tenement*

A substantial extension or alteration in the user of a prescriptive right may destroy the right,[7] but if the alteration of the dominant tenement does not impose any additional burden on the servient tenement, the easement is not extinguished, as where a fulling mill is altered to grind corn,[8]

---

[1] *Liggins v. Inge* (1831), 7 Bing. 682; *Davies v. Marshall, supra.*
[2] *French Hoek Comrs. v. Hugo* (1885), 10 A.C. 336.
[3] *Crossley v. Lightowler* (1867), 16 L.T. 438.
[4] *Mason v. Hill* (1833), 5 B. & Ad. 1.
[5] *Bower v. Hill* (1835), 1 Hodg. 45.
[6] *Deeds (John S.) & Sons Ltd. v. British Electricity Authority and Croydon Corporation* (1950), 114 J.P. 533.
[7] *Royal Mail Steam Packet Co. v. George & Branday*, [1900] A.C. 480.
[8] *Luttrell's Case* (1601), 4 Co. Rep. 86.

or the dimensions of a mill wheel are altered,[1] or there is a minute change in the course of a stream.[2] However, the easement will be destroyed if there is an encroachment by the dominant owner which renders the easement necessarily more injurious to the servient owner; a mill owner having a right to divert water cannot divert more water by altering his sluices,[3] and a riparian owner who has an easement to pollute water must not increase the pollution.[4]

An easement exists for the benefit of the dominant owner alone, and a servient owner acquires no right to insist on its continuance or to ask for damages in its abandonment.[5] But a person who constructs for his own use an artificial watercourse whether on his own or another person's land is, in the absence of agreement to the contrary, bound to keep the watercourse in such state of repair as will prevent damage to the servient tenement, and if he fails to do so, he is liable for any damage which may result.[6]

---

[1] *Saunders v. Newman* (1818), 1 B. & Ald. 258.
[2] *Hall v. Swift* (1838), 4 Bing. 381; *see also Hale v. Oldroyd* (1845), 14 M. & W. 789; *Watts v. Kelson* (1871), 6 Ch. App. 166.
[3] *Bealey v. Shaw* (1805), 6 East 208.
[4] *McIntyre v. McGavin*, [1893] A.C. 268.
[5] *Mason v. Shrewsbury Rly. Co.* (1871), 25 L.T. 239.
[6] *Buckley v. Buckley*, [1898] 2 Q.B. 608.

CHAPTER 7

ARTIFICIAL WATERCOURSES

Typical examples of artificial watercourses are to be found:—

where water from a spring is conveyed by a banked-up open channel to a farmhouse for domestic and farming purposes[1];

by the discharge of waste water from a mine or factory;

by means of an artificial cut to a natural stream[2];

where water is diverted from a river through a goit to work a mill wheel[3];

in canals, sewers and water mains, which are species of artificial watercourses entirely of statutory origin.

Distinction between natural and artificial watercourses

At one time the view was held that there was no particular difference at law between natural and artificial watercourses,[4] but this statement was later held to be too broad.[5] The present position was expressed by Sir Montague Smith in delivering judgment in *Rameshur Pershad Narain Singh v. Koonj Behari Pattuk*[6]:—

> " The right to the water of a river flowing in a natural channel through a man's land, and the right to water flowing to it through an artificial watercourse con-structed on his neighbour's land, do not rest on the same principle. In the former case each successive riparian owner is *prima facie* entitled to the unimpeded flow of the water in its natural course, and to its

---

[1] *Roberts v. Richards* (1881), 44 L.T. 271.
[2] *Gaved v. Martyn* (1865), 13 L.T. 74.
[3] *Burrows v. Lang*, [1901] 2 Ch. 503.
[4] *Magor v. Chadwick* (1840), 11 Ad. & El. 571.
[5] *Wood v. Waud* (1849), 3 Ex. 748.
[6] (1878), 4 A.C. 121.

[127]

reasonable enjoyment as it passes through his land, as a natural incident of his ownership of it. In the latter case any right to the flow of the water must rest on some grant or arrangement, either proved or presumed, from or with the owners of the lands from which the water is artificially brought, or on some other legal origin ".

The right to an artificial watercourse does not arise as a natural right of property, but must be established as an easement (except where an artificial stream is constructed and used by an owner solely on his own land)[1] either by grant,[2] long continued enjoyment or under statute, and the measure and extent of the right thus acquired, and the rights of the parties concerned, are governed by the terms of the grant, the type of user, or the provisions of the statute in each case.[3]

Bowen, L.J., remarked in *Chamber Colliery Co. v. Hopwood*[4] that in general there were two kinds of prescriptive rights claimed to enjoy an artificial watercourse. First of all a man might claim a right to continue the enjoyment of a discharge on to his land of an artificial channel made by somebody else above.[5] Then there might be a claim to discharge water flowing along an artificial cut upon another person's land below.[6]

Any proposition that the right to watercourses, arising from enjoyment, is the same whether they are natural or artificial, cannot be sustained. The right to artificial watercourses, as against the party creating them, depends upon the character of the watercourse, whether it is of a permanent or temporary nature, upon the circumstances under which it was presumably created, and the mode in which it has in fact been enjoyed.[7]

---

[1] *Bunting v. Hicks* (1894), 70 L.T. 455; *Holker v. Porritt* (1875), 33 L.T. 125; *Beeston v. Weate* (1856), 5 E. & B. 986.

[2] *Wood v. Saunders* (1875), 10 Ch. App. 583.

[3] *Sharp v. Waterhouse* (1857), 7 E. & B. 816; *Crossley v. Lightowler* (1867), 16 L.T. 438.

[4] (1886), 55 L.T. 449.

[5] *Ivimey v. Stocker* (1866), 1 Ch. App. 396; *Greatrex v. Hayward* (1853), 8 Ex. 291.

[6] *Carlyon v. Lovering* (1857), 1 H. & N. 784; *Brown v. Dunstable Corpn.*, [1899] 2 Ch. 378.

[7] *Wood v. Waud* (1849), 3 Ex. 748; *Baily & Co. v. Clark, Son & Morland*, [1902] 1 Ch. 649.

Permanent artificial watercourses

Riparian rights identical with those attaching to natural streams may be acquired by prescription in artificial watercourses of a permanent character. These rights depend on the character of the watercourse and the purpose for which it was constructed. If the watercourse is of a permanent nature and constructed for lasting purposes and for the general benefit of those in its vicinity and not merely with the temporary and private object of benefiting the property of those by whom it was constructed, riparian rights may be acquired in its waters just as in a natural stream.[1] In an Australian case,[2] it was held that in the absence of grant, prescription, or implication of law, riparian rights do not exist in an artificial watercourse.

A watercourse, though artificial, may have been originally made under such circumstances and have been so used as to give all the rights that the riparian owners would have had if it had been a natural stream.[3] Again, if a watercourse is partly natural and partly artificial, but nobody can tell when the artificial portion was made, the watercourse may be deemed to be natural, or if in part artificial, to have been made so as to give all the rights of a riparian owner to the proprietor on the banks and his predecessors.[4]

A prescriptive right to the flow of water along an artificial cut over the soil of another may be acquired if the circumstances under which the cut was made show that it was intended to be of a permanent character.[5] But in no case can the owner of the servient tenement acquire, by the mere existence of the easement, a right as against the owner of the dominant tenement to continue the diversion of a stream, since the easement exists for the benefit of the dominant tenement

---

[1] *Blackburne v. Somers* (1879), 5 L.R. Ir. 1.

[2] *Gartner v. Kidman,* [1962] A.L.R. 620.

[3] *Sutcliffe v. Booth* (1863), 27 J.P. 613; *Nuttall v. Bracewell* (1866), L.R. 2 Exch. 1; *Rameshur Pershad Narain Singh v. Koonj Behar Pattak* (1878), 4 App. Cas. 121, P.C.; *Baily & Co. v. Clark, Son & Morland,* [1902] 1 Ch. 649; *Manug Bya v. Manug Kyi Lyo* (1925), L.R. 52 Ind. App. 385, P.C.; *Epstein v. Reymes* (1972), 29 D.L.R. (3rd), (Supreme Court of Canada).

[4] *Roberts v. Richards* (1881), 44 L.T. 271.

[5] *Gaved v. Martyn* (1865), 13 L.T. 74.

alone and the servient owner acquires no right to insist on its continuance, or to ask for damages for its abandonment.[1]

In *Baily & Co. v. Clark, Son & Morland*,[2] it was held that in the case of an artificial watercourse, the origin of which was unknown, the proper inference from the user of the water and from other circumstances might be that the channel was originally constructed upon the condition that all the riparian proprietors should have the same rights, including a right to use the water for manufacturing purposes, as they would have had if the stream had been a natural one. In such a case it appears that a riparian owner is entitled to natural rights and prescriptive rights.

In a slightly later case,[3] where the plaintiffs and their predecessors in title had constantly used the water of an artificial channel for nearly 250 years, the court decided that where water flows through an artificial channel past the lands of several owners to serve the purposes of an owner lower down, the proper grant to presume, in the absence of all evidence as to the conditions upon which the channel was originally made, would be a grant of an easement or right to the running of water and *prima facie* every owner on the banks of such a channel would be entitled to the moiety of the bed of the channel adjoining his land.

Temporary artificial watercourses

In *Arkwright v. Gell*,[4] a case dealing with an artificial stream which drained certain mines, the court decided that the artificial stream was one of a temporary character, having its continuance only whilst the convenience of the mine owners required it and made with the sole object of getting rid of a nuisance to the mines; accordingly, the owners on the banks of the stream could not compel the mine owners to continue the discharge. Again, no action will lie for an injury by the diversion of an artificial watercourse, where it is obvious

---

[1] *Mason v. Shrewsbury Rly.* (1871), 25 L.T. 239.
[2] [1902] 1 Ch. 649.
[3] *Whitmores (Edenbridge) Ltd. v. Stanford*, [1909] 1 Ch. 427.
[4] (1839), 5 M. & W. 203.

from the nature of the case that the enjoyment of the water-course depends upon temporary circumstances and is not of a permanent character, and where the interruption is by a person who stands in the nature of a grantor.[1]

A right to a flow of water along an artificial cut over the soil of another person cannot be acquired under the Prescription Act, 1832, unless the circumstances under which the cut was made show that it was intended to be of a permanent character.[2] In *Burrows v. Lang*,[3] an ancient watercourse diverted from a natural stream and constructed and maintained solely for the purpose of a mill was held to be constructed for a special temporary purpose, and a purchaser of the mill acquired no right either by implied grant or under statute to the use of the water in the watercourse. In *Greatrex v. Hayward*,[4] the court decided that a flow of water for twenty years from a drain made for agricultural improvements did not give a right to a neighbour so as to preclude the owner from altering the level of the drain; the drain was clearly of a temporary character and was dependent upon the mode in which the defendant might adopt in draining his land.

A number of other decisions followed in the wake of *Wood v. Waud* and *Greatrex v. Hayward*. A person who makes an artificial cut and so brings water to a stream which did not go there before, may *prima facie* cut it off if he chooses.[5] In *Hanna v. Pollock*,[6] the defendant's right to an artificial drain was held to be permissive only since the drain was an artificial one, not of a permanent character, but open to alteration or removal at the plaintiff's pleasure. No prescriptive right can be acquired to receive water overflowing from a tank along an artificial stream which had been constructed for a temporary purpose only.[7] The meaning of " temporary purpose " is not confined to a purpose that happens to last in fact for a few

---

[1] *Wood v. Waud* (1849), 18 L.J. Ex. 305; *see also Greatrex v. Hayward* (1853), 8 Ex. 291.
[2] *Gaved v. Martyn* (1865), 13 L.T. 74.
[3] [1901] 2 Ch. 503.
[4] (1853), 8 Ex. 291.
[5] *Brymbo Water Co. v. Lesters Lime Co.* (1894), 8 R. 329.
[6] [1900] 2 I.R. 664.
[7] *Bartlett v. Tottenham* (1932), 45 L.T. 686.

years only, but includes a purpose which is temporary in the sense that it may within the reasonable contemplation of the parties come to an end.[1]

Pollution of artificial watercourses

In general, the pollution of water in an artificial channel falls into the same category as the diversion or obstruction of an artificial watercourse, namely that only a riparian owner can sue in respect of injury caused by pollution. Thus, where it can be concluded that an artificial watercourse was made in such circumstances and has been so used as to give the owners on the banks riparian rights, they will have the same remedies to prevent pollution as have the owners on the banks of a natural stream: *Sutcliffe v. Booth*,[2] which concerned an action by one riparian owner against another for the pollution and diversion of a watercourse: held that it was a misdirection to tell the jury that if the stream were artificial and made by the hand of man, the plaintiff had no right of action, since the circumstances under which the stream was constructed showed that the owners had acquired riparian rights in it.

The position of non-riparian owners as respects the pollution of artificial watercourses is illustrated in the following decisions.

In *Whaley v. Laing*,[3] a mere licensee using water from a canal was held to be unable to sue the defendant, who polluted the canal water, since the licensee had no legal right to the water. *Stockport Waterworks Co. v. Potter*,[4] decided that the plaintiffs, who possessed certain non-riparian land and the right to use conduits on land bordering a natural stream, had no natural rights with regard to the stream and could not sue a riparian owner on the stream who polluted

---

[1] *Arkwright v. Gell* (1839), 5 M. & W. 203; *Burrows v. Lang*, [1901] 2 Ch. 503.

[2] (1863), 27 J.P. 613.

[3] (1857), 2 H. & N. 476.

[4] (1864), 3 H. & C. 300.

the stream so that the water flowing through the conduits was also polluted. The judgment in the Stockport case was approved and followed in *Ormerod v. Todmorden Mill Co.*,[1] where it was held that a water company, not being riparian owners, who took water from a natural stream by means of conduits had no natural rights which enabled them to sue a higher riparian owner for polluting the stream whereby the water flowing through the conduits was also fouled. In *Crossley v. Lightowler*,[2] the owner of a mill, which received water from a natural stream by means of an artificial goit, could not sue in respect of the stream being polluted, since he was not a riparian owner on the goit.

However, irrespective of the position that only a riparian owner can sue another riparian owner for the pollution of the water flowing past his land, no one is entitled at common law to use his land so as to send foul water by an artificial channel or otherwise on to his neighbour's property.

It was decided in an early case[3] that if filth is created on a man's land, then he whose it is must keep it there, that it may not trespass. In *Womersley v. Church*,[4] the defendant was restrained from using his cesspool in such a manner so as to cause water percolating through his property and polluting an adjoining well. This was followed by *Humphries v. Cousins*,[5] where water and sewage came on to the defendant's land by an artificial drain made for the defendant's convenience, and flooded the plaintiff's adjoining premises; the defendant was held liable, although unaware of the drain's existence and therefore of his liability to repair it.

In the case of *Ballard v. Tomlinson*,[6] the plaintiff and defendant were adjoining landowners and each had a deep

---

1 (1883), 47 J.P. 532.

2 (1867), 16 L.T. 638; *see also Dickinson v. Shepley Sewerage Board* (1904), 68 J.P. 363; *Fergusson v. Malvern U.D.C.* (1908), 72 J.P. 273.

3 *Tenant v. Goldwin* (1703), Salk. 21.

4 (1867), 17 L.T. 190.

5 (1877), 2 C.P.D. 239.

6 (1885), 29 Ch. D. 115; *see also Hodgkinson v. Ennor* (1863), 4 B. & S. 229.

well in his own land, the plaintiff's land being at a lower level than the defendant's. The defendant turned sewage into his well and polluted the water which percolated underground from his property to the plaintiff's land, and consequently the water which came into the plaintiff's well from such percolating water when he used his well by pumping became adulterated with the defendant's sewage. Held: that the plaintiff had a right of action against the defendant for polluting the source of supply, although until the plaintiff appropriated it he had no property in the percolating water under his land and although he appropriated the water by the artificial means of pumping. But it may be possible to establish a right to discharge dirty water.[1]

---

[1] *Cawkwell v. Russell* (1856), 26 L.J. Ex. 34.

CHAPTER 8

UNDERGROUND AND PERCOLATING WATER

The law relating to underground or subterranean water is stated in *Chasemore v. Richards*[1]:—

" The law as to water flowing in a certain and definite channel has been conclusively settled in a series of decisions, in which the whole subject has been fully and satisfactorily considered, and the relative rights and duties of riparian owners have been carefully adjusted and established. The principles of these decisions appear to me to be applicable to all water flowing in a certain and defined course, whether in an open visible stream or in a known subterranean channel. But it appears to me that the principles which apply to flowing water in streams or rivers . . . are wholly inapplicable to water percolating through underground strata, which has no certain course, no defined limits, but which oozes through the soil in every direction in which the rain penetrates ".

In dealing with underground water then, a distinction must be drawn between water which flows in a known and defined subterranean channel and water which percolates through the soil having no defined course.

PERCOLATING UNDERGROUND WATER

The General Rule—No riparian rights in underground percolating water

The owner of land through which water flows in a subterranean course has no right or interest in it which enables

---

1 (1859), 7 H.L. Cas. 349.

him to maintain an action against a landowner, who in carrying on mining operations in his own land in the usual manner, drains away the water from the land of the first owner and leaves his well dry.[1] In *Chasemore v. Richards*,[2] an owner who had for more than sixty years enjoyed the use of a stream which was mainly supplied by percolating underground water, lost the use of the stream after an adjoining landowner had dug on his own ground an extensive well for supplying water to local inhabitants, many of which had no title as landowners to the use of the water. Held: the first owner had no right of action. The position can perhaps be best summed up by referring to two Irish cases—*Ewart v. Belfast Poor Law Comrs.*[3]: underground water not flowing in a known channel is not the subject of property or capable of being granted—*Black v. Ballymena Comrs.*[4]: subterranean water can only be the subject of riparian rights when flowing in known and defined channels.

In *R. v. Metropolitan Board of Works*,[5] a landowner was held not to be entitled to compensation under statute for the abstraction of water from underground springs, which rose in his land and fed his ponds, by a sewer constructed under the statute in neighbouring land, since the abstraction of underground percolating water was not actionable. Where a landowner grants the surface of the ground to another person, but retains the minerals beneath, lessees of the minerals are not responsible if in working the minerals they drain the water from the surface.[6]

Abstraction of percolating water in a well or after it has reached the surface

It is clear that no action will lie for the interception of underground percolating water before it reaches a well,[7] but what is the position if the water is drawn off as a result of

---

[1] *Acton v. Blundell* (1843), 12 M. & W. 324; *Hammond v. Hall* (1840), 10 Sim. 551.
[2] (1859), 7 H.L. Cas. 349.
[3] (1881), 9 L.R. Ir. 172.
[4] (1886), 17 L.R. Ir. 459; *Blackrod U.D.C. v. Crankshaw (John) Co. Ltd.* (1913), 136 L.T. Jo. 239.
[5] (1863), 3 B. & S. 710.
[6] *Ballacorkish Co. v. Harrison* (1873), 29 L.T. 658.
[7] *Brain v. Marfell* (1879), 41 L.T. 455.

operations in adjoining land when the water is actually in the well or has got to the surface ? Where water has actually percolated into and is in a well and has been abstracted by workings in adjacent property, again, no action will lie.[1]

As regards water which has reached the surface; in *Dudden v. Clutton Union*,[2] a natural stream of water arose from a spring which served the plaintiff's well and the defendants sank a well in their ground for a workhouse and caught the water at the spring head by tanks before it flowed into the natural channel. Held: that this was not taking underground percolating water, but water after it had arrived at the spring head, and the defendants were guilty of a wrongful diversion. This decision was held not to be affected by the fact that the source of the spring has been built round and formed into a well, thus resulting in an artificial channel for a short distance.[3]

Although a landowner will not in general be restrained from drawing off the subterranean water in the adjoining land, yet he will be restrained, if in so doing, he draws off the water flowing in a defined surface channel through the adjoining land.[4] That decision should be contrasted with *English v. Metropolitan Water Board*,[5] where the defendants in pumping a well lowered the general level of the water in the neighbouring soil so that the soil became dry. This caused the water in a nearby stream to leak through the bed and sides and the supply to a lower riparian owner was seriously diminished. None of the water that leaked out ever reached the defendants' well. Held: that the riparian owner had no right of action against the defendants because the injury was caused by withdrawal of support and not by abstraction from the stream.

Restrictions on underground abstraction

A landowner is entitled to sink a borehole or well on his land to intercept water percolating underground through his own property, although the effect is to interfere with the

---

[1] *New River Co. v. Johnson* (1860), 24 J.P. 244.
[2] (1857), 1 H. & N. 627.
[3] *Mostyn v. Atherton* (1899), 81 L.T. 356.
[4] *Grand Junction Canal Co. v. Shugar* (1871), 24 L.T 402.
[5] [1907] 1 K.B. 588.

supply of underground water to nearby springs, since the interference is to percolating water and not to water flowing in a defined stream. If the landowner's act is a lawful one, it is immaterial what his motives may be in doing so, and cannot render the act unlawful.[1] But subject to certain exceptions, it is an offence to abstract water from underground strata except in pursuance of a licence granted by the water authority. Further, it is prohibited to begin to (a) construct a well, borehole or other work whereby water may be abstracted from underground strata, or (b) extend any such well, borehole or other work or (c) install or modify machinery or apparatus whereby additional quantities of water may be abstracted from underground strata by means of a well, borehole or other work, unless the abstraction or additional quantities of water is authorised by a licence, and the construction, extension, installation or modification as above fulfils the requirement of that licence as to the means whereby water is authorised to be abstracted (see Chapter 11).

Springs and Wells

A spring of water, both in law and in ordinary language, is a natural source of water of a definite and well marked extent,[2] or, as stated in *Brain v. Marfell*,[3] " a spring is not an artificial space, but a natural chasm in which water has collected, and from which is either lost by percolation or rises in a defined channel ". The moment water of a spring issues from the ground and rises into a defined channel it constitutes a watercourse,[4] and water as it issues from a spring or well is not to be considered as the produce of the soil so as to make the right to take it *in alieno solo* for domestic purposes a *profit a prendre*; such right is an easement only and may be claimed by custom.[5] After twenty years uninterrupted enjoyment of a spring of water an absolute right to it is gained by the owner of the land in which it issues above

1 *Bradford Corpn. v. Pickles*, [1895] A.C. 587; *South Shields Waterworks v. Cookson* (1845), 15 L.J. Ex. 315; *Langbrook Properties v. Surrey County Council* (1969), 113 S.J. 983.
2 *Taylor v. St. Helens Corpn.* (1877), 6 Ch. D. 264.
3 (1879), 41 L.T. 457.
4 *Dudden v. Clutton Union* (1857), 1 H. & N. 627.
5 *Race v. Ward* (1855), 19 J.P. 563; *Smith v. Archibald* (1880), 5 A.C. 489.

ground and an adjoining owner cannot lawfully cut a drain whereby the supply of water to the spring is diminished.[1] Nor may a person cut trenches in his land so as to interrupt the natural flow of water from surface springs to his neighbour's property.[2] A right to take water from a well by reason of the occupation of a dwellinghouse, and for the more convenient occupation thereof, is an interest in land.[3]

Support from underground water

Whilst at common law an owner cannot withdraw from his neighbour the support of adjacent soil,[4] there is no right to the support of subterranean water: *Popplewell v. Hodgkinson*,[5] where the defendant by excavations drained the plaintiff's land so that the soil subsided and cottages thereon became thereby cracked and damaged; held: that the plaintiff had no right of action, because he was entitled to drain his soil if for any reason it became necessary or convenient for him to do so. But this does not apply to the loss of support due to removing wet sand and running silt.[6] In a Canadian case[7] it has been held that a right of support from subsurface waters exists (1) where the land is in its natural state and the water has been performing the duties of natural support, or (2) where a building, obviously dependent upon the support of the water, had been severed from " the ownership " of the land, or (3) where the claim was for a building which had for twenty years enjoyed the support of the water.

WATER FLOWING IN A DEFINED UNDERGROUND CHANNEL

Water flowing in a known and definite underground channel is placed in the same category as water flowing in a visible

---

[1] *Balston v. Bensted* (1808), 1 Camp. 463.
[2] *Ennor v. Barwell* (1860), 3 L.T. 170.
[3] *Tyler v. Bennett* (1836), 5 Ad. & El. 377.
[4] *New Moss Colliery v. Manchester Corpn.*, [1908] A.C. 117.
[5] (1869), L.R. 4 Ex. 248; *Elliot v. North Eastern Ry. Co.* (1863), 10 H.L.C. 333.
[6] *Jordeson v. Sutton, etc., Gas Co.*, [1899] 2 Ch. 217. *See also Salt Union v. Brunner*, [1906] 2 K.B. 822; *Fletcher v. Birkenhead Corpn.*, [1907] 1 K.B. 205; *Trinidad Asphalt Co. v. Ambard*, [1899] A.C. 594.
[7] *Rade v. K. & E. Sand and Gravel (Sarina)*, (1969) 10 D.L.R. (3d) 218, Ontario High Court.

stream on the surface.[1] In *Dickinson v. Grand Junction Canal Co.*,[2] it was said " if the course of a subterranean stream were well known, as is the case with many which sink underground, pursue for a short space a subterranean course, and then emerge again, it could never be contended that the owner of the soil under which the stream flowed, could not maintain an action for the diversion of it, if it took place under such circumstances as would have enabled him to recover had the stream been wholly above ground ". There is no reason to doubt that a subterranean flow of water may in some circumstances possess the very same characteristics as a body of water running on the surface.[3]

In order to apply the rule as to riparian rights to subterranean water, it must flow not only in a defined channel but in a known channel, giving to the word " known " a sense beyond what is conveyed by the word " defined ": *Ewart v. Belfast Poor Law Guardians*,[4] in which case water was only discovered by deep excavations made in the land under which the water flowed, and even then it was a matter of controversy and doubt whether there was any defined channel. A " defined " channel means " a contracted and bounded channel, although the course of the stream may be undefined by human knowledge ", and " known " means " the knowledge by reasonable inference from existing and observed facts in the natural or pre-existing conditions of the surface of the ground " and is not synonymous with " visible", nor is it restricted to knowledge derived from exposure of the ground by excavation.[5] If underground water flows in a defined channel into a well supplying a stream above ground, but the existence and course of that channel are not known and cannot be ascertained except by subsequent excavation, the lower riparian owners on the banks of the stream have no right of action for the abstraction of the underground water. [6]

---

1 *Chasemore v. Richards* (1859), 7 H.L. Cas. 349.
2 (1852), 7 Ex. 300.
3 *M'Nab v. Robertson*, [1897] A.C. 129.
4 (1881), 9 L.R. Ir. 172.
5 *Black v. Ballymena Comrs.* (1886), 17 L.R. Ir. 459.
6 *Bradford Corpn. v. Ferrand*, [1902] 2 Ch. 655, as considered in *Bleachers Assocn. Ltd. v. Chapel-en-le-Frith R.D.C.*, [1933] 1 Ch. 356.

PERCOLATING WATER ON THE SURFACE

Water flowing on the surface in a more or less defined channel usually constitutes a natural watercourse, although it may occasionally run dry,[1] but water which squanders itself over an undefined area and having no certain supply and no definite course is not a watercourse,[2] and does not give rise to riparian rights or acquired rights. The owner of land has an unqualified right to drain it for agricultural purposes in order to get rid of mere surface water, and a neighbouring proprietor cannot complain that he is thereby deprived of such water which would otherwise have come to his land. A right to water percolating through the banks of a stream cannot be claimed as an easement.[3]

In *Broadbent v. Ramsbotham*,[4] the plaintiff's well for more than fifty years had been watered by the water of a brook, which was supplied by a pond filled by rain, a shallow well supplied by underground water, a swamp and a well formed by a stream springing out of the side of a hill, the waters of all which occasionally overflowed and ran down the defendant's land in no definite channel into the brook. Held: that the defendant had a right to appropriate the surface water which flowed over his land in no definite channel, although the water was thereby prevented from reaching the brook which it had previously supplied.

The flow of water from a drain made for the purposes of agricultural improvements for twenty years does not give a right to the person, through whose land it flows, to the continuance of the flow so as to preclude the owner of the land drained from altering the level of his drain for the improvement of his land and thus cutting off the supply.[5] In *Bartlett v. Tottenham*,[6] the plaintiff was not entitled to the overflow from a tank set up to supply cattle since the overflow was only temporary. In the absence of a prescriptive right, the

---

[1] *R. v. Oxfordshire* (1830), 1 B. & A. 301; *Stollmeyer v. Trinidad Lake Petroleum Co.*, [1918] A.C. 491.
[2] *Rawstron v. Taylor* (1855), 11 Ex. 254.
[3] *Roberts v. Fellowes* (1906), 94 L.T. 279.
[4] (1856), 11 Ex. 602.
[5] *Greatrex v. Hayward* (1853), 8 Ex. 291.
[6] [1932] 1 Ch. 114.

court will not restrain the draining of gravel pits into a stream to the injury of watercress beds supplied by that stream.[1]

POLLUTION OF PERCOLATING WATER

Whilst the abstraction or diversion of percolating water is not actionable, a person who pollutes underground percolating water is liable to an action and may be restrained by injunction.

In *Hodgkinson v. Ennor*,[2] the plaintiff owned a paper mill and had an immemorial right to the supply of water from a cavern which was fed by rainwater running through underground passages. The defendant, an adjoining owner, in the process of lead working, discharged polluted water from pits through natural rents in the limestone rock to the cavern. The court held that the plaintiff had a right of action based on *Tenant v. Goldwin*,[3] namely that you must not injure your neighbour's property. In *Womersley v. Church*,[4] the defendant was restrained from using his cesspool in such a manner as to pollute water percolating through his land and supplying an adjacent well. The subject was further reviewed in *Ballard v. Tomlinson*,[5] which is dealt with on p. 133.

---

[1] *Weeks v. Heward* (1862), 10 W.R. 557.
[2] (1863), 4 B. & S. 229.
[3] (1703), Salk. 21.
[4] (1867), 17 L.T. 190.
[5] (1885), 29 Ch. D. 115.

CHAPTER 9

FERRIES

Ferries are but a variant of several types of crossings to which rivers and watercourses are habitually subject, namely:—fords, ferries, tunnels and bridges. As to bridges, see OBSTRUCTIONS TO NAVIGATION—BRIDGES, pp. 71, 72 and STRUCTURES OVER WATERCOURSES, pp. 233, 234.

DEFINITION, NATURE AND ORIGIN OF FERRIES

A public ferry is a public highway of a special description[1] and is an exclusive right to carry passengers across a river or arm of the sea from one vill to another, or to connect a continuance line of road leading from one township or vill to another. It is not a servitude imposed upon a district or large area of land, and is wholly unconnected with the ownership or occupation of land. A ferry exists in respect of persons using a right of way, where the line of way is across water; there must be a line of way on land coming down to a landing stage on the water's edge, or where the ferry is from or to a vill, from or to one or more landing places in the vill.[2]

The owner of a ferry must have a right to use the land on both sides of the water for the purpose of embarking and disembarking his passengers, but he need not have any property in the soil on either side.[3] The ferry owner may be said to have a right to make a special use of the highway, but he cannot be said to have the occupation of the highway.[4]

A floating bridge, which consists of a vessel propelled by steam from one side of a river to the other and kept on its

---

[1] *Huzzey v. Field* (1835), 5 Tyr. 855.
[2] *Newton v. Cubitt* (1862), 12 C.B.N.S. 32; *Ipswich (Inhabitants) v. Browne* (1581), Sav. 11 Ex. Ch.
[3] *Peter v. Kendal* (1827), 6 B. & C. 703; *Williams v. Jones* (1810), 12 East 346; *R. v. St. Mary Pembroke* (1851), 15 J.P. Jo. 336.
[4] *R. v. Nicholson* (1810), 12 East 330.

course by chain laid down across the bed of the river, is in substance a ferry and not a bridge.[1] A ferry may exist over a tidal creek which at low water could be traversed on foot,[2] and a ferry may be a one-way ferry, where the owners of opposite manors each have a ferry.[3]

Franchise ferries are of two types; point to point or from vill to vill. In the case of a point to point ferry, which is the more common kind, the exclusive right is only to ferry persons coming along a public right of way to a landing place and desiring to cross to a landing place on the opposite bank and continue their journey along another public way.[4] A vill to vill ferry is an exclusive right of ferriage from one vill to another throughout the area of the vills.[5] A point to point ferry has fixed terminii which cannot be varied to any substantial extent, whilst a vill to vill ferry may have more than one terminii on either side and can be varied within the limits of the vills.[6]

A ferry is *publici juris* and a franchise which no one can erect without a licence from the Crown and once a ferry has been erected, another ferry cannot be erected without an *ad quod damnum*. If a second ferry is erected without a licence, the Crown formerly had a remedy by a *quo warranto*, and the former grantee has a remedy by action.[7] All ancient ferries have their origin in a royal grant, or in prescription, which presumes a royal grant,[8] or by statute. *See Pim v. Curell,*[9] on a grant of ferry rights by the Crown. A jury may presume that a ferry has a legal origin from a user of thirty-five years and a variation in the amount of ferriage will not avoid the franchise.[10] A charter from the Crown granting rights of ferriage over certain rivers only conveys ferries existing at the date of the grant and does not confer on the grantee the

---

[1] *Ward v. Gray*, (1865) 12 L.T. 305.
[2] *Layzell v. Thompson* (1926), 91 J.P. 89.
[3] *General Estates Co. v. Beaver*, [1914] 3 K.B. 918; *Giles v. Groves* (1848), 12 Q.B. 721.
[4] *Hammerton v. Dysart (Earl)*, [1916] 1 A.C. 57; *Cowes U.D.C. v. Southampton, etc., Steam Packet Co.*, [1905] 2 K.B. 287.
[5] *General Estates Co. v. Beaver, supra.*
[6] *Hammerton v. Dysart (Earl), supra; Hemphill v. M'Kenna* (1845), 8 I.L.R. 43.
[7] *Blissett v. Hart* (1744), Willes 508.
[8] *Simpson v. A.-G.*, [1904] A.C. 476.
[9] (1840), 6 M. & W. 234.
[10] *Trotter v. Harris* (1828), 2 Y. & J. 285; *Layzell v. Thompson, supra.*

right to create new ferries over those rivers.[1] A ferry, being an incorporeal hereditament, must be transferred by deed.[2] A ferry may be granted in more or less extensive terms and where it is clear from the terms of the grant that it was intended to grant the ferriage only from one definite place to another definite place, the ferry owner cannot apply his franchise to another landing place some distance from the original place, merely because it is more convenient.[3]

Many of the more important modern ferries are established and worked under local Acts of Parliament, and by the Ferries (Acquisition by Local Authorities) Act, 1919, a local authority may purchase by agreement or accept the transfer of an existing ferry[4] which is within the area of the local authority or which serves the inhabitants of that area.[5] The local authority is empowered to work, maintain and improve the ferry thus acquired, to charge tolls or to free the ferry from tolls, and must make regulations, subject to confirmation by the Secretary of State for the Environment, as to the working of the ferry for the protection from injury of passengers and for the general public.[6] New road-ferries[7] may be provided and maintained by the Secretary of State, and, with the Secretary of State's approval, by a local highway authority,[8] who are empowered to improve a road-ferry provided by them,[9] and to acquire by agreement or compulsorily land required by them for the purpose of providing or improving a road-ferry.[10] A ferry undertaking, other than one acquired under the Ferries (Acquisition by Local Authorities) Act, 1919, may have their statutory charges revised by an order made by the Secretary of State.[11]

---

[1] *Londonderry Bridge Comrs.* v. *M'Keever* (1890), 27 L.R. Ir. 464.
[2] *Mayfield v. Robinson* (1845), 7 Q.B. 486; *Peter v. Kendal* (1827), 6 B. & C. 703.
[3] *Matthews v. Peache* (1855), 20 J.P. 244.
[4] " Existing ferry " is defined by s. 1 (4) of the Ferries (Acquisition by Local Authorities) Act, 1919.
[5] Ferries (Acquisition by Local Authorities) Act, 1919, s. 1.
[6] *Ibid.*, ss. 1, 2.
[7] " Road-ferry " is defined in s. 295 (1) of the Highways Act, 1959.
[8] Highways Act, 1959, s. 26 (3).
[9] *Ibid.*, s. 107.
[10] *Ibid.*, s. 220.
[11] Transport Charges, etc. (Miscellaneous Provisions) Act, 1954, s. 6.

Where proposals have been approved by the Secretary of State relating to a long-distance route in accordance with the National Parks and Access to the Countryside Act, 1949, including proposals for the provision and operation of a ferry, the highway authority for either or both of the highways to be connected by the ferry has power to provide and operate the ferry and do all such things as appear to them expedient for the purpose of operating the ferry. The highway authority may, with the approval of the Secretary of State, make arrangements with any person to provide and operate the ferry and make such contributions as may be agreed with that person. Nothing herein shall be construed as conferring on the highway authority an exclusive right to operate a ferry, nor authorise the doing of anything which apart from this provision would be actionable by any person having an exclusive right to operate a ferry without his consent.[1]

RIGHTS AND OBLIGATIONS OF OWNER OF FERRY

Tolls

A franchise of ferry is a toll franchise for the owner to take a reasonable toll,[2] unless by custom the inhabitants of a particular district have a right to pass a certain ferry free of toll.[3] The Crown have a general prerogative of exemption from payment of tolls,[4] even in respect of tolls created by statute.[5]

Maintenance of Ferry

A ferry owner is under the obligation of always providing proper boats with competent boatmen and all other things necessary for the maintenance of the ferry in an efficient state and condition for the use of the public, and this he is bound to do under pain of indictment.[6] In an early case,[7] it was said that a ferry owner was bound to sustain the ferry for the ease of the lieges. A right of ferry is in derogation of common right, for by common right any one entitled to cross a river

---

[1] National Parks and Access to the Countryside Act, 1949, s. 53.
[2] *A.-G. v. Simpson*, [1901] 2 Ch. 671; *Hammerton v. Dysart (Earl)*, [1916] 1 A.C. 57. *Hix v. Gardiner* (1614), 2 Bulst. 195.
[3] *Payne v. Partridge* (1690), 1 Salk. 12.
[4] *Westover v. Perkins* (1859), 2 E. & E. 57; *Cooper v. Hawkins*, [1904] 2 K.B. 164.
[5] *A.-G. v. Cornwall County Council* (1933), 97 J.P. 281.
[6] *Letton v. Goodden* (1866), 14 L.T. 296.
[7] *Nedeport (Prior) v. Weston* (1443), 2 Roll. Abr. 140. pl.4.

in a boat is entitled to carry passengers too. Within the limits of an ancient ferry no one is permitted to convey passengers across but the owner of the ferry and no one may disturb the ferry. The ferry carries with it an exclusive right or monopoly and in consideration of that monopoly the ferry owner is bound to have his ferry always ready.[1]

If the ferry owner fails to maintain the ferry and keep it in repair, he is liable to indictment for misdemeanour and the Crown may on the ground of neglect repeal the franchise by *scire facias* or a private person who has suffered special damage may bring an action.[2] It is no excuse for neglect that a ferry owner has erected a bridge across the river for common passage, which is more convenient than the ferry, because an owner is not entitled to suppress the ferry and put up a bridge in its place without licence and *ad quod damnum*. But an action will not lie against the ferryman for not keeping a boat for the ferry unless some special damage ensues.[3]

It appears to be the present position for the courts not to grant an injunction to require the owner of a ferry to continue to operate it; *see Pelly v. Woodbridge U.D.C.*,[4] where the court refused to grant an interlocutory mandatory injunction restraining the local authority from discontinuing a public ferry. In *A.-G. (Allen) v. Colchester Corporation*,[5] where a corporation ceased to work their franchise ferry because it operated at a loss, a mandatory injunction was not granted because the court could not compel the performance of personal services or the doing of a continuous act requiring the continuous employment of people, and as the ferry could only be maintained at a loss, it was inequitable to order the defendants to continue working it. The declaration sought was not made because no useful purpose would be achieved by it. In *Gravesham Borough Council v. British Railways Board*[6] the court stated that an injunction in such cases would only be granted in exceptional cases.

---

1 *Simpson v. A.-G.*, [1904] A.C. 476.
2 *Peter v. Kendal* (1827), 6 B. & C. 703.
3 *Payne v. Partridge, supra.*
4 (1950), 114 J.P. Jo. 666.
5 [1955] 2 All E.R. 124.
6 (1977) Law Society's Gazette, 8th March, 1978, p. 249.

Liability for Loss or Injury

The owner of a ferry is liable for any injury caused by negligence to passengers,[1] goods[2] or animals[3] carried on the ferry boat, and the owner of a ferry for carriages is bound to convey carriages and their contents.[4] As to the liability of a ferry boat in collision in fog, *see The Lancashire*.[5] If a ferryman surcharges a barge, a passenger may cast the things out of the barge in case of necessity for the safety of the passengers, and the owners have their remedy against the ferryman. If there is no surcharge and danger accrued only by act of God, no default being in the ferryman, everyone ought to bear his own loss.[6] A ferry owner is liable as a common carrier in respect of goods carried by him.[7]

DISTURBANCE OF FERRIES

Where a franchise of ferry exists, it confers an exclusive and absolute right of ferry and of taking tolls between fixed points, and if another person sets up a new ferry upon the same river near to the first ferry so as to impair it, the first owner has a right of action.[8] The mere act of the defendants carrying passengers in another boat otherwise likely to use the original ferry is a disturbance of the franchise.[9] The owner of a ferry has a cause of action against any one who sets up a new ferry either in the line of the old one or in another line so near as to make it an alternative way of carrying between substantially the same points. But where a new ferry is set up in proximity to an old ferry the question is whether the new traffic is *de facto* part of the old ferry or is really new traffic requiring new facilities and such as would not naturally use the highway which the old ferry serves. In the latter

---

[1] *Dalyell v. Tyrer* (1858), E.B. & E. 899.

[2] *Coote v. Lear* (1886), 2 T.L.R. 806.

[3] *Willoughby v. Horridge* (1852), 16 J.P. 761.

[4] *Walker v. Jackson* (1843), 10 M. & W. 161.

[5] (1874), 29 L.T. 927.

[6] *Mouse's Case* (1608), 12 Co. Rep. 63.

[7] *Southcote's Case* (1601), 4 Co. Rep. 83; *Rich v. Kneeland* (1613), Cro. Jac. 330.

[8] *Blissett v. Hart* (1774), Willes 508; *Blacketer v. Gillett* (1850), 9 C.B. 26.

[9] *North & South Shields Ferry Co. v. Barker* (1848), 2 Ex. 136.

case, the owner of the old ferry has no cause of action. Increased traffic in consequence of the growth of population or of a change in character of the district served by the old ferry is not " new traffic " entitling any one to set up a new ferry near the old one.[1]

Where an exclusive ferry connects two points, it does not prevent persons from going by another boat from one point of the old ferry to a different point on the other side, provided that it is not done fraudulently and as a pretence for avoiding the regular ferry.[2] A new ferry which has the effect of taking away passengers from a regular ferry must be injurious,[3] but where the public convenience requires a new passage at such a distance from the old ferry as makes it to be a real convenience to the public, the proximity of the new ferry from the old one does not seem to be actionable.[4]

The owner of a ferry cannot maintain an action for loss of traffic caused by a new highway by bridge or ferry made to provide for new traffic. In *Hopkins v. Great Northern Ry. Co.*,[5] where a railway company under statutory powers constructed a railway bridge and a foot bridge across a river half a mile above an ancient ferry, so that traffic across the ferry fell off and the ferry was given up, the court decided that the ferry owner could not claim for compensation, since he did not have the exclusive right to carry passengers and goods across the river by any means whatever, but only an exclusive right to carry them across by means of the ferry. Also, where a bridge was constructed by private enterprise connecting the same highway as a ferry, so that the ferry owner lost part of the income derived from tolls, it was held that the bridge was not a disturbance of the ferry and the ferry owner had no remedy.[6]

---

[1] *Hammerton v. Dysart (Earl)*, [1916] 1 A.C. 57.

[2] *Tripp v. Frank* (1792), 4 T.R. 666.

[3] *Huzzey v. Field* (1835), 5 Tyr. 855.

[4] *Newton v. Cubitt* (1862), 6 L.T. 860.

[5] (1877), 2 Q.B.D. 224; over-ruling *R. v. Cambrian Ry. Co.* (1871), 25 L.T. 84.

[6] *Dibden v. Skirrow*, [1908] 1 Ch. 41; *Latter v. Littlehampton U.D.C.* (1909), 73 J.P. 426; *Young v. Thank* (1845), 6 L.T.O.S. 146.

In an action for disturbance of a ferry, it is sufficient for the plaintiff to prove that he was in possession of the ferry at the time when the cause of action arose, and it is not necessary for him to allege or prove the payment of a specified sum for passage money.[1]

A corporation empowered by statute to establish and work a steam-ferry, but on whom no obligation to maintain the ferry had been imposed, has no right to an action for an injunction to restrain a person who, without any title, has established a ferry which interferes with the profits of the steam-ferry.[2]

EXTINGUISHMENT OF FERRIES

A franchise of public ferry could formerly be repealed by the Crown by means of a writ of *scire facias* or *quo warranto*,[3] but the latter method has been abolished.[4] The ferryman can surrender his interest in the ferry by giving up his lease.[5] A ferry may also be extinguished under statute, whereby a bridge or modern ferry is authorised to be substituted for an ancient ferry.[6]

---

[1] *Peter v. Kendal* (1827), 6 B. & C. 703.

[2] *Londonderry Bridge Comrs. v. M'Keever* (1890), 27 L.R. Ir. 464; *Bournemouth-Swanage Ferry Co. v. Harvey*, [1930] A.C. 549.

[3] *A.-G. v. Colchester Corpn.*, [1955] 2 All E.R. 124.

[4] See s. 9 of the Administration of Justice (Miscellaneous Provisions) Act, 1938.

[5] *Peter v. Kendal* (1827), 6 B. & C. 703.

[6] *Cory v. Yarmouth & Norwich Ry. Co.* (1844), 3 Hare 593; *North & South Shields Ferry Co. v. Barker* (1848), 2 Ex. 136; *Royal v. Yaxley* (1872), 36 J.P. 680.

CHAPTER 10

WATER MANAGEMENT

THE WATER ACT 1973

The Water Act 1973, which originated from the report of the Central Advisory Water Committee on the Future Management of Water in England and Wales[1] published in 1971 and followed by a White Paper on the Reorganisation of Water and Sewage Services: Government Proposals and Arrangements for Consultation[2] also issued in 1971, received Royal Assent on the 18th July 1973. The 1973 Act has been amended by the Water Charges Act, 1976, and affected by the Water Charges Equalisation Act, 1977, and the three Acts may be cited together as the Water Acts, 1973-1977.[3] The Act does not extend to Scotland nor Northern Ireland except as expressly stated.[4]

The Act, which is more comprehensive and embracing than previous enactments dealing with river and water management, provided for (1) a restatement of the national policy for water related to the responsibilities of the appropriate Ministers therefore; (2) the abolition of river authorities, statutory water boards and joint sewerage boards and committees, and the transfer of their functions to new regional water authorities, who also took over the responsibilities of local authorities for water supply, sewage disposal and sewerage; and (3) a system of charges levied for the services provided by the water authorities.

All river authorities, together with the Conservators of the River Thames, the Lee Conservancy Catchment Board and the Isle of Wight River and Water Authority, all statutory water undertakers (except statutory water companies, joint water boards and committees) and all joint sewerage boards and committees were abolished on the 1st April 1974.[5] The functions of those bodies, together with the functions of local authorities exercisable in relation to water supply, sewage

---

[1] Department of Environment Circular No. 20/71.
[2] Department of Environment Circular No. 92/71.
[3] Water Charges Equalisation Act, 1977, s. 6 (2).
[4] Water Act 1973, s. 40 (4)-(6).
[5] *Ibid.*, 1973, s. 33.

disposal and water supply, were transferred on that date to the water authorities, who also assumed new powers and duties as to recreation and amenity in connection with water.[1]

Property in respect of the transferred functions and associated rights and liabilities were taken over by, and officers were transferred under the review and advice of the Water Services Staff Commission to, the water authorities on the 1st April 1974 under orders made by the Secretary of State.[2]

CENTRAL ORGANISATION

The functions of Ministers

The duty of the Secretary of State for the Environment, the Secretary of State for Wales and the Minister of Agriculture, Fisheries and Food is to promote jointly a national policy for water in England and Wales and to discharge their respective functions to secure the effective execution of that policy by the bodies responsible for such functions. The Secretary of State is required to promote so much of the national policy as relates to:—

(a) the conservation, augmentation, distribution and proper use of water resources, and the provision of water supplies;

(b) sewerage and the treatment and disposal of sewage and other effluents;

(c) the restoration and maintenance of the wholesomeness of rivers and other inland water;

(d) the use of inland water for recreation;

(e) the enhancement and preservation of amenity in connection with inland water; and

(f) the use of inland water for navigation.

The Minister is responsible for the policy in relation to land drainage and fisheries in inland and coastal waters.[3]

---

1 *See* Water Act 1973, Part II (ss. 9-15, 17-22).

2 Water Act 1973, s. 34 (1), (2), Sch. 6; Local Government Act 1972, ss. 254-257, 259, 260.

3 Water Act 1973, s. 1 (1)-(3).

The Secretary of State is under the duty to collate and publish information from which assessments can be made of the actual and prospective demands for water, and of actual and prospective water resources, in England and Wales, and may collaborate with others in doing so whether in England and Wales or elsewhere.[1] The Minister may give water authorities directions of a general character as to the exercise of their fisheries and land drainage functions, and the Secretary of State may do likewise as to the exercise of their other functions, so far as the exercise of such functions appear to affect the execution of the national policy for water or otherwise to affect the national interest. The appropriate Minister must consult the National Water Council before giving a direction.[2]

National Water Council

The National Water Council was established under the Water Act 1973, to consider and advise any Minister on matters relating to the national policy for water and to advise any Minister and the water authorities on any other matter of common interest to them, promote and assist water authorities in the efficient performance of their functions and upon research and forward planning, advise any Minister on matters on which the Council are consulted by him under a requirement imposed by the Act, establish after consultation a national scheme for the testing and approval of water fittings, prepare after consultation a scheme for the training and education of water authority staff, and on request perform services for, or act on behalf of, two or more water authorities and of statutory water companies in respect of matters of common interest.

The Council consists of (a) a chairman appointed by the Secretary of State; (b) the chairmen of the water authorities; and (c) not more than ten other members having special knowledge of matters relevant to water authority functions, of whom up to eight are appointed by the Secretary of State and up to two appointed by the Minister.[3]

---

[1] Water Act 1973, s. 1 (6), (7).
[2] Ibid., s. 5.
[3] Ibid., 1973, s. 4. The administrative and financial powers of the Council are set out in ibid., Sch. 3, Parts II and III.

Water Space Amenity Commission

The Commission was also set up by the Water Act 1973, to advise the Secretary of State on promoting the national policy for water, and the National Water Council and water authorities on the discharge of their respective functions, so far as such matters relate to recreation and amenity, submit to water authorities any proposals appropriate for the discharge of their functions, and encourage and assist water authorities in preparing plans and programmes under their periodic reviews for forward planning, so far as relating to recreation and amenity. The Commission consists of a chairman appointed by the Secretary of State, the chairmen of the water authorities, and not more than ten other members appointed by the Secretary of State after consultation with specified bodies and organisations.[1]

WATER AUTHORITIES

(1) Establishment

There are ten regional water authorities, nine for England[2] and one for Wales,[3] and each was established by an order made by the Secretary of State for the Environment and the Minister of Agriculture, Fisheries and Food, and came into existence on a day appointed by the order.[4] The Ministers may also by order change the name of a water authority or alter the boundaries of their area.[5] The water authorities exercised their functions on and after 1st April 1974 unless otherwise stated.[6]

(2) Constitution of water authorities

A water authority consists of:—

    (a) a chairman appointed by the Secretary of State;

    (b) between two to four members appointed by the Minister of Agriculture, Fisheries and Food with experience of, and capacity in, agriculture, land drainage or fisheries;

---

[1] Water Act 1973, s. 23.
[2] *Ibid.*, s. 2 (1), (2), Sch. 1.
[3] *Ibid.*, s. 2 (1), (2), 3 (10).
[4] *Ibid.*, s. 2 (4).
[5] *Ibid.*, s. 2 (5).
[6] *Ibid.*, s. 39 (1).

(c) members appointed by the Secretary of State with experience of, and capacity in, some matter relevant to the functions of water authorities;

(d) members appointed by local authorities.

The number of members appointed under (b)-(d) above are specified in the order establishing each water authority and the order is framed so that the total number of members appointed by the Secretary of State and the Minister is less than the number of those appointed by local authorities. In appointing members of a water authority, the Minister concerned must have regard to the desirability of their being familiar with the requirements and circumstances of the authority's area. The Ministers may by order vary the membership of a water authority.[1]

In the case of certain water authorities, there are special provisions regarding the appointment of members.[2]

Schedule 3, Part I to the Act deals with the terms of office of members, vacation of office, filling of casual vacancies, disqualification of members, officers, proceedings of committees, contracts, and so forth.[3]

(3) Members of local authorities

If a quarter or more of the population of a metropolitan county is resident within the area of a water authority, the county council may appoint two members, and the district councils within the county may between them appoint two members, of the water authority.

In the case of a non-metropolitan county or of a county in Wales where a quarter or more of the population resides within the area of a water authority, the county council may appoint one member, and the district councils within the county may between them appoint one member, of the water authority.

Where one-sixth or more but less than one-fourth of the population of any county resides within that area, the county council may, after consultation with the district councils within

---

[1] Water Act 1973, s. 3 (1)-(3), (5), (9).
[2] Ibid., s. 3 (4), (7), (8), (10).
[3] Ibid., s. 2 (8).

the county and wholly or partly within that area, appoint one member of the water authority.[1]

A local authority may appoint their members or other persons to a water authority,[2] and can nominate a deputy to attend meetings of the water authority for a member of the water authority appointed by the local authority.[3]

(4) Committees

Water authorities are empowered to arrange for their functions to be discharged by a committee, a sub-committee, an officer of the authority or by another water authority, and two or more water authorities may discharge functions jointly or by a joint committee. Committees and joint committees may delegate functions to a sub-committee or an officer. Functions exercisable by a regional land drainage committee or any local land drainage committee and a water authority's powers for issuing precepts, making drainage charges or borrowing money are outside the scope of the above arrangements.

The number of members of a committee and their term of office must be fixed by the appointing authority or authorities, or, in the case of a sub-committee, by the appointing committee. A committee or joint committee may include persons who are not members of the appointing authority or authorities, provided at least two-thirds of the members appointed are members of the authority or authorities. Advisory committees or joint committees may be appointed and include persons who are not members of the appointing authority or authorities.[4]

(5) Boundaries of water authority areas

The boundaries of a water authority area, and any waters comprised in it which it is necessary to define for the purposes of exercising any of the authority's functions, are defined in an order under section 2 of the Water Act 1973, establishing the

---

[1] Water Act 1973, s. 3 (6).
[2] *Ibid.*, s. 3 (12).
[3] *Ibid.*, s. 2 (8), Sch. 3, para. 15.
[4] *Ibid.*, s. 6. As to regional and local land drainage committees *see* Chap. 12: for regional and local advisory fisheries committees, *see* Chap. 14.

authority or altering the boundaries of the authority's area. Without prejudice to section 17 (2) of the Land Drainage Act 1976, relating to sea defence works for the purposes of a water authority's functions, the seaward boundary of the authority's area is (except as provided by a section 2 order or the following provisions) low-water mark[1] on the coast of the area.[2]

Subject to any section 2 order, where a river, stream or other watercourse,[3] whether natural or artificial or tidal or not, or any creek so far as it does not form part of such a watercourse-discharges into the sea,[4] the whole of the mouth of the water, course within a line from low-water mark at the seaward extremity of one bank to low-water mark at the seaward extremity of the other bank, or the whole of the creek within such a line (as the case may be) forms part of a water authority area, and, if both banks are in the same such area, form part of that water authority area.   The same applies to the entrance to a dock on the coast.   But if the banks of the watercourse or creek or the sides of the dock are in different water authority areas, a section 2 order may designate the area in which any part of the watercourse, creek or dock is to be comprised.[5]

Subject to any section 2 order, for the purposes of a water authority's fisheries functions, the authority area includes those tidal waters and parts of the sea adjoining the coast of the area in which Her Majesty's subjects have the exclusive right of fishing, and any question arising as to the extent of the area of a water authority is determined by the Minister of Agriculture, Fisheries and Food, whose decision is final.[6]

For the purposes of Part II of the Control of Pollution Act 1974, relating to the pollution of water, the area of a water

---

1 " low-water mark " means low-water mark of ordinary spring tides. (Water Act 1973, s. 2 (7), Sch. 2, para. 1 (3).)

2 *Ibid.*, Sch. 2, paras. 1 (1), 2 (1).

3 " Watercourse " is defined in footnote 1 on p. 174.   (*Ibid.*, s. 38 (1).)

4 " Sea " includes any bay, estuary or arm of the sea.   (*Ibid.*, s. 2 (7), Sch. 2, para. 1 (3).)

5 *Ibid.*, Sch. 2, para. 2 (2)-(4).

6 *Ibid.*, s. 2 (7), Sch. 2, para. 4.

authority includes all controlled waters[1] off the coast of the area which is the authority's area apart from this provision, and any question as to whether any place is included in the area of a water authority is determined by the Secretary of State.[2]

(6) Maps of water authority areas

As soon as practicable after the coming into force of an order establishing a water authority or altering a water authority area, the Secretary of State must send the authority one or more maps which are their area map in relation to their functions, except their land drainage functions, or notify them of such maps. The area maps have to be kept at the principal office of the authority, who must provide reasonable facilities for inspecting them and taking copies of and extracts from the maps. Any local authority whose area is wholly or partly within a water authority area is entitled on application to be furnished with a copy of the map on such payment as the authorities may agree. An area map is conclusive evidence for all purposes as to the boundaries of the water authority area in relation to any functions.[3]

(7) Functions exercised by water authorities

The powers and duties transferred to or conferred on water authorities by the Water Act 1973 comprise those concerned with:—

(a) water supply[4];

(b) sewerage and sewage disposal[5];

(c) water conservation[6];

(d) land drainage[7];

---

[1] " Controlled waters " means the sea within three nautical miles from any point on the coast measured from low-water mark of ordinary spring tides, such other parts of the territorial sea adjacent to Great Britain as are prescribed by regulations and any other tidal waters in Great Britain. (Control of Pollution Act, 1974, s. 56 (1).)

[2] *Ibid.*, s. 56 (4).

[3] Water Act 1973, s. 2 (7), Sch. 2, paras. 6, 7, 12, 13. As to the main river map of a water authority, *see* p. 218.

[4] *See* p. 159.

[5] *See* p. 161.

[6] *See* Chap. 11.

[7] *See* Chap. 12.

(e) control of pollution[1];

(f) fisheries[2];

(g) navigation, where applicable[3];

(h) water recreation.[4]

(8) Water supply

All statutory water undertakers existing immediately before 18th July 1973, except statutory water companies,[5] joint water boards,[6] joint water committees[6] and existing local authorities and other bodies exercising functions not affected by the Water Act 1973, were abolished on 1st April 1974,[7] and the duty to supply water within their areas was imposed on the water authorities.[8] The water authorities are empowered subject to certain provisions[9] to exercise any functions exercisable by statutory water undertakers as such under any enactment or instrument. These functions, together with the functions exercisable by local authorities under Part IV of the Public Health Act 1936 relating to water supply, are no longer applicable (with certain exceptions) to local authorities.[10]

It is the duty of local authorities (other than a county council or the Greater London Council) to ascertain periodically the sufficiency and wholesomeness of water supplies in their area and to notify the water authority of any insufficiency or unwholesomeness in such supplies.[11]

---

[1] See Chap. 15.
[2] See Chap. 14.
[3] See Chap. 4.
[4] See p. 162.
[5] " Statutory water company " means a company authorised immediately before 18th July 1973 by any local statutory provision to supply water or a company in whom the assets of any company so authorised have subsequently become vested. (Water Act 1973, s. 38 (1).)
[6] " Joint water board " and " joint water committees " mean respectively a joint board and a joint committee which have been constituted under s. 9 of the Water Act 1945 and on which a statutory water company is represented. (Ibid., s. 38 (1).)
[7] Ibid., s. 33.
[8] Ibid., s. 11 (1).
[9] Ibid., s. 11 (7), (8).
[10] Ibid., s. 11 (6), (9).
[11] Ibid., s. 11 (2), (10). As to the duty of a water authority to supply water for domestic purposes to premises, see ibid., s. 11 (3)-(5).

Where a water authority area includes the whole or part of the limits of supply of a statutory water company, the authority must discharge their duties of water supply within those limits through the company. Where this situation would have applied on 1st April 1974, a water authority were required on or before 1st November 1973, or such later date as the Secretary of State might authorise, to conclude arrangements with the company whereby the company undertook to supply water on behalf of the authority. The arrangements could include (1) the management or operation of sources of supply; (2) the supply of water in bulk by or to the company; (3) the company's charges for the supply of water. If arrangements were not concluded within a specified period, the terms were settled by the Secretary of State and these were binding on the authority and the company. Arrangements in force may be varied by agreement or in default by the Secretary of State.[1]

It is the duty of a water authority on whose behalf water is being supplied by a statutory water company to take all reasonable steps for making water available to the company to enable them to meet the foreseeable demands of consumers within their limits of supply. Consequently, any statutory duty imposed on a company to supply water, except for fire and other public purposes, ceased to have effect.[2]

Statutory water undertakers[3] are empowered to make agreements with other water undertakers to supply water outside their limits of supply, and where they supply water outside their limits of supply under such an agreement, the enactments relating to that part of their limits of supply which is contiguous to the area being supplied under the agreement are applied to that area.[4]

---

[1] Water Act 1973, s. 12 (1)-(5). As to when the Secretary of State must not settle or vary arrangements, see ibid., s. 12 (6). As to supply of water in bulk and default powers, see ibid., s. 12 (9)-(11), Sch. 4.

[2] Ibid., s. 12 (7), (8).

[3] That expression refers to water authorities, statutory water companies, joint water boards and joint water committees. (Ibid., s. 11 (6).)

[4] Ibid., s. 13 (1)-(3). Where different enactments apply, see ibid., s. 13 (4).

(9) Sewerage and sewage disposal

It is the duty of every water authority to provide, inside or outside their area, such public sewers as may be necessary for effectually draining their area, and also to provide, inside or outside their area, sewage disposal works or otherwise as may be necessary for effectually dealing with the contents of their sewers.[1] The relevant statutory provisions[2] relating to the functions of sewerage, sewage disposal and trade effluent control conferred on local authorities are exercisable, as modified,[3] by water authorities.[4]

A water authority and every local authority[5] whose area is wholly or partly situated in the water authority's area must endeavour to make arrangements for the local authority to discharge as respects their area the water authority's sewerage functions, other than those relating to sewage disposal and the maintenance or operation of sewers vested in a joint sewerage board or the Greater London Council. The arrangements require the local authority to carry out an annual programme of sewerage functions approved by the water authority, provide for the vesting of public sewers in the water authority, require the local authority to provide vehicles for maintaining sewers, provide for the water authority to reimburse the local authority their expenses incurred in discharging functions, provide for the local authority to conduct legal proceedings on behalf of the water authority, and provide for the transfer of the local authority officers to the water authority and their compensation who suffer loss as a result of any variation or ending of the arrangements.

If arrangements between a water authority and a local authority were not entered into by a specified date, the terms were settled by the Secretary of State and these are binding on both authorities, unless they conclude that in the interests of

---

[1] Water Act 1973, s. 14 (1). The same duty previously imposed on local authorities by ss. 14 and 16 of the Public Health Act 1936 has ceased to have effect (*ibid.*).

[2] As set out in *ibid.*, s. 14 (2).

[3] *See ibid.*, s. 14 (3)-(7).

[4] *Ibid.*, s. 14 (2).

[5] Usually a district council or London borough council. (*Ibid.*, s. 15 (10).)

efficiency it would be inexpedient to enter into any arrangements or to be bound by arrangements settled by the Secretary of State. The parties may agree to vary or end any arrangements in force, or in default the Secretary of State may do so. Subject to the terms of the arrangement, a local authority may discharge their sewerage functions by a committee, sub-committee or an officer.[1]

(10) Recreational functions

Every water authority and all other statutory water undertakers may take steps to secure the use of water and land associated with water for the purposes of recreation and all such undertakers are under the duty to take such steps as are reasonably practicable for putting their rights to the use of water and land associated with water to the best use for such purposes. In doing so, such undertakers shall consult the water authority in whose area the land or water in question is situated and take account of any proposals formulated by the authority for discharging their duty.

A water authority may, with the consent of the owner of an inland water[2] which they have no right to use for recreational purposes or of land associated therewith, and of any other person having a right to use the water or an estate or interest in the land, use the land or water for such purposes.

In exercising their above functions, a water authority must not obstruct or otherwise interfere with navigation without the consent of any harbour or navigation authority.[3] When the Secretary of State by order[4] authorises a water authority to carry out works for or connected with the construction or operation of a reservoir in England, or confers compulsory powers for that purpose on a water authority, and it appears

---

[1] As to the duty of a water authority to provide public sewers to be used for domestic purposes for draining premises in their area, *see* Water Act, 1973, s. 16.

[2] " Inland water " is defined in footnote [5] on p. 177.

[3] " Harbour authority " means any person in whom are vested under the Harbours Act 1964 or by another Act or by an order or instrument (except a provisional order) made under another Act or by a provisional order powers or duties of improving, maintaining or managing a harbour. (Harbours Act 1964, s. 57 (1); Water Act 1973, s. 20 (4).)

[4] *I.e.*, an order made under s. 23 of the Water Act 1945 or s. 67 of the Water Resources Act 1963.

to him that the works may permanently affect the area and are not primarily intended to benefit the local inhabitants, he may include in the order provision of recreational facilities or other leisure-time occupation for the benefit of such inhabitants.[1]

(11) Nature conservancy and amenity

In formulating or considering proposals relating to the discharge of any functions of water authorities, such authorities and the appropriate Minister or Ministers must have regard to the desirability of:—

(a) preserving natural beauty, conserving flora, fauna and geological or physiographical features of special interest and protecting buildings and other objects of architectural, archaeological or historic interest and take into account any effect which the proposals would have on the beauty of, or amenity in, any rural or urban area or on such flora, fauna, features, buildings or objects;

(b) preserving public rights of access to areas of mountains, moor, heath, down, cliff or foreshore and other places of natural beauty and take into account any effect which the proposals would have on the preservation of such rights of access.

Where the Nature Conservancy Council are of opinion that an area of land, not being land for the time being managed as a nature reserve, is of special interest by reason of its flora, fauna or geological or physiological features and may at any time be affected by schemes, operations or activities of a water authority, the Council must notify that fact to the water authority in whose area the land is situated.[2]

---

[1] Water Act 1973, s. 20. As to recreational functions in Wales, see ibid., s. 21. As to recreation and amenity functions in and around Greater London, see ibid., s. 25.

[2] Ibid., s. 22.

(12) Periodical reviews, plans and programmes

As soon as practicable after 1st April 1974, every water authority, in consultation with any water authority or authorities likely to be affected by the following matters, must:—

(a) carry out a survey of the water in their area, the existing management of that water, the purposes for which it is being used and its quality in relation to its existing and likely future uses, and prepare a report setting out the results of the survey;

(b) prepare an estimate of the future demand for the use of the water over the next twenty years or other period as the appropriate Minister or Ministers may direct;

(c) prepare a plan as to action to be taken during that period by the authority (whether by way of executing works or securing the execution of works by other persons or otherwise) for securing more efficient management of water in the area, including the meeting of future demands for water and the use of water and restoring or maintaining the wholesomeness of rivers and other inland or coastal waters in their area.

A water authority may require a statutory water company supplying water in their area to undertake a survey and estimate and formulate proposals in the part of the water authority area within the company's limits of supply and submit a report thereon to the water authority.

Each water authority must keep under review their report or estimate and plan and revise these either by way of amendment or by making a fresh survey, estimate and plan at intervals of not more than seven years or as appropriate having regard to changes which have occurred since the previous survey or last revision. Land drainage functions are outside the scope of a periodical survey and estimate, but each water authority are required to carry out a survey of their area in relation to such functions from time to time or as the Minister may direct.

In the light of their most recent survey and plan, a water authority are required to prepare one or more programmes of a general nature for the discharge of their functions over a period of not more than seven years for submission for the approval of the appropriate Minister or Ministers. A programme which relates to the supply of water must take account of any proposed operations by a statutory water company, a joint water board or joint water committee and involving a substantial outlay on capital account.

In carrying out the above duties, a water authority have to consult with every local authority whose area is wholly or partly included in the water authority area, and also have regard to any structure plans, local plans and development plans prepared for any part of the area under the Town and Country Planning Act 1971.

A water authority or other statutory water undertakers, must, in carrying out a project involving substantial outlay on capital account, act in accordance with any approved programme for the time being applicable to the discharge of their functions or the carrying out of their operations.

Each water authority shall make arrangements for carrying out research and related activities (either by the authority or others) in respect of matters affecting their functions and may subscribe or otherwise financially contribute to an organisation formed for that purpose.[1]

(13) Emergencies

Where an emergency or disaster involving destruction of or damage to life or property occurs or is imminent, or there is reasonable ground for apprehending such an emergency or disaster, and a water authority are of opinion that it is likely to affect the whole or part of their area or all or some of their inhabitants in a way connected with the discharge of their functions, the authority shall assist any county or district council in taking action calculated to avert, alleviate or eradicate in the water authority area or among their inhabitants the effects or potential effects of the event.[2]

---

[1] Water Act 1973, s. 24.

[2] *Ibid.*, s. 28.

(14) Dealings in land

A water authority are empowered to acquire by agreement, or compulsorily on being authorised by the appropriate Minister or Ministers,[1] any land,[2] or any interest in or right over land, required for any purpose connected with the performance[3] of any of their functions, but land outside their area and not immediately required for a particular purpose may only be acquired by agreement with the consent of the appropriate Minister or Ministers. Interests in or rights over land may be acquired by way of the creation of new interests or rights as well as interests or rights already in existence before their acquisition.[4]

A water authority may sell, exchange or let land vested in them which is not required for the purposes of any of their functions, but the consent of the appropriate Minister or Ministers is necessary for the disposal of land (a) which was acquired by the water authority compulsorily or by agreement at a time when they were authorised to acquire it compulsorily, or (b) at less than the best price, consideration or rent that can reasonably be obtained, having regard to any restrictions or conditions subject to which the land is disposed of.[5]

(15) Powers of entry and inspection

A person duly authorised by a water authority in writing may at any reasonable time (a) enter upon any land[6] for the purpose of performing any of the functions of the authority,

---

[1] As to the appropriate Minister or Ministers, see p. 179.

[2] " Land " includes land covered by water (Water Resources Act, 1963, s. 135 (1)).

[3] " Performance " in relation to functions, includes the exercise of powers as well as the performance of duties (ibid., s. 135 (1)).

[4] Water Resources Act, 1963, ss. 65, 66; Compulsory Purchase Act, 1965, s. 39 (3), Sch. 7. The power to acquire land under these sections includes the power to provide housing accommodation for persons employed by a water authority (Water Act, 1973, s. 2 (8), Sch. 3, para. 13 (a)). Section 65 of the Water Resources Act, 1963, enables land to be acquired for the purpose of protecting water against pollution (ibid., s. 68). As to compulsory works orders conferring powers of compulsory acquisition, see ibid., s. 68, Sch. 8, Part II. As to the purchase or lease of fisheries, fishing weirs, etc., see s. 28 (6), Sch. 3, Part III, of the Salmon and Freshwater Fisheries Act, 1975.

[5] Water Resources Act, 1963, s. 70.

[6] For the purposes of a water authority's functions relating to river pollution, the above provisions regarding entry apply to vessels as well as land (ibid., s. 111 (5)).

whether in relation to that land or not; (b) for the purpose of
determining whether, and if so in what manner, any of the
authority's functions are to be performed in relation to any
land, or whether any statutory provision relating to any such
functions is being or has been complied with, enter upon any
land and inspect or survey the land and inspect any articles
thereon.[1] Paragraph (b) above is exercisable in a water authority area for the purpose of inspecting local Acts, statutory
orders, awards or other documents in the possession of any
body relating to functions of that body which are or have
been exercisable in that area, and the person carrying out
such an inspection may take copies of, or extracts from, such
documents.[2]

Where a justice of the peace is satisfied on sworn information
in writing (a) that an authorised person has been refused entry
on land, or that refusal is apprehended, or that the land is
unoccupied or that the occupier is temporarily absent, or that
the case is one of urgency, or that an application for admission
would defeat the object of the entry, and (b) that there is
reasonable ground for entry upon the land for the purpose for
which entry is required, the justice may by warrant under his
hand authorise such person to enter the land, if need be by
force.[3] A warrant continues in force until the purpose for
which entry is required has been satisfied.[4]

A person authorised to enter upon land or a vessel must, if
so required, produce evidence of his authority before entering,
and he may take with him on to the land or vessel such other
persons and such equipment as may be necessary. Except in
an emergency, admission to land used for residential purposes
and admission with heavy equipment to any other land cannot
be demanded as of right unless seven days' written notice has
been given to the occupier, but a person is not entitled to enter
or remain on land occupied by statutory water undertakers
unless he complies with any reasonable requirements imposed

---

[1] Water Resources Act, 1963, s. 111 (1).
[2] *Ibid.*, s. 111 (6).
[3] *Ibid.*, s. 111 (3).
[4] *Ibid.*, s. 111 (4).

by the undertakers for the purpose of protecting water against pollution; any question as to what requirements are reasonable shall, in case of dispute, be determined by the Secretary of State, whose decision is final. A person who enters any premises which are unoccupied, or of which the occupier is temporarily absent, must leave the premises effectually secured against trespassers as he found them.[1]

The wilful obstruction of a person acting in the exercise of his powers of entry renders the offender guilty of an offence and liable on summary conviction to a fine not exceeding £20. A person who, in pursuance of the powers of entry or of a warrant issued thereunder, is admitted into a factory, workshop or workplace discloses to any person any information obtained by him therein regarding any manufacturing process or trade secret, or a member or officer of a water authority, to whom any information so obtained is disclosed by reason of his official position, discloses that information to any other person, he is, unless the disclosure is made in the performance of his duty, liable on summary conviction to a fine not exceeding £100, or to imprisonment for a term not exceeding three months, or both.[2]

Any person interested in land or chattels which are damaged in the exercise of any power of entry is entitled to compensation from the water authority, and where in the consequence of the exercise of any such power a person is disturbed in his enjoyment of any land or chattels he is also entitled to compensation from the water authority; any dispute as to a right of compensation, or as to the amount thereof, is determined by the Lands Tribunal.[3]

FINANCIAL PROVISIONS

General Powers

Every water authority are required to discharge their functions as to secure that, taking one year with another, their

---

[1] Water Resources Act, 1963, s. 112 (1)-(5).

[2] Ibid., s. 112 (6), (7).

[3] Ibid., s. 112 (8), (9).

revenue is not less than sufficient to meet their total outgoings properly chargeable to revenue account, and the Secretary of State with Treasury approval and after consulting the National Water Council may by order direct:—

(a) that an authority shall discharge their functions during a specified period to achieve a rate of return on the value of their net assets (as defined by the Secretary of State) at such rate as the Secretary of State specifies in the direction as being a reasonable rate for the authority to achieve;

(b) that an authority shall in the discharge of their functions be under any other financial obligation as the Secretary of State may think fit.

The draft of an order made under paragraph (b) above must be laid before and approved by resolution of each House of Parliament.[1]

Water charges

Section 30 of the Water Act, 1973, which deals with the raising of water charges, has been amended by the Water Charges Act, 1976. Section 1 of the 1976 Act required water authorities to refund charges for sewerage or sewage disposal paid under the Water Authorities (Collection of Charges) Order, 1974,[2] or the Water Authorities (Collection of Charges) Order, 1975,[3] on hereditaments not connected to sewers at the beginning of the financial years 1974-75 or 1975-76. This situation arose from *Daymond v. South West Water Authority*[4] which decided that section 30 (1) of the Water Act, 1973, did not empower water authorities to charge a person for sewerage services of which he did not avail himself and that the Secretary of State could not enlarge the authorities' powers by the 1974 Order. Section 1 of the 1976 Act similarly required the refunding of water rates or charges paid for the two years on hereditaments for which no supply of water was available. Section 2 of that Act overrode the effects of the Daymond case by reinforcing the powers of water authorities to charge under section 30 (1) of the 1973 Act in the manner explained below.

[1] Water Act 1973, s. 29.
[2] S.I. 1974 No. 448.
[3] S.I. 1975 No. 396.
[4] [1976] 1 All E.R. 39, H.L.

A water authority are empowered to fix such charges for the services performed, facilities provided or rights made available by them (including separate charges for separate services, facilities or rights or combined charges for a number of services, facilities or rights) as they think fit, and to demand, take and recover such charges—

(a) for services performed, facilities provided or rights made available in the exercise of any of their functions, from persons for whom they perform the services, provide the facilities or make the rights available, and

(b) without prejudice to head (a) above—

(i) for services performed, facilities provided or rights made available in the exercise of functions under section 14 of the Water Act, 1973 (relating to sewerage and sewage disposal), from persons liable to be rated in respect of the hereditaments mentioned below, and

(ii) for services performed, facilities provided or rights made available in the exercise of the functions mentioned below, from all persons liable to be rated in respect of hereditaments in their area or particular classes of such persons.[1]

Head (b) (i) above applies to a hereditament[2] if—

(a) it is drained by a sewer or drain connecting, either directly or through an intermediate sewer or drain, with a public sewer provided for foul water or surface water or both, or

(b) the person liable to be rated in respect of the hereditament has the use, for the benefit of the heredita-

---

[1] Water Act, 1973, s. 30 (1), as substituted by s. 2 (1) of the Water Charges Act, 1976; *see also* the Water Authorities (Collection and Refunding of Charges) Order, 1976 (S.I. 1976 No. 514) and the Water Authorities (Collection of Charges) Order, 1977 (S.I. 1977 No. 315).

[2] For " hereditament " *see* s. 115 (1) of the General Rate Act, 1967 (Water Act, 1973, s. 30 (11); Water Charges Act, 1976, s. 2 (2)).

ment, of facilities which drain to a sewer or drain so connecting, or

(c) it is subject to special rating.[1] [2]

The functions mentioned in head (b) (ii) are those under—

(i) the Rivers (Prevention of Pollution) Acts, 1951-1961;

(ii) sections 20-22 of the Water Act, 1973 relating to recreation, nature conservation and amenity;

(iii) the Control of Pollution Act, 1974;

(iv) the Salmon and Freshwater Fisheries Act, 1975;

(v) a local statutory enactment conferring functions analogous to those in (i)-(iv) above, and

(vi) a local statutory enactment conferring navigation functions.[3]

A water authority may fix any of their charges by means of a charges scheme or by agreement with any person, and may fix their charges by reference to such criteria and adopt such system for calculating their amount as they consider appropriate, provided that:—

(a) in fixing charges regard shall be had to the cost of performing services, providing facilities or making available rights.

(b) whilst different charges may be made for the same service, facility or right in different cases, each water authority are required to take steps to ensure that not later than 1st April, 1981, their charges shall not show undue preference to, or unduly discriminate against, any class of persons.

(c) after consultation with the National Water Council, the Secretary of State may give directions to water authorities as to the criteria to be applied or the system to be adopted.[4]

---

[1] For " special rating " see s. 30 (11) of the Water Act, 1973 (added by s. 2 (2) of the Water Charges Act, 1976) and s. 3 (3) of the latter Act.
[2] Water Act, 1973, s. 30 (1A); as substituted by s. 2 (1) of the Water Charges Act, 1976.
[3] Water Act, 1973, s. 30 (1B); as substituted by s. 2 (1) of the Water Charges Act, 1976.
[4] Water Act, 1973, s. 30 (2)-(6).

In introducing a new system of charges a water authority may make such transitional charging arrangements as they think fit for a period of up to five years. Nothing in any enactment passed before the Water Act, 1973, shall operate so as to oblige a water authority to fix separate charges for separate services, facilities or rights. A local statutory provision (other than one expressly providing that no charge shall be made for a service, facility or right) cannot limit the discretion of a water authority, or of a statutory water company through whom a water authority are supplying water, as to the charges they make, whether the provision specifies the charges, or fixes maximum charges, or otherwise. Such a limitation in a local statutory provision ceased to have effect on 1st April, 1974, but water authorities and companies must, in fixing charges up to 1st April, 1981, have regard to any special relevant circumstances and any likely differences in the levels of charges if the provision had continued to apply.[1]

The powers conferred on a water authority by section 30 of the Water Act, 1973, include power to charge all persons liable to be rated in respect of hereditaments in their area or particular classes of such persons for any services performed, facilities provided or rights made available in the exercise of functions specified in section 30 (1B) above.[2]

A local authority may agree to collect and recover on behalf of a water authority any charges payable for services performed, facilities provided or rights made available in the local authority's area by the water authority and such charges may be demanded, collected and recovered by the local authority in like manner and together with the general rate.[3]

Water Charges Equalisation Fund

The Secretary of State may by order[4] direct a statutory water undertaker whose financing costs[5] for 1978 or any subsequent

---

[1] Water Act, 1973, s. 30 (7)-(10).
[2] Water Act, 1973, s. 30 (11); added by s. 2 (3) of the Water Charges Act, 1976.
[3] Water Act, 1973, s. 32A, inserted by s. 38 of the Local Government Act, 1974.
[4] *See* the Water Charges Equalisation Order, 1977 (S.I. 1977 No. 2165).
[5] *See* s. 1 (4) of the Water Charges Equalisation Act, 1977.

year are, in proportion to the number of premises to which an unmeasured supply of water is provided, less than the average of the financing costs of all statutory water undertakers in England and Wales to pay an equalisation levy to the National Water Council. For each year for which an equalisation levy is payable, the Secretary of State must by order direct the Council to pay equalisation payments[1] to those statutory water undertakers whose financing costs for that year exceed the average financing costs of statutory water undertakers. Equalisation payments equal in the average the equalisation levies and any discrepancy is adjusted by the Secretary of State each year. Orders are made after consultation with the National Water Council and are subject to approval by resolution of the House of Commons.

In fixing water charges a water authority must treat equalisation levies and payments respectively as additions to and reductions of the cost to the authority in the corresponding accounting period of providing water supplies on an unmeasured basis. The amount of an equalisation levy or payment which a statutory water company is entitled to pay or receive in respect of any year must be passed on in full in the form of increased or reduced charges to the persons to whom water is supplied by the company on an unmeasured basis in the corresponding accounting period.[2]

Charges schemes

A water authority may make a charges scheme for the charges to be paid for any services performed, facilities provided or rights made available by them and the Secretary of State may give directions to water authorities as to the services, facilities or rights to be covered by the scheme. Schemes must be framed to show the method by which and the principles on which charges are to be made and shall be published in such manner as will secure adequate publicity for them. A charges scheme may revoke or amend a previous scheme and a scheme

---

[1] See ibid., s. 2 (2).
[2] Water Charges Equalisation Act, 1977, ss. 1-4.

does not affect the power of a water authority to make an agreement about charges which they were empowered to make before the Water Act, 1973, and in particular relating to (*a*) the reception and disposal of trade effluents; (*b*) the supply of water for non-domestic purposes; and (*c*) special charges in respect of spray irrigation.[1]

Meters

Where charges are payable to a water authority by reference to the volume of water supplied to premises or the volume of effluent[2] discharged therefrom the authority may install on the premises a meter for measuring that volume and subject to any regulation the register of the water is *prima facia* evidence of the volume. Regulations made by the Secretary of State may provide for the installation of meters, their connection, disconnection, maintenance, authentification, testing and other related matters. Provision is made for entry on premises by an officer authorised by a water authority for the purpose of installing, connecting, disconnecting, examining and testing meters.[3]

Annual reports of water authorities

Each water authority are required to make to the Secretary of State and the Minister of Agriculture, Fisheries and Food as soon as possible after the end of each financial year a report on the discharge of their functions during that year in such form and containing such information as may be directed and of their policy and programme. A copy of the report must be sent to the National Water Council and every local authority whose area is wholly or partly situated in the water authority area. The Ministers have to lay a copy of the report before each House of Parliament.[4]

---

[1] Water Act 1973, s. 31.

[2] " Effluent " means any liquid, with or without particles of matter in suspension therein. (*Ibid.*, s. 32 (9).)

[3] *Ibid.*, s. 32 (1)-(6).

[4] Water Act 1973, s. 2 (8), Sch. 3, para. 40.

Loans and Grants.

The Secretary of State may with Treasury approval make grants to a water authority, who may also borrow money temporarily or for capital purposes.[1]

---

[1] *See* further Water Act, 1973, s. 2 (8), Sch. 3, Part. III, paras. 34-37.

CHAPTER 11

WATER RESOURCES

INTRODUCTION

The Water Resources Act, 1963, received Royal Assent on 31st July, 1963, following a White Paper on Water Conservation in England and Wales,[1] which itself was the consequence of two interim reports presented respectively in 1959 and 1960 and a final report in 1962 by the Sub-Committee of the Central Advisory Water Committee on the Growing Demand for Water. The purpose of the Act was to promote measures for the conservation, augmenting and securing the proper use of water resources in England and Wales through the establishment of river authorities and the Water Resources Board and to confer on them and the former Minister of Housing and Local Government new functions in relation to water resources; to provide for controlling the abstraction and impounding of water, and to secure the protection and proper use of inland waters and water in underground strata.[2] The Act has been slightly amended by the Water Resources Acts of 1968 and 1971, and the Acts may be cited together as the Water Resources Acts, 1963 to 1971.[3]

The Acts apply throughout England and Wales and do not extend to Scotland or Northern Ireland,[4] except as otherwise provided by sections 126 and 137 of the 1963 Act. They do not apply to anything done by or on behalf of the Crown or to land occupied by a government department or in respect of

---

[1] Cmnd. 1963/62.
[2] Water Resources Act, 1963, preamble, ss. 1, 4.
[3] Water Resources Act, 1971, s. 3 (1).
[4] Water Resources Act, 1963, s. 137.

the Crown,[1] and there are special provisions regarding telegraphic lines,[2] ecclesiastical property[3] and inland waters owned or managed by British Waterways Board.[4]

River authorities were replaced by water authorities and the Water Resources Board was abolished under the Water Act, 1973.

MEANING OF WATER RESOURCES

In the Act " water resources ", in relation to any area, means water for the time being contained in any source of supply in that area, and " source of supply ", in relation to any area, means either of the following, that is to say—(a) so much of any inland water[5] (other than an inland water falling within section 2 (3)), as is situated in that area, and (b) any underground strata[6] in that area.[7] For the purposes of the Act water for the time being contained in (i) a well, borehole or similar work, including any adit or passage constructed in connection with it for facilitating the collection of water in the well, borehole or work, or (ii) any excavation into underground strata, where the level of water in the excavation depends wholly or mainly on water entering it from such strata, is treated as water contained in the underground strata into which the well, borehole or work was sunk, or the excavation was made, as the case may be.[8] Except as provided in the

---

1 Water Resources Act, 1963, s. 123.
2 *Ibid.*, s. 130.
3 *Ibid.*, s. 132.
4 *Ibid.*, s. 131; Water Act, 1973, s. 40 (3), Sch. 9.
5 " Inland water " means any of the following—(a) so much of any river, stream or other watercourse, whether natural or artificial and whether tidal or not, as is within any of the water authority areas; (b) any lake or pond, whether natural or artificial, and any reservoir or dock (not falling under head (a) above) and is within any of the water authority areas, and (c) so much of any channel, creek, bay, estuary or arm of the sea (not falling within heads (a) or (b) above) and is within any of the water authority areas, and any reference to an inland water includes a reference to part of an inland water (Water Resources Act, 1963, s. 135 (1)).
6 " Underground strata " means strata subjacent to the surface of any land, and (subject and without prejudice to s. 2 (2) of the Act) any reference to water contained in any underground strata is a reference to water so contained otherwise than in a sewer, pipe, reservoir, tank or other underground works constructed in any such strata (*ibid.*, s. 135 (1)).
7 *Ibid.*, s. 2 (1).
8 *Ibid.*, s. 2 (2).

previous sentence, an inland water which either (1) is a lake, pond or reservoir which does not discharge to any other inland water, or (2) is one of a group of two or more lakes, ponds or reservoirs (whether near to or distant from each other) and of watercourses[1] or mains connecting them, where none of the inland waters in the group discharges to any inland water outside the group, does not constitute a source of supply for the purposes of the Act.[2]

THE MINISTERS UNDER THE ACT

The Secretary of State for the Environment is concerned with functions relating to water resources, river pollution and navigation, and the Minister of Agriculture, Fisheries and Food is responsible for land drainage and fisheries.[3]

Any one or more of the above Ministers may hold a local inquiry in connection with any matter arising under the Act or otherwise in connection with any of the functions of water authorities.[4] The Secretary of State is authorised to give directions to water authorities regarding their functions under the Act, and the appropriate Minister or Ministers may give directions to water authorities in relation to their functions regarding land drainage, fisheries or pollution prevention for securing the effective performance of any of their new functions under the Act.[5]

The Ministers may hold a local inquiry when it appears that a water authority have failed to perform any of their functions and may by order declare the water authority to be in default. The order may contain directions as to the performance of the functions and if the defaulting water authority

---

[1] " Watercourse " includes all rivers, streams, ditches, drains, cuts, culverts, dykes, sluices, sewers and passages through which water flows, except (a) mains and water fittings within the meaning of Sched. 3 to the Water Act, 1945, (b) water authority sewers, and (c) any such adit or passage as is mentioned in s. 2 (2) (a) of the Act of 1963 (Water Resources Act, 1963, s. 135 (1)).

[2] *Ibid.*, s. 2 (3).

[3] *Ibid.*, s. 135 (2); The Secretary of State for the Environment Order, 1970 (S.I. 1970 No. 168), art. 2 (1), Sch. 1.

[4] Water Resources Act, 1963, s. 109.

[5] *Ibid.*, s. 107; Water Act, 1973, s. 40 (3), Sch. 9.

fail to comply with any such direction, the Ministers may by order transfer the function to the appropriate Minister, or in the case of a function under the Act, transfer the function to an adjoining water authority.[1] There is provision for the repeal, amendment or adaptation by ministerial order of local enactments which are inconsistent with the provisions of the Act or with anything done in the performance of functions under the Act,[2] and the Secretary of State may make regulations for any purpose for which regulations are authorised or required to be made under the Act.[3]

In the Act " the appropriate Minister or Ministers ", in relation to anything required or authorised to be done by or for the purposes of any provision of the Act, means such one or more of the Ministers, namely, the Secretary of State and the Minister of Agriculture, Fisheries and Food, as is or are concerned with the functions in relation to which, or for the purposes of which, that thing is required or authorised to be done, and, where it means either one or both of those Ministers, means the Ministers in question acting jointly.[4]

WATER AUTHORITIES AND CONSERVATION

Water Conservation

It is the duty of each water authority to take all such action as they may from time to time consider necessary or expedient, or as directions under the Water Act, 1973, or the Water Resources Act, 1963, may require them to take for the purpose of conserving, redistributing or otherwise augmenting water resources[5] in their area, of securing the proper use of such resources, or of transferring such resources to the area of another water authority.[6] The Water Act, 1973, imposes the

---

1 Water Resources Act, 1963, s. 108; Water Act, 1973, s. 40 (3), Sch. 9.

2 Water Resources Act, 1963, s. 133.

3 *Ibid.*, s. 134.

4 Water Resources Act, 1963, s. 135 (2).

5 The reference to action for the purpose of augmenting water resources includes a reference to action for the purpose of treating salt water (whether from the sea or elsewhere) by any process for removing salt or other impurities (Water Act 1973, s. 10 (2)).

6 *Ibid.*, s. 10 (1).

further duty on water authorities to undertake periodical surveys of the water in their area and the purposes for which it is used, prepare estimates of future demands for the use of water, and prepare plans as to action required by way of executing works to meet future demands for water and the use of water; and, in the light of such surveys and plans, the water authorities shall prepare programmes, with particulars of any projects, for the discharge of their functions over a period of not more than seven years.[1]

Under provisions (now repealed)[2] of the Water Resources Act, 1963, the former river authorities were required to prepare schemes for obtaining and recording measurements and particulars of rainfall, evaporation of water, the flow level or volume of inland waters, and other matters affecting water resources in their area. River authorities were also empowered to formulate proposals for investigating the presence, quantity and quality of water in underground strata and ascertaining the effect of abstracting such water on abstraction from other underground or surface sources. Presumably, water authorities will continue and expand such schemes and proposals.

Inspection of records

Each water authority must provide reasonable facilities for the inspection of any records kept by them of the rainfall, the evaporation of water and the flow, level and volume of inland water and water in underground strata in their area, and for the taking of copies of, and extracts from, such records. These facilities are available free of charge to all local authorities and internal drainage boards wholly or partly comprised within the water authority area, and are also available to all other persons on payment of such reasonable fees as the authority may determine.[3]

---

[1] Water Act 1973, s. 24.

[2] *See* ss. 15, 18 of the Water Resources Act 1963 which were repealed (and not replaced) by the Water Act 1973, s. 40 (3), Sch. 9.

[3] Water Resources Act, 1963, s. 16; Water Act, 1973, s. 40, Sch. 8, para. 77, Sch. 9.

Gauges and records kept by other persons

A person, other than a water authority, who proposes to install a gauge for measuring and recording the flow, level or volume of an inland water in a water authority area is required (1) to notify the water authority of his proposal and not to begin the work of installation within the period of three months from the date of service of the notice or such shorter period as the water authority may allow, and (2) not more than one month after the work is completed to notify the water authority where the records obtained from the gauge are to be kept. But this provision does not apply to a gauge installed solely for the benefit of fishermen or to a gauge which is removed within 28 days after it is installed. A water authority is entitled to inspect, at all reasonable hours, records kept by other persons of the flow, level or volume of any inland water within the water authority area and to take copies of, or extracts from, such records. A person who contravenes the provisions concerning the installation of a gauge, or who without reasonable excuse refuses or fails to permit inspection or copying of records, is guilty of an offence and liable on summary conviction to a fine not exceeding £20.[1]

Minimum acceptable flows

As soon as practicable after 1st April, 1965, each water authority has to consider (a) for which inland waters in their area minimum acceptable flows ought to be determined, and (b) whether, for the purpose of determining minimum acceptable flows for such waters, they ought to be dealt with simultaneously or successively, and if successively, how they should be grouped or arranged and in what order.[2]

The next step is for the water authority as soon as practicable to prepare and submit to the Secretary of State a draft statement or series of such statements indicating with respect to each inland water for which minimum acceptable flows are to be determined (a) the control points at which the flow of water is to be measured and the method of measurement to be used

1 Water Resources Act, 1963, s. 17.
2 *Ibid.*, s. 19 (1); Water Act, 1973, s. 40 (3), Sch. 9.

at each point, and (*b*) the proposed minimum acceptable flow at each control point. Before preparing a draft statement for a particular inland water, the water authority must consult (1) any statutory water undertakers having the right to abstract water from the inland water, or from underground strata where it appears that the level of water in such strata depends on the flow of the inland water and the exercise of the right to abstract may be substantially affected; (2) any internal drainage boards from whose drainage district water is discharged into the inland water or in whose district any part of it is situated; (3) any navigation, harbour or conservancy authority having functions in relation to the inland water, or any such authorities having functions in relation to any other inland water where changes in the flow of the inland water in question may affect the flow of the other inland water, or, if the inland water in question or the other inland water is a tidal water and there are no such authorities, the Secretary of State; and (4) the Central Electricity Generating Board.[1]

In determining the minimum acceptable flow to be specified in relation to an inland water, the water authority must have regard to the character of the inland water and its surroundings (and, in particular, any natural beauty which the inland water and its surroundings may possess) and to the flow of water therein from time to time. The flow so specified shall not be less than the minimum which in the water authority's opinion is needed for safeguarding the public health and for meeting (in respect both of quantity and quality) the requirements of existing lawful uses of the inland water, whether for agriculture, industry, water supply or other purposes, and the requirements of land drainage, navigation and fisheries, both in relation to the inland water and other inland waters whose flow may be affected by changes in the flow of the inland water.[2]

Each water authority have to keep under review any approved statements of minimum acceptable flows relating to inland waters in their area and at intervals not exceeding seven

---

[1] Water Resources Act, 1963, s. 19 (3), (4).

[2] *Ibid.*, s. 19 (5). The procedure for the submission and approval of draft statements of minimum acceptable flows is set out in *ibid.*, Sched. 7, Parts I and IV (*ibid.*, s. 19 (6)).

years shall submit to the Secretary of State a draft statement in substitution for a current statement, or proposals for amending a current statement, as they consider appropriate in consequence of the review. Each river basin in a water authority area is to be dealt with separately, but all inland waters comprised in one basin are to be taken together.[1]

The Secretary of State may himself prepare proposals for amending any statement after consulting the water authority in whose area the inland water is situated, except where he is acting on the application of the water authority.[2]

Where it appears to a water authority, in the case of a partcular inland water, that it would be appropriate to measure the level or volume, either instead of, or in addition to, the flow, the water authority may determine that sections 19 and 20 of the Act shall apply in relation to such inland water.[3]

CONTROL OF ABSTRACTION OF WATER

Part IV of the Act provides for the control of the abstraction of water from both inland waters and underground strata by means of a system of licensing operated by the water authorities, and this control procedure has very largely superseded the common law rights to abstract water[4] which existed prior to the Act.

Different types of licences to abstract

The Act made provision for four different kinds of licences, namely—

(1) *A licence of right* which was granted to existing abstractors or those having a statutory entitlement to abstract, that is to say, persons (a) who were entitled to abstract from a source of supply by virtue of a statutory provision (other than an order under the

---

1 Water Resources Act, 1963, s. 20.
2 *Ibid.*, s. 21; Water Act, 1973, s. 40 (3), Sch. 9.
3 Water Resources Act, 1963, s. 22; Water Act, 1973, s. 40 (3), Sch. 9.
4 *See* pp. 89-94.

Water Act, 1958) in force on 1st April, 1965, or
(*b*) who had, otherwise than by virtue of a statutory
provision, abstracted water from a source of supply
at any time within the period of five years ending
with 1st April, 1965. Provided that such a person
applied to the river authority before 1st July, 1965,
on the appropriate form and with the prescribed
evidence, he was entitled to the grant of a licence of
right and there was no provision for refusing to grant
the licence.[1] A licence of right cannot be applied
for or granted after 1st July, 1965.

(2) *A licence other than a licence of right.* As from 1st
July, 1965, a person who proposes to abstract water
from a source of supply has to obtain from the water
authority a licence, which to distinguish it from a
licence of right, is referred to as a licence other than a
licence of right. The procedure in applying for this
type of licence is different to that involving a licence
of right, since notice of intention to apply for a
licence other than a licence of right has to be publicly
advertised and a copy of the notice must be served on
specified bodies where the abstraction is to be from
an inland water. Further, when determining the
licence application the water authority must have
regard to certain factors (specified in section 29[2]) and
may decide either to grant the licence or to refuse it.

(3) *A licence under section* 56 (2). Where an application
was made to a river authority before 1st July, 1965,
in respect of a statutory provision which came into
force after 1st April, 1965, and, apart from the Act,
would authorise a person to do anything which is
restricted by section 23, *i.e.* in respect of abstracting
water, the river authority was required to grant such
person a licence to abstract containing provisions

---

[1] Water Resources Act, 1963, s. 33. *See ibid.*, ss. 34 and 35, as to the determination of licences of right for statutory and non-statutory users.

[2] *See* p. 194.

corresponding as nearly as may be to those of the statutory provision.[1]

(4) *A licence under section* 131 (4). This relates to licences to abstract granted to the British Waterways Board in respect of water sold under contract from inland waters owned or managed by the Board.[2]

The licences described under heads (3) and (4) above represent rather special examples, and since licences of right (head (1) above) cannot now be applied for or granted, these three types of licences will not be considered further. It should be noted that once a licence of right or a licence other than a licence of right has been granted, there is little practical difference between them, except that under section 29 (2) a water authority must not grant a licence other than a licence of right which authorises the abstraction of water so as to derogate from protected rights.[3]

The provisions of the Act referred to hereafter in this chapter relating to licences to abstract are accordingly confined to licences other than a licence of right, unless otherwise specifically stated.

Restrictions of abstraction of water

As from 1st July, 1965, unless a person is exempt from the licensing provisions of the Act by virtue of sections 24 or 25,[4] section 23 (1) provides that—

" no person shall abstract[5] water from any source of supply[6] in a water authority area, or cause or permit any other person so to abstract any water, except in

---

[1] Water Resources Act, 1963, s. 56 (2).

[2] *Ibid.*, s. 131.

[3] As to protected rights, *see* p. 190.

[4] As to exemptions from licensing, *see* p. 187.

[5] " Abstraction ", in relation to water contained in any source of supply in a water authority area, means the doing of anything whereby any of that water is removed from that source of supply and either (*a*) ceases (either temporarily or permanently) to be comprised in the water resources of that area, or (*b*) is transferred to another source of supply in that area, and " abstract " is to be construed accordingly (Water Resources Act, 1963, s. 135 (1)).

[6] " Source of supply " is defined on p. 177.

pursuance of a licence under this Act granted by the water authority and in accordance with the provisions of that licence ".

Section 23 (2) enacts that where by virtue of section 23 (1) the abstraction of water contained in any underground strata is prohibited except under licence, no person shall after 1st July, 1965, begin, or cause or permit any other person to begin, to (a) construct a well, borehole or other work whereby water may be abstracted from such strata, or (b) extend any such well, borehole or other work, or (c) install or modify any machinery or apparatus whereby additional quantities of water may be abstracted from such strata by means of a well, borehole or other work, unless the abstraction of the water, or the additional quantities of water, as the case may be, is authorised by a licence, and the well, borehole or other work as constructed or extended, or the machinery or apparatus as installed or modified, fulfils the requirements of the licence as to the means whereby water is authorised to be abstracted.

The above restrictions have effect notwithstanding anything in any other enactment contained in any Act passed before 31st July, 1963, or in any statutory provision[1] made or issued, whether before or after that date by virtue of such an enactment, but do not apply to the doing of anything authorised by an order under the Water Act, 1958, whether made before or after 31st July, 1963.[2]

Any person who contravenes section 23 (1) or (2), or who (in circumstances not constituting such a contravention) does not comply with a condition or requirement imposed by a licence of which he is the holder, is guilty of an offence and on conviction on indictment or on summary conviction is liable to a fine, which on summary conviction shall not exceed £1,000.[3]

---

[1] " Statutory provision " means a provision, whether of a general or a special nature, contained in, or in any document made or issued under, any Act, whether of a general or a special nature (Water Resources Act, 1963, s. 135 (1)).

[2] *Ibid.*, 1963, ss. 23 (3), 128 (1).

[3] *Ibid.*, s. 49; Criminal Law Act, 1977, s. 28 (2).

Exceptions from licensing control

In order to keep the system of licensing control to practical proportions, section 24 provides that a licence to abstract water from a source of supply is not required in the following cases—

(a) Any abstraction of a quantity of water not exceeding 1,000 gallons, if it does not form part of a continuous operation, or of a series of operations, whereby in the aggregate more than 1,000 gallons are abstracted.

(b) Abstraction from an inland water by or on behalf of an occupier of land contiguous[1] to that water at the point of abstraction for use on a holding consisting of that land with or without other land held therewith for the domestic purposes of the occupier's household and/or agricultural[2] purposes other than spray irrigation.[3]

(c) Abstraction from underground strata by or on behalf of an individual for the domestic purposes of his household.

(d) Abstraction from a source of supply (i) in the course of, or resulting from, any operations for purposes of

---

[1] Land is taken to be contiguous to an inland water notwithstanding that the land is separated from it by a towpath or by any other land used, or acquired for use, in connection with the navigation of the inland water, if such other land does not comprise buildings or works other than a lock, pier, wharf, landing-stage or similar works (Water Resources Act, 1963, s. 135 (7)).

[2] " Agriculture " includes horticulture, fruit growing, seed growing, dairy farming, the breeding and keeping of livestock (including any creature kept for the production of food, wool, skins or fur, or for the purpose of its use in the farming of land), the use of land as grazing land, meadow land, osier land, market gardens and nursery grounds, and the use of land for woodlands where such use is ancillary to the farming of land for other agricultural purposes, and " agricultural " is construed accordingly (ibid., s. 135 (1)).

[3] " Spray irrigation " means the irrigation of land or plants (including seeds) by means of water or other liquid emerging (in whatever form) from apparatus designed or adapted to eject liquid into the air in the form of jets or spray (ibid., s. 135 (1)). See also the Spray Irrigation (Definition) Order, 1965 (S.I. 1965, No. 1010).

land drainage,[1] or (ii) otherwise necessary to prevent interference with any mining, quarrying, engineering, building or other operations, whether underground or on the surface, or to prevent damage to works resulting from any such operations. This exception applies where water is abstracted in the course of any operations mentioned under paragraph (ii) above from an excavation into underground strata, where the level of water therein depends wholly or mainly on water entering it from such strata, and the abstraction is necessary as mentioned in paragraph (ii) notwithstanding that the water is used for the purposes of the operations.

(e) In the case of any abstraction of water from underground strata which falls under heads (c) or (d) above, a licence which would otherwise be required under section 23 (2) does not apply to the construction or extension of a well, borehole or other work, or the installation or modification of machinery or other apparatus for the purpose of abstracting the water.

(f) Any transfer of water from one inland water to another in the course of, or resulting from, any operations carried out by a navigation,[2] harbour[3] or

---

[1] " Land drainage " includes the protection of land against erosion or encroachment by water, whether from inland waters or from the sea, and also includes warping and irrigation other than spray irrigation (Water Resources Act, 1963, s. 24 (10); Water Act, 1973, s. 40 (2), Sch. 8, para. 78).

[2] " Navigation authority " means a person or body of persons (whether corporate or unincorporate) having a duty or power imposed or conferred by or under an enactment to manage or maintain a canal, whether navigable or not, or to manage or maintain an inland navigation other than a canal, whether natural or artificial and whether tidal or not (*ibid.*, s. 135 (1)).

[3] " Harbour authority " means a person or body of persons (whether corporate or unincorporate), who, not being a navigation authority, is or are a harbour authority as defined by s. 3 (5) of the Oil in Navigable Waters Act, 1955 (*ibid.*, s. 135 (1)).

conservancy authority[1] in the performance[2] of their functions as such an authority.

(g) Abstraction by machinery or apparatus installed on a vessel, where the water is abstracted for use on that or any other vessel.

(h) Anything done for firefighting purposes[3] or for the purpose of testing apparatus used for such purposes or of training or practice in the use of such apparatus.

(i) Abstraction, or the construction or extension of a well, borehole or other work, or the installation or modification of machinery or other apparatus, for the purpose (i) of ascertaining the presence of water, or the quality or quantity of water, in underground strata, or (ii) of ascertaining the effect of abstracting water from the well, borehole or other work in question on the abstraction of water from, or the level of water in, any other well, borehole or other work or an inland water, if it is carried out with the consent of the water authority and in compliance with any conditions imposed by the authority.

Besides the specific exemptions from the requirement of a licence to abstract given in section 24, further exceptions from licensing are available under section 25. On the application of a water authority in relation to all sources of supply in their area, or of a navigation, harbour or conservancy authority having functions in relation to an inland water, the Secretary of State may by order except one or more sources of supply in a water authority area from the restriction imposed by section 23 (1) on the grounds that the restriction so imposed is not

---

[1] " Conservancy authority " means a person or body of persons (whether corporate or unincorporate) having a duty or power imposed or conferred by or under an enactment to conserve, maintain or improve the navigation of a tidal river, and not being a navigation or harbour authority (Water Resources Act, 1963, s. 135 (1)).

[2] " Performance ", in relation to functions, includes the exercise of powers as well as the performance of duties, and " perform " is construed accordingly (ibid., s. 135 (1)).

[3] " Fire-fighting purposes " means the purposes of the extinction of fires and the protection of life and property in case of fire (ibid., s. 24 (8); Fire Services Act, 1947, s. 38 (1)).

needed in relation to the source or sources of supply in question. The applicant authority must first consult with the other authorities concerned, and any one order so made is limited to one water authority area and cannot extend to a source of supply outside that area.[1]

Finally, under the Spray Irrigation (Definition) Order, 1965,[2] specified methods of spray irrigation carried out in connection with weed or pest control and the spreading of nutrients are excepted from licensing.

Protected rights to abstract water

Since the Act has largely replaced the common law rights with respect to the abstraction of water[3] by means of a system of statutory licensing, the Act has created statutory rights referred to as " protected rights " to ensure that licence holders and certain categories of abstractors who are exempt from licensing control may lawfully exercise their rights to abstract under the Act.

In the case of the holder of a licence to abstract water, he is taken to have a right to abstract to the extent authorised by the licence and in accordance with the provisions contained in it. In the case of exempted categories under section 24 (2) or (3), a person is taken to have a right to abstract to the extent specified in those subsections. That is to say, under section 24 (2) water may be taken from an inland water by or on behalf of an occupier of land contiguous to that inland water at the place where the abstraction is effected in so far as the water is taken for use on a holding consisting of that land with or without other land held therewith for use on such holding for either or both the domestic purposes of the occupier's household and agricultural purposes other than spray irrigation. Similarly, under section 24 (3) water may be abstracted from underground strata in so far as the water is

---

[1] Water Resources Act, 1963, s. 25; Water Act, 1973, s. 40 (3), Sch. 9. Part I and, where applicable, Part IV of Sch. 7 to the Water Resources Act, 1963, have effect in relation to an application made under *ibid.*, s. 25, subject to the provisions of s. 25 (5)-(8).

[2] S.I. 1965, No. 1010.

[3] *See* pp. 89-94.

abstracted by or on behalf of an individual as a supply of water for the domestic purposes of his household.[1]

It will be noted later that section 29 (2) prohibits a water authority from granting a licence authorising the abstraction of water so as to derogate from any rights which, at the time when the application is determined, are protected rights. This means that a licence must not be granted so as to allow its holder to abstract water in such a way, or to such an extent, as to prevent a person entitled to a protected right from abstracting water to the extent permitted in accordance with the protected right.[2]

A breach of the duty imposed by section 29 (2) (*i.e.* if a licence is granted which authorises an abstraction of water so as to derogate from a protected right) does not invalidate the grant or variation of a licence, but any person entitled to a protected right may seek enforcement of his right by bringing a civil action against the water authority (but not against any other person) for damages for breach of statutory duty; the duty cannot be enforced by criminal proceedings or by prohibition or injunction.[3]

Where a water authority are directed by the Secretary of State to grant or vary a licence which authorises derogation from protected rights, this will be treated as a breach of statutory duty on the part of the water authority, and the duty of the water authority in complying with the Secretary of State's direction does not afford any defence in an action brought against the water authority for breach of their statutory duty; however, this provision does not apply to a direction given in consequence of an appeal against the decision of the water authority on an application for the grant of a licence of right.[4]

In an action brought against a water authority for breach of statutory duty, there are two possible defences. Firstly, the

---

[1] Water Resources Act, 1963, s. 26 (1).

[2] *Ibid.*, s. 26 (2). As to the curtailment of a protected right to which the occupier of a holding is entitled under *ibid.*, s. 24 (2), *see ibid.*, s. 55.

[3] *Ibid.*, s. 50 (1).

[4] *Ibid.*, s. 50 (2).

J

authority may prove that the fact that the abstraction authorised by the licence granted or varied by the authority derogated from the protected right was wholly or mainly attributable to exceptional shortage of rain or to an accident or other unforeseen act or event not caused by, and outside the control of, the water authority.[1] Secondly, there is the defence open to a water authority under section 50 (4) (5) where the plaintiff is the holder of, or has applied for, a licence of right. As to the powers of the Secretary of State to indemnify water authorities in certain cases, see section 51.

Who may apply for a licence

No application for a licence to abstract water can be entertained unless it is made by a person entitled to make the application in accordance with the undermentioned provisions.[2]

A person may apply to abstract water from an inland water if, at the place or places at which the proposed abstractions are to be effected, either (i) he is the occupier of land contiguous to such inland water, or (ii) he satisfies the water authority that he has, or will have at the time when the proposed licence is to take effect, a right of access to such land.[3]

In relation to abstractions from underground strata, a person may apply for a licence if either (i) he is the occupier of land consisting of or comprising such underground strata, or (ii) in a case where water contained in an excavation into underground strata is, by virtue of section 2 (2) (b) of the Act of 1963, treated as water contained in such underground strata, he satisfies the water authority that he has, or will have at the time when the proposed licence is to take effect, a right of access to land consisting of or comprising such underground strata.[4]

An occupier of land for the purposes of the two previous paragraphs includes (a) a person who satisfies the water authority that he has entered into negotiations to acquire an interest

---

1 Water Resources Act, 1963, s. 50 (3).
2 Ibid., s. 27 (1).
3 Ibid., s. 27 (2).
4 Water Resources Act, 1968, s. 1 (1).

in land that will entitle him to occupy that land, and (b) a person who satisfies the water authority that by virtue of any enactment the compulsory acquisition by that person of such land has either been authorised or can be authorised and has been initiated, i.e. that a draft order or order has been submitted to the appropriate Minister and that the draft order if made or the order if confirmed will authorise that person to acquire that land compulsorily.[1]

Procedure in applying for a licence

A water authority cannot entertain an application for a licence unless the procedure for publication of the application referred to in section 28 is complied with.[2] The applicant is required to publish a notice[3] of his proposal in the London Gazette and for each of two successive weeks in one or more newspapers circulating in the locality of the proposed points of abstraction, and where the licence applied for is for abstraction from an inland water, a copy of the notice must be served on any navigation, harbour or conservancy authority having functions in relation to the inland water at any proposed point of abstraction, and also on any internal drainage board within whose district any point of abstraction is situated. The notice, in addition to giving details of the intended abstraction, names a place within the locality in which any point of abstraction is to be situated where a copy of the application and of any map, plan or other document submitted with the application may be inspected by the public free of charge, and states that any person may make written representations to the water authority with respect to the application within a period of not less than 28 days from the date on which the notice is first published in a newspaper and not less than 25 days from the date on which it is published in the London Gazette. The application form[4]

---

[1] Water Resources Act, 1963, s. 27 (4); Water Resources Act, 1968, s. 1 (2)-(5).

[2] Publication was not required in the case of an application for a licence of right, see p. 184.

[3] The notice is form N1 in Sch. 2 to the Water Resources (Licences) Regulations, 1965 (S.I. 1965, No. 534).

[4] The form is model form 1 or 2 in Sch. 1 to the Water Resources (Licences) Regulations, 1965.

is then sent to the water authority accompanied by a map[1] and with the prescribed evidence of publication of the notice.[2]

Determination of licence application

Where an application for a licence to abstract water is made to a water authority, the provisions of section 29 have effect. In the first instance, the water authority must not a grant a licence which would authorise the abstraction of water so as to derogate from any rights which are protected rights[3] at the time when the application is determined.[4]

Next, in dealing with the application, the water authority must have regard to (a) any written representations received by them within the prescribed period for making such representations arising from the notice previously published in the London Gazette and newspapers, and (b) the applicant's requirements as far as they appear to be reasonable to the water authority.[5]

Thirdly, where the application relates to abstraction from an inland water, the water authority must have regard to the need to secure that the flow at any control point will not be reduced below the minimum acceptable flow[6] already determined for the inland water at that point, or (if it is already less than the minimum acceptable flow) will not be further reduced below that minimum acceptable flow.[7] However, if the application is made at a time when no minimum acceptable flow has been determined for such inland water, the water authority is required to have regard to the considerations by

---

[1] As to the map, see reg. 6 (2) of the Water Resources (Licences) Regulations, 1965.

[2] The prescribed evidence consists of copies of the newspapers containing the notice and a declaration signed by or on behalf of the applicant that the notice has been published in the London Gazette and that the appropriate authorities have been served with the notice where the abstraction is to be from an inland water (see the Water Resources (Licences) Regulations, 1965, reg. 6 (4)).

[3] As to protected rights, see p. 190.

[4] Water Resources Act, 1963, s. 29 (2).

[5] Ibid., s. 29 (3), (4).

[6] As to minimum acceptable flow, see p. 181.

[7] Water Resources Act, 1963, s. 29 (6).

reference to which a minimum acceptable for the inland water would fall to be determined.[1]

Finally, where the application relates to abstraction from underground strata, the water authority is to have regard to the requirements of existing lawful uses of water abstracted from such strata, whether for agriculture, industry, water supply or other purposes, and if it appears to the water authority that the proposed abstraction is likely to affect the flow, level or volume of an inland water, the considerations in the previous paragraph regarding minimum acceptable flow or notional m.a.f. shall apply as if the application related to abstraction from that inland water.[2]

Subject to the above provisions (and to the provisions of the Act which follow hereafter) the water authority may (a) grant a licence containing such provisions as they consider appropriate, or (b) if, having regard to the provisions of the Act, they consider it necessary or expedient to do so, may refuse to grant a licence.[3]

Matters specified in the licence

Every licence to abstract water must—

(1) Make provision as to the quantity of water authorised to be abstracted in pursuance of the licence from the source of supply during a specified period or periods, including provision as to the way in which such quantity is to be measured or assessed.

(2) Make provision for determining, by measurement or assessment, what quantity of water is to be taken to have been abstracted during any such period by the licence holder from the source of supply.

(3) Indicate the means whereby water is authorised to be abstracted by reference either to specified works, machinery or apparatus or to works, machinery or apparatus fulfilling specified requirements.

---

[1] Water Resources Act, 1963, s. 29 (5).
[2] *Ibid.*, s. 29 (7).
[3] *Ibid.*, s. 29 (8).

(4) Specify the land on which, and the purposes for which, water abstracted is to be used, except in the case of a licence granted to a water authority or to water undertakers.

(5) Specify the person to whom the licence is granted.

(6) State whether the licence is to remain in force until revoked or is to expire at a specified time.

The same licence may make different provision with respect to the abstraction of water (a) during different periods, (b) from the same source of supply but at different points or by different means, (c) for use for different purposes. Two or more licences may be granted to the same person to be held concurrently in respect of the same source of supply, if the licences authorise the abstraction of water at different points or by different means.[1]

Effect of the licence

Where an action is brought against a person in respect of water abstracted from a source of supply, it is a defence for him to prove that the abstraction was in pursuance of a licence and that the provisions of the licence were complied with, but this does not exonerate a person from an action for negligence or breach of contract. Subject to the provisions of the Act regarding succession to licences and the variation of licences, the person to whom a licence to abstract water is granted is for the purposes of the Act the holder of the licence.[2]

Succession to licences

Where the holder of a licence is the occupier of the whole of the land specified in the licence as the land on which water abstracted in pursuance of the licence is to be used, and either, being an individual, he dies, or by reason of any other act or event the original holder, whether an individual or not, ceases to be the occupier of the whole of the land and does not continue to occupy any part of it and (either immediately after

---

[1] Water Resources Act, 1963, s. 30.

[2] *Ibid.*, s. 31.

his death or the occurrence of such other act or event or subsequently) another person as successor becomes the occupier of the whole of the land, then the successor becomes the holder of the licence. But if the successor fails to give notice to the water authority of the change in occupation of the land within one month from the date on which he became the occupier, he ceases to be the holder of the licence at the end of that period (and in that event he would need to apply for a new licence in the prescribed manner). Upon being given notice by the new licence holder, the water authority must vary the licence accordingly.[1]

Reference of licence applications to the Secretary of State

The Secretary of State may give directions, either to a particular water authority or to water authorities generally, or relating either to a particular application or to applications of a class specified in the direction, requiring applications for licences to be referred to him instead of being dealt with by water authorities. A direction may also be given exempting from the operation thereof such classes of applications specified in the direction in such circumstances as may be so specified. Before determining an application referred to him, the Secretary of State may, and must if so requested by the applicant or the water authority, hold a local inquiry or hearing. The Secretary of State's decision on an application referred to him is final, and where the decision is that a licence is to be granted, it shall include a direction to the water authority to grant a licence containing such provisions as may be specified in the direction.[2]

Appeals to the Secretary of State

Where an applicant for a licence is dissatisfied with the water authority's decision, or by reason of the water authority's failure to notify him of their decision or that the application has been referred to the Secretary of State (in accordance with directions given under section 38) within three months

---

[1] Water Resources Act, 1963, s. 32. *See also* the Water Resources (Succession to Licences) Regulations, 1969 (S.I. 1969, No. 976).

[2] *Ibid.*, s. 38; Water Act, 1973, s. 40 (2), Sch. 8, para. 79.

from the date of receipt of the application, or within such extended period as may be agreed upon in writing between the applicant and the water authority, the applicant may give written notice of appeal to the Secretary of State within one month from the date of receipt of notice of the water authority's decision, or within three months from the date of receipt of the application (or any agreed extension thereof), as the case may be, or within such longer period as the Secretary of State may at any time allow.

The applicant must also serve a copy of the notice of appeal on the water authority, and provide the Secretary of State with copies of the licence application, all relevant maps and particulars supplied to the authority, the notice of the decision (if any) and all other relevant correspondence with the authority. The water authority is required to serve a copy of the notice of appeal on any person who made written representations with respect to the application before it was determined by the water authority, and the Secretary of State in determining the appeal must take any further representations received from such persons into account.

The Secretary of State may, and must if so requested by the applicant or the water authority, hold a local inquiry or hearing before determining an appeal. The decision of the Secretary of State on appeal is final and where he decides to grant, vary or revoke a licence, the decision shall include a direction to the water authority accordingly.[1]

Revocation and variation of licences

A licence holder may apply to the water authority to revoke the licence, and thereupon the authority must revoke it accordingly. Or a licence holder may apply to the water authority for a variation of his licence, in which case sections 28, 29 and 38-41 of the Act are applied with the necessary modifications, except that where the proposed variation is limited to reducing the quantity of water authorised to be

---

[1] Water Resources Act, 1963, ss. 39-41; Water Resources (Licences) Regulations, 1965 (S.I. 1965, No. 534), reg. 12.

abstracted, publication of notice of the variation and the consideration of written representations by the water authority under sections 28 and 39 (4) do not apply.[1] Should a water authority propose to revoke or vary a licence they have granted, the procedure under sections 43 and 44 applies.

Temporary restriction on spray irrigation

If it appears necessary to a water authority by reason of exceptional shortage of rain or other emergency to impose a temporary restriction on the abstraction of water used for the purpose of spray irrigation, the water authority may serve a notice on the holder of a licence which authorises abstraction for that purpose (or for that purpose together with other purposes) reducing, during a specified period, the quantity of water authorised to be abstracted for that purpose. A notice cannot be served in respect of abstraction from underground strata unless such abstraction is likely to affect the flow, level or volume of an inland water. Where two or more such licences authorise abstraction from the same source of supply either at the same point or at points which are not far distant from each other, like notices must be served on all the licence holders in respect of the same period and the reductions imposed by the notices must represent as nearly as practicable the same proportion of the quantity of water authorised by the licences to be abstracted for spray irrigation.[2]

Register of applications and licences

Every water authority must keep a register in such manner and containing such information as may be prescribed by regulations[3] regarding applications made for the grant, revocation or variation of licences, the way in which applications have

---

[1] Water Resources Act, 1963, s. 42. As to the payment of compensation by a river authority, where they have revoked or varied a licence under *ibid.*, s. 44, *see ibid.*, s. 46. As to where an owner of fishing rights in respect of an inland water may apply to the Secretary of State for revocation or variation of a licence, *see ibid.*, s. 47.

[2] *Ibid.*, s. 45.

[3] *See* the Water Resources (Licences) Regulations, 1965 (S.I. 1965, No. 534), reg. 17.

been dealt with and as to the persons becoming licence holders under section 32 dealing with succession to licences. The register must also contain information about applications made by the water authority to abstract or impound water and licences granted or deemed to be granted. A register shall be available for public inspection at all reasonable hours.[1]

Charges for licences

Charges are payable to a water authority for the abstraction of water under a licence and are fixed by a charges scheme · made by the authority.[2] No charges are leviable for water authorised by a licence to be abstracted from underground water for agricultural purposes other than spray irrigation.[3] The holder of a licence, where the purposes for which water is used consist of or include spray irrigation and the water is to be used on land of which the holder is the occupier, may apply to a water authority to enter into an agreement with him for a period of at least five years for the charges to be based partly on the quantity of water authorised to be abstracted and partly on the quantity measured or assessed as being abstracted. If the authority refuse to make an agreement, or if the licence holder objects to the terms of an agreement as proposed by the authority, either party may refer the question in dispute to the Secretary of State, whose decision is final.[4]

A person who is liable to pay charges to a water authority for the abstraction of water under a licence may apply to the authority to make an agreement with him for the exemption from or reduction in the charges having regard to:—

   (a) the extent to which any works constructed or to be constructed by that person have made or will make a beneficial contribution towards fulfilling the purposes of the functions conferred on the water authority by section 9 of the Water Act, 1973;

---

[1] Water Resources Act, 1963, s. 53.
[2] Water Act 1973, s. 30 (1), (2). As to a charges scheme, see p. 173.
[3] Water Resources Act 1963, s. 60 (6); Water Act 1973, s. 40 (2), Sch. 8, para. 80 (3).
[4] Water Resources Act 1963, s. 63; Water Act 1973, s. 40, Sch. 8, para. 81, Sch. 9.

(b) any financial assistance which that person has rendered or agreed to render towards the carrying out of works by the water authority in performing those functions;

(c) any other material consideration.

If the water authority refuse to make an agreement with an applicant or he objects to the terms of an agreement as proposed by the authority, either party may refer the question in dispute to the Secretary of State, whose decision is final.[1]

If the charges payable under a licence are not paid within fourteen days after written demand served on the licence holder, the water authority may by notice in writing suspend the operation of the licence until the charges have been paid.[2]

Abstraction and impounding of water by water authorities

Part IV of the Act is applied to the abstraction of water by water authorities from sources of supply in their areas, and to the construction or alteration by water authorities of impounding works in their areas subject to such exceptions and modifications as may be prescribed by regulations. Any such regulations may in particular provide for securing that (a) a licence required by a water authority shall be granted, or deemed to be granted, by the Secretary of State and not by the water authority; (b) in such cases and subject to such conditions as may be prescribed, a licence required by a water authority shall be deemed to be granted by the Secretary of State unless he requires that an application for the licence shall be made to him by the water authority; and (c) where a licence is deemed to be granted under paragraph (b) above, the water authority shall give notice of that fact as may be prescribed.[3]

---

[1] Water Resources Act 1963, s. 60 (1)-(5); Water Act 1973, s. 40 (2), Sch. 8, para. 80 (1), (2).

[2] Water Resources Act 1963, s. 64 (2); Water Act 1973, s. 40 (3), Sch. 9.

[3] Water Resources Act, 1963, s. 52; *see also* the Water Resources (Licences) Regulations, 1965 (S.I. 1965, No. 534), regs. 13-15.

CONTROL OF IMPOUNDING OF WATER

Restrictions on impounding works

As from 1st July, 1965, section 36 (1) of the Act provides that—

> " no person shall . . . begin, or cause or permit any other person to begin, to construct or alter any impounding works[1] at any point in an inland water in a water authority area . . . unless—
>
> > (a) a licence under this Act granted by the water authority to obstruct or impede the flow of that inland water at that point by means of impounding works is in force, and
> >
> > (b) the impounding works will not obstruct or impede the flow of the inland water except to the extent, and in the manner, authorised by the licence, and
> >
> > (c) any other requirements of the licence, whether as to the provision of compensation water or otherwise are complied with ".

Any person who contravenes section 36 (1), or who (in circumstances not constituting such a contravention) does not comply with a condition or requirement imposed by a licence of which he is the holder, is guilty of an offence and on conviction on indictment or on summary convictions is liable to a fine, which on summary conviction shall not exceed £1,000.[2]

A licence to impound is not, however, required, in the following circumstances—

> (1) If the construction or alteration of any impounding works, or the obstruction or impeding of the flow of the inland water resulting from the construction or alteration of the works, is authorised (in whatsoever

---

[1] " Impounding works " means either of the following—(a) any dam, weir or other works in an inland water whereby water may be impounded, and (b) any works for diverting the flow of an inland water in connection with the construction or alteration of any dam, weir or other works falling under head (a) above (Water Resources Act, 1963, s. 36 (6)).

[2] *Ibid.*, s. 49; Criminal Law Act, 1977, s. 28 (2).

terms, and whether expressly or by implication) by virtue of a statutory provision,[1] other than one which is not contained in, or made or issued under, the Water Resources Act, 1963, or the Water Act, 1958.[2]

(2) Where impounding works are constructed or altered in the course of the performance by a navigation, harbour or conservancy authority of their functions as such an authority.[3]

Where a licence to impound is necessary under the Act of 1963, it should be noted that the consent of the drainage board may also be required under section 28 of the Land Drainage Act, 1976,[4] or that the consent of the water authority is necessary under section 29 of that Act.[5]

General provisions as to licences to impound

The person to whom a licence to impound is granted (and no other person) is for the purposes of the Act the holder of the licence.[6] In any action brought against a person in respect of an obstruction or impeding of the flow of an inland water at any point by means of impounding works, it is a defence for him to prove that the flow was so obstructed or impeded in pursuance of a licence to impound, and in the manner specified in such licence, and to an extent not exceeding the extent so specified and that any other requirements of the licence were complied with, but this does not exonerate a person from an action for negligence or breach of contract.[7] A water authority may grant a combined licence to include impounding works and to abstract the water.[8]

---

[1] " Statutory provision " means a provision, whether of a general or a special nature, contained in, or in any document made or issued under, any Act, whether of a general or a special nature (Water Resources Act, 1963, s. 135 (1)).
[2] Ibid., s. 36 (2), (3).
[3] Ibid., s. 36 (4).
[4] See p. 232.
[5] See p. 233.
[6] Water Resources Act, 1963, s. 37 (1).
[7] Ibid., s. 37 (2).
[8] Ibid., s. 37 (3).

A water authority have a duty not to grant a licence to impound which would authorise the holder to obstruct or impede the flow of an inland water by means of impounding works in such a way, or to such an extent, as to prevent a person entitled to a protected right from abstracting water to the extent permitted by such right.[1]

The provisions of sections 28 and 29 as to the publication and determination of an application for a licence to abstract have effect in relation to applications for licences to impound.[2]

FURTHER POWERS AND FUNCTIONS

Compulsory powers for works

Where in the performance of their water resources functions a water authority propose to carry out any engineering or building operations,[3] and it appears to them that for the purpose of carrying out such operations they need compulsory powers, whether consisting of or including powers of compulsory acquisition or not, the authority may apply to the Secretary of State for an order. Subject to the prescribed procedure,[4] the Secretary of State may make an order conferring on the authority compulsory powers for the purpose of carrying out the works in question.[5]

If it appears appropriate to the Secretary of State to facilitate the performance of the water resources functions of a water authority, he may on the application of the authority make an order, subject to such conditions as may be specified in the order, authorising the authority to discharge water into an inland water or underground strata. A person who suffers

---

[1] Water Resources Act, 1963, ss. 26 (2), 36 (6).

[2] *Ibid.*, s. 37 (5).

[3] " Engineering or building operations " (without prejudice to the generality of that expression) includes the construction, alteration, improvement or maintenance of any reservoir, watercourse, dam, weir, well, borehole or other works, the closure or removal of any reservoir, watercourse, dam, weir, well, borehole or other works, the construction, alteration, improvement, maintenance or demolition of any building or structure, and the installation, modification or removal of any machinery or apparatus (Water Resources Act, 1963, s. 135 (1)).

[4] *See ibid.*, s. 67 (2), Sch. 8.

[5] *Ibid.*, s. 67.

damage attributable to such a discharge is entitled to recover compensation from the authority. A water authority and a statutory water undertaking may with the consent of the Secretary of State, enter into an agreement respecting the discharge of water from any works belonging to the undertakers.[1]

Without prejudice to any other powers, conferred on them by or under the Water Resources Act, 1963, or any other Act, a water authority are empowered to carry out such engineering or building operations as they consider necessary or expedient for the purposes of any of their functions.[2]

For the purpose of doing anything in the performance of their water resources functions certain provisions of the Water Act, 1945, have effect in relation to water authorities.[3]

Agreements for facilitating performance of water resources functions

A water authority may enter into an agreement with statutory water undertakers, any local authority or the owner or occupier of any land with respect to one or more of the following matters:—

(a) the execution by any party to the agreement of works within the water authority area in connection with the performance of their water resources functions;

(b) the maintenance by any party to the agreement of works executed in pursuance of the agreement;

(c) provision for the water authority to use or have access to any land within their area for any purpose connected with the performance of their water resources functions;

---

1 Water Resources Act, 1971, s. 1.
2 Water Resources Act, 1963, s. 69 (1).
3 These provisions being ss. 9, 12-17, 19, 20, 22, 28, 67 and 68 of Sch. 3 to the Water Act 1945 as modified by Sch. 9 to the Water Resources Act 1963. Section 61 of the Land Drainage Act 1930 has effect in relation to these provisions.
4 Water Resources Act, 1963, s. 69 (3), (4).

(*d*) the manner in which any reservoir in the water authority area is to be operated.

The Secretary of State may direct that in specified cases a water authority or authorities shall not enter into an agreement except with his consent. Arrangements may be made for an agreement with an owner of land to be registered as a land charge.[1]

Borings not requiring licences

A person who proposes to construct a well, borehole or other work to be used solely for the purpose of abstracting, to the extent necessary to prevent interference with the execution or operation of any underground works, water contained in underground strata, or proposes to extend any such well, borehole or other work, must, before he begins to construct or extend the work, give notice of his intention in the prescribed form[2] to the water authority.

Similarly, a person proposing to construct or extend a boring for purpose of searching for or extracting minerals must give prior notice to the water authority in the prescribed form.[2]

On receiving such notice, the water authority may serve a conservation notice on such person requiring him to take reasonable measures for conserving water as specified in the notice, being measures which, in the authority's opinion, will not interfere with the protection of the underground works or with the winning of minerals, as the case may be.

The person on whom the conservation notice is served may appeal in writing to the Secretary of State on the grounds (*a*) that the measures required are not reasonable, and/or (*b*) that the measures would interfere with the protection of the underground works or with the winning of minerals. The Secretary of State may confirm, quash or vary the conservation notice and his decision is final. A person who contravenes

---

[1] Water Resources Act 1963, s. 81; Water Act 1973, s. 40 (3), Sch. 9.

[2] *See* the Water Resources (Miscellenous Provisions) Regulations, 1965 (S.I. 1965, No. 1092), regs. 7, 8, Sch.

any of the above provisions or fails to comply with a conservation notice is guilty of an offence and liable on conviction on indictment or on summary conviction to a fine, which on summary conviction shall not exceed £1,000.[1]

Byelaws for protecting water resources

A water authority may for the purposes of their functions relating to water resources or land drainage[2] or fisheries make byelaws prohibiting inland waters in their area from being usèd for boating (whether with mechanically propelled boats or otherwise), swimming or other recreational purposes, or regulating the way in which such inland waters may be used for any of those purposes.

Byelaws made in respect of inland water may include provision prohibiting the use of the inland waters by boats which are not registered with the water authority and for the authority to make reasonable charges in respect of the registration of boats.

Byelaws as to inland waters shall not apply to:—

(a) any tidal waters.

(b) any inland waters where functions are exercisable by, a navigation, harbour or conservancy authority other than the water authority.

(c) any inland water as defined by section 2 (3) of the Water Resources Act, 1963.[3]

(d) any reservoir belonging to and operated by statutory water undertakers other than the water authority.

A person who contravenes, or fails to comply with, any byelaws is guilty of an offence and liable on summary conviction to a fine not exceeding £20: if the contravention or failure to comply is continued after the conviction, he is guilty of a further offence and liable on summary conviction to a fine not exceeding £5 for each day on which it is so continued. Without prejudice to any such proceedings, a

---

1 Water Resources Act, 1963, s. 78; Criminal Law Act, 1977, s. 28 (2).

2 " Land drainage " includes defence against water (including sea water), irrigation other than spray irrigation, warping and the provision of flood warning systems (Water Resources Act, 1963, s. 135 (1); Water Act, 1973, s. 40 (2), Sch. 8, para. 85).

3 See p. 177.

water authority may take such action as they consider necessary to remedy the effect of any contravention of, or failure to comply with the byelaws, and may recover their reasonable expenses in doing so from the person in default.[1]

Power to require information

A water authority may give directions requiring a person who is abstracting water from a source of supply in their area, to give such information to the authority as to the abstraction, at such times and in such form, as specified in the directions. A person who has been given directions and considers them to be unreasonable or unduly onerous may make representations thereon to the Secretary of State, who may direct the water authority to revoke or modify them, but the right to make such representations does not apply to directions requiring the occupier of land to give prescribed particulars as to the quantity of water abstracted by him or on his behalf from a source of supply in the water authority area. A person who fails to comply with directions given by a water authority is guilty of an offence and liable on summary conviction to a fine not exceeding £20.[2]

Contributions between water authorities and other bodies

Where it appears to a navigation, harbour or conservancy authority,[3] on the application of a water authority, that works constructed or maintained by a water authority in performing their water resources functions have made or will make a beneficial contribution towards the performance of the functions of the authority to whom the application is made, that authority must contribute to the river authority such sums, on such terms and conditions, as may be agreed appropriate towards the expenditure incurred or to be incurred by the water authority in constructing or maintaining such works. If the navigation or other authority refuse to contribute, or the parties are

---

[1] Water Resources Act 1963, s. 79; Water Act 1973, s. 40 (2), Sch. 8, para. 82; Control of Pollution Act, 1974, s. 108 (2), Sch. 4.

[2] Water Resources Act, 1963, s. 114; Control of Pollution Act, 1974, s. 108 (2), Sch. 4.

[3] These authorities are defined in footnotes 2, 3 on p. 188 and footnote 1 on p. 189.

unable to agree as to the contribution or the terms and conditions concerned, either party may refer the matter in dispute to the Secretary of State who may either determine the matter themselves or refer it to arbitration. Conversely, a navigation, harbour or conservancy authority may apply to a water authority for a contribution in respect of works constructed or maintained by the applicants which appear to have made or will make a beneficial contribution towards the fulfilment of the purposes of the water resources functions of the water authority.[1]

---

1 Water Resources Act, 1963, s. 91.

CHAPTER 12

LAND DRAINAGE

The main purposes of land drainage are:—(a) the improvement of agricultural land; (b) the protection of land (including urban areas and property generally) from flooding and inundation of water, whether fresh or sea water; and (c) the conservation of water in rivers for riparian owners and other users.

These objectives are achieved by the periodic cleansing, scouring and improvement of the channels of rivers, streams and watercourses and the removal of obstructions therefrom; the maintenance and erection of dams, weirs and sluices for controlling the flow of water; and the execution of drainage and flood relief schemes for improving river channels and lowering the water levels therein or by the construction of new channels where desirable. Such drainage works are normally carried out by drainage authorities (*i.e.* water authorities or internal drainage boards) upon the watercourses under their jurisdiction, but drainage work is also done on other watercourses by local authorities exercising land drainage functions, or by farmers and private landowners. In addition, coast protection works, mainly in the form of sea walls and flood embankments, are effected either by water authorities under the Land Drainage Act, 1976, or by maritime local authorities under the Coast Protection Act, 1949.[1]

A brief summary of land drainage legislation up to the passing of the Land Drainage Act, 1930, is given on pp. 36 and 37.

---

[1] *See* COAST PROTECTION AND SEA DEFENCE, on pp. 36 to 42.

LAND DRAINAGE LEGISLATION SINCE 1930

The Land Drainage Act, 1930, established drainage districts with a drainage board for each district to exercise a general supervision over all matters relating to the drainage of land within that district and possessing the powers and performing the duties conferred or imposed by the Act. The drainage districts originally consisted of:—

(a) Catchment areas, the drainage of which was directed to the rivers or arterial drains specified in Schedule 1 to the Act and the drainage boards for which were the catchment boards constituted in accordance with Part II of the Act;

(b) Drainage districts, other than catchment areas, constituted either within or outside catchment areas for such areas " as derive benefit or avoid damage as a result of drainage operations ",[1] and under the jurisdiction of drainage boards, or internal drainage boards where the drainage district was within a catchment area;

(c) Drainage districts or drainage areas constituted under the Land Drainage Act, 1861, or under that Act as amended, or under any other enactment relating to the drainage of land, and the drainage boards or drainage authorities of such districts or areas were treated as if they had been constituted under the Land Drainage Act, 1930, as the drainage boards of those districts or areas.[2]

However, on the passing of the River Boards Act, 1948, considerable changes were effected to the Land Drainage Act, 1930, and the structure of drainage authorities set up under that Act underwent a twofold operation. Firstly, catchment boards and catchment areas were superseded by river boards and river board areas, except as regards the Thames and Lee catchment areas. Secondly, although drainage authorities

---

[1] This phrase is explained in a document issued by the Minister of Agriculture and Fisheries in 1933 known as the " Medway letter ".

[2] Land Drainage Act, 1930, ss. 1-3.

other than catchment boards were left largely undisturbed, the ultimate result of the establishment of river board areas for practically the whole of England and Wales meant that external drainage districts were included in the river board areas and became internal drainage districts.

The River Boards Act, 1948, provided for two types of drainage district:—(i) river board areas under river boards, and (ii) drainage districts within river board areas under the jurisdiction of internal drainage boards.

The Land Drainage Act, 1961, did not affect the structure of drainage boards, but amended and added to their land drainage functions.

The Water Resources Act, 1963, completed the repeal of the River Boards Act, 1948,[1] and the thirty-two river boards were abolished and replaced by twenty-seven river authorities (established under the 1963 Act), to whom were transferred the land drainage and other functions previously exercised by the river boards, and the river authorities also assumed the new functions of water resources contained in the 1963 Act.[2] The provisions of the 1963 Act, suitably adapted, were applied to the Thames and Lee catchment areas as if they were river authority areas.[3] In relation to Greater London the London Government Act, 1963, provided that the Greater London Council exercises land drainage functions in respect of metropolitan watercourses and the London borough councils as regards non-metropolitan watercourses.[4]

Finally, the Water Act, 1973, abolished the river authorities, together with the Thames Conservancy and the Lee Conservancy Catchment Board, and established regional water authorities who on 1st April, 1974, took over the land drainage and other functions hitherto exercisable by the river authorities.[5] In the London excluded area (comprising so much of

---

1 Water Resources Act, 1963, s. 136, Sch. 14, Part I.
2 *Ibid.*, s. 5, Sch. 3.
3 *Ibid.*, s. 125, and orders made thereunder.
4 London Government Act, 1963, s. 62, Sch. 14.
5 Water Act, 1973, ss. 2, 9, 33.

Greater London and any adjoining area as does not for the purpose of exercising land drainage functions lie within any water authority area[1]) land drainage continues to be exercised by the Greater London Council and London borough councils.[2] Internal drainage boards are not affected by the Act.

LAND DRAINAGE ACT, 1976

The statute law with respect to land drainage is contained in the Land Drainage Act, 1976, which applies to England and Wales, but does not extend to Scotland or Northern Ireland.[3]

Nothing in the Land Drainage Act, 1976, shall affect or prejudice the provisions of the Salmon and Freshwater Fisheries Act, 1975, or any rights, powers or duties conferred or imposed thereby, and in the exercise of the powers conferred by the 1976 Act, due regard must be had to the fishery interests.[4] Provision is made for the protection of nationalised undertakings,[5] and the Act is applied to land belonging to the Crown and Government departments with certain reservations.[6] Nothing in the Act shall be taken to authorise any person to execute any works or do any thing in contravention of the provisions of the Ancient Monuments Acts, 1913-1972.[7]

Nothing in the Land Drainage Act, 1976, affects the powers exercisable by a drainage authority or local authority under a local Act as they existed immediately before the commencement of the 1976 Act. Local Act provisions for protecting any authority or person which applied immediately before the coming into force of the 1976 Act, in relation to powers under an enactment re-enacted by the 1976 Act exercised by a drainage authority or local authority, apply to the like extent in

---

1 Water Act, 1973, s. 38 (1).
2 Land Drainage Act, 1976, s. 105, Sch. 5, para. 3 (2).
3 *Ibid.*, s. 118 (3).
4 *Ibid.*, s. 113; but *see Proctor v. Avon & Dorset River Board* [1953], C.P.L. 562: (*i.e.* a drainage board requiring entry on land to improve existing works do not need consent from those having merely an incorporeal right in the water and not on the banks).
5 Land Drainage Act, 1976, s. 112.
6 *Ibid.*, s. 115.
7 *Ibid.*, s. 111.

relation to powers exercised by such an authority under the corresponding provision of the 1976 Act.[1]

" The Minister " for the purposes of the Land Drainage Act, 1976, is the Minister of Agriculture, Fisheries and Food,[2] although another Minister may be expressly referred to.[3]

The Land Drainage Act, 1976, being a consolidation measure, has not substantially affected or altered the basic drainage functions of water authorities or internal drainage boards and these functions continue to be exercised in relation to the London excluded area[4] by the Greater London Council and other authorities subject to the provisions of Schedule 5 to the 1976 Act. It should be noted that in this Act " drainage authority " means a water authority or an internal drainage board, whilst " drainage body " is defined as a drainage authority or any other body having power to make or maintain works for the drainage of land.[5]

INTRODUCTION TO DRAINAGE AUTHORITIES

Water authorities and land drainage

(1) *General supervision and discharge of functions by committees*

A water authority must exercise a general supervision over all matters relating to land drainage in their area and arrange for their regional land drainage committee (without prejudice to any scheme for the appointment of local land drainage committees) to discharge all their land drainage functions except the raising of drainage charges,[6] the levying of precepts,[7] the borrowing of money[8] and making an application for a water charges option order.[9] An authority may give their regional committee directions on exercising land drainage

---

[1] Land Drainage Act, 1976, s. 114; and *see Belton v. Crowle District Drainage Board* (1935), 153 L.T. 466, where it was stated that the corresponding provision in a previous Land Drainage Act did not refer to provisions in local Acts concerned with rating.

[2] *Ibid.*, s. 116 (1).

[3] *Ibid.*, s. 88.

[4] *See* p. 212.

[5] Land Drainage Act, 1976, ss. 17 (7), 116 (1).

[6] *See* p. 243.

[7] *See* p. 240.

[8] *See* p. 175.

[9] *See* p. 244.

functions other than one of their internal drainage functions,[1] which appears to affect materially the authority's management of water for purposes other than land drainage.[2]

(2) *Regional land drainage committees*

The regional committee consists of:—

(*a*) a chairman who is one of the authority members appointed by the Minister of Agriculture, Fisheries and Food.

(*b*) a number of other members appointed by the Minister with experience of, and capacity in, or special knowledge of land drainage or agriculture and related matters.

(*c*) two members appointed by the authority.

(*d*) other members appointed by or on behalf of the constituent councils[3] any part of which are in the water authority area.

A water authority determine the total number of members of their regional committee, and may vary the number from time to time.   The total number must be not less than eleven nor more than seventeen, except where the authority determine that the committee shall consist of more than seventeen and the Minister confirms this by order.

When the number of members has been fixed, the Minister by order specifies the number of members to be appointed to the committee by or on behalf of the constituent councils, and the Minister must have regard to the proportion which the estimated penny rate product of the area of each council within the water authority area bears to the aggregate of the penny rate products of all the councils within the area.   The order is framed so that the total number of members (including the chairman) appointed by the Minister and by the water authority

---

[1] As to " internal drainage functions ", *see* s. 1 (3) of the Land Drainage Act, 1976.
[2] Land Drainage Act, 1976, s. 1 (1), (2).
[3] A constituent council is a county council or London borough council (Land Drainage Act, 1976, s. 2 (6)).

is one less than the number of those appointed by or on behalf of the councils.[1]

A person nominated by one or more councils to act as a deputy for a member of a regional committee appointed by or on behalf of the council or councils, may attend and vote at a meeting of the committee instead of that member.[2]

(3) *Local land drainage committees*

Any local land drainage schemes (which provide in a water authority area for the creation of one or more local land drainage districts and for constituting a local land drainage committee for each district) in force immediately before the coming into operation of the Land Drainage Act, 1976, continue in force.

A regional committee may at any time submit to the water authority a local land drainage scheme for any part of their area for which there is no scheme in force, after consulting the county and district councils, any part of which falls within the area to which the scheme will relate and also with appropriate organisations representative of land drainage or agriculture. The water authority must send any scheme submitted to them to the Minister, who may approve the scheme to come into operation on a date fixed by him.

A scheme shall provide that any local committee consists of between eleven and fifteen members (unless the regional committee recommend more than fifteen and the Minister so approves) comprising:—

(*a*) a chairman appointed from among their own members by the regional committee;

(*b*) other members appointed by the regional committee, being persons with knowledge and experience of land drainage or agriculture;

(*c*) members appointed by or on behalf of the constituent councils, any part of which is in the local land drainage district.

---

[1] Land Drainage Act, 1976, ss. 2, 3.
[2] *Ibid.*, s. 3 (9), Sch. 1, para. 12 (1).

The total number of members appointed to a local committee by the regional committee must be one less than the number appointed by or on behalf of the councils.[1]

A person nominated by one or more councils to act as a deputy for a member of a local committee appointed by or on behalf of the council or councils may attend and vote at a meeting of the committee instead of that member.[2]

Internal drainage boards

Internal drainage districts continue for the purpose of the drainage of land; internal drainage boards are bodies corporate and exercise a general supervision over all matters relating to the drainage of land within their district and have such other powers and perform such other duties as conferred or imposed on internal drainage boards by the Land Drainage Act, 1976. Internal drainage districts are such areas as derive benefit or avoid danger as a result of drainage operations.[3]

An internal drainage board consists of members elected in accordance with the provisions of the Land Drainage (Election of Drainage Boards) Regulations, 1938,[4] and to be qualified for membership a person must be the owner of not less than four hectares of land situate in the electoral district, or the occupier of not less than eight hectares of such land, or the owner or occupier of land of an annual value of £30 or upwards, or a person nominated as a candidate by an owner or body of owners qualified as above.[5] The persons who are entitled to vote at the election of members of an internal drainage board are those who at the date of election own or occupy land on which a drainage rate has been levied in the year immediately preceding.[6] Provisions relating to the members and proceedings of internal drainage boards are set out in Part I of Schedule 2 to the Land Drainage Act, 1976.

---

[1] Land Drainage Act, 1976, ss. 4, 5.
[2] Ibid., s. 3 (9), Sch. 1, para. 12 (1).
[3] Ibid., s. 6.
[4] S.R. & O. 1938 No. 558 as amended by S.I. 1977 No. 366.
[5] Land Drainage Act, 1976, s. 7 (2), Sch. 2, Part I, para. 1 (1) as amended by the Land Drainage Act, 1976 (Amendment) Regulations, 1978 (S.I. 1978 No. 319).
[6] Ibid., Sch. 2, Part II, para. 22.

Main rivers and their control

(1) *Control of main rivers*

The powers conferred by the Land Drainage Act, 1976, on drainage authorities,[1] so far as concerns main rivers,[2] their banks[3] and drainage works[4] in connection with main rivers, are exercisable solely by water authorities. Any question arising hereunder, or section 17,[5] 21[6] or 23[7] of the Land Drainage Act, 1976, whether any work is, or whether any proposed work will if constructed be, a drainage work in connection with a main river, must be referred to the Minister of Agriculture, Fisheries and Food for decision or, if either of the parties so requires, to arbitration.[8]

(2) *Main river maps*

A " main river map " means a map of a water authority's area relating to the water authority's land drainage functions (*a*) which shows by a distinctive colour the extent to which any watercourse[9] in that area is to be treated as the main river or part of the main river for the purposes of the Land Drainage Act, 1976, and (*b*) which indicates by a distinctive colour or otherwise which (if any) of those watercourses are watercourses designated in a scheme made under section 50. The main

---

[1] " Drainage authority " means a water authority or internal drainage board (Land Drainage Act, 1976, ss. 17 (7), 116 (1)).

[2] " Main river " means a watercourse shown as such on a main river map and includes any structure or appliance for controlling or regulating the flow of water into, in or out of the channel, being a structure or appliance situated in the channel or in any part of the banks of the channel (other than a structure or appliance vested in or controlled by an internal drainage board (*ibid.*, s. 8 (3)).

[3] " Banks " means banks, walls or embankments adjoining or confining, or constructed for the purposes of or in connection with, any channel or sea front, and includes all land between the bank and low-water mark (Land Drainage Act, 1976, s. 116 (1)).

[4] " Drainage works " are not defined, but " drainage " includes defence against water (including sea water), irrigation, other than spray irrigation, and warping (*ibid.*, s. 116 (1)).

[5] *See* p. 223.

[6] *See* p. 228.

[7] *See* p. 228.

[8] Land Drainage Act, 1976, s. 8.

[9] " Watercourse " includes all rivers and streams and all ditches, drains, cuts, culverts, dikes, sluices, sewers (other than public sewers within the meaning of the Public Health Act, 1936) and passages, through which water flows (Land Drainage Act, 1976, s. 116 (1)).

river maps at the commencement of the 1976 Act are either those maps kept by the former river authorities and catchment boards or new maps sent to water authorities by the Minister of Agriculture, Fisheries and Food. The map is conclusive evidence for all purposes as to what is the main river and as to the boundaries of the water authority area in relation to their land drainage functions.

Where (a) a water authority area is altered so as to affect any particulars shown on the main river map, or (b) the Minister confirms a scheme under section 50, or (c) a water authority apply to the Minister for variation of their map so far as it shows the extent to which a watercourse is to be treated as the main river, the Minister shall either require the water authority to send him the main river map and alter the map and send it back to the water authority, or prepare a new map and send it to the water authority or notify the authority that he does not intend to vary their map.   Before altering a map, or preparing a new map, the Minister is required to give notice of his intention to do so to persons affected and to consider any objections made to him.

The main river map must be kept at the principal office of the water authority, who shall provide reasonable facilities for its inspection, and for taking copies of, and extracts from, the map.[1]

Transfers of functions and reorganisation of internal drainage districts

(1) *Schemes for transfer to water authority of functions in relation to main river*

A water authority may at any time and must if directed by the Minister of Agriculture, Fisheries and Food prepare and submit to him for confirmation a scheme making provision for the transfer from any drainage body to the water authority of all rights, powers, duties, obligations and liabilities (including liabilities incurred in connection with works) over or in connection with the main river, and of any property held by the

---

[1] Land Drainage Act, 1976, s. 9.   As to maps of water authority areas, *see* p. 158.

drainage body for the purpose of, or in connection with, any functions so discharged, and for any matters supplemental to or consequential on such transfer. The scheme is subject to confirmation by the Minister by order.

Where liabilities incurred in connection with drainage works are transferred under a scheme from a local authority to the water authority, the authority may require the local authority to contribute towards the discharge of the liabilities. If the amount of the contributions is not agreed between the authority and the local authority, it must be determined by a single arbitrator agreed on between them or, in default of such agreement, by the Minister of Agriculture, Fisheries and Food and the Secretary of State acting jointly.[1]

(2) *Schemes for reorganisation of internal drainage districts and for conferring functions on water authority*

A water authority may at any time and must if directed by the Minister of Agriculture, Fisheries and Food submit to him for confirmation a scheme for the constitution of new internal drainage districts and boards, the abolition or reconstitution of existing districts and boards, the abolition of commissioners of sewers, the alteration of boundaries of existing districts, the amalgamation of an existing district with another district, the making of alterations in or additions to local Acts and awards where this is necessary or expedient for enabling the area affected by the local Act or award to be drained effectively, and the transfer to a water authority or internal drainage board of any property, rights, powers, duties, obligations and liabilities vested in or to be discharged by the water authority or internal drainage board affected by the scheme. The scheme is subject to confirmation by the Minister by order.[2]

(3) *Order for transfer of functions to water authority*

On a petition presented in that behalf to the Minister of Agriculture, Fisheries and Food by a water authority, he may by order transfer to the authority the powers, duties, liabilities,

---

[1] Land Drainage Act, 1976, s. 10.
[2] *Ibid.*, s. 11.

obligations and property (including maps, deeds and other documents) of the drainage board of any internal drainage district, and thereupon the water authority shall become the drainage board of that district.[1]

(4) Orders for transfer to internal drainage board of functions conferred or transferred

Where, whether by virtue of a scheme under section 11 of the Land Drainage Act, 1976, or an order under section 12 thereof, a water authority are the drainage board of an internal drainage district and a petition for constituting an internal drainage board for that district is made to the water authority by a sufficient number of qualified persons, *i.e.* owners and occupiers of land in the district in respect of which a drainage rate is levied,[2] or by a rating authority in whose case an agreement made with the drainage board of the district under section 81 of the Land Drainage Act, 1976, is in force, the Minister of Agriculture, Fisheries and Food may by order constitute an internal drainage board for that district and transfer to it the property and liabilities of the water authority vested in or incurred by them in their capacity as the drainage board for that district.   The water authority must send a copy of the petition to the Minister, who will consider the views of the authority before making an order.[3]

Review of boundaries, supervision and exercise of functions in default

(1) Review of boundaries of internal drainage district

Where the boundaries of an internal drainage district in a water authority area have for a period exceeding ten years been neither altered nor reviewed as hereafter mentioned, the water authority must review those boundaries on a petition for their alteration being made to the authority by a sufficient number[4] of owners and occupiers of land in the district in respect of

---

[1] Land Drainage Act, 1976, s. 12.
[2] " Sufficient number of qualified persons ", *see* further s. 116 (2) of the Land Drainage Act, 1976.
[3] Land Drainage Act, 1976, s. 13.
[4] " Sufficient number of qualified persons ", *see* s. 116 (2) of the Land Drainage Act, 1976.

which a drainage rate is levied or by a rating authority in whose case an agreement made with the drainage board of the district under section 81 of the Land Drainage Act, 1976, is in force. On receiving a petition the water authority must inform the Minister of Agriculture, Fisheries and Food and give notice in one or more local newspapers that representations may be made to the water authority. In carrying out a review the water authority is required to consult the internal drainage board and to consider any representations duly made to them, and within six months after the petition was made or such longer time as the Minister may allow the water authority must inform the Minister whether, as a result of the review, they propose to submit to him a scheme under section 11 of the Land Drainage Act, 1976. A water authority is not required to carry out a review or publish a notice on a petition which in the opinion of the Minister is frivolous.[1]

(2) *Supervision of internal drainage boards and districts*

A water authority may for securing the efficient working and maintenance of existing drainage works within the area and the construction of such new drainage works as may be necessary, give such general or special directions as they consider reasonable for the guidance of the internal drainage boards with respect to their powers and duties as such.

A water authority may give consent (which is not to be unreasonably withheld) subject to reasonable conditions for an internal drainage board to construct drainage works or alter existing drainage works within the water authority area, if such will in any way affect the interests of, or the working of any drainage works belonging to, another internal drainage board. Any question as to whether the consent of the water authority is unreasonably withheld or whether any condition subject to which such consent was given was reasonable must be referred to the Minister of Agriculture, Fisheries and Food for decision. An internal drainage board may by agreement with the water authority construct or alter any structure, appliance or channel for the discharge of water from their district into the main river.

---

[1] Land Drainage Act, 1976, s. 14.

If an internal drainage board acts in contravention of the above provision, the water authority may themselves execute any works and do any things necessary to prevent or remedy any damage resulting from the action of the internal drainage board and recover from that board summarily as a civil debt the expenses reasonably incurred in exercising that power.[1]

(3) *Exercise by water authority of functions in default*

Where a water authority is of the opinion that any land in their area is injured or likely to be injured by flooding or inadequate drainage which might be remedied wholly or partially by an internal drainage board exercising its powers, and which either are not being exercised at all, or are not being exercised to the necessary extent, the water authority may exercise all or any of those powers. Before exercising such powers in default, the water authority is required to give thirty days' written notice of their intention to do so, and if the drainage board object, the water authority must obtain the consent of the Minister of Agriculture, Fisheries and Food before exercising the powers. The Minister may hold a public local inquiry with respect to the objection. In exercising the powers of an internal drainage board, a water authority is entitled to inspect and take copies of any deeds, maps, books and other documents in the possession of the internal drainage board relating to land drainage. A water authority may, on the application of the council of a county or London borough whose area is wholly or partly within the water authority area, direct that the powers conferred by this provision shall be exercised by that council instead of by the authority. If the water authority refuse the application, the council may appeal to the Minister, who may require the authority to comply with the application.[2]

POWERS OF DRAINAGE AUTHORITIES
Carrying out drainage works
(1) *General drainage powers*

Every drainage authority acting within their area are empowered to—

---

[1] Land Drainage Act, 1976, s. 15.
[2] *Ibid.*, s. 16.

K

(a) **Maintain existing works,** that is to say, cleanse, repair or otherwise maintain in a due state of efficiency an existing watercourse[1] or drainage work[2];

(b) **Improve existing works,** that is to say, deepen, widen, straighten or otherwise improve an existing watercourse, or remove or alter mill dams, weirs or other obstructions to watercourses, or raise, widen or otherwise improve any existing drainage work;

(c) **Construct new works,** that is to say, make a new watercourse or drainage work or erect machinery or do any other act not hereinbefore referred to, required for the drainage of the area.

These powers do not authorise a water authority to do any work otherwise than in connection with the main river, save that the power of a water authority to maintain, improve or construct drainage works against sea water or tidal water is exercisable anywhere in the water authority area, irrespective of whether they are works in connection with the main river, and the water authority area is deemed to extend beyond the low-water mark. Where a water authority area abuts on the sea or on an estuary the water authority concerned may construct all such works and do all such things in the sea or in that estuary as may, in their opinion, be necessary to secure an adequate outfall for the main river. A drainage authority desiring to execute drainage works for the benefit of their area in lands outside that area may exercise the powers conferred on landowners under section 93[3] of the Land Drainage Act, 1976.[4]

These powers do not impose a duty upon authorities to carry out drainage works, but merely confer a power to do so, and whether they exercise that power is a matter entirely within their own discretion.[5] If an authority decide not to exercise

---

1 " Watercourse " is defined in footnote 9 on p. 218.
2 As to " drainage work ", *see* footnote 4 on p. 218.
3 *See* p. 250.
4 Land Drainage Act, 1976, s. 17 (1)-(4).
5 *East Suffolk Catchment Board v. Kent* (1941), 105 J.P. 129; *Smith v. Cawdle Fen Comrs.*, [1938] 4 All E.R. 64; *Gillett v. Kent Rivers Catchment Board*, [1938] 4 All E.R. 810.

their powers they are not liable to a member of the public for damage he sustains by reason of the failure to exercise that power. Should the authority exercise their powers the only duty which they owe to a member of the public is not thereby to add to the damage that he would have suffered if they had done nothing.[1]

Section 17 does not authorise a person to enter on the land of any person except for the purpose of maintaining existing works,[2] but an authority requiring entry on land for improving existing works does not have to obtain consent of persons having only an incorporeal right in the water and not on the bank.[3]

Any development by a water authority established under the Water Act, 1973, in connection with the improvement, maintenance or repair of watercourses or drainage works constitutes permitted development under the Town and Country Planning General Development Order, 1977,[4] article 3, Schedule 1, class 16, and may be undertaken without planning permission being required.

(2) Compensation for injury

Where injury is sustained by a person by reason of a drainage board exercising its powers under section 34 of the Land Drainage Act, 1930, the board is liable to make full compensation to the injured person, and in case of dispute the amount of the compensation must be determined by the Lands Tribunal.[5] The word " injury " refers to actual damage as a result of work carried out by a board which would have been unlawful apart from the powers conferred by section 17 (1), and a person who sustains injury through drainage works has no right of action based on nuisance and his only remedy is a claim for compensation under section 17 (5).[6]

---

[1] *East Suffolk Catchment Board v. Kent, supra.*
[2] Land Drainage Act, 1976, s. 17 (6).
[3] *Proctor v. Avon & Dorset River Board* [1953], C.P.L. 562.
[4] S.I. 1977, No. 289, as amended by S.I. 1977 No. 1781.
[5] Land Drainage Act, 1976, s. 17 (5).
[6] *Marriage v. East Norfolk Rivers Catchment Board* (1949), 113 J.P. 362.

Section 17 (5) extends to injury sustained by a person by reason of an internal drainage board exercising the power of entry conferred by section 39 of the Land Drainage Act, 1976.[1]

But if damage is caused by work done under section 17 (1) in a negligent or unreasonable manner, or where the damage is caused by work not authorised thereby it seems that the remedy lies by an action based on negligence and not by a claim for compensation.[2] Provided that a board act within the scope of the powers conferred on them by section 17 (1), a riparian owner whose legal rights will thereby be violated, cannot bring an injunction in the absence of negligence by the board.[3]

The assessment of compensation due to a landowner for injury caused by a board in exercise of their powers under section 17 is not a condition precedent to the board exercising their powers, nor to make assessment a condition of the right of entry on the land.[4] Where claims for compensation under section 17 (5) in cases of dispute are referred to and determined by the Lands Tribunal, it is for the arbitrator to determine not only the *quantum* of compensation but also whether the claimant is entitled to compensation.[5] A reference to the Lands Tribunal under section 17 of the Land Drainage Act, 1976, and section 1 (3) (*b*) of the Lands Tribunal Act, 1949, is an arbitration under an Act of Parliament within the meaning of section 27 (6) of the Limitation Act, 1939, and a right to compensation may be barred by section 27 and section 2 (1) (*d*) of that Act; accordingly, a claim under section 17 must be brought within six years from the date on which the cause of action accrued.[6]

---

1 Land Drainage Act, 1976, s. 39 (4).
2 *Ash v. Great Northern, etc., Rl. Co.* (1903), 67 J.P. 417; *Roberts v. Charing Cross Rly.* (1903), 87 L.T. 732; *R. v. Darlington L.B.* (1865), 29 J.P. 419; *Coe v. Wise* (1866), 30 J.P. 484.
3 *Proctor v. Avon & Dorset River Board* [1953], C.P.L. 562; *Marriage v. East Norfolk River Catchment Board, supra.*
4 *Symes v. Essex Rivers Catchment Board* (1937), 101 J.P. 179.
5 *Marriage v. East Norfolk Rivers Catchment Board, supra; Rhodes v. Airedale Drainage Comrs.* (1876), 35 L.T. 46.
6 *Vincent v. Thames Conservators* (1953), 4 P. & C.R. 66; *see also Robson v. Northumberland & Tyneside River Board* (1952), 3 P. & C.R. 150, where the Statutes of Limitation were not invoked.

Other decisions on claims made under section 17 (5) against drainage boards include *Scutt & Screeton v. Lower Ouse Internal Drainage Board,*[1] *Lovegrove v. Isle of Wight River Board,*[2] *Jones v. Mersey River Board,*[3] *Oakes v. Mersey River Board,*[4] *Birch v. Ancholme Drainage Board,*[5] *Rippingale Farms Ltd. v. Black Sluice Internal Drainage Board,*[6] *Glazebrook v. Gwynedd River Board,*[7] *Burgess v. Gwynedd River Authority,*[8] *Welsh National Water Development Authority v. Burgess.*[9]

(3) *Maintenance of the flow of watercourses*

Where a watercourse is in such a condition that the proper flow of water is impeded, the drainage authority; *i.e.* in relation to a watercourse, not being main river, in an internal drainage district, the internal drainage board, and in relation to any other watercourse, the water authority, may by notice served on (1) a person having control of the part of the watercourse where the impediment occurs; or (2) the owner or occupier of land adjoining that part; or (3) a person to whose act or default the condition is due, require that condition to be remedied. The consent of the owner or occupier of the land must be obtained before a notice is served requiring a person to carry out work on land not owned or occupied by him. This provision does not apply where the condition is attributable to subsidence due to mining operations (including brine pumping), nor to a watercourse (not being main river) under the jurisdiction of a conservancy, harbour or navigation authority[10] which is exercising its powers except with the authority's consent.[11]

Drainage works concerning more than one drainage authority

(1) *Drainage works on boundary of water authority area*

Drainage works in connection with the main river may be carried out by a water authority on or near the boundary of

---

[1] (1953), 4 P. & C.R. 71.
[2] (1956), J.P.L. 211.
[3] [1957] 3 All E.R. 375.
[4] (1957), J.P.L. 824.
[5] (1958), J.P.L. 257.
[6] [1963] 1 W.L.R. 1347.
[7] (1964), 15 P. & C.R. 75.
[8] Ref. 18/1970 (1972) 24 P. & C.R. 150.
[9] (1974), J.P.L. 665.
[10] These authorities are defined in the footnotes on pp. 188 and 189.
[11] Land Drainage Act, 1976, ss. 18, 19.

their area notwithstanding that they are or include works in the area of another water authority, but where such works are works in connection with the main river of both water authority areas only one authority may carry out the works. If the water authorities fail to agree which of them is to carry out the works, the question must be determined by the Minister of Agriculture, Fisheries and Food. The water authority carrying out the works is entitled to such contribution towards the cost thereof from the other authority as may be agreed between them or in default of agreement, by the Minister.[1]

(2) *Arrangements between drainage authorities*

A water authority may enter into an agreement with an internal drainage board for the carrying out by the board, on such terms as to payment or otherwise as specified in the agreement, of any work in connection with the main river which the water authority are authorised to carry out, but not within another internal drainage district. Also, a drainage authority for any area may, with the consent of the drainage authority for an adjoining area, execute and maintain in the adjoining area any works which the first-mentioned authority might perform, on such terms as to payment or otherwise as may be agreed between the authorities, or may agree to contribute to the expenses of the execution or maintenance of works by the drainage authority of an adjoining area.[2]

Arrangements with other persons and powers as respects obligations and rights of other persons

(1) *Arrangements with other persons generally*

A drainage authority may by agreement with any person execute at his expense, whether within or outside their area, drainage works which that person is entitled to execute.[3]

(2) *Arrangements with certain authorities*

A water authority may enter into an agreement with the council of a county, district or London borough or with a

---

1 Land Drainage Act, 1976, s. 20.
2 *Ibid.*, s. 21.
3 *Ibid.*, s. 22.

navigation authority[1] for the carrying out by the council or authority, on such terms as to payment or otherwise as may be specified in the agreement, of any work in connection with the main river which the river authority are authorised to carry out.

With the approval of the Minister of Agriculture, Fisheries and Food and of the Secretary of State a drainage authority may, with a view to improving the drainage of their area, enter into an arrangement with a navigation or conservancy authority[2] for (a) transferring to the authority the whole or part of the undertaking, rights, powers, duties of, or property vested in, the navigation or conservancy authority as such; (b) the authority altering or improving any works of the navigation or conservancy authority; (c) the authority making payments to the navigation or conservancy or *vice versa* in respect of any matter provided for by the arrangement. The authority must give notice in the appropriate form of any intended arrangement, and, also, when an arrangement has been made.[3]

Note also that under the Water Resources Act, 1963, a water authority may apply to the Secretary of State and the Minister of Agriculture, Fisheries and Food acting jointly for an order transferring to the authority (*inter alia*) (a) any functions of a navigation, conservancy or harbour authority,[4] in so far as they are exercisable in the water authority area; (b) any property of any such authority which is situated in the

---

[1] " Navigation authority " means any person or body having powers under any Act of Parliament to work or maintain a canal or other inland navigation (including a navigation in tidal water (Land Drainage Act, 1976, s. 116 (1)).

[2] " Conservancy authority " includes all persons or bodies of persons, corporate or incorporate, entrusted with the duty or invested with the power of conserving, maintaining, or improving the navigation of a tidal river (Merchant Shipping Act, 1894, s. 742; Land Drainage Act, 1976, s. 116 (1)).

[3] Land Drainage Act, 1976, s. 23. *See* Land Drainage (River Authorities) General Regulations, 1965 (S.I. 1965 No. 443), reg. 5; Land Drainage (General) Regulations, 1932 (S.R. & O. 1932 No. 64), reg. 2.

[4] These authorities are defined in footnotes [2] and [3] on p.188 and footnote [1] on p. 189.

water authority area. Or a navigation, conservancy or harbour authority may themselves apply for an order.[1]

(3) *Enforcement of obligations to repair watercourses, bridges, etc.*

The Land Drainage Act, 1976, did not operate to release any person from any obligation to which he was before the passing of the Act subject by reason of tenure, custom, prescription or otherwise,[2] and the general wording of the Act did not transfer any such obligations.[3]

If a person, who by reason of any such obligation, is liable to do any work in relation to a watercourse, bridge or drainage work (whether by way of repair, maintenance or otherwise), fails to do the work, the drainage authority may serve a notice on that person requiring him to do the necessary work with all reasonable and proper dispatch. Should the person fail to comply with the notice within seven days the drainage board may do the work and recover their reasonable expenses so incurred.[4]

(4) *Variation of awards*

Where an award made under statute contains a provision affecting or relating to the drainage of land in a water authority area (including a provision affecting the powers or duties of a drainage body or other person as to the drainage of land) the water authority may, and must if so directed by the Minister of Agriculture, Fisheries and Food on an application as hereafter mentioned, submit to the Minister for confirmation a scheme for revoking, varying or amending that provision. The Minister may by order confirm the scheme with or without modifications.

---

[1] Water Resources Act, 1963, s. 82; Water Act, 1973, s. 40, Sch. 8, para. 83, Sch. 9. An order is made in accordance with the 1963 Act, Sch. 10 (*ibid.*, s. 82 (3)).

[2] Land Drainage Act, 1976, s. 24 (1).

[3] *North Level Comrs. v. River Welland Catchment Board* (1938), 102 J.P. 82; *see also A.-G. v. St. Ives R.D.C.*, [1961] 1 All E.R. 265; *see* further, REPAIR OF SEA WALLS AND RIVER BANKS, pp. 39 to 42.

[4] Land Drainage Act, 1976, s. 24 (2), (3).

An application may be made to the Minister for a direction as mentioned above by a person who is under an obligation imposed by the award or by a drainage authority, but an application cannot be entertained unless the applicant has requested the water authority to submit a scheme and the authority have either refused to do so within six months or have submitted a scheme different from that so requested.[1]

(5) Commutation of obligations

Where a person is under an obligation imposed on him by reason of tenure, custom, prescription or otherwise to do any work in connection with the drainage of land (whether by way of repairing banks or walls, maintaining watercourses or otherwise) then (a) if the work is in connection with the main river, the water authority for the area concerned must take steps to commute the obligation; and (b) in any other case, the water authority or the internal drainage board for the internal drainage district concerned, may commute the obligation with the consent of the Minister of Agriculture, Fisheries and Food. The obligations do not extend to purely contractual obligations,[2] nor to voluntary payments paid under contract.[3] Where a water authority or internal drainage board propose to commute an obligation to which this provision applies they are required to give in such manner as the Minister may direct,[4] a notice of any proposal to commute any such obligation, the terms on which it is to be commuted and of the time within which objection to the proposal may be made. The person on whom the obligation is imposed may within one month of the notice notify the authority of his objection to the proposal and the question whether the authority shall proceed to commute the obligation must be referred to the Minister whose decision is final.[5]

---

[1] Land Drainage Act, 1976, s. 25.
[2] *Eton R.D.C.* v. *Thames Conservators* (1950), 114 J.P. 279.
[3] *Re Fitzherbert Brockhole's Agreement, River Wyre Catchment Board v. Miller* (1939), 103 J.P. 379.
[4] *See* the Land Drainage (General) Regulations, 1932 (S.R. & O. 1932, No. 64), regs. 1, 8; the Land Drainage (River Authorities) General Regulations, 1965 (S.I. 1965 No. 443), reg. 4.
[5] Land Drainage Act, 1976, s. 26.

(6) *Power to vary navigation rights*

A drainage authority may apply to the Minister of Agriculture, Fisheries and Food in the case of a navigation authority which is not exercising at all, or is not exercising to the necessary extent, the powers vested in it, to revoke, vary or amend by order the provisions of any local Act relating to navigation rights over, or to the powers and duties of the navigation authority[1] with respect to, any canal, river or navigable waters within the drainage district. The order may be made by the Minister if it appears desirable with a view to securing the better drainage of any land, and after consultation with the Secretary of State, but an order cannot be made so as to affect tidal waters[2] except with the consent of the Secretary of State for Trade.[3]

Control of obstructions in and structures in, over or under watercourses

(1) *Obstructions in watercourses*

A person must not (*a*) erect a mill dam, weir or other like obstruction to the flow of a watercourse (not being part of the main river) or raise or otherwise alter any such obstruction in a drainage authority area; (*b*) erect a culvert that would be likely to affect the flow of a watercourse (not being main river) or alter a culvert in a manner that would be likely to affect any such flow, without the consent in writing (not to be unreasonably withheld) of the drainage authority. If the drainage authority fail within two months after receiving an application for consent to notify the applicant in writing of their decision, the authority are deemed to have consented thereto. Any question as to whether the consent is unreasonably withheld shall be referred to arbitration. An obstruction with is erected or raised or otherwise altered in contravention of this provision is deemed to be a nuisance, and the drainage authority may serve a notice on the person by whom the obstruction has been erected or

---

1 " Navigation authority " means any person or body having powers under any Act of Parliament to work or maintain a canal or other inland navigation (including a navigation in tidal waters) (Land Drainage Act, 1976, s. 116 (1)).

2 " Tidal waters " means any waters within the ebb and flow of the tide at ordinary spring tides (*ibid.*, s. 27 (4)).

3 *Ibid.*, s. 27.

raised or otherwise altered, requiring him to abate the nuisance within a specified time, and if that person makes default in so doing, the authority shall cause a complaint relating to the nuisance to be made before a justice, who shall thereupon issue a summons requiring that person to appear before the magistrates' court. These powers do not apply to works under the control of a navigation authority,[1] harbour authority[1] or conservancy authority,[1] or to works executed or maintained under statutory powers.[2]

(2) Structures in, over or under watercourses

A person cannot (i) erect a structure in, over or under a watercourse which is part of the main river, nor (ii) erect or alter a structure designed to contain or divert the floodwaters of any part of the main river, except with the consent of and in accordance with plans and sections approved by the water authority; and (iii) a person cannot, without the consent of the water authority, carry out any works of alteration or repair on a structure in, over or under such a watercourse if the work is likely to affect the flow of water in the watercourse or to impede a drainage work. These restrictions under heads (i) and (iii) above do not apply (1) to a work executed under section 15 of the Public Health Act, 1936, or sections 19 or 20 of Schedule 3 to the Water Act, 1945 (which relate to the provision of sewers and water mains); or (2) to a work executed in an emergency, but the person executing emergency work must as soon as practicable inform the water authority.

A consent or approval is not to be unreasonably withheld and consent may be given subject to reasonable conditions as to the time at which and the manner in which a work is to be carried out. Consent or approval which is neither given nor refused within two months after application therefor is made is deemed to have been given. Any question whether consent or approval is unreasonably withheld or whether a condition imposed is reasonable must (a) if the parties agree to arbitration, be referred to a single arbitrator agreed between

---

[1] These authorities are defined in the footnotes on pp. 188 and 189.
[2] Land Drainage Act, 1976, s. 28.

them or, in default of agreement, appointed by the President of the Institute of Civil Engineers; (b) if the parties do not agree to arbitration, be referred to and determined by the Minister of Agriculture, Fisheries and Food and the Secretary of State acting jointly.

If a person executes work in contravention of this provision the water authority may remove, alter or pull down the work and recover from that person the expenses incurred in doing so. Nothing herein shall affect any enactment requiring the consent of a Government department for erecting a bridge or any powers exercisable by a Government department in relation to a bridge.[1]

Schemes for drainage of small areas

Where the council of a county or London borough or a water authority (hereafter called " the authority ") are of opinion that land within their area is capable of improvement by drainage works, but that the constitution of an internal drainage district would not be practicable for that purpose, the authority may make a scheme for executing such drainage works as appear to them desirable. Before an authority other than a water authority make a scheme they have to consult the water authority. The estimated expenses of the scheme must not exceed £50 for each hectare, but the Minister of Agriculture, Fisheries and Food may exempt a scheme from that limit if it appears to him that the works proposed are urgently required in the public interest, and he may by order approved by a resolution of each House of Parliament vary that limit.

The owners and occupiers of land within the area to which the scheme relates, and any other persons who appear to be affected by the scheme, must be notified in the prescribed manner[2] by the authority of their intention to make the scheme and of the time within which objections to the scheme may be made. In the event of objections being made, the scheme cannot be made unless the draft scheme is confirmed by the

---

[1] Land Drainage Act, 1976, s. 29.
[2] *I.e.*, as the Minister may prescribe by the Drainage Schemes (Notices) Regulations, 1965 (S.I. 1965 No. 445).

Minister after holding a public inquiry or hearing. The scheme has to be registered in the register of local land charges.[1] In relation to any works executed in pursuance of a scheme a council have all the powers (exercisable subject to the same restrictions) of an internal drainage board under sections 17 and 33 of the Land Drainage Act, 1976. The expenses incurred by an authority in executing drainage works (up to the maximum amount recoverable by the authority as stated in the scheme), and any expenses for maintaining such works, are recoverable by the authority from the several owners of the lands to which the scheme relates according to the apportionment provided for by the scheme.[2]

Flood warning systems

A water authority are empowered (a) to provide and operate a flood warning system for their area; (b) both within and outside their area to provide, install and maintain apparatus required for the purposes of such a system; (c) to carry out within their area any other engineering or building operations[3] so required; and (d) to adapt for the purposes of such a system any apparatus or works to which a hydrometric scheme[4] made by the authority relates. Before exercising within the area of another water authority any power conferred under head (b) above other than the power to maintain apparatus, the water authority must consult with that other authority. A flood warning system is defined as meaning any system whereby, for the purpose of providing warning of any danger of flooding, information respecting rainfall[5] as measured at a particular place within a particular period, or the level or flow of an inland water[6] at a particular time, or other matters appearing

---

[1] See the Local Land Charges Rules, 1977 (S.I. 1977 No. 985).

[2] Land Drainage Act, 1976, ss. 30, 31, as amended by the Land Drainage Act 1976 (Amendment) Regulations, 1978 (S.I. 1978 No. 319). For local authorities, see s. 100.

[3] " Engineering or building operations " includes the construction, alteration, improvement, maintenance or demolition of any building or structure, and the installation, modification or removal of any machinery or apparatus (Land Drainage Act, 1976, s. 32 (5)).

[4] As to hydrometric schemes, see p. 180.

[5] " Rainfall " includes any fall of snow, hail or sleet (Land Drainage Act, 1976, s. 32 (5)).

[6] " Inland water " is defined in footnote 5 on p. 177.

to the authority to be relevant for that purpose, is obtained and transmitted, whether automatically or otherwise, with or without provision for carrying out calculations based on any such information and for transmitting the results of such calculations.[1]

Incidental powers

(1) *Disposal of spoil*

A drainage authority may, without making payment therefor, appropriate and dispose of any matter removed in the course of executing any work for widening, deepening or dredging a watercourse, and may deposit any matter so removed on the banks[2] of the watercourse, or on such width of land adjoining the watercourse as is sufficient to enable the matter to be removed and deposited by mechanical means in one operation, unless the matter so deposited would constitute a nuisance under Part III of the Public Health Act, 1936. Where injury is sustained by a person by reason of a drainage authority exercising their powers in depositing matter, the authority may compensate him, and if the injury could have been avoided if those powers had been exercised with reasonable care, the authority is liable to make full compensation to the injured party under section 17 (5)[3] of the Land Drainage Act, 1976. A drainage authority and a local authority may enter into an agreement for the local authority to dispose of matter removed as aforesaid on payment by the drainage authority.[4]

(2) *Byelaws*

A drainage authority may make byelaws for securing the efficient working of the drainage system in their area or district, and in particular for—

> (*a*) Regulating the use and preventing the improper use of watercourses, banks or works vested in or under

---

1 Land Drainage Act, 1976, s. 32. As to grants for flood warning systems, *see* p. 250. As to power of Greater London Council to provide flood warning system, *see* p. 252.

2 " Banks " is defined in footnote 3 on p. 218. On the meaning of " banks ", *see Jones v. Mersey River Board*, [1957] 3 All E.R. 375; *Oakes v. Mersey River Board* (1957), J.P.L. 824. *See also* pp. 9 and 10.

3 *See* p. 225.

4 Land Drainage Act, 1976, s. 33.

their control or for preserving the same from damage or destruction; but such byelaws must not prevent reasonable facilities being afforded to enable a watercourse being used by stock for drinking purposes;

(b) Regulating the opening of sluices and floodgates in connection with the above works;

(c) Preventing the obstruction of a watercourse vested in or under their control by the discharge of any liquid or solid matter into the watercourse or by reason of such matter being allowed to flow or fall into it;

(d) Compelling persons having control of a watercourse vested in or under the control of the board or of any watercourse flowing into the same, to cut vegetable growths in or on the bank of the watercourse and, when cut, to remove them.

In addition, a water authority may make such byelaws as the authority consider necessary for securing the proper defence against sea water or tidal water of any part of their area.

A person who contravenes, or fails to comply with, any byelaw is liable on summary conviction to a fine not exceeding £400 and a further fine not exceeding £40 for every day on which the contravention or failure is continued after conviction. If a person acts in contravention of, or fails to comply with, any byelaw, the drainage authority may, without prejudice to any proceedings before mentioned, take such action as may be necessary to remedy the effect of the contravention or failure, and may recover the expenses reasonably incurred by them in doing so from the person in default. No byelaw shall conflict or interfere with the operation of byelaws made by a navigation, harbour or conservancy authority.[1] Byelaws are made in accordance with Schedule 4 to the Land Drainage Act, 1976.

(3) *Power of water authorities to acquire accretions of land resulting from drainage works*

If the Minister of Agriculture, Fisheries and Food certifies that, as a result of drainage works executed or proposed to

---

[1] Land Drainage Act, 1976, s. 34.

be executed by a water authority in connection with the tidal waters of the main river or any drainage works transferred from a drainage body to the water authority, there has been or is likely to be an accretion of land, the water authority may acquire either by agreement or compulsorily such accretion or land to which it will be accreted and other land reasonably required for reclaiming the accretion or for its enjoyment when reclaimed.[1]

(4) *Power of internal drainage board to acquire land*

An internal drainage board is empowered, for any purpose in connection with the performance of any of its functions to acquire land,[2] whether inside or outside its area, by agreement or compulsorily if authorised by the Minister of Agriculture, Fisheries and Food. These powers include the acquisition of interests in or rights over land by way of securing the creation of new interests or rights as well as by acquiring interests or rights already in existence.[3] An internal drainage board may also dispose of land held, but, except in the case of a letting or assignment not exceeding seven years, the consent of the Minister is required (*a*) where land is disposed of for a consideration less than the best that can reasonably be obtained; and (*b*) where the land being disposed of was acquired under compulsory powers.[4] A water authority can acquire land for any of its functions under sections 65 and 66 of the Water Resources Act, 1963.[5]

(5) *Powers of entry of internal drainage boards*

Without prejudice to any other enactment conferring powers of entry, a person authorised by an internal drainage board may, after producing his authority if so required, enter land, and take with him other persons and necessary equipment, for exercising any function of the board. Except in an emergency, admission to land cannot be demanded as of right, unless

---

1 Land Drainage Act, 1976, s. 36.
2 " Land " includes water and any interests in land or water and any easement or right in, to or over land or water (Land Drainage Act, 1976, s. 116 (1)).
3 *Ibid.*, s. 37; *see also* the Internal Drainage Boards (Acquisition of New Interests and Rights) Regulations, 1977 (S.I. 1977 No. 84).
4 *Ibid.*, s. 38.
5 *See* p. 166.

written notice of intended entry has been given to the occupier, and, if the land is used for residential purposes, or admission is demanded with heavy equipment, has been given not less than seven days before the demand is made. Compensation is payable under section 17 (5) of the Land Drainage Act, 1976, for injury sustained by reason of the exercise of the power of entry. Anyone intentionally obstructing or impeding a person exercising the above rights is liable to a fine not exceeding £200.[1]

RESTORATION AND IMPROVEMENT OF DITCHES

(1) *Power of Agricultural Land Tribunal to order cleansing of ditches, etc.*

Where a ditch[2] is in such condition as to cause injury to, or to prevent the improvement of the drainage of, any land, the Agricultural Land Tribunal[3] may, on the application of the owner or occupier of the land, order the owner or occupier of the land abutting on or through which the ditch passes, or any other person having a right to carry out the work specified in the order, to cleanse the ditch, remove matter impeding the flow of water therein or otherwise put it in proper order and protect is as specified in the order. The order is sufficient authority for the person named therein to do the work specified therein and to enter land so specified.[4] Where work specified in an order has not been carried out at the expiration of three months or such longer time as specified in the order, the Minister of Agriculture, Fisheries and Food or a drainage body authorised by him may carry out the work, and enter any land which it is necessary to enter for that purpose, and may also recover from the person named in the order the

---

[1] Land Drainage Act, 1976, s. 39. *See also Pattinson v. Finningley I.D.B.* [1970] 1 All E.R. 790 (under the Land Drainage Act, 1961, s. 40 (1), a drainage board could enter land to exercise any function and not merely to maintain existing works).
[2] " Ditch " includes a culverted and a piped ditch but does not include a watercourse vested in or under the control of a drainage body (Land Drainage Act, 1976, s. 40 (4)).
[3] As to composition and powers of the Tribunal for hearing applications, *see* s. 42 of the Land Drainage Act, 1976.
[4] Land Drainage Act, 1976, s. 40.

reasonable expenses incurred in doing the work which ought to have been done by him.[1]

(2) *Power of Agricultural Land Tribunal to authorise drainage works on adjoining land*

Where the drainage of any land requires work to be carried out in connection with a ditch passing through other land, or the replacement or construction of such a ditch, or the alteration or removal of any drainage work in connection therewith, the Agricultural Land Tribunal may on the application of the owner or occupier of the land to be drained make an order authorising him to carry out such work specified in the order and for that purpose to enter any land so specified.[2]

(3) *Supplementary provisions as to powers of entry and compensation*

A person entitled under Part III of the Land Drainage Act, 1976, to enter land may take with him such other persons and equipment as may be necessary, but before entry not less than seven days' notice in writing must be given to the occupier. A person who sustains injury by reason of the exercise of any power conferred under Part III, apart from a power exercised in or for the purpose of the execution of work required by an order under Part III, is entitled to full compensation from the person exercising the power, and in case of dispute the amount of compensation must be determined by the Lands Tribunal.[3]

RAISING OF REVENUE BY DRAINAGE AUTHORITIES

Power of water authorities to require payment of their land drainage expenses by local authorities

Not later than the February immediately preceding each financial year[4] each water authority has to estimate the amount

---

[1] Land Drainage Act, 1976, s. 43.
[2] *Ibid.*, s. 41.
[3] *Ibid.*, s. 44.
[4] Financial year, *i.e.* year ending on 31st March.

of the " qualifying expenses "[1] for that year in respect of each local land drainage district in their area and apportion the estimated amount among the councils of the counties or London boroughs any part of whose area is comprised in that district on the basis of the estimated penny rate product[2] for that year for the respective relevant areas.

The estimated penny rate product as determined for any area for any year, and any information relevant to such determination which may be specified in the rules under which the determination is made,[3] must be notified to the water authority at such time and in such manner as may be so specified.

A water authority may issue precepts to local authorities requiring payment of the amounts apportioned, and must prepare in such form as the Minister may direct a statement of the purposes to which the amount demanded by the precept issued is intended to be applied and of the basis on which it is calculated. A local authority shall not be liable to pay the amount demanded by precept until they have received a statement.

If at any time during a financial year it appears to a water authority that the aggregate amount for which they have issued precepts for that year in respect of a local land drainage

---

[1] " Qualifying expenses " are ascertained in accordance with s. 45 of the Land Drainage Act, 1976. In general terms these expenses consist of over a financial year—

the expenses of performing the land drainage functions of a water authority (excluding expenditure paid for out of any reserve, replacement or sinking fund or by local authority precept)

PLUS

an appropriate proportion of the expenses of administration, research and related activities, any amounts allocated to reserve and payments defraying National Water Council expenditure

PLUS

any new working capital required

PLUS or MINUS

any excess or deficiency from the aggregate amount brought forward from a previous financial year.

[2] For calculation of estimated and actual penny rate, *see* s. 45 (3) of the Land Drainage Act, 1976.

[3] That is, the rules made under s. 113 (1) (*c*) of the General Rate Act, 1967.

district will fall short of the qualifying expenses for that year, the authority must estimate the amount of the deficiency and apportion the estimated amount in the same way as the amount estimated for qualifying expenses and issue precepts for the estimated amount of the deficiency.

The aggregate amount for which precepts in respect of a local land drainage district may be issued for any one financial year to a local authority must not, unless special consent[1] has been obtained, exceed 1.7 times the appropriate penny rate for that part of the area of the local authority as is comprised in the local land drainage district for the financial year in which the precept is to be issued.   Where a water authority borrow money under the Water Act, 1973, if a special resolution[1] is passed, the foregoing provision has effect during the currency of the loan, as if for the refernece to 1.7 times the appropriate penny rate there is substituted a reference to such greater amount as may be specified in the resolution.

A water authority is required as soon as practicable after the end of each financial year to calculate the excess or deficiency between the amount demanded by precept issued by the authority to a local authority in respect of a relevant area and the amount so demanded from the local authority under the apportionment of the estimated amount of the qualifying expenses.   If the calculation shows an excess such amount is recoverable by the local authority from the water authority, and if it shows a deficiency such amount is recoverable by the water authority from the local authority.[2]

As soon as practicable after the end of each financial year each water authority has to ascertain the actual amount of their qualifying expenses for that year for each local land drainage district in their area and determine whether and how far the aggregate amount for which precepts have been issued for that year to the local authorities exceeds or falls short of

---

[1] " Special consent " and " special resolution " mean respectively a consent given and resolution passed by a majority of the whole number of the local authority members of the local land drainage committee of the local land drainage district (Land Drainage Act, 1976, s. 46 (7)).
[2] Land Drainage Act, 1976, ss. 45, 46.

the actual amount of the qualifying expenses. Any excess or deficiency must be brought forward to the following financial year or the next financial year thereafter (at the option of the water authority) and deducted or added in ascertaining the qualifying expenses in respect of the district concerned for the financial year to which it is brought forward.[1]

Power of water authorities to raise drainage charges

A water authority may raise drainage charges at an amount per hectare of agricultural land and agricultural buildings in so much of their area as does not fall under an internal drainage district (excluding rough grazing land and woodlands other than commercial woodlands) and levied on the occupiers or owners of the land.[2]

A **general drainage charge** may be levied to raise revenue by a water authority at an amount per hectare of land in a local land drainage district on the occupiers, provided that the regional land drainage committee for the authority's area have recommended that the charge should be raised. The amount of the charge must be ascertained and particulars thereof specified in an order made by the Minister.[3]

A **special drainage charge** may be raised where it appears to a water authority that the interests of agriculture in the water authority's area or any part of it require drainage works to be carried out in connection with watercourses in the area. The water authority may submit to the Minister for confirmation a scheme designating the watercourses and any watercourses connected with them, and making provision for raising a special drainage charge to meet the expenses of drainage works in connection with the designated watercourses and expenses arising from such works.[4]

A scheme may designate the whole or any part of the water authority area for the purposes of the charge, and if the scheme

---

1 Land Drainage Act, 1976, s. 47.
2 *See* definitions in s. 89 of the Land Drainage Act, 1976.
3 Land Drainage Act, 1976, ss. 48, 49, as amended by the Land Drainage Act, 1976 (Amendment) Regulations, 1978 (S.I. 1978 No. 319).
4 *Ibid.*, s. 50 (1), (2).

is confirmed the designated watercourses are to be treated as part of the main river. Copies of the scheme must be sent to county and district councils affected, any internal drainage board and agricultural interests in the area. Before submitting a scheme a water authority have to consult agricultural interests in the area so designated, and a scheme which designates a watercourse within an internal drainage district must be submitted with a statement that the drainage board for that district have consented to the designation or that they have not consented together with reasons why the watercourse should nevertheless be designated. The Minister cannot confirm the scheme unless satisfied that it is reasonable and financially sound.[1] The amount of the charge is determined by the water authority's regional land drainage committee but must not exceed the maximum amount specified in the scheme or such greater amount as may be authorised by order made by the Minister on the application of the water authority, nor ten pence or such other amount as may be submitted by order made by the Minister by statutory instrument and approved by resolution of the House of Commons.[2]

A drainage charge is raised by resolution of a water authority for a year ending on the 31st March and before or during the year for which it is raised. The Minister is empowered to make regulations[3] prescribing the forms of drainage charge and of demands for drainage charges.[4] There are provisions for the publication, amendment and recovery of drainage charges, power to require information, reduced liability for drainage charges and other matters.[5]

Alternative power of water authorities to make water charges option order

At any time after 31st March, 1978, a water authority may apply to the Minister of Agriculture, Fisheries and Food for the Minister and the Secretary of State for the Environment

---

[1] Land Drainage Act, 1976, s. 50 (3)-(9).
[2] Ibid., s. 51.
[3] See the Drainage Charges (Forms) Regulations, 1969 (S.I. 1969 No. 469).
[4] Land Drainage Act, 1976, s. 53.
[5] See ibid., ss. 52, 54-61.

to make a charges option order which will have the effect that the powers to levy general drainage charges[1] and to raise precepts on local authorities[2] will cease to have effect in relation to the water authority's area and be repealed. When a water charges option order comes into force the appropriate provisions relating to financial provisions and the raising of water charges[3] shall apply to the water authority area in relation to their land drainage functions. The Ministers cannot make an order unless satisfied that the water authority's regional land drainage committee recommended the authority to make the application and that making the order would be in the public interest.[4]

Power of internal drainage boards to raise drainage rates

The expenses of an internal drainage board under the Land Drainage Act, 1976, or any other Act (including any contribution made by the board towards expenses of the water authority), in so far as they are not met by contributions from the water authority,[5] are raised by means of drainage rates, which are assessed and levied by the board on the occupiers of hereditaments in the drainage district. A drainage rate is either an **owner's rate** levied for defraying expenses incurred in connection with new works or the improvement of existing works and charges in respect of contributions to be made by the internal drainage board to the water authority, or an **occupier's rate** raised to defray any other expenses or charges. Both types of rates are assessed and levied on the occupier of hereditaments, who may recover from the owner any amount he has paid on account of an owner's drainage rate. After consultation with the water authority, an internal drainage board may levy differential rates in particular cases, or determine that no rates shall be levied in respect of hereditaments which by reason of their height above sea level or for any other reason ought to be wholly exempted.[6]

---

[1] *See* ss. 48, 49 of the Land Drainage Act, 1976.
[2] *See ibid.*, ss. 45-47.
[3] *See* ss. 29-32 of the Water Act, 1973; pp. 169-172.
[4] Land Drainage Act, 1976, s. 62.
[5] Under s. 84 (4) of the Land Drainage Act, 1976.
[6] Land Drainage Act, 1976, s. 63; *see also* s. 68.

The procedure as to the assessment, incidence, operation and recovery of drainage rates, the publication and amendment of rates, appeals against rates and rating in urban areas are dealt with in sections 64-83 of the Land Drainage Act, 1976.[1]

Miscellaneous revenue-raising powers

(1) *Contributions by internal drainage boards to water authorities and vice versa*

A water authority shall by resolution require each internal drainage board to make such contribution towards the expenses of the water authority as the latter considers fair. The water authority may issue a precept to the internal drainage boards requiring payment of the amount to be contributed, and must send with the precept a statement in a form[2] prescribed by the Minister of Agriculture, Fisheries and Food of the purposes to which the amount demanded by the precept is intended to be applied and of the basis upon which it is calculated. There is no obligation upon an internal drainage board to pay the amount demanded until the statement has been received, and the water authority may enforce compliance with the precept issued by *mandamus*. There is a right of appeal to the Minister by an internal drainage board or by the council of a county or London borough within or partly within the water authority area against the amount of the contribution. Where, whether by virtue of section 11 or 12 of the Land Drainage Act, 1976, a water authority are the drainage board of an internal drainage district, they may by resolution allocate a corresponding amount of revenue in lieu of making a contribution to the drainage board.

An internal drainage board may apply to the water authority for a contribution towards their expenses, if it appears to the internal drainage board that owing to the quantity of water which their district receives from land at a higher level, or by reason of the time which will elapse before their district

---

[1] *See also* the Drainage Rates (Forms) Regulations, 1977 (S.I. 1977 No. 357); the Drainage Rates (Appeals) Regulations, 1970 (S.I. 1970 No. 1152); the Registers of Drainage Boards Regulations, 1968 (S.I. 1968 No. 1672).

[2] *See* the River Authorities (Precepts on Internal Drainage Boards) Regulations, 1969 (S.I. 1969 No. 438); the Catchment Boards (Precepts) Regulations, 1962 (S.I. 1962 No. 548).

obtains relief from the operations of the water authority on the main river, it is fair that the water authority should contribute. The internal drainage board may appeal to the Minister of Agriculture, Fisheries and Food if the water authority refuse to contribute, or as to the amount of any contribution.[1]

(2) *Power of internal drainage boards to borrow*

With the sanction of the Minister of Agriculture, Fisheries and Food, an internal drainage board may borrow on the security of any property vested in them or rates to be levied by or contributions to be paid to them for the purpose of defraying the costs, charges or expenses incurred by them in the execution of the Land Drainage Act, 1976, or without the Minister's sanction to discharge loans contracted under the Land Drainage Act, 1976, or previous enactments repealed thereby. Money may be borrowed for such period not exceeding fifty years as the board, with the sanction of the Minister, may determine in each case.[2]

(3) *Power of drainage authorities to levy navigation tolls*

Where any navigable waters within a drainage authority area are not subject to the control of a navigation, harbour or conservancy authority[3] the drainage authority for the area may apply to the Secretary of State for the Environment for an order imposing tolls in respect of the navigation of vessels in those waters. An order cannot be made unless the Secretary of State is satisfied that the cost of the maintenance or works in connection with the waters in question has been or will be increased as a result of the use of such waters for purposes of

---

[1] Land Drainage Act, 1976, ss. 84-86.

[2] *Ibid.*, s. 87. As to borrowing by local authorities, *see* p. 253. For borrowing by water authorities, *see* p. 175.

[3] " Navigation authority " means any person or body having powers under any Act of Parliament to work or maintain a canal or other inland navigation (including a navigation in tidal water) (Land Drainage Act, 1976, s. 116 (1)). " Conservancy authority " includes all persons or bodies of persons, corporate or incorporate, entrusted with the duty or invested with the power of conserving, maintaining, or improving the navigation of a tidal river. " Harbour authority " includes all persons or bodies of persons, corporate or incorporate, being proprietors of, or interested with, the dealing or invested with the power of constructing, managing, regulating, maintaining, or lighting a harbour. (Merchant Shipping Act, 1894, s. 742; Land Drainage Act, 1976, s. 116 (1)).

navigation. Tolls payable in respect of the navigation of a vessel in such waters may be demanded from the person in charge of the vessel by an authorised person and, if not paid on demand, may be recovered from either the person in charge of the vessel or the owner thereof.[1]

POWERS OF THE MINISTER AND LOCAL AUTHORITIES

Powers of the Minister

(1) Grants to water authorities

Grants may be made by the Minister of Agriculture, Fisheries and Food towards the expenditure incurred by water authorities, in the improvement of existing drainage works[2] or the construction of new drainage works, of such amounts as the Treasury may from time to time sanction. But no grants will be made unless the plans for the improvement or construction have been approved by the Minister and he is satisfied that the work is being properly carried out, and grants are made subject to such conditions as may, with treasury approval, be prescribed.[3]

Grants may be made to water authorities by the Minister with Treasury approval (a) in advance of expenditure on drainage works approved under the preceding paragraph, and (b) on preliminary expenses on drainage works not subsequently carried out, and in respect of head (b) the Minister may with Treasury approval make advances to a water authority on account of the expenditure.[4]

The Minister may also, with Treasury approval, make grants and advances to water authorities towards expenditure incurred in connection with the improvement of existing works and the construction of new works for (a) the acquisition of land and rights over land under sections 65 and 66 of the Water Resources Act, 1963; (b) providing housing accommodation

---

[1] Land Drainage Act, 1976, s. 88.
[2] Grants are not available towards works of maintenance.
[3] Land Drainage Act, 1976, s. 90 (1), (2). See the Land Drainage (Grants) Regulations, 1967 (S.I. 1967 No. 212).
[4] Ibid., s. 90 (3)-(5).

for employees of a water authority[1] in controlling works which require the employee to reside in the vicinity of the works; (c) making payments for compensation under section 17 (5) of the Land Drainage Act, 1976; (d) paying compensation under section 33 (4) of the 1976 Act, for unavoidable injury arising from the deposit of matter on river banks. In addition, grants or advances can be made in executing works (other than maintenance works of a routine kind) for rebuilding or repairing bridges maintained by a water authority.[2]

Where a water authority under section 22 of the Land Drainage Act, 1976, execute by agreement with and at the expense of any other person, drainage works which that person is entitled to execute, the Minister may, with Treasury approval, make grants to the water authority in respect of the cost of works so executed by the authority.[3]

As to grants to water authorities by the Secretary of State under the Water Act, 1973, *see* p. 175. As to grants for flood warning systems, *see* p. 250.

(2) Grants to other drainage bodies

The Minister of Agriculture, Fisheries and Food may make grants of such amounts and subject to such conditions as may be approved by the Treasury towards expenditure incurred by internal drainage boards and all other drainage bodies except water authorities in carrying out drainage schemes.

Grants may be made to drainage bodies by the Minister with Treasury approval (a) in advance of expenditure on drainage works approved under the preceding paragraph, and (b) on preliminary expenses on drainage works not subsequently carried out, and in respect of head (b) the Minister may with Treasury approval make advances to a drainage body on account of the expenditure.

The Minister may also, with Treasury approval, make grants and advances to an internal drainage board towards expenditure in carrying out works (other than maintenance works of a

---

1 *See* the Water Act, 1973, s. 2 (8), Sch. 3, Part I, para. 13.
2 Land Drainage Act, 1976, s. 90 (6).
3 *Ibid.*, s. 90 (7).

routine kind) for rebuilding or repairing bridges maintained by a board.

Further, the Minister may, with Treasury approval, make grants to an internal drainage board or a local authority towards the cost of works executed by the board or authority under sections 22 or 99 of the Land Drainage Act, 1976 (which empower a board or authority by agreement to carry out drainage works for other persons).[1]

(3) Grants towards cost of flood warning systems

The Minister of Agriculture, Fisheries and Food may make grants, subject to conditions as he may impose with Treasury approval, of such amounts as the Treasury may sanction, towards expenditure incurred by water authorities or the Greater London Council in (a) providing or installing apparatus or carrying out other engineering or building operations for the purposes of a flood warning system, or (b) adapting for such purposes apparatus or works to which a hydrometric scheme relates. No grants are payable in respect of any work unless it has been approved by the Minister and he is satisfied that it is properly carried out. The Minister may with Treasury approval make advances on account of expenditure about to be incurred.[2]

(4) Power to authorise landowners to execute drainage works

Where a person is unable to execute drainage works which would improve his land by reason of the objection or disability of another person whose land would be affected by the works, he may apply in the prescribed form[3] to the Minister of Agriculture, Fisheries and Food for an order authorising him to execute such works.[4]

---

[1] Land Drainage Act, 1976, s. 91.
[2] Ibid., s. 92. As to flood warning systems, see p. 235.
[3] See the Land Drainage (General Regulstions) 1932 (S.R. & O. 1932 No. 64), reg. 6.
[4] Land Drainage Act, 1976, s. 93.

(5) *Other powers of the Minister*

The Minister of Agriculture, Fisheries and Food is empowered for the purposes of the Land Drainage Act, 1976, to—

(a) provide by regulations[1] for the payment of compensation to officers or other employees of a drainage body, internal drainage board or water authority who suffer loss of employment or diminution of emoluments attributable to specified provisions of the Act[2];

(b) make regulations for prescribed matters[3];

(c) hold inquiries as necessary or desirable.[4]

Powers of local authorities

(1) *General drainage powers*

The council of a county, district or London borough as respects any land which is within their area have all the powers conferred on internal drainage boards by section 18 of the Land Drainage Act, 1976, relating to the maintenance of watercourses, but where a watercourse is in a water authority area the council must first notify the water authority or internal drainage board.[5]

(2) *Powers to undertake drainage works against flooding*

For the purpose of preventing flooding or remedying or mitigating damage caused by flooding the council of a district or London borough are given all the powers conferred on drainage boards by sections 17 (1), (4),[6] 33[7] and 34[8] of the Land Drainage Act, 1976, and those councils may acquire land compulsorily in the exercise of these powers. Provision is made for county councils to exercise these functions where they are not exercised by district councils. Under this provision a

---

1 *See* the Land Drainage (Compensation) Regulations, 1977 (S.I. 1977 No. 339).
2 Land Drainage Act, 1976, s. 94.
3 *Ibid.*, s. 95.
4 *Ibid.*, s. 96.
5 *Ibid.*, s. 97.
6 *See* p. 224.
7 *See* p. 236.
8 *See* p. 237.

council cannot execute drainage works in connection with the main river, nor execute drainage works in connection with a watercourse except with the consent (which is not to be unreasonably withheld) of and in accordance with reasonable conditions imposed by the water authority. Any question whether the consent of a water authority is unreasonably withheld or whether conditions thereby imposed are reasonable must be referred to and determined by the Minister of Agriculture, Fisheries and Food and the Secretary of State acting jointly.[1]

(3) *Power to execute drainage works by agreement with other persons*

The council of a county or London borough (and the Greater London Council as regards the main metropolitan watercourses) may by agreement with any person execute at his expense, within the council's area, any drainage works which he is entitled to execute.[2]

(4) *Schemes for drainage of small areas*

The provisions of section 30[3] of the Land Drainage Act, 1976, apply to the council of a county or London borough besides a water authority, and before making a scheme the council must consult the water authority for the area concerned. In relation to works executed under a scheme, a council is given the powers of an internal drainage board under sections 17[4] (general drainage powers) and 33[5] (disposal of spoil) of the Act.[6]

(5) *Power of Greater London Council to provide flood warning system*

The G.L.C. has power to provide and operate a flood warning system for the London excluded area, subject to consultation with the water authority as to the installation of any apparatus.[7]

---

[1] Land Drainage Act, 1976, s. 98.
[2] *Ibid.*, s. 99.
[3] *See* p. 234.
[4] *See* p. 223.
[5] *See* p. 236.
[6] Land Drainage Act, 1976, s. 100.
[7] *Ibid.*, s. 101.

(6) *Power to contribute to expenses of drainage works*

A local authority may contribute towards the expenses of the execution or maintenance of drainage works by a drainage body such amount as appears to the local authority to be proper, having regard to the public benefit to be derived therefrom.[1]

(7) *Powers of entry*

Section 39[2] of the Land Drainage Act, 1976, applies to local authorities and their functions under that Act as it applies to, and to the functions of, internal drainage boards.[3]

(8) *Power to borrow*

The council of a county or London borough may borrow for the purposes of the Land Drainage Act, 1976.[4]

---

[1] Land Drainage Act, 1976, s. 102.
[2] *See* p. 238.
[3] Land Drainage Act, 1976, s. 103.
[4] *Ibid.*, s. 104.

CHAPTER 13

FISHERIES AT COMMON LAW

TYPES OF FISHERIES

The kinds of fisheries more commonly encountered are several fishery, common fishery, common of fishery, free fishery, territorial fishery, exclusive fishery and corporeal and incorporeal fisheries.

A fishery, which is a right to fish in one's own, or in another person's water, may exist either apart from or as incident to the ownership of the soil over which the water flows.[1] The general principle is that fisheries are in their nature mere profits of the soil over which the water flows and that the title to a fishery arises from the right to the soil.[2] Where the soil under the water and the right to fish in the water are in the same ownership the fishery is known as a **corporeal** or **territorial** fishery, but if the fishery is severed from the soil it becomes a *profit a prendre in alieno solo* and an **incorporeal** hereditament or fishery. A person may be the owner of a corporeal fishery although he has no land adjacent thereto.[3]

A person who has the sole and exclusive right of fishing either with or without the soil is said to have an **exclusive, several** or **free**, right of fishery, and the expressions " sole and exclusive " and " free " are taken to be equivalent to a several fishery.[4]

Common fishery is the right of the public to fish in tidal waters and common of fishery is a right for one or more persons to fish in common with the owner of the fishery.

---

[1] *Hanbury v. Jenkins*, [1901] 2 Ch. 401.
[2] *A.-G. for British Columbia v. A.-G. for Canada*, [1914] A.C. 153.
[3] *Marshall v. Ulleswater Steam Navigation Co.* (1863), 3 B. & S. 732.
[4] *Holford v. Bailey* (1849), 13 Q.B. 426; *Gipps v. Woollicot* (1697), 3 Salk. 360; *Malcomson v. O'Dea* (1863), 10 H.L.C. 593.

Any apparent conflict between the variety of these terms can be narrowed down by the classification of rights of fisheries and fishing into (1) public fisheries, or the public right of fishery in the sea and tidal waters where not appropriated as a several fishery, and (2) private fisheries comprising several fisheries and common of fishery.

Originally tidal and non-tidal fisheries were vested in the Crown as the owner of the kingdom. Whilst a several fishery in tidal waters may have been granted by the Crown to a subject before Magna Charta, the Crown retained the soil and fishing of many such fisheries as parcels of manors as part of the Crown estates. Where a non-tidal fishery was granted by the Crown to a subject as parcel of a manor, the owner might sell the soil and fishery as a whole or in parts, or retain the soil and convey an incorporeal fishery, or create a common of fishery by permitting other persons to fish with him.

PUBLIC FISHERIES

The subjects of the Crown are entitled as of right not only to navigate but to fish in tidal waters, whether on the high seas, the foreshore or in creeks, estuaries and tidal rivers, and by reason of the provisions of Magna Charta no restriction can be put upon that right of the public by an exercise of the prerogative in the form of a grant or otherwise.[1]

Fishing on the high seas and in tidal waters

The right to fish on the high seas is open and common to everyone without any limitations, apart from special custom or usage of a particular country,[2] and except such restrictions as have been imposed by Act of Parliament or in accordance with conventions with foreign states as confirmed by statute.[3]

---

[1] A.-G. for British Columbia v. A.-G. for Canada, [1914] A.C. 153.

[2] Hogarth v. Jackson (1827), 2 C. & P. 595; Fennings v. Grenville (Lord) (1808), 1 Taunt. 241.

[3] A.-G. for British Columbia v. A.-G. for Canada, supra; Smith v. Cooke (1914), 112 L.T. 864.

Formerly, within the limits of territorial waters, *i.e.* a distance of three nautical miles measured from low water mark,[1] by international law the public as subjects of the realm had the right to fish to the exclusion of the subjects of other states,[2] except where a tidal fishery was known to exist, and subject to any restrictions imposed by Parliament.[3] Since the right of fishing in the sea is common to all the Queen's subjects, a prescription for such a right annexed to certain tenements is bad.[4]

Now under the Fishery Limits Act, 1976, British fishery limits extend to 200 miles from the baselines from which the breadth of the territorial sea adjacent to the United Kingdom, the Channel Islands and the Isle of Man is measured. Foreign fishing boats registered in a country designated by order may fish in areas within British fishery limits designated in the order and for descriptions of fish so registered. Foreign fishing boats not so registered cannot enter British fishery limits except for a purpose (and only during its fulfilment) recognised by international law or by a convention between Her Majesty's Government in the United Kingdom and the government of the country to which the boat belongs and the boat cannot fish or attempt to fish while within the limits.[5]

Fishery on the foreshore

The public right to fish in tidal waters *prima facie* includes the right to fish upon the seashore between high and low water mark, unless such general right is abridged by the existence of an exclusive right to fish in some individual.[6] The ownership of the foreshore is *prima facie* vested in the Crown, subject to the public rights of fishing and navigation which are the only public rights known to the common law

---

[1] Territorial Waters Jurisdiction Act, 1878, s. 7; *see also* the *Anglo-Norwegian Fisheries Case*, [1952] 1 T.L.R. 181.

[2] *R. v. Keyn* (1876), 2 Ex D. 63.

[3] *See* the Sea Fisheries Regulation Act, 1966; the Sea Fisheries (Shellfish) Act, 1967.

[4] *Ward v. Creswell* (1741), Willes 265.

[5] *See* further p. 19.

[6] *Bagott v. Orr* (1801), 2 Bos. & P. 472.

in the sea itself.[1] The public have no rights over the fore-shore when not covered by the tide, except such as are ancillary to their rights of fishing and navigation in the sea; when covered by the tide the foreshore is part of the sea and the only rights of the public in or over it are the rights of fishing and navigation and rights ancillary thereto.[1]

The public common law rights with respect to the sea independent of usage are rights upon the water, not upon the land, of passage and fishing on the sea and on the fore-shore, when covered with water; and in order to exercise those rights, the public have a means of getting to and upon the water only by and from such places as have been appointed by necessity and usage. The public have no general right of lading, unlading, landing or embarking where they please upon the foreshore or the land adjoining thereto, except in cases of peril or necessity,[2] or under statute.

Fishermen in pursuit of their lawful calling are not at liberty to use the soil above high water mark for approaching or leaving their boats, carrying their fish or otherwise.[3] The general rule is that the public are entitled to enter upon the foreshore when dry for the purposes of navigation and fishing, but have no other rights of entry without the consent of the Crown or its lessees.[4] An immemorial user of the foreshore in tidal and navigable waters, by the owners of fishing boats and other craft, by fixing moorings in the soil, for the purpose of attaching their boats to them, may be supported either as an ordinary incident of the navigation of such waters, or on a presumption of a legal origin by grant from the Crown of the foreshore subject to such user, or by concession by a former owner of the foreshore to all persons navigating the waters to use it for fixing moorings.[5] The public may take shell fish found on the foreshore.[6] As to the taking of mussels

---

[1] *Fitzhardinge (Lord) v. Purcell*, [1908] 2 Ch. 139; *Malcomson v. O'Dea* (1863), 10 H.L.C. 593; *A.-G. v. Chambers* (1854), 23 L.T.O.S. 238.

[2] *Blundell v. Catterall* (1821), 5 B. & Ald. 268.

[3] *Ilchester (Earl) v. Rashleigh* (1889), 61 L.T. 477; *Ward v. Cresswell* (1741), Willes 265; *Aiton v. Stephen* (1876), 1 A.C. 459.

[4] *Llandudno U.D.C. v. Woods*, [1899] 2 Ch. 705.

[5] *A.-G. v. Wright*, [1897] 2 Q.B. 318.

[6] *Bagott v. Orr* (1801), 2 Bos. & P. 472.

from a natural bed on the foreshore, *see R. v. Howlett, R. v. Howlett.*[1]

A fisherman has no right, as incidental to his exercise of the public right of fishing, to appropriate a portion of the foreshore for the storage of his oysters to the exclusion of the rest of the public.[2] But if oysters stored in ponds on the foreshore become polluted with sewage discharged to the sea by a local authority and are rendered unfit, the owner of the ponds may maintain an action for trespass against the local authority.[3] An immemorable custom for fishermen of a parish to spread their nets to dry upon private land has been held to be a valid custom,[4] although the user of the kinds of nets has varied from time to time.[5] A claim may be established to take fish by way of toll from fishermen landing on a beach in consideration of the claimant furnishing and maintaining a capstan and windlass on the beach for drawing fishing boats out of the water.[6]

The common right of fishing in the sea must be exercised in a reasonable and lawful manner[7] and may be carried out with lines and lawful nets,[8] but not with fixed engines on the margins of the shore,[9] since the right to erect fixed engines on the foreshore indicates the ownership of a several fishery therein and of the soil.[10]

Several fishery in tidal waters

To the general principle that the public have a " liberty in the sea and creeks or arms thereof ", Lord Hale made the exception " unless in such places, creeks or navigable rivers

---

1 (1968), 112 S.J. 150.

2 *Truro Corpn. v. Rowe*, [1902] 2 K.B. 709.

3 *Foster v. Warblington U.D.C.*, [1906] 1 K.B. 648.

4 *Lockwood v. Wood* (1844), 6 Q.B. 50; *Ipswich (Inhabitants) v. Browne* (1581), Sav. 11, 14; *Gray v. Bond* (1821), 2 B. & B. 667.

5 *Mercer v. Denne*, [1905] 2 Ch. 538.

6 *Falmouth (Earl) v. Penrose* (1827), 6 B. & C. 385; *Falmouth (Lord) v. George* (1828), 5 Bing. 286.

7 *Whelan v. Hewson* (1871), I.R. 6 C.L. 283.

8 *Warren v. Matthews* (1703), 1 Salk. 357; *Kintore v. Forbes* (1828), 4 Bli. N.S. 483.

9 *Pery v. Thornton* (1899), 23 L.R. Ir. 402; *Bevins v. Bird* (1865), 12 L.T. 306.

10 *Rawstorne v. Backhouse* (1867), 17 L.T. 441.

where either the King or some other particular subject has granted a proprietary exclusive of that common liability ". This passage refers to certain special cases of which instances are to be found in well-known English decisions where separate and exclusive rights of fishing in tidal waters have been recognised as the property of the owner of the soil. In all such cases the proof of the existence and enjoyment of the right has of necessity gone further back than the date of Magna Charta.[1] The right to exclude the public from tidal waters and to create a several fishery existed in the Crown and might lawfully have been exercised by the Crown before Magna Charta and the several fishery could lawfully be afterwards made the subject of a grant by the Crown to a private person, either together with or distinct from the soil.[2] But since Magna Charta no grant by the Crown of part of the bed of the sea or of a tidal navigable river can operate to the detriment of the public right of fishing.[3] The public cannot lay claim to fish in a several tidal fishery because a fluctuating and uncertain body cannot claim a *profit a prendre*.[4]

A fishery in tidal waters is not a royal franchise and does not on coming into the hands of the Crown by escheat, forfeiture, etc., merge in the Crown.[5]

Royal fisheries

The public right to fish in tidal waters does not extend to taking Royal fish—whales, sturgeons and porpoise—caught in the water or found on the shore, which belong to the Crown and no subject can have them without special grant from the Crown.[6] *See also* ROYAL FISH, p. 34.

Limits of tidal part of a river

The right of fishing in a tidal river is *prima facie* a public right,[7] whilst the fishing in a non-tidal river is the subject of

---

[1] *A.-G. for British Columbia v. A.-G. for Canada*, [1914] A.C. 153.
[2] *Malcomson v. O'Dea* (1863), 10 H.L.C. 593.
[3] *Fitzhardinge (Lord) v. Purcell*, [1908] 2 Ch. 139.
[4] *Goodman v. Saltash Corpn.* (1882), 7 A.C. 633; *Murphy v. Ryan* (1868), I.R. 2 C.L. 143.
[5] *Northumberland (Duke) v. Houghton* (1870), 22 L.T. 491.
[6] *Royal Fishery of Banne Case* (1610), Dav. Ir. 35; *Warren v. Matthews* (1703), 1 Salk. 357.
[7] *R. v. Stimpson* (1863), 4 B. & S. 301.

property and must have an owner and cannot be vested in the public generally.[1] When, then, does a river cease to be tidal and become non-tidal ? It was stated in *Horne v. Mackenzie*,[2] that " the thing to be looked to is the fact of the absence or of the prevalence of the fresh water, though strongly impregnated by salt. Now, where this fresh water prevails then the river is non-tidal ". In *Reece v. Miller*,[3] it was held that a river could not be considered to be tidal at a point where the water was not salt and at ordinary tides was unaffected by any tidal influence, although on occasions of very high tides the rising of salt water dammed back the fresh water and caused it to rise and fall with the flow and ebb of the tide.

It appears that a river is to be regarded as non-tidal from the point of view of fishing where the water is unaffected by the action of ordinary tides, as opposed to tidal waters where there is a horizontal ebb and flow caused by the ordinary sea tide.[4]

Fisheries and navigation

See NAVIGATION VERSUS FISHING, p. 65.

Fishing in non-tidal waters

The Crown is not of common right entitled to the soil of non-tidal waters[5] and if the Crown were both owner of the bed of a non-tidal river and of the right of fishing, the right of fishing would be a proprietary and not a prerogative right.[6] Nor can a right of fishery by the public exist in such waters at law.[7] This principle applies to non-tidal navigable rivers,[8]

---

1 *A.-G. for British Columbia v. A.-G. for Canada*, [1914] A.C. 153.
2 (1839), 6 Cl. & Fin. 628.
3 (1882), 8 Q.B.D. 626; *see also Brown v. Ellis* (1886), 50 J.P. 326; *Micklethwait v. Vincent* (1892), 67 L.T. 225.
4 *West Riding of Yorkshire Rivers Board v. Tadcaster R.D.C.* (1907), 97 L.T. 436; *see also Calcraft v. Guest*, [1898] 1 Q.B. 759; Stuart Moore's " History and Law of Fisheries ", pp. 102-107; *Cross v. Minister of Agriculture*, [1941] I.R. 55; *Ingram v. Percival*, [1968] 3 All E.R. 657.
5 *Johnson v. O'Neill*, [1911] A.C. 552.
6 *Devonshire (Duke) v. Pattinson*, [1887] 20 Q.B.D. 263.
7 *Hudson v. MacRae* (1863), 4 B. & S. 585; *Reece v. Miller* (1882), 8 Q.B.D. 626; *Murphy v. Ryan* (1868), I.R. 2 C.L. 143; *Wells v. Hardy* [1964] 1 All E.R. 953.
8 *Pearce v. Scotcher* (1882), 46 L.T. 342.

although rendered statutably navigable by artificial means,[1] and a legal right for the public to fish in a non-tidal river cannot be obtained by custom,[2] prescription or otherwise.[3] The public have no right as members of the public to fish in a non-tidal river; they may fish by licence or indulgence or good nature of the owner of the fishery, but they have no right to fish themselves as the public.[4]

PRIVATE FISHERIES

A private fishery may be either a several fishery or a common of fishery.

Several fisheries

A several fishery means an exclusive right to fish in a given place and may exist either apart from or as incident to the ownership of the soil over which the river flows. Where a several fishery is proved to exist, the owner of the fishery is to be presumed in the absence of evidence to the contrary, to be the owner of the soil, whether it is a navigable river or a non-navigable river.[5] In order to constitute a several fishery, it is requisite that the party claiming it should so far have the right of fishing, independent of all others, as that no person should have a co-extensive right with him in the subject claimed.[6]

A several fishery is not an exclusive right for the owner to take all the fish in a given place, but is divisible since the owner may reserve to himself the right to take all floating fish and grant to another the sole right to fish for oysters,[7] or the other party may be entitled to fish at certain periods of the year.[8] A several fishery may be leasehold or freehold and may be appurtenant to or parcel of a manor,[9] or appurtenant

---

[1] *Mussett v. Burch* (1876), 35 L.T. 486; *Hargreaves v. Diddams* (1875), 32 L.T. 600.
[2] *Pearce v. Scotcher* (1882) 9 Q.B.D. 162.
[3] *Smith v. Andrews*, [1891] 2 Ch. 678.
[4] *Blount v. Layard*, [1891] 2 Ch. 681.
[5] *Hanbury v. Jenkins*, [1901] 2 Ch. 401; *Hindson v. Ashby*, [1896] 2 Ch. 1.
[6] *Seymour v. Courtenay* (1771), 5 Burr. 2814.
[7] *Seymour v. Courtenay, supra*; *Rogers v. Allen* (1808), 1 Camp. 309.
[8] *Goodman v. Saltash Corpn.* (1882), 7 A.C. 633.
[9] *A.-G. v. Emerson*, [1891] A.C. 649; *Rogers v. Allen, supra*.

to a tenement or land,[1] and the general law of conveyancing, that where a riparian owner, who is also owner of the soil under a river *ad medium filum*, makes a grant of his land on the banks of the river, the soil *ad medium filum* passes by the grant, applies to land of any tenure, whether freehold or leasehold.[2] A several fishery cannot be appurtenant to a several pasture,[3] but is capable of being a right in gross.[4]

Common of fishery

A common of fishery or common piscary is an incorporeal right of fishing where the owner of the right fishes in common with the owner of the river bed or in common with other persons who enjoy the same right.

A common of fishery (which must be distinguished from common fishery or the public right to fish in tidal waters) may be either a common appendant, common appurtenant or a common in gross. A common appendant is a right in respect of arable land granted to a freehold tenant prior to the Statute Quia Emptores of 1289. A common of piscary appurtenant is a right of fishing attached to a particular tenement or premises and may be claimed by grant, custom or prescription and arises by act of parties and does not usually attach by tenure. The right cannot as a rule be severed or enjoyed apart from the dominant tenement and passes with the dominant tenement to each successive owner. A common of piscary appurtenant is limited to the needs of the occupants of the tenement.[5] Common in gross may be claimed by grant or prescription and is not connected with the ownership of land. A custom for commoners, copyholders and ancient freeholders of a manor and their tenants and the dwellers in the parish and manor to have common of fishery over the lord's waste of the manor and to take away fish as a *profit a prendre* is unreasonable and bad.[6]

---

[1] *Hayes v. Bridges* (1795), 1 Ridg. L. & S. 390.
[2] *Tilbury v. Silva* (1890), 45 Ch. D. 98; *Grove v. Portal*, [1902] 1 Ch. 727.
[3] *Edgar v. English Fisheries Special Comrs.* (1870), 35 J.P. 822.
[4] *Staffordshire Canal Navigation v. Bradley*, [1912] 1 Ch. 91; *Neill v. Devonshire (Duke)* (1882), 8 A.C. 135.
[5] *Payne v. Ecclesiastical Comrs. & Landon* (1913), 30 T.L.R. 167; *Harris v. Chesterfield (Earl)*, [1911] A.C. 623.
[6] *Allgood v. Gibson* (1876), 34 L.T. 883.

How private fisheries may be claimed

A person who claims a private fishery must show the foundation of his claim, since *prima facie* the right is in all the King's subjects, or in the owner of the soil. In the case of a private river, the lord's having the soil of it is good evidence that he has the right of fishing and it puts the proof in those that claim *liberam piscarium*. But in the case of a tidal river and in an arm of the sea, there *prima facie* it is common to all, and if any appropriates the privilege to himself, the proof lies in his side.[1]

(1) Claim by express grant

The use of the word " several " or " *separalis piscoria* " is not necessary to create a several fishery,[2] but a fishery would not pass by the word " soil ".[3]

The owner of a corporeal fishery (who has both the soil and fishery) may dispose of it by conveyance or lease in the ordinary way, and an incorporeal fishery must be conveyed by deed under seal.[4] A corporeal fishery comprising the fee simple in the river bed at a specified place and the right to take fish in the water above such bed is land, not a right appurtenant to land, and cannot be transferred merely by a conveyance of other land and rights appurtenant to such land.[5] *Prima facie*, the grant of a fishery passes the soil, since the owner of a fishery, in the absence of evidence to the contrary, is presumed to be the owner of the soil.[6] The owner of a several fishery in ordinary cases and where the terms of the grant are unknown, may be presumed to be the owner of the soil, but where the terms of the grant are known and convey no more than an incorporeal hereditament the presumption is destroyed.[7]

---

[1] *Fitzwalter's (Lord) Case* (1674), 1 Mod. Rep. 105.
[2] *Hanbury v. Jenkins*, [1901] 2 Ch. 401; *Beaufort (Duke) v. Aird (John) & Co.* (1904), 20 T.L.R. 602.
[3] *Scratton v. Brown* (1825), 4 B. & C. 485.
[4] *Bird v. Higginson* (1837), 6 Ad. & El. 824.
[5] *Hesketh v. Willis Cruisers* (1968) 19 P. & C.R. 573, C.A.
[6] *A.-G. v. Emerson*, [1891] A.C. 643; *Hindson v. Ashby*, [1896] 2 Ch. 1.
[7] *Somerset (Duke) v. Fogwell* (1826), 5 B. & C. 875.

(2) *Lease or licence*

A lease of a fishery may be granted with the soil as a corporeal hereditament or as an incorporeal right without the soil. A lease or licence of a fishery must be granted by deed,[1] but if a fishery is let by an agreement not under seal, the landlord may recover the rent for the use and occupation of the fishery.[2] An incorporeal hereditament can only be conveyed by deed.[3] By a lease of land, whether agricultural or other land, through which a river runs, the right of fishing in the river unless expressly reserved to the lessor passes to the tenant and the lessor cannot prosecute persons for unlawfully taking fish in the river.[4]

Strictly speaking, a reservation and exception in a lease of a right of fishing operates as a re-grant by the lessee to the landlord.[5] A grant by deed of the right of fishing is not a licence to fish, but a right to fish and carry away the fish caught and the grantees have a right of action against anyone who wrongfully interferes with their right.[6] In *Re Vickers' lease, Pocock v. Vickers*,[7] a clause in a fishing lease that the owner should retain for her own use a rod in the fishing was construed as a contractual right only which ended on her death. Where a right of fishing is let together with corporeal hereditaments under the same lease and the lessee uses both for his trade, he is entitled to security of tenure for both under the Landlord and Tenant Act.[8] A licence which is not made under seal merely gives the licensee a right to fish and not to take away the fish caught, because a right to take

---

[1] *Fuller v. Brown* (1849), 13 J.P. 445; *Bird v. Gt. Eastern Ry. Co.* (1865), 13 L.T. 365.

[2] *Holford v. Pritchard* (1849), 3 Ex. 793.

[3] *Somerset (Duke) v. Fogwell, supra; Bird v. Higginson* (1837), 6 Ad. & Ed. 824.

[4] *Jones v. Davies* (1902), 86 L.T. 447.

[5] *Doe d. Douglas v. Lock* (1835), 2 Ad. & El. 705.

[6] *Fitzgerald v. Firbank*, [1897] 2 Ch. 96; *Wickham v. Hawker* (1840), 7 M. & W. 63; *Nicholls v. Ely Beet Sugar Factory Ltd.*, [1931] 2 Ch. 84.

[7] [1947] Ch. 420.

[8] *Whitley v. Stumbles*, [1930] A.C. 544.

away fish is an interest in land and has to be granted under seal.[1]

(3) *Prescription*

In the case of non-tidal rivers the presumption is that the owner of the bed has the right to fish in the stream.[2] In arms of the sea and tidal rivers the right of fishing is public and common and whilst a proprietor of land may have an exclusive right of fishing, such right is not to be presumed, but on the contrary, *prima facie*; but it is capable of being proved. The Crown may grant a several fishery in a tidal river or in an arm of the sea; if it may be granted, it may be prescribed, for a prescription implies a grant. But it cannot be presumed, it must be proved.[3] A prescription must be proved as extensively as it is claimed.[4]

A prescriptive right to a several fishery in a tidal river cannot be supported by custom as being a claim to a *profit a prendre*, nor can it be claimed by the inhabitants of ancient tenements in a borough, since a fluctuating and uncertain body cannot claim a *profit a prendre*.[5] Nor can a *profit a prendre* be claimed by prescription on behalf of a large and indefinite class described as " owners and occupiers ".[6] A prescriptive right may be claimed at common law or under the Prescription Act, 1832, but rights in gross are not within that Act.[7]

Evidence of Title to Fisheries

(1) *Fisheries in tidal waters*

Title to a fishery in tidal waters must be shown to have existed prior to the reign of Henry II, because Magna Charta made illegal all grants by the Crown of a several fishery in

---

[1] *Webber v. Lee* (1882), 9 Q.B.D. 315.
[2] *Blount v. Layard*, [1891] 2 Ch. 681.
[3] *Carter v. Murcot* (1768), 4 Burr. 2162.
[4] *Rogers v. Allen* (1808), 1 Camp. 309.
[5] *Goodman v. Saltash Corpn.* (1882), 48 L.T. 239; *Mills v. Colchester Corpn.* (1868), L.R. 3 C.P. 575.
[6] *Tilbury v. Silva* (1890), 45 Ch. D. 98; *Harris v. Chesterfield (Earl)*, [1911] A.C. 623.
[7] *Shuttleworth v. Le Fleming* (1865), 19 C.B.N.S. 687.

tidal waters which had not been in existence in that reign. In the absence of an express grant or charter by the Crown, a prescriptive right must be shown. If evidence is given of long enjoyment of a fishery, to the exclusion of others, of such a character as to establish that it has been dealt with as of right as a distinct and separate property, and that there is nothing to show that its origin was modern, a reasonable presumption is that it became such in due course of law and must therefore have been created before legal memory.[1]

(2) *Fisheries in non-tidal waters*

Title to the ownership of a fishery in non-tidal waters may be proved in the same way as ownership of a fishery in tidal waters, but although evidence of the early history of a fishery may be useful or necessary in defining boundaries, or to show that the fishery is attached to the soil, etc., generally speaking title to a fishery in non-tidal waters need not be proved further back any more than title to any other kind of property.[2]

(3) *Documentary evidence*

In giving evidence of his title to a fishery the claimant should produce the grant and all other documents relating to the fishery, with evidence of possession and actual user of the fishery for a period sufficient to establish his right. In *Mannall v. Fisher*[3] a corporation claimed the exclusive right of fishery in a haven and their lessees brought an action against two fishermen for an invasion of that right. The plaintiffs offered as evidence a charter of Elizabeth I confirming former charters of the corporation and giving them powers to make byelaws for the preservation of the fish in the haven, a statute for the preservation of the haven, a record of an action brought by the corporation in 1792 against a fisherman for dredging for oysters in their water and a book containing entries of payments made to the corporation for licences to fish in the haven.

---

[1] *Malcomson v. O'Dea* (1863), 10 H.L.C. 593.

[2] *See* Stuart Moore's " *History and Law of Fisheries* ", p. 143.

[3] (1859), 23 J.P. 375; *see also Neill v. Devonshire (Duke)* (1882), 8 A.C. 135; *Lord Advocate v. Lovat* (1880), 5 A.C. 273; *Tighe v. Sinnott*, [1897] 1 Ir. R. 140; *Johnston v. O'Neill*, [1911] A.C. 552.

Held: that the jury were warranted in finding upon this evidence that the corporation had the right claimed.

Other documents which have been admitted by the courts to prove possession of fisheries are ancient documents coming out of proper custody and purporting upon the face of them to show exercise of ownership, such as old leases and counterparts,[1] old licences of court rolls,[2] collectors' accounts showing receipts of rent,[3] proceedings and decrees of former suits in respect of fisheries,[4] entries in rate books,[5] and land tax assessments.[6] Proof of payment of rent under a lease is sufficient evidence of a private right of fishing.[7]

(4) Evidence of possession

Evidence of actual user and enjoyment by a plaintiff of a right of several fishery in a tidal river for 110 years prior to an action is of itself alone satisfactory evidence upon which a jury would be amply justified in presuming that the right had existed from time immemorial, and consequently that there must have been a valid grant of the fishery by the Crown anterior to Magna Charta. It is for the defendant to establish either that the right was in fact created since the time of legal memory and Magna Charta, or that at some period subsequent thereto no such fishery was in existence.[8] In other cases, proof of enjoyment of a tidal fishery for fifty years[9] and twenty years[10] have been held sufficient to establish ownership.

Without evidence of possession and enjoyment, even the clearest apparent title to a several fishery, on paper only, would not exclude the public right of fishing in tidal waters.

---

1 *Malcomson v. O'Dea* (1863), 10 H.L.C. 593.
2 *Rogers v. Allen* (1808), 1 Camp. 309; *A.-G. v. Emerson,* [1891] A.C. 649.
3 *Percival v. Nanson* (1851), 7 Ex. 1.
4 *Neill v. Devonshire (Duke), supra; Johnston v. O'Neill, supra.*
5 *Smith v. Andrews,* [1891] 2 Ch. 678.
6 *Doe d. Strode v. Seaton* (1834), 2 A. & E. 171.
7 *Gabbett v. Clancy* (1845), 8 I.L.R. 299; *Greenbank v. Sanderson* (1884), 49 J.P. 40.
8 *Northumberland (Duke) v. Houghton* (1870), 22 L.T. 491; *see also Leconfield v. Lonsdale* (1870), 23 L.T. 155.
9 *R. v. Downing* (1870), 23 L.T. 398.
10 *Halse v. Alder* (1874), 38 J.P. 407.

If the fishery of a whole river is what has been sometimes called a " *unum quid* ", there can be no doubt that evidence of acts of ownership and enjoyment in any part of it would be applicable to the whole.[1] In actions involving a mere trespasser where an individual fishes in a non-tidal river, it is only necessary to prove actual possession.[2] Recitals in documents as to a grant by the Crown are no evidence of what is there recited, though actual possession in conformity therewith constitutes a *prima facie* title.[3] Possession must be considered in every case with reference to the peculiar circumstances; the acts which imply possession in one case may be wholly inadequate to prove it in another.[4]

Evidence of possession to support a claim of ownership of a several fishery include the use of fixed engines on the foreshore and bed of a tidal navigable river,[5] the taking of fish with nets in a river by the claimant,[6] granting or taking a lease of a fishery,[7] or receiving rent under a fishery lease.[8] Acts by riparian owners, such as placing stakes and wattles on the soil of a river to prevent erosion by flood, cutting weeds, taking gravel and making cattle pens in the stream, are also *prima facie* acts of ownership.[9]

Presumptions as to ownership of fisheries

(1) *In tidal waters*

Prima facie the Crown is entitled to every part of the foreshore of the sea between high and low water mark and of the soil of tidal rivers so far as the tide flows and reflows and the right of fishery thereover is *prima facie* in the public.[10] But proof of the ownership of a several fishery over part of the foreshore raises a presumption against the Crown that the

---

1 *Neill v. Devonshire (Duke), supra.*
2 *Bristow v. Cormican* (1878), 3 A.C. 648.
3 *Bristow v. Cormican* (1878), 3 A.C. 641.
4 *Lord Advocate v. Lovat* (1880), 5 A.C. 273.
5 *Fitzhardinge (Lord) v. Purcell,* [1908] 2 Ch. 139; *Edgar v. English Fisheries Special Comrs.* (1870), 23 L.T. 732.
6 *Lord Advocate v. Lovat, supra.*
7 *R. v. Alfresford* (1786), 1 T.R. 358; *Ecroyd v. Coulthard,* [1898] 2 Ch. 358.
8 *Greenback v. Sanderson* (1884), 49 J.P. 40.
9 *Hanbury v. Jenkins,* [1901] 2 Ch. 401.
10 *Malcomson v. O'Dea* (1863), 10 H.L.C. 593.

freehold of the soil of that part of the foreshore is vested in the owner of the several fishery.[1] Where a subject is owner of a several fishery in tidal waters he may be presumed to be the owner of the soil.[2]

(2) *In non-tidal waters*

The right of fishing in non-tidal waters or in inland streams is presumptively vested in the several riparian owners *ad medium filum aquae*, and if the same person is the owner of both banks he has the entire fishing to the extent of the length of his land.[3] In the case of a private river running through a manor, the presumption is that each owner of land within the manor on the bank of the river has the right of fishing in front of his land, and if the lord claims a several fishery he must make out that claim by evidence.[4] Where a river divides two properties, there is a presumption that the true line of division is the middle of the river.[5]

If a several fishery is proved to exist, the owner of the fishery is presumed, in the absence of evidence to the contrary, to be the owner of the soil over which his fishery extends, whether it is a navigable river or one neither public nor navigable,[6] but a several fishery may exist independently of the ownership of the soil.[7]

(3) *Rebuttal of presumptions*

These presumptions are rebuttable on proof of surrounding circumstances in relation to the particular property which negative the possibility that the claimant has the exclusive right to the bed of the river or the fishery therein.[8] Thus, where it was attempted to raise a presumption that a right of several fishery within a manor passed to the lord by a deed as appurtenant to the manor, that presumption was rebutted

---

[1] *A.-G. v. Emerson*, [1891] A.C. 649; *Beaufort (Duke) v. Aird (John) & Co.* (1904), 20 T.L.R. 602.

[2] *Somerset (Duke) v. Fogwell* (1826), 5 B. & C. 875.

[3] *Tracey Elliott v. Morley (Earl)* (1907), 51 S.J. 625.

[4] *Lamb v. Newbiggin* (1844), 1 Car. & Kir. 549.

[5] *Chesterfield (Lord) v. Harris*, [1908] 2 Ch. 397.

[6] *Hanbury v. Jenkins*, [1901] 2 Ch. 401; *Hindson v. Ashby*, [1896] 2 Ch. 1; *Holford v. Bailey* (1849), 13 Q.B.D. 426; *Somerset (Duke) v. Fogwell* (1826), 5 B. & C. 875; *Partheriche v. Mason* (1774), 2 Chit. 658.

[7] *Marshall v. Ulleswater Steam Navigation Co.* (1863), 3 B. & S. 732.

[8] *Devonshire (Duke) v. Pattinson* (1887), 20 Q.B.D. 263.

by proof that, before the date of that deed, owners of land within the manor and on the bank of the river had the right of free fishery therein.[1]

Boundaries of fisheries

The extent in length of a fishery up and down a river is determined by the length of riparian land belonging to the owner of the fishery, or by the limits assigned to the fishery by the particular conveyance, grant, lease or licence, or by its user and enjoyment in the case of a presumed grant. In *Stephens v. Snell*[2] it was held that the extent in length of a manorial fishery was the bounds of the manor.

As regards the width of a fishery in a non-tidal river, the respective riparian owners are presumed to be the owners of the soil of one half of the stream and are entitled to fish the river *ad medium filum aquae*, unless the same person owns both banks when he has the fishing *prima facie* over the entire bed in proportion to the extent of his land.[3] The *medium filum* of a non-tidal stream is apparently a line running down the centre of the river at the ordinary state of the river, *i.e.* the midline of the usual flow of the river without regard to periods of flood water or drought.[4]

The ascertainment of the *medium filum* of a tidal river containing fish is apt to present some difficulty. In some rivers with wide estuaries, such as the Thames and Humber, the riparian manors, which include the fisheries, are limited to their respective foreshores, and here it is easy to determine the width of such fisheries. But in tidal rivers with narrow estuaries, *e.g.* the Tyne, Severn and Trent, the manors and fisheries extend to midstream, and here there are two alternative methods for ascertaining the width of the fisheries. The

---

[1] *Lamb v. Newbiggin, supra.*

[2] [1939] 3 All E.R. 622.

[3] *Tracey Elliott v. Morley (Earl)* (1907), 51 Sol. Jo. 625; *Waterford Conservators v. Connolly* (1889), 24 I.L.T. 7.

[4] *Hindson v. Ashby*, [1896] 1 Ch. 78; and *see* Stuart Moore's "*Law and History of Fisheries*", pp. 114-118.

medium filum may be taken to be the middle of the river at its state of low water, when the upper river discharges to the sea through the low water channel which winds between the shores of the river, but nevertheless provides a readily ascertainable line for finding the boundary between the riparian manors and fisheries. Secondly, the *medium filum* may be drawn down the centre of the river between ordinary high water mark on each side, when the bed and shores are covered by the waters of the sea. There is no English decision on this point, but it has been argued that the middle line of a tidal river should be drawn down the centre of the channel at ordinary low water.[1]

Fisheries on the foreshore are usually limited to the foreshore of the manors, but occasionally a deep-sea fishery, such as an oyster bed, will be found to extend below low water mark.[2]

A several fishery in a tidal river, the waters of which have permanently receded from one channel and flow in another, cannot be followed from the old to the new channel.[3] But where a river channel gradually and imperceptibly over a period of years changes its course, an exclusive right of fishery over the whole bed of the river will follow the change in course.[4] So also, where two persons each have an exclusive right to fish in an estuary, each to the middle thread of a river running through it, and the river changes its course through the estuary, the limit of each fishery will then be the middle of the new channel of the river.[5]

Fisheries in lakes and ponds

The Crown is not of common right entitled to the soil or fisheries of an inland non-tidal lake, irrespective of its size,

---

[1] *See* Stuart Moore's " *Law and History of Fisheries* ", chapter XX; Hale's First Treatise, " *De Jure Maris* " at p. 354; *Pearce v. Bunting* (1896), 60 J.P. 695; *Thames Conservators v. Smeed Dean & Co.*, [1897] 2 Q.B. 334; *Miller v. Little* (1879), 4 L.R. Ir. 304.

[2] *Gann v. Free Fishers of Whitstable* (1865), 11 H.L.C. 192; *Foreman v. Free Fishers of Whitstable* (1869), L.R. 4 H.L. 266; *Loose v. Castleton* (1978) *The Times*, 21st June.

[3] *Carlisle Corpn. v. Graham* (1869), 21 L.T. 333.

[4] *Foster v. Wright* (1878), 44 J.P. 7; *Hindson v. Ashby*, [1896] 2 Q.B. 1.

[5] *Miller v. Little* (1879), 4 L.R. Ir. 304.

and no right can exist in the public to fish in such waters,[1] whether they are navigable or not.[2] If a pond is situate in one ownership *prima facie* the right of fishing is vested in the owner,[3] and where a lake lies between a number of manors it appears that the right of fishery is divided *ad medium filum aquae*.[4] A person may construct a fish-pond on his own land, but he cannot do so on a common if this disturbs the commoners' rights.[5]

Fisheries in canals and reservoirs

The right of fishery in a canal or reservoir is usually regulated by the provisions of the statute under which the canal or reservoir is constructed; thus, the owners of land on either side may have the sole, exclusive and several right of fishing in so much of the canal as was made over or through their land,[6] together with the right to use the towpath and banks of the canal in exercise of their rights.[7] The public have no right to fish in a canal.[8] If a non-tidal stream is rendered statutably navigable the public acquire no right to fish therein.[9]

Fishing paths

A fishery owner is not of right entitled to land nets or walk along the river bank for purposes of fishing unless he is the owner of the bank or has the consent of the owner of the soil,[10] but a prescriptive right to do so may be presumed depending

---

[1] *Johnston v. O'Neill*, [1911] A.C. 552; *Bristow v. Cormican* (1878), 3 A.C. 641.

[2] *Bloomfield v. Johnston* (1868), I.R. 8 C.L. 68; *R. v. Burrow* (1869), 34 J.P. 53; *Pery v. Thornton* (1889), 23 L.R. Ir. 402.

[3] *Clarke v. Mercer* (1859), 1 F. & F. 492.

[4] *Marshall v. Ulleswater Steam Navigation Co.* (1863), 3 B. & S. 732.

[5] *Reeve v. Digby* (1638), Cro. Car. 495.

[6] *Grand Union Canal Co. v. Ashby* (1861), 6 H. & N. 394; *Snape v. Dobbs* (1823), 1 Bing. 202.

[7] *Staffordshire & Worcestershire Canal Navigation v. Bradley*, [1912] 1 Ch. 91.

[8] *Mussett v. Birch* (1876), 35 L.T. 486.

[9] *Hargreaves v. Diddams* (1875), 32 L.T. 600; *Pearce v. Scotcher* (1882), 9 Q.B.D. 162.

[10] *Ipswich v. Browne* (1581), Savil 11, 14.

upon the evidence of user.[1] Where a fishery goes with the soil
of a river the right of a fishing-path may be appurtenant, and
in the case of an incorporeal right of fishing an incorporeal
right of way along both banks of a river may be appendant,
since the one is capable of union with the other without any
incongruity.[2]

The public have no right to fish from river banks which are
in private ownership, although they may have a right to fish
in the river[3]; and they cannot fish from a public highway
besides a river,[4] nor from a towpath.[3] As to the use of a
towing path by adjoining owners to fish in a canal, see *Staffordshire & Worcestershire Canal Navigation v. Bradley*.[5] In tidal
waters the public may use the foreshore for fishing[6] and
fishermen may be presumed to have a right to land nets on the
shore above ordinary high water mark.[7]

Weirs obstructing fisheries

The erection of weirs in navigable rivers was forbidden from
early times under statute. Magna Charta c. 23 (1225) enacted
that " all weirs from henceforth shall be utterly put down in
the Thames and Medway and throughout all England except
by the sea coast ", and similar declarations were made in
slightly later statutes.[8] These provisions have been held to
apply only to navigable rivers,[9] and a weir is not illegal in
such a river if it can be shown to have been granted by the
Crown before the time of Edward I.[10] Therefore, fishing
weirs may exist in non-navigable rivers although of a more
recent date than the reign of Edward I, and a right to such
weirs in private waters may be acquired by grant from other

---

[1] *Gray v. Bond* (1821), 2 B. & B. 667; *Shuttleworth v. Le Fleming* (1865),
19 C.B.N.S. 687.
[2] *Hanbury v. Jenkins*, [1901] 2 Ch. 401.
[3] *Ball v. Herbert* (1789), 3 T.R. 253.
[4] *Harrison v. Rutland (Duke)*, [1893] 1 Q.B. 142.
[5] [1912] 1 Ch. 91.
[6] *Blundell v. Catterall* (1821), 5 B. & Ald. 268.
[7] *Gray v. Bond* (1821), 2 B. & B. 667.
[8] 25 Edward III, st. 4, c. 4 (1350); 45 Edward III, c. 2 (1371); 17 Richard
II, c. 9 (1393); 1 Henry IV, c. 12 (1399); 4 Henry IV, c. 11 (1402); 12 Edward
IV, c. 7 (1472).
[9] *Leconfield v. Lonsdale* (1870), 23 L.T. 155.
[10] *Williams v. Wilcox* (1838), 8 Ad. & El. 314.

riparian owners, or by enjoyment or by any other means by which such rights may be constituted.[1] Once the right to an ancient weir has been proved, it must not be raised, altered or enlarged, nor converted from a brushwood to a stone weir.[2] *See also* sections 6 to 18 of the Salmon and Freshwater Fisheries Act, 1975, pp. 281 to 286.

Remedies for disturbance of fisheries

An action will lie for the disturbance of a fishery,[3] and at common law stealing fish from a private pond is an indictable offence.[4] A right to fish and carry away the fish caught is a *profit a prendre* and an incorporeal hereditament and the owner has a right of action for an injunction and damages against anyone who unlawfully does any act which disturbs the exercise or enjoyment of that right.[5] Disturbance of a several fishery is an invasion of a legal right and it is not necessary to prove pecuniary loss, but the injury to the legal right carries with it the right to damages.[6] *See also Rawson v. Peters*[7] where a canoeist disturbed fish in a river and interfered with an incorporeal fishery, though no damage was caused and nobody fishing at the time. The plaintiff was awarded nominal damages with liberty to apply to the county court for an injunction.

Causing water to overflow another person's fishery although done by an act on the party's own soil is a trespass,[8] and an interference with the free passage of fish up a river by a landowner erecting weirs across the river so that fish are prevented from reaching the upper portions of the river constitutes an injury to the owners of the upper waters and gives rise to an

---

[1] *Rolle v. Whyte* (1868), 7 B. & S. 116.

[2] *Chester Mill Case* (1610), 10 Co. Rep. 137b; *Weld v. Hornby* (1806), 7 East 195.

[3] *Child v. Greenhill* (1639), Cro. Car. 553; *Smith v. Kemp* (1693), 2 Salk. 637; *Holford v. Bailey* (1849), 13 Q.B. 426.

[4] *Gray's Case* (1594), Owen 20; *R. v. Steer* (1704), 6 Mod. Rep. 183.

[5] *Fitzgerald v. Firbank*, [1897] 2 Ch. 96; *Granby (Marquis) v. Bakewell U.D.C.* (1923), 87 J.P. 105.

[6] *Nicholls v. Ely Beet Sugar Factory Ltd.*, [1931] 2 Ch. 84.

[7] *The Times*, Nov. 2, 1972, C.A.

[8] *Courtney v. Collet* (1697), 12 Mod. Rep. 164.

action for damages and will be restrained by injunction.[1]
The courts will grant an injunction to restrain a person from
enclosing the bed of a river, the effect of which being to
destroy a fishery.[2] An angling association supporting an
action for pollution brought by a member has been held not
to be guilty of maintenance.[3] *See also* POLLUTION OF FISH-
ERIES, p. 344.

Taking or destroying fish

The Theft Act, 1968, provides as follows—

(1) Subject to paragraph (2) below, a person who unlawfully takes[4] or destroys, or attempts to take or destroy,
any fish[5] in water[6] which is private property or in
which there is any private right of fishery is liable on
summary conviction to a fine not exceeding £50 or,
for an offence committed after a previous conviction
of an offence under this paragraph, to imprisonment
for a term not exceeding three months or to a fine
not exceeding £100 or to both.

(2) Paragraph (1) above does not apply to taking or
destroying fish by angling in the daytime, *i.e.* in the
period beginning one hour before sunrise and ending
one hour after sunset, but a person who by angling
in the daytime unlawfully takes or destroys, or
attempts to take or destroy, any fish in water which
is private property or in which there is any private
right of fishery is liable on summary conviction to a
fine not exceeding £20.

(3) The court by which a person is convicted of an
offence under this provision may order the forfeiture
of anything which, at the time of the offence, he had
with him for use for taking or destroying fish.

---

[1] *Hamilton v. Donegal (Marquis)* (1795), 3 Ridg. P.R. 267; *Weld v. Hornby,*
supra; Barker v. Faulkner (1898), 79 L.T. 24; *Pirie & Sons Ltd. v. Kintore*
(Earl), [1906] A.C. 478; *Fraser v. Fear* (1912), 107 L.T. 423.
[2] *Bridges v. Highton* (1865), 11 L.T. 653.
[3] *Martell v. Consett Iron Co. Ltd.,* [1955] 1 All E.R. 481; the offence of
maintenance was, however, abolished by the Criminal Law Act, 1967, s. 13,
Sch. 4, Parts I and II.
[4] Catching fish with the object and intention of replacing them in the river
constitutes a " taking " (*Wells v. Hardy* [1964] 1 All E.R. 953).
[5] The Act applies to any kind of fish (*Caygill v. Thwaite* (1885) 49 J.P. 614;
Leavett v. Clark [1915] 3 K.B. 9).
[6] The Act applies to tidal and non-tidal waters (*Paley v. Birch* (1867) 8
B. & S. 336).

(4) Any person may arrest without warrant anyone who is, or whom he, with reasonable cause, suspects to be, committing an offence under paragraph (1) above, and may seize from any person who is, or whom he, with reasonable cause, suspects to be, committing any offence under this provision anything which on that person's conviction of the offence would be liable to be forfeited under paragraph (3) above.[1]

Property in fish

At common law fish in a running river are *ferae naturae* and cannot be stolen or become the subject of property in the possession of the owner of a private fishery until they are caught and brought into actual possession.[2] But the taking of fish from an enclosed pond or private lake, where they cannot swim away and the property is not lost, is larceny at common law,[3] and a fish which has been taken and captured in a net may be stolen.[4] Fish caught at sea and deposited dead in the hold of a vessel are held to be in the possession of the owner of the vessel and a person who takes them may be convicted of larceny.[5] Royal fish, namely, whales, sturgeon and porpoise, are the property of the Crown or its grantees whether taken at sea or on the shore and do not belong to the finder. Oysters and mussels and cockles in or on a bed within the limits of a several oyster and mussel and cockle fishery granted under the Sea Fisheries Act, 1868,[6] and oysters in or on a private oyster bed, are the absolute property of the grantee or owner of the bed.[7]

---

[1] Theft Act, 1968, s. 32 (1), Sch. 1, para. 2.

[2] *R. v. Hundsdon* (1781), 2 East, P.C. 611.

[3] *R. v. Steer* (1704), 6 Mod. Rep. 183; *Gray v. Trowe* (1601), 75 E.R. 1043.

[4] *Young v. Hitchens* (1844), 6 Q.B. 606.

[5] *R. v. Mallison* (1902), 86 L.T. 600.

[6] This Act has been repealed and replaced by the Sea Fisheries (Shellfish) Act, 1967.

[7] Sea Fisheries (Shellfish) Act, 1967, s. 7.

CHAPTER 14

FISHERIES UNDER STATUTE

THE SALMON AND FRESHWATER FISHERIES ACT, 1975

The statute law relating to salmon and freshwater fisheries is contained in the Salmon and Freshwater Fisheries Act, 1975 (hereafter described as " the Act ") which came into force on 1st August, 1975,[1] and extends only to England and Wales except as otherwise expressly provided,[2] and has local or limited application to the River Esk, and Solway Firth, and does not apply to the River Tweed.[3]

The legal rights of conservators or other persons to dredge, scour, cleanse or improve a navigable river, canal or other inland navigation are not affected by anything in the Act.[4]

The Minister of Agriculture, Fisheries and Food is charged to promote jointly with the Secretary of State for the Environment a national policy for water in England and Wales and it is also the duty of the Minister to secure the effective execution of so much of that policy as relates to fisheries in inland and coastal waters.[5]

Fishery functions of water authorities

(1) Transfer of fishery functions to water authorities

As from 1st April, 1974, the functions of fisheries, which immediately before that date had been exercisable by river authorities, were transferred to the water authorities established under the Water Act, 1973.[6] It is the duty of every water

---

1 Salmon and Freshwater Fisheries Act, 1975, s. 43 (4).
2 *Ibid.*, s. 43 (2), (3).
3 *Ibid.*, s. 39.
4 *Ibid.*, s. 42 (8).
5 Water Act, 1973, s. 1 (1), (3).
6 *Ibid.*, s. 9.

authority to maintain, improve and develop the salmon fisheries, trout fisheries, freshwater fisheries and eel fisheries in the area for which they exercise functions under the Act, and to establish advisory committees of persons who appear to them to be interested in any such fisheries in that area and consult them as to the manner in which the authority are to discharge their fisheries duty as above. Each authority must establish a regional advisory committee for the whole of the area and such local advisory committees as the authority consider necessary to represent the fishery interests in different parts of the area.[1]

For the purposes of a water authority's functions relating to fisheries, the water authority area includes those tidal waters and parts of the sea adjoining the coast of such area in which Her Majesty's subjects have the exclusive right of fishing, and any question as to the extent of a water authority area shall be determined by the Minister of Agriculture, Fisheries and Food.[2]

(2) Powers of water authorities

Under the Act water authorities have the following powers and duties:—

    (1) To grant fishing and general licences upon payment of licence duties[3] (see further pp. 290 to 292).

    (2) To make and enforce byelaws for the protection, preservation and improvement of fisheries; this is a permissive power, subject to water authorities being under a duty to make byelaws fixing the annual close season and weekly close time for fishing for salmon and trout other than rainbow trout. Byelaws may be made to apply to the whole or part of the water authority area, or to the whole or parts of the year. Any person who contravenes or fails to comply with the provisions of any byelaw is guilty of an offence.[4] The procedure for making byelaws is contained in

---

[1] Salmon and Freshwater Fisheries Act, 1975, s. 28 (1), (2).
[2] Water Act, 1973, s. 2 (7), Sch. 2, para. 4.
[3] Salmon and Freshwater Fisheries Act, 1975, s. 25, Sch. 2.
[4] See, further, ibid., s. 28 (3), Sch. 1, Sch. 3, Part II.

section 36 (3) of, and Schedule 7 to, the Water Act, 1973.

(3) To purchase or take on lease either by agreement or compulsorily any dam[1] fishing weir,[1] fishing mill dam,[1] fixed engine[1] or other artificial obstruction, and any fishery attached to or worked in connection with any such obstruction, and remove or alter the obstruction, or use or work in any lawful manner the obstruction for fishing purposes and exercise any fishery rights so acquired. The provisions of Part VI of the Water Resources Act, 1963 (which, *inter alia*, empower water authorities to acquire land in connection with the performance of any of their functions) have effect for this purpose.[2]

(4) To construct and maintain fish passes in dams or in connection therewith, and abolish, alter, restore or substitute existing fish passes or free gaps with the consent of the Minister provided that no injury is done to the milling power or to the supply of water or to a navigable river, canal or other inland navigation.[3] A water authority may purchase the bank adjoining a dam for making or maintaining a fish pass.[4]

(5) To place and maintain gratings with the consent of the Minister in watercourses or other channels for conveying water for any purpose from waters frequented by salmon or migratory trout.[5]

(6) To take legal proceedings in respect of offences against the Act, or for enforcing the provisions of the Act or for the protection of the fisheries in their area from injury by pollution or otherwise.[6]

---

[1] These terms are defined on p. 280.
[2] Salmon and Freshwater Fisheries Act, 1975, s. 28 (3), Sch. 3, Part III, paras. 37 (*a*), 38.
[3] *Ibid.*, s. 10.
[4] *Ibid.*, Sch. 3, Part III, para. 37 (*b*).
[5] *Ibid.*, s. 15.
[6] *Ibid.*, Sch. 3, Part III, para. 39 (1) (*a*).

(7) To purchase or lease by agreement any fishery, fishing rights or establishment for the artificial propagation or rearing of salmon, trout or freshwater fish, and use, work or exercise the same by themselves, their lessees or persons duly authorised by them.[1]

Definitions

The following definitions are assigned to expressions used in the Salmon and Freshwater Fisheries Act, 1975[2]—

" the Minister " means the Minister of Agriculture, Fisheries and Food;

" dam " includes any weir or other fixed obstruction used for the purpose of damming up water;

" fishing mill dam " means a dam used or intended to be used partly for the purpose of taking or facilitating the taking of fish, and partly for the purpose of supplying water for milling or other purposes[3];

" fishing weir " means any erection, structure or obstruction fixed to the soil either temporarily or permanently across, or partly across, a river or branch of a river, and used for the exclusive purpose of taking or facilitating the taking of fish;

" mill " includes any erection for the purpose of developing water power, and the expression " milling " has a corresponding meaning;

" fixed engine " includes (a) stake net, bag net, putt, putcher; and (b) any fixed implement or engine for taking or facilitating the taking of fish; and (c) any net secured by anchors and any net or other implement for taking fish fixed to the soil, or made stationary in any other way; and (d) any net placed or suspended in any inland or tidal waters unattended by the owner or a

---

[1] Salmon and Freshwater Fisheries Act, 1975, Sch. 3, Part III, para. 39 (1) (b).

[2] Ibid., s. 41 (1).

[3] For cases on the meaning of fishing mill dam, see Garnett v. Backhouse (1867), 8 B. & S. 490; Pike v. Rossiter (1877), 37 L.T. 635; Moulton v. Wilby (1863), 2 H. & C. 25; Rossiter v. Pike (1878), 4 Q.B.D. 24.

person duly authorised by the owner to use the same for taking salmon or trout, and any engine, device, machine or contrivance, whether floating or otherwise, for placing or suspending such last-mentioned net or maintaining it in working order or making it stationary[1];

" salmon " means all fish of the salmon species[2];

" trout " means any fish of the salmon family commonly known as trout and includes " migratory trout " and char;

" migratory trout " means trout which migrate to and from the sea;

" freshwater fish " means any fish living in fresh water exclusive of salmon and trout and of any kinds of fish which migrate to and from tidal water and of eels[2];

" immature " in relation to salmon means that the salmon is of a length of less than twelve inches measured from the tip of the snout to the fork or cleft of the tail, and in relation to any other fish means that the fish is of a length less than such (if any) as may be prescribed by byelaw;

" unclean " in relation to any fish mean that the fish is about to spawn or has recently spawned and has not recovered from spawning.

Prohibitions on taking and destroying fish

(1) Prohibited implements

A person must not use any of the following instruments, that is to say:—

---

[1] For cases on fixed engines and the meaning thereof, *see Olding v. Wild* (1866), 14 L.T. 402; *Holford v. George* (1868), 18 L.T. 817; *Gore v. English Fisheries Comrs.* (1871), 24 L.T. 702; *Oswald v. M'Call*, [1919] S.C. 584; *Irish Society v. Fleming*, [1912] I.R. 287, H.L.; *Irish Society v. Harold* (1912), 46 I.L.T. 273; *Crossfield v. Rogers & Gibson* (1897), 31 I.L.T. 464; *Watts v. Lucas* (1871), 24 L.T. 128; *Vance v. Frost* (1894), 58 J.P. 398; *Percevil v. Stanton*, [1954] 1 All E.R. 392.

[2] *See also* definition in s. 10 (1) of the Diseases of Fish Act, 1937.

    (i) a firearm within the meaning of the Firearms Act, 1968[1];

    (ii) an otter lath or jack,[2] wire or snare;

    (iii) a crossline[3] or setline[3];

    (iv) a spear, gaff, stroke-haul, snatch[4] or other like instrument[5];

    (v) a light;

for the purpose of taking or killing salmon, trout or freshwater fish. Nor may a person having in his possession any instrument mentioned above intending to use it to take or kill any such fish, or throw or discharge a stone or other missile for the purpose of taking or killing or facilitating the taking or killing of any such fish. A person who contravenes this provision is guilty of an offence, unless he proves to the satisfaction of the court that the act was done for the purpose of the preservation or development of a private fishery and with the previous written permission of the water authority for the area in which the act was done. But this provision does not apply to a person using a gaff (consisting of a plain metal hook without a barb) or tailer as auxiliary to angling with a rod and line, or having such a gaff or tailer in his possession intending to use it as aforesaid.[6]

(2) Taking unclean or immature fish, disturbing spawn, etc.

    A person who knowingly[7] takes, kills or injures, or attempts

---

[1] " Firearm " means a lethal barrelled weapon of any description from which any shot, bullet or other missile can be discharged. (*See* further s. 57 (1) of the Firearms Act, 1968.)

[2] " Otter lath or jack " includes any small boat or vessel, board, stick, or other instrument, whether used with a hand line, or as auxiliary to a rod and line, or otherwise for the purpose of running out lures, artificial or otherwise (Salmon and Freshwater Fisheries Act, 1975, s. 1 (3)). *See also Allen* v. *Parker* (1891), 30 L.R. Ir. 87, on " otter ".

[3] " Crossline " means a fishing line reaching from bank to bank across water and having attached to it one or more lures or baited hooks and " setline " means a fishing line left unattended in water having attached to it one or more lures or baited hooks. (Salmon and Freshwater Fisheries Act, 1975, s. 1 (3)).

[4] " Stroke haul or snatch " includes any instrument or device, whether used with a rod and line or otherwise, for the purpose of foul hooking any fish (Salmon and Freshwater Fisheries Act, 1975, s. 1 (3)).

[5] On the meaning of " instrument ", *see Jones* v. *Davies* (1902), 86 L.T. 447; *Maw* v. *Holloway*, [1914] 3 K.B. 594.

[6] Salmon and Freshwater Fisheries Act, 1975, s. 1.

[7] Ignorance of fact may be a defence: *Hopton* v. *Thirwell* (1863), 9 L.T. 327. As to evidence of intention, *see Davies* v. *Evans* (1902), 86 L.T. 419.

to take, kill or injure salmon, trout or freshwater fish which is unclean[1] or immature,[1] or who buys, sells or exposes for sale, or has in his possession any such fish or part of such fish is guilty of an offence, but not if he takes a fish accidentally and returns it to the water with least possible injury. The wilful disturbance of spawn or spawning fish, or any bed, bank or shallow on which such spawn or fish may be is also an offence, but without prejudice to the legal right of any person to take materials from any waters. For the purpose of fishing for salmon, trout or freshwater fish, it is an offence for anyone to use fish roe, or to buy, sell or expose for sale, or have in his possession roe of salmon or trout. It is not an offence under these provisions if such acts are done for artificial propagation, or for some scientific purpose or for the preservation or development of a private fishery, and for which the previous written permission has been obtained of the water authority for the area.[2]

(3) Nets

It is an offence for any person to shoot or work a seine or draft net for salmon[3] or migratory trout[3] in any waters across more than three-fourths of the width thereof. It is also an offence for a person, except in a place where smaller dimensions are authorised by byelaw, to take or attempt to take salmon or migratory trout with any net having a mesh of less dimensions than two inches in extension from knot to knot (the measurement to be made on each side of the square), or eight inches measured round each mesh when wet, except in the case of a landing net in use as auxiliary to angling with rod and line; the placing of two or more nets the one behind the other, or near to each other in such manner as practically to diminish the mesh of the nets used, or the covering of the nets with canvas, or the using of any other device so as to evade this provision with respect to the mesh of nets, is deemed to be a contravention of this provision.[4]

---

1 These terms are defined on p. 281.
2 Salmon and Freshwater Fisheries Act, 1975, s. 2.
3 These terms are defined in p. 281.
4 Salmon and Freshwater Fisheries Act, 1975, s. 3. As to the use of nets, see *Davies v. Evans* (1902), 86 L.T. 419; *Dodd v. Armor* (1867), 31 J.P. 773; *Moses v. Raywood*, [1911] 2 K.B. 271.

(4) Matter injurious to fish

It is an offence for a person to cause[1] or knowingly permit[2] to flow, or to put or knowingly permit to be put, into any waters containing fish, or into any tributaries[3] thereof, any liquid or solid matter to such an extent as to cause the waters to be poisonous or injurious to fish or the spawning grounds, spawn or food of fish. But this does not apply to any act done in exercise of a legal right or in continuation of a method in use in connection with the same premises prior to the 18th July, 1923, if the court is satisfied that the best practicable means have been used within a reasonable cost to prevent such matter from doing injury to fish or to the spawning grounds, spawn or food of fish. Proceedings can only be instituted by the water authority or a person who has first obtained a certificate from the Minister that he has a material interest in the waters alleged to be affected.[4] Any entry of matter into a stream or controlled waters authorised by a consent or in consequence of an act so authorised consent given under Part II of the Control of Pollution Act, 1974, and is in accordance with any conditions to which the consent is subject does not constitute an offence under the foregoing provision.[5]

(5) Prohibition of use of explosives, poisons or electrical devices and of destruction of dams, etc.

A person must not use in or near any waters (including waters adjoining the coast of England and Wales and within the exclusive fishery limits of the British Islands[6]) any explosive

---

[1] On "causes to flow", see *Alphacell Ltd. v. Woodward* [1972] 2 All E.R. 1475, distinguishing *Moses v. Midland Ry. Co.* (1915), 84 L.J.K.B. 2181; *Price v. Cromock*, [1975] 2 All E.R. 113.

[2] On "knowingly permit", see *West Riding of Yorkshire Council v. Holmfirth*, [1894] 2 Q.B. 842.

[3] For cases on the meaning of "tributary", see *Merricks v. Cadwallader* (1881), 46 L.T. 29; *Hall v. Reid* (1882), 48 L.T. 221; *Harbottle v. Terry* (1882), 47 J.P. 136; *George v. Carpenter*, [1893] 1 Q.B. 505; *Evans v. Owen*, [1895] 1 Q.B. 237; *Stead v. Nicholas*, [1901] 2 K.B. 163; *Cook v. Clareborough* (1903), 70 J.P. 252; *Moses v. Iggo*, [1905] 1 K.B. 516.

[4] Salmon and Freshwater Fisheries Act, 1975, s. 4; as to radioactivity, *see* p. 346.

[5] Control of Pollution Act, 1974, s. 54.

[6] *See* the Fishery Limits Act, 1964, on p. 19.

substance, poison or other noxious substance,[1] or any electrical device, with intent thereby to take or destroy fish, except where a person uses a substance or device for a scientific purpose or for protecting, improving or replacing stocks of fish, and with the written permission of the water authority for the area, and permission given by a water authority for the use of a noxious substance must also be approved by the Minister of Agriculture, Fisheries and Food. Nor may a person without lawful excuse destroy or damage any dam,[2] floodgate or sluice with intent thereby to take or destroy fish.

A person who contravenes any of the above provisions, or who for the purpose of contravening the first above-mentioned provision, has in his possession an explosive or noxious substance or an electrical device, is guilty of an offence.[3]

Obstructions to passage of fish

(1) Fixed engines

A person who (a) places a fixed engine[4] in any inland or tidal waters[5]; or, (b) uses an unauthorised fixed engine for taking or facilitating the taking of salmon or migratory trout or for detaining or obstructing the free passage of such fish in such waters is guilty of an offence, and engines so used or placed may be taken possession of or destroyed by a person acting under directions to that effect given by the water authority for the area. An unauthorised fixed engine means any fixed engine other than (i) a fixed engine certified in pursuance of the Salmon Fishery Act, 1865, to be a privileged fixed engine or (ii) a fixed engine which was in use for taking salmon or migratory trout during the open season of 1861 in

---

1 " Poison or . . . noxious material ". This under s. 9 of the Salmon and Freshwater Fisheries Act, 1923 (now replaced by the above provision) covered anything put into water which was injurious to the health or life of fish or which rendered their capture more easily (*R. v. Antrim Justices*, [1906] 2 I.R. 298).

2 " Dam " is defined on p. 280.

3 Salmon and Freshwater Fisheries Act, 1975, s. 5.

4 For definition of " fixed engine " and cases thereon, *see* p. 280.

5 As to the extent of tidal waters, under this provision, *see Ingram v. Percival* [1968] 3 W.L.R. 663.

pursuance of an ancient right or mode of fishing as lawfully exercised during that season by virtue of a grant or charter or immemorial usage.[1,2,3]

(2) Fishing weirs

No unauthorised fishing weir, *i.e.* one which was not lawfully in use on 6th August, 1861, by virtue of a grant or charter or immemorial usage, shall be used for taking or facilitating the taking of salmon or migratory trout. A fishing weir[4] extending more than half-way across a river at its lowest state of water must not be used for taking salmon or migratory trout unless it has a free gap or opening in the deepest part of the river between the points where it is intercepted by the weir and (*a*) the sides of the gap are in a line with and parallel to the direction of the stream at the weir; and (*b*) the bottom of the gap is level with the natural bed of the river above and below the gap; and (*c*) the width of the gap in its narrowest part is not less than one-tenth part of the width of the river. A free gap need not be more than 40 feet wide and must not be less than 3 feet wide. A person using a weir in contravention of this provision or making any alteration in the bed of a river in such manner as to reduce the flow of water through a free gap is guilty of an offence.[5]

(3) Fishing mill dams

An unauthorised fishing mill dam, *i.e.* one which was not lawfully in use on 6th August, 1861, by virtue of a grant or charter or immemorial usage, must not be used for taking or facilitating the taking of salmon or migratory trout. A fishing mill dam[4] must not be used for taking salmon or migratory trout unless it has a fish pass of such form and

---

[1] As to the legality of ancient fishing weirs and dams, *see Robson v. Robinson* (1783), 3 Doug. K.B. 306; *Williams v. Wilcox* (1838), 8 Ad. & El. 314; *Rolle v. Whyte* (1868), L.R. 3 Q.B. 286; *Leconfield v. Lonsdale* (1870), L.R. 5 C.P. 657; *Pirie & Sons Ltd. v. Kintore*, [1906] A.C. 468; *Fraser v. Fear* (1912), 107 L.T. 423.

[2] On " immemorial usage ", *see Bevins v. Bird* (1865), 12 L.T. 304; *Olding v. Wild* (1866), 14 L.T. 402.

[3] Salmon and Freshwater Fisheries Act, 1975, s. 6.

[4] This term is defined on p. 280.

[5] Salmon and Freshwater Fisheries Act, 1975, s. 7.

dimensions as approved by the Minister and is maintained in such a condition and has constantly running through it such a flow of water as will enable such fish to pass up or down. A person who uses an unauthorised fishing mill dam as above, or uses or attempts to use a dam without a fish pass as above, is guilty of an offence. If a fishing mill dam has not a fish pass attached to it as required by law, the right to use the dam for taking fish is deemed to have ceased and is for ever forfeited, and the water authority for the area may remove from it any cage, crib, trap, box, cruive or other obstruction to the free passage of the fish.[1]

(4) Duty to make and maintain fish passes

Where in waters frequented by salmon or migratory trout, a new dam is constructed or an existing dam is raised or otherwise altered so as to cause increased obstruction to the passage of such fish, or any other obstruction to the passage of such fish is created, increased or caused, or a dam which from any cause has been destroyed or taken down to the extent of one-half its length has been rebuilt or reinstated, the owner or occupier of the dam or obstruction must make and maintain a fish pass for such fish on being required by the water authority for the area, of such form and dimensions as the Minister may approve. Failure to do so renders the owner or occupier guilty of an offence. The water authority are empowered to do any work required and to enter upon the dam or obstruction and recover their expenses from the person in default.[2]

(5) Water authority may construct and alter fish passes

With the written consent of the Minister, a water authority may construct and maintain in a dam or in connection with a dam a fish pass of a form and dimensions approved by the Minister without injury to the milling power, water supply of or to any navigable river or canal, and may also with like consent abolish, alter, substitute or restore an existing fish pass or free gap without injury as before. If a person injures such

---

[1] Salmon and Freshwater Fisheries Act, 1975, s. 8.
[2] *Ibid.*, s. 9.

M

a new or existing fish pass he must pay the water authority the expenses incurred in repairing the injury.[1]

(6) Minister's consents and approvals for fish passes

Any consent or approval given by the Minister to or in relation to a fish pass may be given provisionally until the Minister indicates that the fish pass is functioning satisfactorily, and he may revoke his consent or approval given provisionally after giving the applicant not less than 90 days' notice of his intention to do so. Where the Minister approves a fish pass and does not revoke his approval, it is deemed to be a fish pass in conformity with the Act.[2]

(7) Penalty for injuring or obstructing fish pass or free gap

Any person who wilfully alters or injures a fish pass, or does any act whereby salmon or migratory trout are obstructed or liable to be obstructed in using a fish pass or whereby a fish pass is rendered less efficient, or alters a dam or the river bed or banks so as to render a fish pass less efficient, or uses a contrivance or does any act liable to scare, hinder or disturb salmon or migratory trout from passing through a fish pass is guilty of an offence, and is liable to pay any expenses incurred (recoverable in a summary manner) in restoring the fish pass to its former state of efficiency. The owner or occupier of a dam is deemed to have altered it if it is damaged, destroyed or allowed to fall into a state of disrepair, and if after notice is served on him by the water authority he fails to repair or reconstruct it within a reasonable time so as to render the fish pass as efficient as before the damage or destruction. If a person (a) does any act for preventing salmon or migratory trout from passing through a fish pass, or takes, or attempts to take, a salmon or trout in passing through a fish pass; or (b) places an obstruction, uses a contrivance, or does any act whereby salmon or trout may be scared, deterred or in any way prevented from freely entering and passing up and down a free gap at all periods of the year, he is guilty of an offence.[3]

---

1 Salmon and Freshwater Fisheries Act, 1975, s. 10.
2 *Ibid.*, s. 11.
3 *Ibid.*, s. 12.

(8) Sluices

The sluices of dams for drawing off water which would otherwise flow over the dam in waters frequented by salmon or migratory trout must be kept shut on Sundays and at all times when water is not required for milling purposes in such manner as to cause the water to flow through any fish pass in or connected with the dam or, if there is no fish pass, over the dam unless written permission is granted by the water authority for the area, except in cases of flood or for purposes of milling or navigation.[1]

(9) Gratings

Gratings must be placed and maintained at the expense of the owner of the undertaking or mill occupier across conduits or artificial channels through which water is diverted from waters frequented by salmon or migratory trout for purposes of a mill or of a water or canal undertaking to prevent the descent of such fish, unless an exemption is granted by the water authority for the area. Unless exempted, gratings must also be placed and maintained across such conduits or channels to prevent salmon or migratory trout entering the outfall. If a person without lawful excuse fails to place or maintain a grating in accordance with this provision he is guilty of an offence. Gratings must not be placed so as to interfere with the passage of boats on a navigable canal.[2]

(10) Boxes and cribs in weirs and dams

No fishing weir or fishing mill dam can be used for taking salmon or migratory trout by means of cribs or boxes unless the latter comply with the requirements of the Act, namely, that (a) the upper surface of the sill of the box or crib must be level with the bed of the river; (b) the bars or inscales of the heck or upstream side of the box or crib—(i) must not be nearer to each other than 2 inches; (ii) must be capable of being removed; and (iii) must be placed perpendicularly; (c) there must not be attached to any such box or crib any spur or tail wall, leader or outrigger of a greater length than 20 feet from the upper or lower side of the box or crib.[3]

---

[1] Salmon and Freshwater Fisheries Act, 1975, s. 13.
[2] *Ibid.*, s. 14.
[3] Salmon and Freshwater Fisheries Act, 1975, s. 16.

(11) Taking salmon or trout above or below an obstruction

Salmon or trout must not be taken or killed, or attempted to be taken or killed, except with rod and line, or scared or disturbed within 50 yards above or 100 yards below a dam or any artificial or natural obstruction, or within such other distance as may be prescribed by byelaw, or in any waters under or adjacent[1] to or communicating with a mill, or in the head race or tail race of a mill, or in any artificial channel connected with any such dam or obstruction. But this does not apply to a legal fishing mill dam not having a crib, box or cruive, or to a fishing box, coop, apparatus, net or mode of fishing in connection with and forming part of such a dam or obstruction for purposes of fishing.[2]

Close seasons: sale and export of fish

(1) Salmon

Subject to any byelaws the annual close season for salmon is the period between the 31st August and the 1st February following; the close season for fishing with a rod and line is the period between the 31st October and the 1st February, and that for fishing with putts and putchers is the period between 31st August and the 1st May following; the weekly close time for salmon is from 6 a.m. on Saturday to 6 a.m. on the following Monday. Any person fishing for, taking, killing or attempting to take or kill salmon (*a*) except with a rod and line or putts and putchers during the annual close season or weekly close time; or (*b*) with a rod and line during the annual close season for rod and line; or (*c*) with putts and putchers during the annual close season for putts and putchers, is guilty of an offence, unless done for the artificial propagation of fish or for some scientific purpose, with the previous permission of the water authority.[3] An angler regularly staked out nets to catch plaice, cod, etc., and during the close season he found one dead salmon in a net and a live one in another net. He was charged under section 19 for taking salmon. Held: he was fishing for other fish and had no intention of catching salmon. An intention was required to catch salmon.[4]

---

[1] On "adjacent", *see Wellington Corpn. v. Lower Hull Corpn.*, [1904] A.C. 775.
[2] Salmon and Freshwater Fisheries Act, 1975, s. 17.
[3] *Ibid.*, s. 19 (1)-(3), Sch. 1.
[4] *Cain v. Campbell* [1978] Crim. L.R. 292.

Fixed engines must be removed or rendered incapable of taking or obstructing the passage of salmon during the annual close season and during the close season for putts and putchers, and also (except in the case of putts and putchers) during the weekly close time. No obstructions must be placed during the annual close season or weekly close time to deter salmon from passing up a river.[1]

A person must not buy, sell, or expose for sale, or have in his possession[2] for sale salmon between the 31st August and the 1st February following, unless it has been canned, frozen, cured, salted, pickled, dried or otherwise preserved outside the United Kingdom, or so treated in the United Kingdom between the 1st February and the 31st August, or caught as a clean salmon beyond such limits, or caught as a clean and mature salmon within such limits if its capture by net instrument or device was lawful at the time and in the place where it was caught.[3]

(2) Trout

Subject to any byelaws the annual close season for trout (not rainbow trout) is the period between the 31st August and the 1st March following, and the annual trout close season for rod and line is the period between the 30th September and the 1st March following; the weekly close time for trout is from 6 a.m. on Saturday until 6 a.m. on the following Monday. Any person who fishes for, takes, kills, or attempts to take or kill trout other than rainbow trout (a) except with a rod and line during the annual close season or weekly close time for trout; or (b) with a rod and line during the annual trout close season for rod and line, is guilty of an offence, unless done for the artificial propagation of fish, the stocking or restocking of waters, or for some scientific purpose,[4] with the previous permission of the water authority in whose area the act was done.[5] The provisions of section 20 penalising the obstruction of salmon during the annual close season or weekly close

---

1 Salmon and Freshwater Fisheries Act, 1975, s. 20.
2 Actual physical possession is not necessary: *M'Attee v. Hogg* (1903), 5 F. (Ct. of Sess.) 67; *see also Birkett v. McGlassons Ltd.*, [1957] 1 All E.R. 369.
3 Salmon and Freshwater Fisheries Act, 1975, s. 22.
4 *See Price v. Bradley* (1885), 50 J.P. 150.
5 Salmon and Freshwater Fisheries Act, 1975, s. 19 (1), (4), (5), Sch. 1.

time apply to migratory trout. Trout must not be bought, sold or exposed for sale or had in one's possession for sale between the 31st August and the 1st March following, unless it has been canned, frozen, cured, salted, pickled, dried or otherwise preserved outside the United Kingdom, or so treated in the United Kingdom between the 1st March and the 31st August, or caught as a clean trout beyond such limits, or caught as a clean and mature trout within such limits if its capture by net or device was lawful at the time and in the place where it was caught.[1]

(3) Export and consignment of salmon and trout

Unclean[2] salmon or trout, or salmon and trout caught during the time at which their sale is prohibited where such fish were caught, cannot be exported or entered for export. Salmon or trout intended for export between the 31st August and the 1st May following must be entered for that purpose with the proper officer of customs before shipment.[3] Salmon or trout cannot be consigned or sent by common or other carrier unless contained in a package conspicuously marked on the outside with the word salmon or trout, as the case may be, and an authorised officer may open any package suspected to contain salmon or trout and detain it if not so marked, or where a marked package is being dealt with contrary to law.[4]

(4) Freshwater fish

The annual close season for freshwater fish is the period between the 14th March and 16th June except in waters for which a close season is dispensed with or a different season is substituted by byelaws. The annual close season for rainbow trout for any waters is that fixed by byelaws. During the annual close seasons as above freshwater fish or rainbow trout

---

1 Salmon and Freshwater Fisheries Act, 1975, s. 22.
2 " Unclean " is defined on p. 281.
3 Salmon and Freshwater Fisheries Act, 1975, s. 23.
4 *Ibid.*, s. 24.

cannot be fished for, taken or killed, or attempted to be taken
or killed in an inland water and eels cannot be fished for by a
rod and line in such water, but this does not apply (*a*) to the
owner or occupier of a several fishery where salmon or trout
are specially reserved, removing eels, freshwater fish or rainbow
trout not so preserved; (*b*) to a person fishing with rod and
line in a several fishery with written permission of the owner
or occupier; (*c*) to a person fishing with rod and line for eels
in waters where such fishing is authorised by byelaw; (*d*) to
taking freshwater fish or trout for scientific purposes, or taking
freshwater fish for bait, in a several fishery with written permission of the owner or occupier or in any other fishery except
where the taking would contravene a byelaw.[1]

Before 25th June in any year it is forbidden to hang, fix or
use in waters frequented by salmon or migratory trout any
baskets, nets, traps or devices for catching eels, or place[2] in
inland waters any device to catch or obstruct fish descending a
river. Between the 1st August and the 1st March following
baskets, traps or devices for taking fish must not be placed
upon the apron of a weir.[3] But eel baskets not exceeding ten
inches in diameter, constructed to be fished with bait, and not
used at a dam or other obstruction or in a conduit or artificial
channel by which water is deviated from a river, or any device
for taking eels as may be authorised by the water authority for
the area with the consent of the Minister are not prohibited.[4]

Regulation of fisheries

An application to the Minister for an order for the general
regulation of the salmon, trout, freshwater and eel fisheries
may be made by a water authority, a county council, the
owners of one-fourth at least in value of the several fisheries
proposed to be regulated, a majority of persons licensed to fish
in public waters or an association sufficiently representative of
fishing interests within the area of the proposed order. An
order may provide (*inter alia*) for defining the area within

---

[1] Salmon and Freshwater Fisheries Act, 1975, s. 19 (6)-(8), Sch. 1.
[2] For meaning of " place ", *see Briggs v. Swanwick* (1883), 47 J.P. 564.
[3] As to what is meant by " apron of a weir ", *see Maw v. Holloway*, [1914]
3 K.B. 594.
[4] Salmon and Freshwater Fisheries Act, 1975, s. 21.

which the order is to apply; the rating of several fisheries; the erection and working by the water authority or their lessees of fixed engines for catching salmon or migratory trout, the modification of any provisions of the Act in relation to fisheries in the area; the modification of local fishery Acts; and any incidental, consequential or supplemental provisions.[1] An order is made in accordance with the procedure set out in Schedule 3, Part I, paras. 5-13.

Transfer of fish

A person is guilty of an offence if he introduces any fish or spawn of fish into an inland water, or has in his possession any fish or spawn of fish intending to introduce it into an inland water, unless he first obtains the written consent of the water authority within whose area any part of the water is situated.[2]

Licences to fish

A water authority must by a licensing system regulate fishing for salmon and trout in their area, and also fishing for freshwater fish of any description or eels except so far as excused by the Minister. A fishing licence entitles the person to whom it is granted and no others to use an instrument specified in the licence to fish for any fish of a description, in an area and for a period so specified.

A fishing licence to use an instrument other than a rod and line to fish for salmon or trout also authorises the use of the instrument for that purpose by the duly authorised servants or agents of the person to whom it is granted, but not exceeding the specified number.[3] A fishing licence to use a rod and line entitles the licensee to use as ancillary to that use a gaff, consisting of a plain metal hook without a barb, or a tailer or landing net. A licence to use any instrument to fish for salmon authorises the use of that instrument to fish for trout, whilst a licence in respect of any instrument to fish for salmon or trout authorises the use of that instrument to fish for freshwater fish and eels.

---

[1] Salmon and Freshwater Fisheries Act, 1975, s. 28 (3)-(6), Sch. 3, Part I, paras. 1-4.

[2] *Ibid.*, s. 30.

[3] *See ibid.*, Sch. 2, para. 13.

A general licence may be granted to any person or association entitled to an exclusive right of fishing in any inland waters to fish in those waters subject to any conditions agreed between the water authority and the licensee, and the licence entitles the licensee and any person (unless disqualified) authorised by him in writing or, in the case of an association, by its secretary so to fish.[1]

A water authority may by order confirmed by the Minister limit for a period not exceeding ten years from the coming into operation of the order the number of fishing licences to be issued in any one year for fishing in any part of their area for salmon or trout other than rainbow trout with any instrument so specified other than rod and line. An order may provide for the selection of the applicants to whom such licences are to be issued where the number of applicants exceeds the number of licences which may be granted. An order may be revoked by the Minister, or by an order made by the water authority and confirmed by the Minister.[2]

A person in any place in which fishing for fish of any description is regulated by a licensing system who fishes for or takes fish of that description otherwise than by means of an instrument which he is entitled to use for that purpose by virtue of a licence or otherwise than in accordance with the conditions of the licence is guilty of an offence. A person is also guilty of an offence if in such a place he has in his possession with intent to use it for such purposes an instrument other than one which he is authorised to use for that purpose by virtue of such a licence.[3]

Except where the water authority grant an exemption in special cases, a duty is payable in respect of a licence and is fixed by the authority and with the approval of the Minister if written objection is made to the proposed duty by an interested party. Different duties may be fixed depending on the instrument, period, parts of the area, descriptions of fish and classes of licence holder. Temporary licences may be granted for up to fourteen days. The sum payable on a general licence is agreed between the authority and the licensee. Upon payment

---

[1] See the Salmon and Freshwater Fisheries Act, 1975, s. 25.
[2] Ibid., s. 26 (1), (7). As to confirmation of an order, see ibid., s. 26 (2)-(6).
[3] Ibid., s. 27.

of the duty, a licence must be granted to every applicant who is not disqualified from holding one.[1]

A water bailiff appointed by a water authority or any constable may require a person fishing, or whom he reasonably suspects of being about to fish or to have within the preceding half hour fished, in a water authority area to produce his licence or other authority to fish and to state his name and address. A person holding a fishing licence for a water authority area may, on producing his licence, require any person fishing in that area to produce his licence or other authority to fish and to state his name and address. Failure so to produce his licence or authority, or to state his name and address, renders the person guilty of an offence unless within seven days he produces the licence or authority at the office of the water authority.[2]

The taking of salmon or trout only by means of a licensed instrument applies to the taking of live or dying fish and not to dead fish.[3] A person fishing with no intention of catching fish does not require a licence.[4] Where the licence is for the use of one instrument a licensee must not use more than one such instrument at the same time, *i.e.* a licence to fish with rod and line does not permit fishing with three rods and lines.[5]

Water bailiffs

A water bailiff appointed by a water authority is empowered to examine any dam, fishing weir, fishing mill dam, fixed engine or obstruction or artificial water course, and for that purpose enter on any land. He can examine any instrument or bait which he has reasonable cause to suspect of having been or being used or likely to be used in taking fish in contravention of the Act, or any container which he has reasonable cause to suspect of having been or being used or likely to be used for holding any such instrument, bait or fish. He can stop and

---

1 Salmon and Freshwater Fisheries Act, 1975, Sch. 2.
2 *Ibid.*, s. 35.
3 *Gazard v. Cooke* (1890), 55 J.P. 102; *Stead v. Tillotson* (1900), 64 J.P. 343.
4 *Marshall v. Richardson* (1889), 60 L.T. 605; *Watts v. Lucas* (1871), 24 L.T. 128. But *see Hill v. George* (1880), 44 J.P. 424; *Short v. Bastard* (1881), 46 J.P. 580; *Moses v. Raywood*, [1911] 2 K.B. 271.
5 *Combridge v. Harrison* (1895), 72 L.T. 592.

search[1] any boat or other vessel used in fishing in a water authority area or any vessel or vehicle which he has reasonable cause to suspect of containing (a) fish caught in contravention of the Act; (b) any such instrument, bait or container[2] as above. He may also seize fish and instruments, vessels, vehicles or other things liable to be forfeited. It is an offence to refuse to allow a water bailiff to make an authorised entry, search or examination or to seize anything which he is authorised to seize, or to resist or obstruct him in the same.[3] Every water bailiff is deemed to be a constable and has the same powers, privileges and liabilities as a constable duly appointed at common law or by statute for the enforcement of the Act, or any order or byelaw made thereunder. The production of evidence of his appointment is sufficient warrant for a water bailiff to exercise the powers conferred on him by the Act.[4] A bailiff is bound to produce his instrument of appointment before attempting to exercise his powers of search, etc.,[5] and the fact that it is so dark that the instrument cannot be read is immaterial.[6] A water bailiff is entitled to take proceedings without being specially authorised to do so by his employers.[7]

A water bailiff or other officer of a water authority may, under a special written order from the authority, at all reasonable times enter, remain upon and traverse any lands not being a dwelling house or curtilage thereof adjoining or near to any waters within the authority area to prevent any offence against the Act.[8] A justice of the peace may authorise a water bailiff or other officer of a water authority to enter and remain on any land situate on or near any waters for not more than twenty-four hours where an offence against the Act is suspected of being or is likely to be committed to detect the persons committing the offence. In addition, a water bailiff or other officer of a water authority or constable may be authorised by warrant to enter suspected premises to detect any offence against the

[1] A person can be convicted although illegally searched: *Jones v. Owens* (1870) 34 J.P. 759.
[2] This includes pockets in clothing: *Taylor v. Pritchard*, [1910] K.B. 320.
[3] Salmon and Freshwater Fisheries Act, 1975, s. 31.
[4] *Ibid.*, s. 36.
[5] *Barnacott v. Passmore* (1887), 19 Q.B.D. 75.
[6] *Cowler v. Jones* (1890), 54 J.P. 660.
[7] *Pollock v. Moses* (1894), 70 L.T. 378.
[8] Salmon and Freshwater Fisheries Act, 1975, s. 32.

Act and seize all illegal nets or other instruments and fish (including eels) on the premises suspected to have been illegally taken.[1]

A water bailiff with assistants may seize without warrant any person illegally taking or killing fish (including eels) by night, *i.e.* between the expiration of the first hour after sunset on any day and the beginning of the last hour before sunrise on the following morning, or found on or near any waters with intent illegally to take or kill fish or having in his possession any instrument prohibited by the Act for the capture of fish, and deliver the offender into the custody of a police officer.[2] The Minister may appoint persons to exercise in a water authority area the powers of a water bailiff under sections 31 to 34 of the Act.[3]

Offences and Penalties

A person guilty of an offence against the Act is in respect of the offences specified in the Table to Part I of Schedule 4 to the Act, liable on summary conviction or on indictment to the maximum punishments by way of fine or imprisonment as specified therein and as modified by the Criminal Law Act, 1977, sections 28 (2), (4), 31 (1), 32 (1), Schedule 6. For the purposes of the Table a person is treated as acting together with another, if both are engaged in committing an offence against section 1 or section 27 of the Act, other than one committed by means of a rod or line or without an instrument, or one is aiding, abetting, counselling or procuring the commission of such an offence by the other. A person guilty of an offence against any provision of the Act not specified in the Table is liable to a fine not exceeding £500.[4]

The court by which a person is convicted of an offence against the Act may order the forfeiture of (*a*) any fish illegally taken by him or in his possession at the time of the offence; (*b*) any instrument, bait or other thing used in the commission of the offence; (*c*) in the case of an offence of unlawful possession of any substance or device in contravention of section 5

---

1 Salmon and Freshwater Fisheries Act, 1975, s. 33.
2 *Ibid.*, s. 34.
3 *Ibid.*, ss. 31-34, 36.
4 *Ibid.*, s. 37, Sch. 4, Part I, para. 1; Criminal Law Act, 1977, s. 31 (1), Sch. 6.

of the Act, such substance or device; and (d) on conviction or indictment, any vessel or vehicle used in or in connection with the commission of the offence or in which any substance or device unlawfully in his possession was contained at the time of the offence. The court may order any object so forfeited to be disposed of as it thinks fit.[1] If a person is convicted of an offence against the Act and is subsequently convicted of any such offence, the court may order that any fishing or general licence he holds shall be forfeited, and that he shall be disqualified for holding and obtaining such a licence or for fishing in a water authority area by virtue of such a licence for a period not exceeding one year as the court thinks fit.[2]

A person who is prosecuted for an offence against the Act, and holds a fishing or general licence must either (a) deliver it to the clerk of the court not later than the day before the date appointed for the hearing, or (b) post it so that in the ordinary course of post it would be delivered not later than that day by letter addressed to the clerk and either registered or sent by recorded delivery service, or (c) have it with him at the hearing. If he is convicted and the court makes an order under Schedule 4, Part II, para. 9, of the Act, the court shall order the licence to be surrendered to it.   Where the offender has not posted or delivered the licence as above and does not surrender it as required then he is guilty of an offence and the licence shall be revoked from the time when its surrender was ordered.[3] Where a court orders a licence to be surrendered, or where a person is disqualified from holding or obtaining a licence, the court shall (a) send notice of the order to the water authority within whose area the offence was committed, unless the authority prosecuted in the case; (b) if the licence has been surrendered, forward it to the authority who may dispose of it as they think fit.[4]

Any offence committed on the sea coast or at sea beyond the ordinary jurisdiction of a magistrates' court shall be

---

1 Salmon and Freshwater Fisheries Act, 1975, Sch, 4, Part II, para. 5.   Schedule 7 to the Customs and Excise Act, 1952, is applied with modifications to vessels and vehicles, liable to forfeiture under *ibid.*, para. 5. (*Ibid.*, Sch. 4, Part II, para. 1.)
2 *Ibid.*, Sch. 4, Part II, para. 9.
3 *Ibid.*, Sch. 4, Part II, para. 10.
4 *Ibid.*, Sch. 4, Part II, para. 11.

deemed to have been committed in any place abutting on such sea coast or adjoining such sea.[1]

A justice of the peace is not disqualified from hearing a case because he is a subscriber to a fish protection society, but he cannot hear a case for an offence committed on his own land or in relation to a fishery which he owns or occupies.[2] A justice is disqualified from adjudicating if present at a meeting which authorised the prosecution,[3] unless he took no part in the decision thereon.[4] On a conviction of an offence against the Act, the clerk of the court must forward a certificate of conviction to the water authority for the area in which the offence was committed within one month.[5]

An officer of a water authority and certain other officers may seize fish bought, sold or exposed for sale in contravention of the Act,[6] and fish seized under the Act may be sold and the proceeds of sale are liable to forfeiture, or if not forfeited are payable on demand to the owner of the fish.[7]

THE DISEASES OF FISH ACT, 1937

The Diseases of Fish Act, 1937, was passed to prevent the spread of the disease known as furunculosis (and such other diseases to which the Act may be extended by Order in Council)[8] among salmon and freshwater fish. The importation of live fish of the salmon family into Great Britain is prohibited, and a licence granted by the Minister of Agriculture, Fisheries and Food is required for the import of live freshwater fish or live eggs of salmon and freshwater fish.[9]

---

[1] Salmon and Freshwater Fisheries Act, 1975, Sch. 4, Part II, para. 2.

[2] *Ibid.*, Sch. 4, Part II, para. 4.

[3] *R. v. Henley*, [1892] 1 Q.B. 504; *R. v. Huggins*, [1895] 1 Q.B. 563.

[4] *R. v. Pwllheli JJ., Ex p. Soane*, [1948] 2 All E.R. 815.

[5] Salmon and Freshwater Fisheries Act, 1975, Sch. 4, Part II, para. 12.

[6] *Ibid.*, Sch. 4, Part II, para. 7.

[7] *Ibid.*, Sch. 4, Part II, para. 8.

[8] *See* s. 13 of the Diseases of Fish Act, 1937. The provisions of this Act have been applied with respect to a disease known as columnaris (Diseases of Fish Order, 1966 (S.I. 1966, No. 944)). *See also* the Diseases of Fish Order, 1973 (S.I. 1973, No. 2093).

[9] Diseases of Fish Act, 1937, s. 1; Diseases of Fish Regulations, 1937 (S.R. & O. 1937, No. 1224), as amended by S.I. 1950, No. 127.

If the Minister is satisfied that any waters are infected with furunculosis, he may by order declare the area to be an infected area, and may prohibit or regulate the transport of live fish, or of eggs of fish or of foodstuff for fish from the area to prevent the spread of infection. The Minister may by written notice give directions to the occupier of any fish farm in the infected area to take all reasonable steps to secure the removal of dead or dying fish from the waters and regulate the disposal thereof.[1]

Where a water authority suspect that any waters, not being a fish farm, are infected, they must forthwith report the facts to the Minister and may take any practicable steps for removing dead and dying fish from the waters. Where an area is declared to be infected, the Minister may authorise a water authority to remove fish from the waters (not being a fish farm), and the water authority must destroy or otherwise properly dispose of all fish removed by them and send the Minister a return of the fish removed.[2]

If a Ministry Inspector suspects that the waters of a fish farm are infected, he must serve a notice on the occupier and no live fish, eggs of fish and foodstuff for fish shall be transported from the fish farm for a period of sixteen days. Should any person who is entitled to take fish, or employed to take care of fish, suspect that the waters are infected, he must report this to the water authority, or to the Minister in the case of a fish farm.[3]

A person guilty of an offence under the Act is liable on summary conviction to a fine not exceeding £20 or, in the case of a second or subsequent conviction, to a fine not exceeding £100, and the court may order to be forfeited any fish, eggs of fish, foodstuff or article in respect of which the offence was

[1] Diseases of Fish Act, 1937, s. 2.
[2] Ibid., s. 3.
[3] Ibid., s. 4.

committed. A water authority have power to take legal proceedings to enforce the Act as respects waters in their area.[1]

THE SEA FISHERIES REGULATION ACT, 1966

Local fisheries committees

Under the Sea Fisheries Regulation Act, 1966, the Minister of Agriculture, Fisheries and Food may on the application of a county council by order (*a*) create a sea fisheries district comprising any part of the sea[2] within the national or territorial waters of the United Kingdom adjacent to England or Wales, either with or without any part of the adjoining coast, and (*b*) define the limits of the district, and the area chargeable with any expenses under the Act, and (*c*) provide for the constitution of a local fisheries committee for the regulation of the sea fisheries carried on within the district.[3] The power to make orders is exercisable by statutory instrument and the draft of such statutory instrument must be laid before Parliament.[4]

The local fisheries committee for a sea fisheries district is a committee of the county council, or a joint committee of such county councils, as determined by the order creating the district, and consists of members appointed by the council, or by the constituent councils in such proportions as so determined, together with additional members, not exceeding the number of members required to be appointed by the council or constituent councils, including one person appointed by each water authority having jurisdiction within the district of the committee, and the rest are persons appointed by the Minister as being

---

[1] Diseases of Fish Act, 1937, s. 8; Water Act, 1973, s. 40 (2), Sch. 8, para. 43.

[2] " Sea " includes the coast up to high water mark (Sea Fisheries Regulation Act, 1966, s. 20 (1)).

[3] Sea Fisheries Regulation Act, 1966, s. 1 (1); Local Government Act, 1972, s. 272 (1), Sch. 30. As to subsequent orders, *see* 1966 Act, s. 1 (1).

[4] Sea Fisheries Regulation Act, 1966, s. 1 (2). As to the making of draft orders, *see ibid.*, s. 4. As to the powers of ratepayers and inhabitants of a county to apply for an order, *see ibid.*, s. 3.

acquainted with the needs and opinions of the fishing interests of the district.[1]

An order constituting a local fisheries committee may contain regulations as to the number and mode of appointment of the members of the committee, and such other matters relating to the constitution of the committee as seem expedient to the Minister.[2]

The expenses of a local fisheries committee, so far as payable by a county council, are, according as the order constituting the committee provides, expenses for general or special county expenses.[3]

Powers of Committees

A local fisheries committee may:—

(a) Enforce any Act relating to sea fisheries[4];

(b) Undertake, with the approval of the Minister of Agriculture, Fisheries and Food, the destruction of predatory fish, predatory marine animals, predatory birds and eggs of such birds[5], where desirable for the preservation and improvement of fisheries[6];

(c) Contribute to the cost of maintaining or improving small harbours used principally by persons engaged in the sea-fishing industry[7];

(d) Institute proceedings for offences under the Prevention of Oil Pollution Act, 1971 if the committee or its

---

[1] Sea Fisheries Regulation Act, 1966, s. 2 (1), (2); Local Government Act, 1972, s. 272, Sch. 30. " Fishing interests " includes all persons interested in fisheries, either as owners of fisheries or interests therein, fishermen, fishing boat-owners, fish curers, fish merchants or otherwise (*ibid.*, s. 2 (2)).

[2] *Ibid.*, s. 2 (5).

[3] *Ibid.*, s. 17 (1).

[4] Sea Fisheries Regulation Act, 1966, s. 13 (5). Sea Fisheries Act, 1968, s. 22 (1), Sch. 1, Part II.

[5] *See also* the Protection of Birds Acts, 1954-1967.

[6] Sea Fisheries Regulation Act, 1966, s. 13 (2).

[7] *Ibid.*, s. 13 (4).

officers are authorised in that behalf under section 19 (6) of that Act;

(e) Stock or restock any public fishery for shellfish.[1]

Byelaws

Subject to any regulations[2] made by the Minister of Agriculture, Fisheries and Food, a local fisheries committee may make byelaws for (inter alia):—

(a) Restricting or prohibiting methods of fishing for sea fish, the use of instruments of fishing for sea fish and for determining the size of mesh, form and dimensions of instruments of fishing for sea fish[3];

(b) Restricting or prohibiting the fishing for or taking of all or any specified kinds of sea fish during specified periods;

(c) The regulation, protection and development of fisheries for all or any specified kinds of shellfish.[4]

The skipper and owner of a vessel used for fishing in any manner constituting a contravention of byelaws referred to in paragraphs (a) or (c) above are each guilty of an offence and liable on summary conviction to a fine not exceeding £50 for a first offence, or £150 for a second offence, or to imprisonment up to three months, or to a fine not exceeding £300, or to both, for a third or subsequent offence.[5] Without prejudice to the operation of the foregoing provision, a person who contravenes a byelaw made by a local fisheries committee

---

[1] Sea Fisheries Regulation Act, 1966, s. 13 (1). " Shellfish " includes crustaceans and molluscs of any kind (ibid., s. 20 (1)).

[2] See the Sea Fisheries (Byelaws) Regulations, 1938 (S.R. & O. 1938, No. 1182).

[3] " Sea fish " means fish of any description found in the sea including shellfish, but does not include (a) fish of the salmon species, or (b) trout which migrate to and from the sea (Sea Fisheries Regulation Act, 1966, s. 20 (1)).

[4] Sea Fisheries Regulation Act 1966, s. 5 (1); Control of Pollution Act, 1974, s. 108 (2), Sch. 4.

[5] Sea Fisheries Regulation Act, 1966, s. 11 (2).

is liable on summary conviction to a fine not exceeding £50 or, in the case of a second or subsequent conviction, to a fine not exceeding £100.[1]

Byelaws are confirmed by the Minister of Agriculture, Fisheries and Food after holding a local inquiry, if he thinks fit,[2] and may be revoked by him if he considers it necessary or desirable for the maintenance or improvement of fisheries, after considering any objection raised by the local fisheries committee and holding a public inquiry, if so required by them.[3]

Byelaws cannot be made so as to prejudicially affect rights of several fishery or rights over the foreshore, nor affect any byelaws made by a water authority in force within a sea fisheries district or the statutory powers of a local authority to discharge sewage.[4]

Where an offence under section 11 of the Sea Fisheries Regulation Act, 1966, is committed on the sea coast or at sea beyond the ordinary jurisdiction of a magistrates' court and not on or from a ship or boat, it is deemed to have been committed within the body of any county having a separate commission of the peace abutting on that sea coast or adjoining that sea, and may be tried and punished accordingly.[5]

Fishery officers

A local fisheries committee may appoint fishery officers[6] for enforcing the byelaws within their district, and such officers may within the limits of their district, or of an adjoining sea fisheries district, water authority area or harbour authority's district, stop and search vessels or vehicles used in fishing or in conveying fish or substances the deposit or discharge of

---

[1] Sea Fisheries Regulation Act, 1966, s. 11 (5).
[2] *Ibid.*, s. 7.
[3] *Ibid.*, s. 8.
[4] *Ibid.*, s. 6.
[5] Sea Fisheries Regulation Act, 1966, s 11 (7).
[6] Fishery officers must be distinguished from British sea fishery officers appointed for the purposes of the Sea Fisheries Acts.

which is prohibited or regulated by the byelaws, examine instruments used in fishing for fish and search containers used in carrying fish and seize sea fish or instruments taken or used in contravention of the byelaws.[1] A person who without reasonable excuse refuses to allow a fishery officer to exercise his statutory powers, or resists or obstructs an officer in the performance of his duty, is liable on summary conviction for each offence to a fine not exceeding £50.[2]

Relations of local fisheries committees with water authorities

Where a proposed sea fisheries district will adjoin or overlap a water authority area, the Minister of Agriculture, Fisheries and Food is required, by the order defining the limits of the district, to draw a line at or near the mouth of every river or stream flowing into the sea or into any estuary within those limits, or at the option of the Minister at or near the mouth of any estuary within those limits, and the sea fisheries district shall not extend into any river, stream or estuary above that line. The order may provide that the water authority shall have the powers of a local fisheries committee with respect to any such river, stream or estuary.[3]

Where an area is under the jurisdiction of a water authority or harbour authority, and a sea fisheries district has not been created for that area or part thereof, the Minister may by order confer on the water authority or harbour authority the powers of a local fisheries committee with respect to that area.[4] Where a water authority or harbour authority have the powers of a local fisheries committee hereunder, those powers shall be exercised subject to the same conditions as if exercised by a local fisheries committee, and the provisions of the Sea Fisheries Regulation Act, 1966, shall apply in relation to byelaws made or officers appointed in exercise of such powers as

---

[1] Sea Fisheries Regulation Act, 1966, s. 10.
[2] Ibid., s. 11 (1).
[3] Ibid., s. 18 (1).
[4] Ibid., s. 18 (2).

if the byelaws were made or the officers appointed by a local fisheries committee.[1]

A county council may pay or contribute to the expenses incurred by a water authority in exercising their powers under the Sea Fisheries Regulation Act, 1966.[2]

---

[1] Sea Fisheries Regulation Act, 1966, s. 18 (3).

[2] Ibid., s. 19; Local Government Act, 1973, s. 272, Sch. 30.

CHAPTER 15

THE CONTROL OF POLLUTION OF WATERS

THE CONTROL OF POLLUTION ACT, 1974

The new statute law concerning the control and prevention of pollution[1] of rivers, coastal waters and underground water is contained in Part II of the Control of Pollution Act, 1974, which largely replaces and repeals the previous legislation on that subject, namely the Rivers (Prevention of Pollution) Acts, 1951-1961, and sections 72-76 of the Water Resources Act, 1963.[2]

The Control of Pollution Act, 1974, which was passed on the 31st July, 1974, applies to England, Wales and Scotland, but does not extend to Northern Ireland except as stated.[3] The Minister for the purposes of Part II of the Act is the Secretary of State for the Environment and the operation and enforcement of the pollution provisions lie with the water authorities subject to directions by and references to the Secretary of State. Part II of the Act comes into force on such date or dates as the Secretary of State may appoint.[4]

The Secretary of State may by order repeal or amend any provision of any local Act passed before the 1974 Act (including

---

[1] Pollution at common law is dealt with on pp. 103-111.

[2] As to the repeal of most of those statutes, *see* the Control of Pollution Act, 1974, s. 108 (1), (2), Schs. 3, 4.

[3] Control of Pollution Act, 1974, s. 109 (3). Provisions applicable to Scotland are not dealt with here.

[4] Control of Pollution Act, 1974, s. 109 (2).

an Act confirming a provisional order) or of any order or other instrument made under an Act so passed if the provision is inconsistent with, or has become unnecessary or requires alteration in consequence of, any provision of the 1974 Act or corresponds to any provision repealed by that Act.[1]

Unless it expressly provides otherwise, the Act does not (a) confer a right of action in civil proceedings (other than for recovery of a fine) in respect of a contravention of the Act or an instrument made under the Act; (b) affect a restriction imposed by or under any other enactment, whether public, local or private; or (c) derogate from a right of action or other remedy (whether civil or criminal) in proceedings instituted otherwise than under the Act.[2]

For the purposes of Part II of the Act the area of a water authority includes all controlled waters[3] off the coast of the area which is the authority's area apart from this provision, and any question as to whether any place is included in the area of a water authority by virtue of this provision is determined by the Secretary of State.[4]   Where an estuary is situated in the areas of two or more water authorities, the Secretary of State may direct the authorities to arrange for a joint committee to discharge their functions relating to the restoration and maintenance of the wholesomeness of rivers and other waters.[5]

---

[1] Control of Pollution Act, 1974, s. 108 (3).

[2] *Ibid.*, s. 105 (2).

[3] " Controlled waters " means the sea within three nautical miles from any point on the coast measured from low-water mark of ordinary spring tides, such other parts of the territorial sea adjacent to Great Britain as are prescribed by regulations and any other tidal waters in Great Britain (*ibid.*, s. 56 (1)).   No regulations have been made for this purpose.

[4] Control of Pollution Act, 1974, s. 56 (4).

[5] Water Act, 1973, s. 17 (5).

CONTROL OF POLLUTION

Control of pollution of rivers, coastal waters, etc.

(a) Offences

A person is guilty of an offence if he causes or knowingly permits—[1]

    (a) any poisonous, noxious or polluting matter[2] to enter[3] a stream[4] or controlled waters[5] or any specified underground water[6]; or

---

[1] " Causes or knowingly permits ". In *Alphacell Ltd. v. Woodward*, [1972] 2 All E.R. 475, H.L., it was said that " causing " must be given a common sense meaning, and anyone could " cause " something to happen intentionally or negligently or inadvertently. In *Impress (Worcester) Ltd. v. Rees*, [1971] 2 All E.R. 357 the company were held not to have caused pollution because this was due to the intervening act of an unauthorised person and was not the conduct of the company. It was held in *Price v. Cromack* [1975] 2 All E.R. 113, that " causing " required some positive act of the defendant as opposed to mere tacit standing by and looking on. For earlier cases *see also Kirkheaton L.B. v. Ainley*, [1892] 2 Q.B. 283; *Southall-Norwood U.D.C. v. Middlesex County Council* (1901), 83 L.T. 742; *Korten v. West Sussex County Council* (1903), 67 J.P. 167; *Butterworth v. West Riding of Yorkshire Rivers Board*, [1909] A.C. 45; *Rochford R.D.C. v. Port of London Authority*, [1914] 2 K.B. 916; *West Riding of Yorkshire Rivers Board v. Linthwaite U.D.C.*, [1915] 2 K.B. 436; *Moses v. Midland Rly. Co.* (1915), 79 J.P. 367; *Smith v. G.W. Rly. Co.* (1926), 135 L.T. 112.

[2] " Poisonous, noxious or polluting "; these expressions are not defined, but *see Dell v. Chesham U.D.C.* (1921), 85 J.P. 186; *Durrent v. Branksome U.D.C.*, [1897] 2 Ch. 291.

[3] " Enters " includes polluting matter discharged to a sewer or channel and passing into a stream; *Kirkheaton L.B. v. Ainsley*, [1892] 2 Q.B. 283; *Butterworth v. West Riding of Yorkshire Rivers Board*, [1909] A.C. 45.

[4] " Stream " includes any river, watercourse or inland water, whether natural or artificial or above or below ground, except (a) any lake or pond which does not discharge into a stream, subject to any regulations (as to which *see* s. 56 (3) of the Act) which provide that any prescribed lake or pond which does not discharge into a stream, or that any lake or pond of a prescribed description which does not discharge into a stream, shall be a stream for the purposes of Part II of the Control of Pollution Act, 1974; (b) any sewer vested in a water authority; and (b) any tidal waters, and any reference to a stream includes a reference to the channel or bed of a stream which is for the time being dry (Control of Pollution Act, 1974, s. 56 (1), (3)). No regulations have been made for this purpose.

[5] " Controlled waters " is defined in footnote [3] on p. 309.

[6] " Specified underground water " means underground water in a water authority area specified, as water which is used or is expected by the authority to be used for any purpose, in a document in a form prescribed by regulations for the purposes of this definition and contains prescribed particulars and of which a copy is kept available, and has for not less than one month been kept available, at the principal office of the authority for inspection by the public free of charge during office hours (*ibid.*, s. 56 (1)). No regulations have been made for this purpose.

(b) any matter to enter a stream so as to tend (either directly or in combination with other matter which he or another person causes or permits to enter the stream) to impede the proper flow of the stream in a manner leading or likely to lead to a substantial aggravation of pollution due to other causes or of the consequences of such pollution; or

(c) any solid waste matter to enter a stream or restricted waters.[1], [2]

A person guilty of an offence under paragraphs (a) or (b) above is liable on summary conviction to imprisonment for a term not exceeding three months or a fine not exceeding £1,000 or both, and on conviction on indictment to imprisonment for a term not exceeding two years or a fine or both. A person guilty of an offence under paragraph (c) above is liable on summary conviction to a fine not exceeding £200.[3]

(b) *Exemptions from offences*

A person is not guilty of an offence under section 31 (1) of the Act if—

(a) the entry in question is authorised by, or is a consequence of an act authorised by, a disposal licence[4] or a consent given by the Secretary of State or a water authority in pursuance of the Act and the entry or act is in accordance with any conditions to which the licence or consent is subject; or

(b) the entry in question is authorised by, or is a consequence of an act authorised by (i) section 34 of the Water Act, 1945 (relating to temporary discharges by water undertakers), or any enactment prescribed by

---

[1] " Restricted waters " means controlled waters in (a) areas designated by regulations as tidal waters for the purposes of this definition; and (b) other areas of a kind prescribed by regulations for the purposes of this definition as areas in which, in the opinion of the Secretary of State, vessels commonly lie at moorings in close proximity to one another (*ibid.*, s. 56 (1)). No regulations have been made for this purpose.

[2] *Ibid.*, s. 31 (1).

[3] Control of Pollution Act, 1974, s. 31 (7); Criminal Law Act, 1977, s. 28 (2); Criminal Law Act, 1977 (Commencement No. 5) Order, 1978 (S.I. 1978, No. 712 (C. 16)).

[4] *I.e.*, a licence to dispose of controlled waste under Part I of the Act.

regulations, or (ii) any provision of a local Act[1] or statutory order[2] which expressly confers power to discharge effluent into water, or (iii) a licence granted under the Dumping at Sea Act, 1974;[3] or

(c) the entry in question is attributable to an act or omission in accordance with good agricultural practice other than an act or omission which (i) is of a kind specified in a notice which is in force when the entry occurred and which was served under section 51 (3) (a) of the Act (relating to notices to abstain from certain agricultural practices) on the occupier or a previous occupier of the place where the act or omission occurs, and (ii) occurs after twenty-eight days from the date entered in the register maintained under section 51 (4) as the date of service of the notice; or

(d) the entry in question is caused or permitted in an emergency in order to avoid danger to the public and, as soon as reasonably practicable after the entry occurs, particulars of the entry are furnished to the water authority in whose area it occurs; or

(e) the matter in question is trade or sewage effluent discharged as mentioned in section 32 (1) (a) of the Act or matter discharged as mentioned in section 32 (1) (b) or (c) and the entry in question is not from a vessel.

Nor is a person guilty of an offence by reason only of his permitting water from an abandoned mine, to enter a stream or controlled waters or any specified underground water.[4]

A person is not by virtue of section 31 (b) or (c) guilty of an offence by reason of his depositing the solid refuse of a

---

[1] " Local Act " includes enactments in a public general Act which amends a local Act (Control of Pollution Act, 1974, s. 31 (9)).

[2] " Statutory order " means an order, byelaw, scheme or award made under an Act of Parliament, including an order or scheme confirmed by Parliament or brought into operation in accordance with special parliamentary procedure (ibid., s. 31 (9)).

[3] I.e., a licence granted by the Minister of Agriculture, Fisheries and Food to dump substances or articles in the sea.

[4] Control of Pollution Act, 1974, s. 31 (2).

mine[1] or quarry[2] on any land so that it falls or is carried into a stream or restricted waters[3] if:—

(a) he deposits the refuse on the land with the consent (which must not be unreasonably withheld) of the water authority in whose area the land is situated, and

(b) no other site for the deposit is reasonably practicable, and

(c) he takes all reasonably practicable steps to prevent the refuse from entering the stream or restricted waters.[4]

(c) Regulations

Regulations[5] may be made providing for the precautions to be taken, by any person having the custody or control of any poisonous, noxious or polluting matter, for the purpose of preventing the matter from entering a stream or controlled waters or any specified underground water. Such regulations may provide that a contravention thereof is an offence subject to a prescribed maximum penalty.[6]

Where it appears to the Secretary of State, with a view to preventing poisonous, noxious or polluting matter from entering any such waters as above, to be appropriate to prohibit or restrict the carrying on in a particular area of activities which he considers are likely to result in pollution of the waters, he may by regulations[7] (a) designate that area; (b) provide that

---

[1] " Mine " means an excavation or system of excavations made for the purpose of, or in connection with, the getting, wholly or substantially by means involving the employment of persons below ground, of minerals (whether in their natural state or in solution or in suspension) or products of minerals (Mines and Quarries Act, 1954, s. 180 (1); Control of Pollution Act, 1974, s. 105 (1)).

[2] " Quarry " means an excavation or system of excavations made for the purpose of, or in connection with, the getting of minerals (whether in their natural state or in solution or in suspension) or products of minerals, being neither a mine nor merely a well or borehole or a well and borehole combined (Mines and Quarries Act, 1954, s. 180 (2); Control of Pollution Act, 1974, s. 105 (1)).

[3] As to " restricted waters ", see footnote 1 on p. 311.

[4] Control of Pollution Act, 1974, s. 31 (3).

[5] No regulations have been made.

[6] Control of Pollution Act, 1974, s. 31 (4).

[7] No regulations have been made.

prescribed activities must not be carried on at any place within the area except with the consent (not to be unreasonably withheld) of the water authority in whose area the place is situated and subject to any reasonable conditions; and (c) provide that a contravention of the regulations is an offence subject to a prescribed maximum penalty.[1]

(d) Byelaws

A water authority may by byelaws provide for prohibiting or regulating the washing or cleansing, in a stream or controlled waters in their area, of things of a specified kind, and a person contravening a byelaw is guilty of an offence and liable on summary conviction to a fine not exceeding £200 or such smaller amount as is specified in the byelaws.[2]

Control of discharges

Section 32 of the Act replaces the powers of control previously exercised by river authorities in respect of discharges of trade and sewage effluents to streams, tidal waters and underground strata[3] and extends and strengthens such powers now in the hands of the water authorities.

(a) Offences

It is made an offence for a person to cause or knowingly permit any trade effluent[4] or sewage effluent[5] or matter described below to be discharged into waters stated below unless such discharge is made with the consent under section 34 of the water authority in whose area the discharge occurs, or in a

---

[1] Control of Pollution Act, 1974, s. 31 (5).   As to the maximum penalties prescribed under *ibid.*, s. 31 (4) and (5), *see ibid.*, s. 31 (8).

[2] Control of Pollution Act, 1974, s. 31 (6).

[3] *I.e.*, the powers previously conferred on river authorities by the Rivers (Prevention of Pollution) Acts, 1951-1961, and ss. 72-76 of the Water Resources Act, 1963.

[4] " Trade effluent " includes any liquid (either with or without particles of matter in suspension in it) which is discharged from premises used for carrying on any trade or industry, other than surface water and domestic sewage, and any land or premises wholly or mainly used (whether for profit or not) for agricultural or horticultural purposes or for scientific research or experiment are deemed to be premises used for carrying on a trade (Control of Pollution Act, 1974, s. 105 (1)).

[5] " Sewage effluent " includes any effluent from the sewage disposal or sewerage works of a water authority (*ibid.*, s. 56 (1)).

case falling within paragraph (a) (iv) below, of the water authority whose area includes the point at which the pipe passes or first passes into or under controlled waters from the sea outside them, and is in accordance with any conditions to which the consent is subject.

The cases covered by the above provision are:—

(a) any trade or sewage effluent to be discharged—
   (i) into a stream,
   (ii) into controlled waters,
   (iii) into any specified underground water,
   (iv) from land in Great Britain through a pipe into the sea outside controlled waters,
   (v) from a building or from plant on to or into any land or into a lake or pond which does not discharge into a stream,

(b) any matter other than trade or sewage effluent to be discharged into any waters referred to in (a) (i)-(iii) above from a sewer or drain,

(c) any matter other than trade or sewage effluent to be discharged into any waters referred to in (a) (i)-(iii) above from a drain which a highway authority or other person is entitled to keep open by virtue of section 103 of the Highway Act, 1959, and in respect of which the water authority in whose area the discharge occurs has within three months from the date of the discharge served a notice on the highway authority or other person stating that this paragraph is to apply to the drain.[1]

A person who is guilty of an offence as above is liable on summary conviction to imprisonment for a term not exceeding three months or a fine not exceeding £1,000, or both, and, on conviction on indictment, to imprisonment for a term not exceeding two years or a fine or both.[2]

---

[1] Control of Pollution Act, 1974, s. 32 (1).

[2] Ibid., s. 32 (7); Criminal Law Act, 1977, s. 28 (2); Criminal Law Act, 1977 (Commencement No. 5) Order, 1978 (S.I. 1978, No. 712 (C. 16)).

(b) Exceptions

The above provisions regarding the control of discharges shall not apply to discharges of a kind or in an area specified in an order which may be made by the Secretary of State before the above provisions came into force, being discharges for which, if the Act had not been passed, consent under the Rivers (Prevention of Pollution) Acts, 1951 to 1961, or section 72 of the Water Resources Act, 1963, would not have been required. An order may be varied or revoked and may require a water authority to publish such information about the order in a manner as is so specified.[1]

Nor do the above provisions regarding control apply to discharges (a) from a vessel, (b) authorised by a licence granted under the Dumping at Sea Act, 1974, or (c) caused or permitted in an emergency to avoid danger to the public if, as soon as reasonably practicable after the discharge occurs, particulars of the discharge are furnished to the water authority in whose area it occurs.[2]

(c) Liability of water authority for sewage discharges

Where any sewage effluent is discharged as mentioned in section 32 (1) (a) from any works or sewer vested in a water authority and the authority did not cause or knowingly permit the discharge but were bound to receive into the works or sewer, either unconditionally or subject to conditions which were observed, matter included in the discharge, the authority are deemed for the purposes of that provision to have caused the discharge.[3]

A water authority are not guilty of an offence under section 32 (1) by reason only of the fact that a discharge from a sewer or works vested in the authority contravenes conditions of a consent relating to the discharge if (a) the contravention is attributable to a discharge which another person caused or permitted to be made into the sewer or works; and (b) the

---

[1] Control of Pollution Act, 1974, s. 32 (3).

[2] *Ibid.*, s. 32 (4).

[3] *Ibid.*, s. 32 (2).

authority either was not bound to receive the discharge into the sewer or works or was bound to receive it subject to conditions which were not observed; and (c) the authority could not reasonably have been expected to prevent the discharge into the sewer or works. Further, a person is not guilty of such an offence in consequence of a discharge which he caused or permitted to be made into a sewer or works vested in a water authority if the authority were bound to receive the discharge there either unconditionally or subject to conditions which were observed.[1]

Control of sanitary appliances on vessels

Previously a river authority was empowered to make byelaws for prohibiting or regulating the keeping or use on specific non-tidal streams of vessels provided with sanitary appliances, and such byelaws could be extended to specified tidal waters or parts of the sea.

The present position is dealt with in section 33 of the Act, which enables a water authority by byelaws[2] to make provision for prohibiting or regulating the keeping or use on a stream or restricted waters[3] in the area of the authority, of vessels[4] of a kind specified in the byelaws which are provided with sanitary appliances[5]; and a person contravening a byelaw is guilty of an offence.[6]

A person who after the end of 1978[7] keeps or uses on a stream any vessel provided with a sanitary appliance shall, subject to the further provision relating to the sealing of vessels or appliances, be guilty of an offence. Thereafter the reference to " stream " in the preceding paragraph shall cease to have effect.[8]

---

1 Control of Pollution Act, 1974, s. 32 (5).
2 Byelaws are made in accordance with the Water Act, 1973, s. 36 (3), Sch. 7, Part II, and the Control of Pollution Act, 1974, s. 108 (1), Sch. 3, para. 30.
3 " Restricted waters " are defined in footnote 1 on p. 333.
4 " Vessel " includes a hovercraft (Control of Pollution Act, 1974, s. 105 (1)).
5 " Sanitary appliance " means a water closet or other prescribed appliance (except a sink, a bath and a shower-bath), which is designed to permit polluting matter to pass into the water on which the vessel in question is for the time being situated (*ibid.*, s. 33 (10)).
6 *Ibid.*, s. 33 (1). As to the application of byelaws made under s. 5 (1) (c) of the Rivers (Prevention of Pollution) Act, 1951, *see ibid.*, s. 33 (2).
7 That date is undoubtedly due to be revised.
8 Control of Pollution Act, 1974, s. 33 (3).

So far as sanitary appliances on vessels within restricted waters are concerned, a water authority have the choice after 1978[1] of continuing with byelaws or of applying for an order.

A water authority or harbour authority[2] can apply to the Secretary of State and the Minister of Agriculture, Fisheries and Food, who acting jointly may make an order after the end of 1978[1] providing that a person who keeps or uses, on any restricted waters in the area of the authority specified in the order, a vessel provided with a sanitary appliance shall, subject to the further provision relating to the sealing of vessels or appliances, be guilty of an offence. When such an order is in force, the water authority cannot exercise in any restricted waters in their area the power to make byelaws for prohibiting or regulating the keeping or use of vessels provided with sanitary appliances. An order may be revoked by the Ministers jointly on the application of or after giving notice to the authority.[3] The Ministers jointly may also by order provide that so much of a stream as is specified therein shall be disregarded for the purposes of section 33 (3) and treated as restricted waters for the purposes of section 33 (4).[4]

At and after the end of 1978 each water authority will be required to arrange at the request of a person in charge of a vessel provided with a sanitary appliance to fix a seal to the vessel or appliance in such a manner that while the seal is affixed matter cannot pass from the appliance into the water on which the vessel for the time being is situated; while the seal is so affixed, the appliance shall be disregarded for the purposes of sections 33 (3) and (4).[5]

Regulations[6] may be made for requiring a person who in prescribed circumstances hires out for payment to another

---

[1] That date is undoubtedly due to be revised.

[2] " Harbour authority " means any person in whom are vested under the Harbours Act, 1964, or by another Act or by an order or instrument (except a provisional order) made under another Act or by a provisional order powers or duties of improving or maintaining or managing a harbour. (Harbours Act, 1964, s. 57 (1); Control of Pollution Act, 1974, s. 33 (10).)

[3] Control of Pollution Act, 1974, s. 33 (4). As to the procedure for making an order, see ibid., s. 33 (6).

[4] Ibid., s. 33 (5).

[5] Ibid., s. 33 (8).

[6] No regulations have yet been made.

person any vessel provided with a sanitary appliance to give to the other person notice in a prescribed form of prescribed provisions made by or under section 33. A person failing to comply with such a requirement is guilty of an offence.[1]

A person guilty of an offence under any of the above provisions is liable on summary conviction to a fine not exceeding £200.[2]

CONSENTS FOR DISCHARGES

Consents and conditions

An application to a water authority for consent for discharges of effluent or other matter must state:—

(a) the place at which the discharges are proposed to be made;

(b) the nature and composition of the matter to be discharged and its maximum temperature at the time when it is to be discharged;

(c) the maximum quantity of the matter to be discharged on any one day and the highest rate of discharge.

A water authority may treat an application for consent for discharges at two or more places as separate applications to discharge at each of the places.[3]

It is the duty of a water authority to give consent to an application either unconditionally or subject to conditions or to refuse it, and not to withhold consent unreasonably. If within the period of three months from the date when an application is received by a water authority, or within such longer period as may at any time be agreed upon in writing between the authority and the applicant, the authority have neither given nor refused consent nor informed the applicant that the application has been transmitted to the Secretary of

---

[1] Control of Pollution Act, 1974, s. 33 (9).
[2] *Ibid.*, s. 33 (11).
[3] *Ibid.*, s. 34 (1).

State under section 35, the authority are deemed to have refused consent.[1]

Where a person has, without the consent of the water authority, caused or permitted matter to be discharged in their area in contravention of section 32 (1) of the Act and a similar contravention by that person is likely, the authority may serve on him an instrument in writing giving consent, subject to conditions, for discharges of a kind so specified. But such a consent does not relate to any discharge which occurred before the instrument giving consent was served on the recipient.[2]

The conditions subject to which a water authority may give their consent shall be such reasonable conditions as the authority think fit, including reasonable conditions as to:—

(a) the places at which the discharges may be made and the design and construction of any discharge outlets;

(b) the nature, composition, temperature, volume and rate of the discharges and the periods during which the discharges may be made;

(c) the provision of facilities for taking samples of the matter discharged and the provision, maintenance and use of manholes, inspection chambers, observation wells and boreholes in connection with the discharges;

(d) the provision, maintenance and testing of meters for measuring the volume and rate of the discharges and apparatus for determining the nature, composition and temperature of the discharges;

(e) the keeping of records of the nature, composition, temperature, volume and rate of the discharges and of records of readings of meters and other recording apparatus provided in accordance with any other condition attached to the consent;

---

[1] Control of Pollution Act, 1974, s. 34 (2).
[2] *Ibid.*, s. 34 (3).

(*f*) the making of returns and the giving of other information to the water authority about the nature, composition, temperature, volume and rate of the discharges; and

(*g*) the steps to be taken for preventing the discharges from coming into contact with any specified underground water.

Consent may be given subject to different conditions in respect of different periods.[1]

A person who, in an application for consent, makes any statement which he knows to be false in a material particular or recklessly makes any statement which is false in a material particular is guilty of an offence and is liable on summary conviction to a fine not exceeding £1,000 or on conviction on indictment is liable to imprisonment for a term not exceeding two years or a fine or both.[2]

References to Secretary of State

It is the duty of a water authority to comply with any direction by the Secretary of State to the authority to transmit to him for determination specified applications for consent for discharges made to the authority, who must also inform each applicant that his application has been transmitted to the Secretary of State. Before determining such an application the Secretary of State may, and must if the water authority or the applicant request him in accordance with regulations[3] to be heard with respect to the application, cause a local inquiry to be held or afford both parties (and any person who has made representations under section 36 (1) (*c*) or (5)) an opportunity of appearing before and being heard by a person appointed by the Secretary of State for the purpose. The Secretary of State determines an application by directing the water authority to refuse their consent or to give the consent

---

[1] Control of Pollution Act, 1974, s. 34 (4).
[2] *Ibid.*, s. 34 (5); Criminal Law Act, 1977, s. 28 (2); Criminal Law Act, 1977 (Commencement No. 5) Order, 1978 (S.I. 1978, No. 712 (C. 16)).
[3] No regulations have been made.

either unconditionally or subject to such conditions as specified in the direction, and the authority must comply with the direction.[1]

Publication of applications for consent

Where a water authority receive an application for consent for a discharge or serve an instrument under section 34 (3), before deciding whether to give or refuse consent in pursuance of the application or after serving the instrument, as the case may be, the authority must—

(a) publish in the form prescribed by regulations[2] notice of the application or instrument in two successive weeks in a newspaper or newspapers circulating in (i) the area or areas in which the places[3] are situated of the discharges, and (ii) the area or areas in the vicinity of any stream or controlled waters likely to be affected by the discharges, and not earlier than the day following that on which the first newspaper publication of the notice is completed publish such a notice in the London Gazette;

(b) send copies of the application or instrument to each local authority[4] in whose area a discharge is the subject of an application or instrument, and in the case of an application or instrument relating to controlled waters or an application relating to the sea outside controlled waters, to the Secretary of State and the Minister of Agriculture, Fisheries and Food; and

(c) consider any written representations relating to the application or instrument made to the authority by any person within the period of six weeks from the date of publication of the notice in the London Gazette.[5]

---

[1] Control of Pollution Act, 1974, s. 35. The provisions of *ibid.*, s. 36, regarding publication and giving notice of applications, etc., apply to applications which are the subject of a direction under s. 35 (*ibid.*, s. 36 (5)).

[2] No regulations have yet been made.

[3] Any place at sea at which it is proposed in an application that a discharge should be made is treated as situated at the point on land nearest to that place (Control of Pollution Act, 1974, s. 36 (1)).

[4] " Local authority " means the council of a county or district, the Greater London Council and a London borough council (*ibid.*).

[5] *Ibid.*, s. 36 (1).

A water authority are entitled to recover from the applicant the cost of publishing a notice of an application in local newspapers and the London Gazette.[1]

A water authority may disregard the requirements as to publication and giving notice in relation to an application (except so far as copies may have to be sent to the Ministers) if the authority propose to give consent to the application and consider that the discharges in question will have no appreciable effect on the water into which they are proposed to be made.[2]

Where a water authority propose to give consent to an application under section 34 in consequence of an application in respect of which representations have been made, the authority must serve notice of their proposal on the person making the representations informing him that he may, within twenty-one days from the date on which the notice was served on him, request the Secretary of State to give a direction under section 35 (1) in respect of the application. The authority shall not give consent before the expiration of that period, and if the person within such period makes a request to the Secretary of State and serves notice of the request on the authority, the authority shall not give consent unless the Secretary of State notifies the authority that he declines to comply with the request.[3]

A consent for any discharges given under section 34 is not limited to discharges by a particular person and extends to the discharges in question which are made by any person.[4]

Regulations[5] may provide that conditions of a prescribed kind to which a consent given under section 34 is subject shall be disregarded for the purposes of sections 31 (2) (a), 32 (1) and 54.[6]

---

[1] Control of Pollution Act, 1974, s. 36 (3).
[2] *Ibid.*, s. 36 (4).   The provisions of s. 36 (1) regarding publication and notices in respect of applications for consent are also waived when the Secretary of State issues a certificate under *ibid.*, s. 42.
[3] *Ibid.*, s. 36 (6).
[4] *Ibid.*, s. 36 (7).
[5] No regulations have yet been made.
[6] Control of Pollution Act, 1974, s. 36 (8).

A person who without reasonable excuse fails to comply with a condition which under section 36 (8) is to be disregarded for the purposes there mentioned is guilty of an offence and liable on summary conviction to a fine not exceeding £400, but no proceedings for such an offence can be brought in England and Wales except by or with the consent of the Director of Public Prosecutions or by the water authority which gave the consent.[1]

Revocation of consents and variation of conditions

A water authority are required to review periodically consents and any conditions thereto, and may, by serving a notice on the person making a discharge under a consent, revoke the consent if it is reasonable to do so, or make reasonable modifications of the conditions, or provide reasonable conditions in the case of an unconditional consent. The Secretary of State may direct a water authority to serve a notice as above containing such provisions as specified in the direction. If the authority fail to serve the notice within such period as the Secretary of State may allow, he may do so on behalf of the authority, and this takes effect as if served by the authority.[2]

Restriction on variation and revocation

Each instrument signifying the consent of a water authority under section 34 of the Act, must specify a period during which a notice revoking the consent or modifying or imposing conditions cannot be served without the written agreement of a person making a discharge in pursuance of the consent. Likewise, each notice of revocation, modification or imposition served under section 37 (1) (except a notice only revoking a consent or conditions served by a water authority) must specify a period during which a subsequent notice cannot be served without the written agreement of a person making a discharge in pursuance of a consent to which the first notice relates. In each case the period must be a reasonable one of

---

1 Control of Pollution Act, 1974, s. 36 (9).
2 *Ibid.*, s. 37.

not less than two years from the date on which the consent takes effect or on which the first notice is served.[1]

Nothing contained above prohibits a notice of revocation, modification or alteration under section 37 (1) being served by a water authority without the written agreement and during the specified period if the authority consider (a) that it is necessary to serve the notice in order to provide proper protection for persons likely to be affected by discharges which could lawfully be made apart from the notice or (b) in the case of a notice relating to a consent given by an instrument served under section 34 (3), that it is appropriate to serve the notice in consequence of representations received under section 36 (1) with respect to the instrument.[2]

Where an authority serve a notice under section 38 (3), they are liable to pay compensation to the recipient of the notice unless it is served in pursuance of section 37 (1) and not by virtue of section 37 (2) and either:—

(a) it states that in the opinion of the authority the notice is required (i) in consequence of a change of circumstances (which may include a change in the information available about the discharges to which the notice relates or as to the interaction of such discharges with other discharges or matter) which has occurred since the date on which the consent took effect or the notice of revocation, etc., was served (as the case may be) and could not reasonably have been foreseen on that date, and (ii) otherwise than in consequence of consents given under section 34 after that date, and states the reasons for the opinion; or

(b) the relevant consent was given by an instrument served under section 34 (3) and the notice is served within three months from the date on which notice of the instrument was published in the London Gazette under section 36 (1).[3]

---

[1] Control of Pollution Act, 1974, s. 38 (1), (2).

[2] *Ibid.*, s. 38 (3).

[3] *Ibid.*, s. 38 (4).

Provision may be made by regulations[1] as to the manner of determining the amount of any compensation payable including the factors to be taken into account in determining the amount.[2]

Appeals to Secretary of State

Any question as to whether (a) a water authority have unreasonably withheld their consent under sections 31 (3) or 34 of the Act or regulations made under section 31 (5) or have given their consent under section 34 or such regulations subject to conditions which are unreasonable; or (b) a notice served under section 37 (1) contains terms (other than a term required by section 38 (2)) which are unreasonable; or (c) the period specified in an instrument or notice under section 38 (1) or (2) is unreasonable, is determined by the Secretary of State. No question relating to a determination of the Secretary of State under section 35 (4) shall be referred to him and any such determination is final.[3]

Where the consent of a water authority in pursuance of regulations made under section 31 (5) is withheld for any activity or is given subject to conditions for any activity and the applicant for the consent obtains a certificate from the Minister of Agriculture, Fisheries and Food stating that the activity in question is a good agricultural practice, any question as to whether the water authority have unreasonably withheld the consent or given it subject to conditions which are unreasonable is determined by the Secretary of State and the Minister acting jointly.[4]

If a water authority serve on any person a notice under section 37 containing a statement as mentioned in section 38 (4) (a), that person or his agent may request the Secretary of State to direct that the statement should be omitted from the notice and the Secretary of State may if he thinks fit comply with the request.[5]

---

[1] No regulations have yet been made.
[2] Control of Pollution Act, 1974, s. 38 (5).
[3] *Ibid.*, s. 39 (1).
[4] *Ibid.*, s. 39 (2).
[5] *Ibid.*, s. 39 (3).

Regulations[1] may be made as to the manner in which and the time within which a question may be referred or a request may be made under the above provisions and as to procedure for dealing with a reference or request.[2]

In a case where (a) a question as to whether a water authority have unreasonably withheld their consent under section 34, or have given their consent under that section subject to conditions which are unreasonable, is referred to the Secretary of State in pursuance of that section; and (b) representations relating to the application for the consent in question were made to the authority in pursuance of section 36 (1) (c), it is the duty of the Secretary of State, before he determines the question, to secure that the authority have served notice of the reference on the persons who made the representations and to take account of any further written representations received by him from those persons within a prescribed period.[3]

Where a question is referred to the Secretary of State and he determines that the consent in question was unreasonably withheld or that the conditions or terms or period in question are or is unreasonable, he shall give the water authority, such a direction as he thinks fit and the authority are required to comply with the direction.[4] A consent which is withheld by a water authority, the conditions subject to which a consent is given, the terms contained in a notice served, and the period specified in an instrument or notice shall be treated as reasonable until the contrary is determined by the Secretary of State on appeal, but where a question as to the reasonableness of the conditions of a consent given in pursuance of regulations made under section 31 (5) is referred to the Secretary of State or to him and the Minister under section 39 on appeal the consent shall be treated as unconditional whilst the reference is pending.[5]

---

[1] No regulations have yet been made.
[2] Control of Pollution Act, 1974, s. 39 (4).
[3] *Ibid.*, s. 39 (5).
[4] *Ibid.*, s. 39 (6).
[5] *Ibid.*, s. 39 (7).

At any stage of the proceedings on a reference to the Secretary of State or to him and the Minister he or they may, and must if so directed by the High Court, state in the form of a special case for the decision of the court any question of law arising in such proceedings, subject to a right of appeal on any judgement of the High Court, to the Court of Appeal which may be brought with the leave of the High Court or the Court of Appeal.[1]

Transitional provisions relating to consents

Regulations[2] may provide that consents for discharges given under the Rivers (Prevention of Pollution) Acts, 1951 to 1961, or section 72 of the Water Resources Act, 1963, shall have effect for any of the purposes of Part II of the 1974 Act as if given under prescribed provisions of section 34 of the 1974 Act, and that conditions to which such consents were subject shall have effect for such purposes as if attached to the consents under prescribed provisions of Part II of the 1974 Act.[3] Applications for such consents pending before the date when section 32 (1) of the 1974 Act comes into force are to be treated after that date as applications for consent made under section 34 of the 1974 Act which were made on the date on which they were actually made,[4] and regulations may provide that appeals pending before that date under the above enactments shall be treated after that date as appeals made under prescribed provisions of Part II of the 1974 Act.[5]

Regulations may also provide that the terms of consents for outlets given under the Rivers (Prevention of Pollution) Act, 1951, and for conditions to which such consents were subject shall have effect, with or without modifications, for any of the purposes of Part II of the 1974 Act as if the terms or conditions were conditions attached to consents given under section 34 of the 1974 Act for discharges from the outlets, or to be treated in some other prescribed manner.[6]

---

1 Control of Pollution Act, 1974, s. 39 (8).
2 No regulations have yet been made.
3 Control of Pollution Act, 1974, s. 40 (1).
4 *Ibid.*, s. 40 (3).
5 *Ibid.*, s. 40 (5).
6 *Ibid.*, s. 40 (2).

Registers

Water authorities are required to maintain, in accordance with regulations,[1] registers containing prescribed particulars of (a) applications made for consent; (b) consents given (except under section 40 (4)) and the conditions subject to which the consents are subject; (c) samples of effluent taken by the authorities under section 113 (1) of the Water Resources Act, 1963, samples of water taken by the authorities, information produced by analyses of the samples and the steps taken in consequence of the information; (d) certificates issued under section 42; (e) notices of which copies have been served on the authorities under section 51 (3) (b) other than notices of rejections of applications.   A water authority must secure that registers are open to inspection by the public free of charge at all reasonable hours, and afford the public reasonable facilities for obtaining copies of entries in the register on payment of reasonable charges.[2]

Exemption from publicity

A person proposing to make or having made an application to a water authority for a consent under section 34 may apply to the Secretary of State within a prescribed period[3] for a certificate providing that section 36 (1) relating to publication of notice of the application and section 41 (1) (a)-(c) and (e) (regarding the entry of particulars in the register maintained by a water authority) shall not apply to the application or to any consent given or conditions imposed or to any sample of effluent taken from a discharge for which consent is given in consequence of the application or to information produced by analysing such a sample.   If the person satisfies the Secretary of State that it would prejudice to an unreasonable degree some private interest by disclosing information about a trade secret, or be contrary to the public interest, if a certificate was not issued, the Secretary of State may issue a certificate to him providing that section 36 (1) and 41 (1) (a)-(c) and (e) do not apply to such things mentioned above as are specified in the

---

[1] No regulations have yet been made.
[2] Control of Pollution Act, 1974, s. 41.
[3] No regulations have yet been made.

certificate. Similarly, if a person makes a discharge which is the subject of a consent given under the River (Prevention of Pollution) Acts, 1951-1961, or section 72 of the Water Resources Act, 1963, the Secretary of State may issue a certificate under the equivalent conditions as above.[1]

FURTHER PROVISIONS

Operations to remedy or forestall pollution

Where it appears to a water authority that pollution injurious to the flora or fauna of a stream in their area has been caused in consequence of discharges made by virtue of a consent given by the authority under section 34 of the Act after the date when this provision comes into force[2] or discharges made by virtue of a variation[3] of a consent under that section which was made by the authority after that date, it is the duty of the authority to exercise their powers under section 37 (1) (relating to revocation of consent and alteration and imposition of conditions) to ensure that further discharges of a kind which caused such injurious pollution[4] are not made under the consent or variation or are not so made after such a period as the authority consider necessary for the purpose of allowing the discharger to secure that the discharges are not of such a kind or to make arrangements for discontinuing the discharges.

Where a period is considered necessary for the purpose above, the authority are required to carry out, as soon as reasonably practicable, appropriate operations to remedy or mitigate the injurious pollution, and also such operations as are necessary to restore the fauna and flora of the stream as far as reasonably practicable in their previous state.[5]

---

[1] Control of Pollution Act, 1974, s. 42.

[2] Section 46 comes into force on such date as the Secretary of State may by order appoint.

[3] " Variation " in relation to a consent, means a modification in pursuance of *ibid.*, s. 37 (1), of the conditions to which the consent is subject or, in the case of an unconditional consent, the subjection of the consent to conditions in pursuance of that subsection. (Control of Pollution Act, 1974, s. 46 (8)).

[4] " Injurious pollution " in relation to a stream, means pollution injurious to the fauna or flora of the stream (*ibid.*, s. 46 (8)).

[5] *Ibid.*, s. 46 (1).

If it appears to a water authority that injurious pollution of a stream has been caused in consequence of discharges made as above, but that further discharges so made after a reasonable period after carrying out operations to restore the flora and fauna will not cause injurious pollution of the stream, then the authority are not required to exercise their section 37 (1) powers, but must carry out remedial operations as soon as reasonably practicable and, after the period previously mentioned, also carry out restoration operations as respects the flora and fauna.[1]

A water authority must perform the duty imposed by section 46 (1) to exercise their powers under section 34 notwithstanding the standstill period of two years referred to in section 38 (1) and (2), but (a) where in the performance of that duty a notice is served in consequence of which compensation would have been payable under section 38 (4) if such notice had been served under section 38 (3), compensation is so payable as if the notice had been so served; and (b) there is no restriction on the powers of the Secretary of State under section 37 (2) (which relates to his power to direct a water authority to revoke a consent or alter or impose conditions).[2]

Where any poisonous, noxious or polluting matter or solid waste matter is likely to enter, or is or was present in, a stream or controlled waters or specified underground water, the water authority for the area (without prejudice to any duty imposed by the foregoing provisions) may carry out in their area or elsewhere appropriate operations (a) in a case where the matter appears, likely to enter such waters, for preventing it from doing so and (b) in a case where the matter appears to be or to have been present in such waters, for removing or disposing of the matter or of remedying or mitigating any pollution caused by its presence in the waters or of restoring the waters (including the fauna and flora in them), so far as reasonably practicable, to their previous state immediately before the matter becomes present in the waters. Nothing in this provision

---

[1] Control of Pollution Act, 1974, s. 46 (2).
[2] *Ibid.*, s. 46 (3).

empowers a water authority to impede or prevent a discharge being made under a consent given under section 34.[1]

Where a water authority carry out any operations under the foregoing provisions they are entitled to recover the costs of doing so (a) in the case of operations under section 46 (1) or (2), from the dischargers in question and (b) in the case of operations under section 46 (4), from any persons who caused or knowingly permitted the matter in question to be present in the place from which it was likely to enter the waters or (as the case may be) to be present in the waters.[2]   However, no costs are payable by a person (i) if he satisfies the court that the costs were incurred unnecessarily; or (ii) for operations in respect of water from an abandoned mine which that person permitted to reach a place mentioned in paragraph (b) above or to enter the waters; or (iii) if he is a person to whom compensation is payable under section 46 (3) in respect of a consent to which the operations in question relate.[3]

In determining the damage suffered in consequence of pollution for which operations have been or may be carried out under section 46, account must be taken of the extent to which it is shown that the damage has been reduced by such operations and of the extent to which it is shown that the damage is likely to be so reduced.[4]

Waste from vessels

Each water authority are required to arrange for collecting and disposing of waste from vessels in their area which need collecting in consequence of section 33 relating to the control of sanitary appliances on vessels, and also to arrange for providing facilities for the washing out of prescribed appliances[5] from vessels in their area.   A water authority may also arrange for the provision of facilities by way of water closets, urinals

---

[1] Control of Pollution Act, 1974, s. 46 (4).
[2] *Ibid.*, s. 46 (5).
[3] *Ibid.*, s. 46 (6).
[4] *Ibid.*, s. 46 (7).
[5] No regulations have yet been made as to appliances.

and wash basins for the use of persons from vessels in their area. A port health authority are empowered to make arrangements with a water authority for any of the above purposes.[1]

Excluding unregistered vessels from rivers

Where it appears to a water authority to be appropriate for preventing the pollution of streams in their area, the authority may make byelaws providing that vessels shall not be used on any such streams specified in the byelaws unless the vessels are registered by the authority in accordance with the byelaws or are exempted from registration. A person causing or knowingly permitting a vessel to be on a stream in contravention of such byelaws is guilty of an offence and liable on summary conviction to a fine not exceeding £50. The byelaws may authorise the authority to make reasonable charges for the registration of vessels and no charges shall be payable by persons in or from registered vessels for those persons using facilities provided under section 47 by or by arrangement with the authority.[2]

Deposits and vegetation in rivers, etc.

It is an offence for a person, except in the exercise of statutory powers relating to land drainage, flood prevention or navigation, without the consent of the water authority (which is not to be unreasonably withheld) to remove from any part of the channel or bed of a stream a deposit accumulated by reason of a dam, weir or sluice holding back the water of the stream and does so by causing the deposit to be carried away in suspension in the water of the stream. It is also an offence if, without the like consent, any substantial amount of vegetation cut or uprooted in a stream, or so near to the stream that it falls into it, is allowed to remain in the stream by the wilful default of a person. A person guilty of such an offence is liable on summary conviction to a fine not exceeding £200. Regulations[3] may provide that a reference to a stream shall be

---

[1] Control of Pollution Act, 1974, s. 47.
[2] *Ibid.*, s. 48.
[3] No regulations have yet been made.

construed as including a reference to such controlled waters as may be prescribed. Any question as to whether the consent of a water authority is unreasonably withheld is determined by the Secretary of State, and any consent given under section 4 of the former Rivers (Prevention of Pollution) Act, 1951, is to be treated as given under this provision.[1]

Pollution problems arising from mine closures

Each water authority may carry out studies for ascertaining what problems relating to the pollution of streams, controlled waters or specified underground water may arise or have arisen through the abandonment of any mine in their area or might arise if a mine were abandoned, and also what steps are likely to be appropriate for dealing with the problems and what the cost of taking such steps would be.[2]

Abstaining from agricultural practices

If a water authority are of opinion that a stream, controlled waters or specified underground water (a) have been or are likely to be polluted in consequence of an act of omission as first mentioned in section 31 (2) (c) of the Act which has occurred at a place in the authority area, or (b) are likely to be polluted if such an act or omission occurs at such a place, the authority may by making written application to the Secretary of State (specifying the kind of act or omission in question and reasons for the opinion), request him to serve a notice on the occupier of the place requesting the occupier to prevent acts or omissions of that kind at that place.[3] The authority must serve a copy of the application on the Minister of Agriculture, Fisheries and Food and on the occupier, and also serve on the occupier a statement that he may within twenty-eight days from the date of service of the statement make written representations to the Secretary of State about the application.[4]

---

1 Control of Pollution Act, 1974, s. 49.
2 *Ibid.*, s. 50.
3 *Ibid.*, s. 51 (1).
4 *Ibid.*, s. 51 (2).

When the Secretary of State has considered any representations made to him about the application, he shall serve on the occupier the notice requested by the application or a notice less restrictive than the request specified in the application or a notice stating that the application has been rejected. The Secretary of State shall also serve on the water authority a copy of the notice served on the occupier.[1] The Secretary of State is empowered to cancel a notice served on an occupier after giving notice of his proposal to do so to the water authority and considering any representations made by the authority.[2]

Charges for discharges

The Secretary of State may, by an order made after consultation with the National Water Council, provide that sections 30 and 31 of the Water Act, 1973 (relating to charges for facilities provided by water authorities and to schemes for payment of charges) shall apply to discharges of trade or sewage effluent made or authorised to be made under a consent given under the Act or the Public Health (Drainage of Trade Premises) Act, 1937.[3]

Discharges by water authorities

Part II of the Act has effect with modifications prescribed by regulations[4] in relation to discharges by a water authority in their area and such regulations may provide for consents required by water authorities for the purposes of Part II as modified to be or be deemed to be given by the Secretary of State.[5]

Legal proceedings

When an offence under the Act which has been committed by a body corporate is proved to have been committed with the consent or connivance of, or to be attributable to any neglect on the part of, a director, manager, secretary or other similar

---

1 Control of Pollution Act, 1974, s. 51 (3).
2 Ibid., s. 51 (5).
3 Control of Pollution Act, 1974, s. 52.   As to the provisions of an order, see ibid.
4 Regulations have not yet been made.
5 Control of Pollution Act, 1974, s. 55.

officer of the body corporate, or any person who was purporting to act in any such capacity, he as well as the body corporate shall be guilty of that offence and liable to be proceeded against and punished accordingly. Where the affairs of a body corporate are managed by its members the above provision applies in relation to the acts and defaults of a member in connection with his functions of management as if he were a director of the body corporate.[1]

Where the commission by any person of an offence under the Act is due to the default of some other person, that other person shall be guilty of the offence, and a person may be charged with and convicted of an offence by virtue of this provision.[2]

A magistrates' court in England and Wales may try an information for an offence under section 31 (1) of the Act or regulations or byelaws made under that section if the information is laid within one year from the commission of the offence.[3]

Rights of entry and inspection

A person authorised by a water authority in writing may at any reasonable time:—

(a) Enter upon any land or vessel[4] for the purpose of (i) performing any function[5] conferred on the authority or that person under the Act, or (ii) determining whether, and if so in what manner, such a function should be performed, or (iii) determining whether any provision of the Act or an instrument made under the Act is being complied with.

(b) Carry out such inspections, measurements and tests on the land or vessel or of any articles on it and take away such samples of the land or articles as he considers appropriate for such a purpose.[6]

---

[1] Control of Pollution Act, 1974, s. 87 (1).
[2] Ibid., s. 87 (2).
[3] Ibid., s. 87 (3).
[4] " Vessel " includes a hovercraft within the meaning of the Hovercraft Act, 1968 (Control of Pollution Act, 1974, s. 105 (1)).
[5] " Functions " includes powers and duties (ibid., s. 98).
[6] Ibid., s. 91 (1).

Where a justice of the peace is satisfied on sworn information in writing (a) that an authorised person has been refused admission to any land or vessel or that refusal is apprehended or that the land or vessel is unoccupied or that the occupier is temporarily absent or that the case is one of emergency or that an application for admission would defeat the object of the entry; and (b) that there is reasonable ground for entry upon the land or vessel for the purpose for which entry is required, the justice may by warrant under his hand authorise that person to enter the land or vessel, if need be by force.[1] But a justice must not issue a warrant unless he is satisfied (i) that admission to the land or vessel was sought after not less than seven days' notice of the intended entry has been served on the occupier; or (ii) that such admission was sought in an emergency and was refused by or on behalf of the occupier; or (iii) that the land or vessel is unoccupied; or (iv) that an application for admission would defeat the object of the entry.[2] A warrant issued continues in force until the purpose for which the entry is required has been satisfied.[3]

A person authorised to enter upon land or a vessel must, if so required, produce evidence of his authority before entering, and he may take with him such other persons and such equipment as may be necessary. Except in an emergency, or where the land or vessel is unoccupied, admission to land or a vessel used for residential purposes and admission to any other land or a vessel with heavy equipment cannot be demanded of right unless seven days' notice of intended entry has been served on the occupier. A person who enters land or a vessel which is unoccupied or of which the occupier is temporarily absent must leave the land or vessel effectually secured against trespassers as he found it.[4]

A water authority are obliged to make full compensation to any person who has sustained damage by reason of an authorised person exercising the powers conferred on him as above,

---

1 Control of Pollution Act, 1974, s. 91 (2).
2 *Ibid.*, s. 91 (3).
3 *Ibid.*, s. 91 (4).
4 *Ibid.*, s. 92 (1)-(4).

or an authorised person failing to perform the duty above to leave the land or vessel as effectually secured against trespassers as he found it, except where the damage is attributable to the default of the person who sustained it. Any dispute as to a person's entitlement to compensation or as to its amount is determined by arbitration.[1]

The wilful obstruction of a person acting in the exercise of his powers of entry renders the offender guilty of an offence and liable on summary conviction to a fine not exceeding £100.[2]

Any reference in the above provisions to an emergency is a reference to a case where a person requiring entry to land or a vessel has reasonable cause to believe that circumstances exist which are likely to endanger life or health and that immediate entry thereto is necessary to verify the existence of those circumstances or to ascertain their cause or to effect a remedy.[3]

Power to obtain information

A water authority may serve a notice on any person requiring him to furnish to them within a period or at times specified in the notice and in a form so specified, any information so specified which the authority reasonably consider they need for the purposes of any fuction conferred on them by the Act. Regulations[4] may provide for restricting the information which may be required and for determining the form in which the information is to be so required. A person who (a) fails without reasonable excuse to comply with the requirements of a notice served on him, or (b) in furnishing information in compliance with a notice, makes any statement, which he knows to be false in a material particular or recklessly makes a statement which is false in a material particular, is guilty of an offence and liable on summary conviction to a fine not exceeding £400.[5]

---

[1] Control of Pollution Act, 1974, s. 92 (5).
[2] Ibid., s. 92 (6).
[3] Ibid., s. 92 (7).
[4] Regulations have not yet been made.
[5] Control of Pollution Act, 1974, s. 93.

Prohibition of disclosure of information

A person who discloses information relating to any trade secret used in carrying on a particular undertaking and the information has been given to him or obtained by him under the Act is guilty of an offence and liable on summary conviction to a fine not exceeding £400, but he is not guilty of such offence if (a) the disclosure is made in the performance of his duty, or with the written consent of a person having a right to disclose the information, or (b) the information is of a kind prescribed for the purposes of this provision and if regulations[1] made for such purposes provide that information of that kind may only be disclosed in pursuance of the regulations to prescribed persons, the disclosure is to a prescribed person.[2]

A person who discloses any information (i) which has been furnished to or obtained by him in connection with an application for consent, or the imposition of conditions, under the former Rivers (Prevention of Pollution) Acts, 1951 or 1961 (including the variation of conditions, and references and applications to the Secretary of State); or (ii) which is derived from samples of effluents (but not samples of waters into which effluent is discharged) taken for the purposes of those Acts, is guilty of an offence, for which he is liable on summary conviction to a fine not exceeding £100 or to imprisonment for a term not exceeding three months or to both, unless the disclosure is made (a) with the consent of the person by whom the information was furnished or from whom it was obtained or, where information is derived from a sample of effluent, of the person making the discharge; or (b) in connection with the execution of those Acts or the Control of Pollution Act, 1974; or (c) for the purposes of any proceedings arising out of the former Acts of 1951 or 1961 (including references and applications to the Secretary of State) or of criminal proceedings whether so arising or not, or for the purpose of any report of any such proceedings.[3]

---

[1] Regulations have not yet been made.
[2] Control of Pollution Act, 1974, s. 94.
[3] Rivers (Prevention of Pollution) Act, 1961, s. 12; Control of Pollution Act, 1974, s. 108 (1), Sch. 3, para. 17.

Sampling and analysis of effluents

A water authority are entitled to obtain and take away samples of any effluent which is passing from any land[1] or vessel into (a) any inland water[2] in the water authority area; (b) any tidal water or part of the sea not comprised in the water authority area but adjoining the coast of that area; (c) any controlled waters[3] adjoining that area, or (d) any underground strata[4] in that area. The result of an analysis[5] of a sample is not admissible as evidence in any legal proceedings in respect of any effluent passing from any land or vessel unless the person taking the sample forthwith notifies to the occupier[6] of the land or the owner or master of the vessel his intention to have it analysed, and there and then divides the sample into three parts, causes each part to be placed in a container which must be sealed and marked and must (a) deliver one part to the occupier; (b) retain one part for future comparison; and (c) if he thinks fit to have an analysis made, submit one part to the analyst.[7] If it is not reasonably practicable for the person taking the sample forthwith to notify to the occupier of the land or the owner or master of the vessel his intention to have it analysed the matters specified in paragraphs (a) to (c) above must be done as soon as is reasonably practicable. A person who wilfully obstructs a person exercising a right of a water authority to obtain and take away samples is guilty of an offence and liable on summary conviction to a fine not exceeding £20.[8]

---

[1] " Land " includes land covered by water (Water Resources Act, 1963, s. 135 (1)).

[2] " Inland water " is defined in footnote 5 on p. 177.

[3] As to controlled waters, *see* footnote 3 on p. 309.

[4] " Underground strata " is defined in footnote 6 on p. 177.

[5] References to an analysis include references to any test of whatever kind and " analysed " and " analyst " are to be construed accordingly (Water Resources Act, 1963, s. 113 (6)).

[6] The occupier is the sewerage authority by whom the sewer is maintained in respect of an effluent passing from a sewer into any water (Water Resources Act, 1963, s. 113 (4)).

[7] It is open to the prosecution to prove pollution in any way they choose; they are not obliged to have samples analysed. *Trent River Board v. Wardle Ltd.*, [1957] Crim. L. R. 196.

[8] Water Resources Act, 1963, s. 113 (1)-(3), (5); Control of Pollution Act, 1974, s. 108 (1), Sch. 3, para. 21.

Samples of effluent

It shall be presumed in any legal proceedings, until the contrary is shown, that any sample of effluent taken at an inspection chamber, manhole or other place provided in compliance with a condition imposed under section 7 of the former Rivers (Prevention of Pollution) Act, 1951, or the former Rivers (Prevention of Pollution) Act 1961, or the Control of Pollution Act, 1974, in relation to any waters is a sample of what was passing from the land or premises to such waters.[1]

A water authority may agree with the occupier of land or premises from which effluent is discharged on the point or points at which the authority in exercise of their rights under section 113 of the Water Resources Act, 1963, or under any other enactment take samples of the effluent passing into any waters, and an agreement shall have effect in relation to the land or premises notwithstanding any change of occupation, but the water authority or occupier may at any time declare that it shall cease to have effect. In default of agreement, the water authority may apply to the Secretary of State, who may, after considering any representations made by the occupier and any other person who appears to the Secretary of State to be interested, fix the point at which samples are to be taken. The Secretary of State may on the application of the water authority or occupier review and vary his decision. In any legal proceedings it shall be presumed, until the contrary is shown, that any sample of effluent taken at a point fixed under the above provisions is a sample of what was passing from the land or premises to any waters.[2]

A water authority are required to maintain a register containing such particulars as the Secretary of State may direct[3] of sampling points fixed as above.[4]

---

[1] Rivers (Prevention of Pollution) Act, 1961, s. 10 (1); Control of Pollution Act, 1974, s. 108 (1), Sch. 3, para. 17.

[2] Rivers (Prevention of Pollution) Act, 1961, s. 10 (2)-(4).

[3] See the Rivers Pollution (Register of Sampling Points) Directions, 1962.

[4] Rivers (Prevention of Pollution) Act, 1961, s. 10 (5).

Special measures for securing proper use of water resources

Any reference in the Water Resources Act, 1963, to action for the purpose of securing the proper use of water resources is (without prejudice to the generality thereof) taken to include action of any description to which this provision applies for the purpose of rendering the quality of the water contained in an inland water more suitable for a particular use for which the water is required. This provision applies (a) to the making and (on the part of the water authority) the performance of an agreement between a water authority and a sewerage authority whereby, in consideration of payments by the water authority, the sewerage authority will secure the removal to a different point, or other alteration, of an outlet from which sewage effluent (within the meaning of Part II of the Control of Pollution Act, 1974) is discharged by the sewerage authority into an inland water in the water authority area; (b) to the carrying out by a water authority of any operations, other than engineering or building operations,[1] which are excepted from this provision by directions given by the Secretary of State either to water authorities generally or to a particular water authority.[2]

Acquisition of land for protection of water against pollution

The purposes for which a water authority may acquire land[3] by agreement or compulsorily under section 65 of the Water Resources Act, 1963, in connection with the performance of any of their functions include land which the water authority require for the purpose of protecting against pollution water in (a) a reservoir owned or operated by the water authority or proposed to be acquired or constructed by them for the purpose of its being operated by them, or (b) underground strata in

---

[1] " Engineering or building operations " (without prejudice to the generality of that expression) includes the construction, alteration, improvement or maintenance or the closure or removal of any reservoir, watercourse, dam, weir, well, borehole or other works, the construction, alteration, improvement, maintenance or demolition of any building or structure, and the installation, modification or removal of any machinery or apparatus (Water Resources Act, 1963, s. 135 (1)).

[2] *Ibid.*, s. 77; Control of Pollution Act, 1974, s. 108 (1), Sch. 3, para. 20.

[3] " Land " includes any interest in or right over land (Water Resources Act, 1963, s. 68 (3)).

their area from which the water authority are for the time being authorised to abstract water in pursuance of a licence granted or deemed to be granted under the Act of 1963.[1]

INDUSTRIAL AND MISCELLANEOUS POLLUTION

Apart from the Control of Pollution Act, 1974, it is an offence under a variety of unrelated statutes for specified trade wastes or particular polluting substances to be discharged or put into watercourses and other waters.

Gas waste

Persons engaged in the manufacture of gas are liable to a penalty of £200 and to a further daily penalty of £20 if they cause or suffer any washing or other substance produced in making or supplying gas to be brought or to flow into a stream, reservoir, aqueduct, pond or place for water, or into a drain or pipe communicating therewith, or if they wilfully do any act connected with the making or supplying of gas whereby the water in any such stream, aqueduct, etc., is fouled.[2]

Where gas which is stored underground pursuant to Part II of the Gas Act, 1965, pollutes any water or interferes with the flow of any water, or displaces water located in or percolating through an underground stratum, and as a result a person is prevented from effectively exercising or enjoying a protected right[3] which was exercisable at the time when the storage authorisation order came into force, the gas authority operating the underground gas storage are obliged to pay compensation or take other steps, such as cleanse the supply of water or provide an alternative supply of water. This provision is without prejudice to the liability of a gas authority in criminal proceedings under Part XIV of Schedule 3 to the Water Act, 1945.[4] Sections 71 and 72 of that Schedule provide penalties

---

[1] Water Resources Act, 1963, s. 68 (1). As to the application of s. 22 (2)-(4) of the Water Act, 1945, as amended by the Water Act, 1973, s. 40 (2), Sch. 8, para. 51, to Water Resources Act, 1963, s. 68, see s. 68 (2).
[2] Public Health Act, 1875, s. 68.
[3] As to protected rights, see p. 190.
[4] Gas Act, 1965, s. 15.

where water supplies, waterworks or water belonging to water undertakers are fouled by washing or other liquid produced in or resulting from the manufacture or supply of gas or the treatment of any residual products of the manufacture of gas.

Protection of water supplies

The Water Act, 1945, contains provisions for protecting water supplies against pollution. Water authorities and other statutory water undertakers are empowered (a) to enter into agreements with landowners or local authorities with a view to draining land or for more effectually collecting, conveying or preserving the purity of water which the undertakers are authorised to take[1]; and (b) to acquire land and execute works thereon, for the purpose of protecting against pollution any surface or underground water belonging to the undertakers or which they are authorised to take.[2] It is an offence to pollute water from a spring, well, borehole or adit which is used or likely to be used for human consumption or domestic purposes, or for manufacturing food or drink for human consumption.[3] Where water from a well, tank or other source of supply which is used or likely to be used for such purposes, is or is likely to become so polluted as to be prejudicial to health, a local authority may take steps to have the source of supply cut off or the use of the water restricted.[4]

Protection of fish and fisheries

It is an offence for a person to cause or knowingly permit to flow, or put or knowingly permit to be put, into any waters containing fish, or into any tributaries thereof, any liquid or solid matter to such an extent as to cause the waters to be poisonous or injurious to fish or the spawning grounds, spawn or food of fish. Proceedings may only be instituted by a water authority or by a person who has a certificate from the

---

[1] Water Act, 1945, s. 15; Water Act, 1973, s. 40, Sch. 8, para. 49, Sch. 9.

[2] Water Act, 1945, s. 22; Water Act, 1973, s. 40 (2), para. 51.

[3] Water Act, 1945, s. 21; Control of Pollution Act, 1974, s. 99, Sch. 2, para. 16.

[4] Public Health Act, 1936, s. 140.

Minister of Agriculture, Fisheries and Food that he has a material interest in the waters alleged to be affected.[1]

It is also an offence for a person to use in or near any waters (including waters adjoining the coast of England and Wales and within the exclusive fishery limits[2] of the British Islands) any explosive substance, any poison or other noxious substance, or any electrical device, with intent thereby to take or destroy fish. This provision does not, however, apply to the use of any substance or device for a scientific purpose, or for the purposes of protecting, improving or replacing stocks of fish, and with the written permission of the water authority; but such permission must not be given by the water authority as respects the use of a noxious substance otherwise than with the approval of the Minister of Agriculture, Fisheries and Food.[3]

The purposes for which byelaws may be made by a water authority under Schedule 3, Part II, para. 31 of the Salmon and Freshwater Fisheries Act, 1975, include the regulation of the deposit or discharge in any waters containing fish of any liquid or solid matter as specified in the byelaws detrimental to salmon, trout or freshwater fish, or the spawn or food of fish.[4]

In relation to oyster, mussel or cockle fisheries it is an offence knowingly to deposit any ballast, rubbish or other substance within the limits of the several fishery or private bed.[5]

---

[1] Salmon and Freshwater Fisheries Act, 1975, s. 4. As to the protection afforded in respect of an offence under s. 4, *see* s. 54 of the Control of Pollution Act, 1974. As to radioactivity, *see* p. 346.

[2] As to exclusive fishery limits, *see* p. 20.

[3] Salmon and Freshwater Fisheries Act, 1975, s. 5.

[4] As to radioactivity in relation to Sch. 3, Pt. II, para. 31 of the Salmon and Freshwater Fisheries Act, 1975, *see* p. 346.

[5] Sea Fisheries (Shellfish) Act, 1967, s .7 (4) (c).

Radioactive waste

Subject to any particular descriptions of radioactive waste[1] which may be excluded by order of the Secretary of State for the Environment, any radioactive waste on or from premises used for the purposes of any undertaking,[2] or arising from mobile radioactive apparatus, shall only be disposed[3] of in accordance with an authorisation granted by the Secretary of State. In particular, the disposal of radioactive waste on or from premises used by the Atomic Energy Authority[4] for the purposes of their undertaking, or on or from premises on a site licensed under the Nuclear Installations Acts, 1965 and 1969, must be authorised by both the Secretary of State and the Minister of Agriculture, Fisheries and Food.[5]

The Secretary of State is empowered to provide or arrange adequate facilities for the safe disposal or accumulation of radioactive waste, and no account must be taken of any radioactivity possessed by any substance[6] or article[7] or by any part of any premises in the exercise, performance or enforcement of certain specified enactments.[8] This prohibition is also applied to any local enactment (*a*) which prohibits or restricts the

---

[1] As to definition of " radioactive waste ", *see* ss. 18 (4) and 19 (1) of the Radioactive Substances Act, 1960.

[2] " Undertaking " includes any trade, business or profession and, in relation to a public or local authority, includes any of the powers or duties of that authority (Radioactive Substances Act, 1960, s. 19 (1)).

[3] Disposal in relation to waste includes the discharge thereof into water (Radioactive Substances Act, 1960, s. 19 (1)).

[4] *See* the Atomic Energy Authority Acts, 1954, 1959 and 1971.

[5] Radioactive Substances Act, 1960, ss. 6, 8.

[6] " Substance " means any natural or artificial substance, whether in solid or liquid form or in the form of a gas or vapour (Radioactive Substances Act, 1960, s. 19 (1)).

[7] " Article " includes a part of an article (*ibid.*, s. 19 (1)).

[8] The enactments in question include s. 2 of the Sea Fisheries Regulation Act, 1888 (now replaced by s. 5 of the Sea Fisheries Regulation Act, 1966), s. 4 and Sch. 3, Pt. II, para. 31 of the Salmon and Freshwater Fisheries Act, 1975, ss. 27, 39, 48, 81, 82, 92, 108 (2), 141, 259 and 261 of the Public Health Act, 1936, the Public Health (Drainage of Trade Premises) Act, 1937, ss. 17 and 21 of the Water Act, 1945, (Radioactive Substances Act, 1960, s. 9 (1)), Sch. 1, Part I; London Government Act, 1963, s. 93 (1), Sch. 18, Part II; Control of Pollution Act, 1974, s. 108 (2), Sch. 4.

disposal or accumulation of waste[1] or of any substances being
a nuisance or prejudicial to health, noxious or polluting, or
(b) which confers or imposes a power or duty on any local
authority, water authority, local fisheries committee, statutory
water undertakers or other public or local authority, or their
officers, to take any action (whether by way of legal proceedings
or otherwise) for preventing, restricting or abating such dis-
posals or accumulations as are mentioned in paragraph (a)
above.   But the Ministers must consult with such authorities in
appropriate cases before granting an authorisation.[2]

Pollution of harbours

It is forbidden under penalty to cast, throw, empty or
unload ballast, stone, slate, gravel, earth, rubbish, wreck or
filth into ports, harbours, havens or navigable rivers from
ships or the shore,[3] or to throw or put ballast, earth, ashes,
stones or other thing into a dock or harbour.[4]

Offensive matter from cemeteries

It is an offence subject to a penalty of £50 for a company or
local authority providing a cemetery under powers which
incorporate the Cemeteries Clauses Act, 1847, to cause or
suffer to be brought or to flow into a stream, canal, reservoir,
aqueduct, pond or watering place, any offensive matter from
a cemetery whereby the water therein is fouled.[5]

Diseased animal carcasses

It is an offence to throw or place, or cause or suffer to be
thrown or placed, into or in a river, stream, canal, navigation

---

[1] " Waste " includes any substance which constitutes scrap material or an
effluent or other unwanted surplus substance arising from the application of
any process, and also includes any substance or article which requires to be
disposed of as being broken, worn out, contaminated or otherwise spoilt (Radioactive Substances Act, 1960, s. 19 (1)).   Any substance or article which, in the
course of the carrying on of any undertaking, is discharged, discarded or otherwise dealt with as if it were waste shall, for the purposes of the Act, be presumed
to be waste unless the contrary is proved (Radioactive Substances Act, 1960,
s. 19 (3)).
[2] *Ibid.*, ss. 8, 9, 10.
[3] Harbours Act, 1814, s. 11.
[4] Harbours, Docks and Piers Clauses Act, 1847, s. 73.
[5] Cemeteries Clauses Act, 1847, s. 20.

or other water, or into or in the sea within three miles of the shore, the carcass of an animal which has died of disease, or been slaughtered as diseased or suspected.[1]

SEWAGE DISPOSAL AND POLLUTION

A good deal of the law on pollution has been concerned with the exercise by local authorities of their public health functions relating to sewage disposal, which functions were transferred to water authorities as from 1st April, 1974, pursuant to the Water Act, 1973, and the following paragraphs must now be construed accordingly.

A local authority could not set up a prescriptive right to discharge the drainage of a whole town into a river, based on the previous practice of a few houses in the town draining to the river.[2]   The fact that a vast population would suffer if the town remained undrained and unless the plaintiff's rights were invaded, is one which the courts could not take into consideration.[3]   In the absence of a prescriptive or other right to do so, a local authority cannot discharge sewage into a brook or a drain.[4]   A local authority have no right at common law, prescription or under the Public Health Acts to discharge sewage into the sea so as to cause a nuisance, by killing fish or damaging oyster beds, and an injunction will be granted to restrain them.[5]   A right cannot be set up either by prescription or under the doctrine of lost grant to cause sewage or trade refuse to fall or flow into a stream and thereby to pollute it, where the right claimed would be in contravention of a statutory prohibition.[6]

---

[1] Diseases of Animals Act, 1950, s. 78 (1) (vii).

[2] *A.-G. v. Luton L.B.* (1856), 20 J.P. 163.

[3] *A.-G. v. Birmingham Corpn.* (1858), 4 K. & J. 528.

[4] *Metropolitan Board of Works v. London & N.W. Ry. Co.* (1881), 17 Ch. D. 246.

[5] *Foster v. Warblington U.D.C.*, [1906] 1 K.B. 648; *Hobart v. Southend Corpn.*, [1906] 75 L.J.K.B. 305; *Owen v. Faversham Corpn.* (1908), 73 J.P. 33.

[6] *Green v. Matthews* (1930), 46 T.L.R. 206; *Butterworth v. West Riding of Yorkshire Rivers Board*, [1909] A.C. 45: *Hulley v. Silversprings Bleaching Co.*, [1922] 2 Ch. 268.

A duty was up to 1st April, 1974, imposed upon local authorities under the Public Health Act, 1936, to provide public sewers as may be necessary for effectually draining their districts and to deal effectually with the contents of their sewers by means of disposal works or otherwise, and they were empowered to provide sewage disposal works and to construct and maintain public sewers. Sewage for this purpose includes both foul water drainage and surface water drainage, but not trade effluents.[1] The final sewage effluent may be discharged to a stream, after it has been so treated at a sewage works as not prejudicially to affect the purity and quality of the water in the stream.[2] The mere existence of a right in one riparian owner to discharge effluent does not create a right in the others to its continued discharge.[3]

In discharging their functions of sewage disposal a local authority must not create a nuisance,[4] and if negligence is proved on the part of the local authority an injured party has a right of action.[5] If, however, the injury is due to the local authority failing or omitting to improve their drainage system or to enlarge sewers in order to cope with an expanding population and flooding thereby results, there is no right of action,[6] but a remedy might be available by complaint to the Minister of Housing and Local Government,[7] together with a claim for compensation under section 322 of the Public Health

[1] As to which, *see* the Public Health (Drainage of Trade Premises) Act, 1937, as amended by the Public Health Act, 1961, Part V, s. 86, Sch. 5.

[2] Public Health Act, 1936, s. 30; *Durrent v. Branksome U.D.C.*, [1897] 2 Ch. 291; *see also Dell v. Chesham U.D.C.* (1921), 85 J.P. 186; *A.-G. v. Ringwood R.D.C.* (1928), 92 J.P. 65; *A.-.G v. Cockermouth L.B.* (1874), 38 J.P. 660.

[3] *Deed (John S.) & Sons v. British Electricity Authority & Croydon Corpn.* (1950), 114 J.P. 533.

[4] Public Health Act, 1936, s. 31.

[5] *Smith v. King's Norton R.D.C.* (1896), 60 J.P. 520; *Lambert v. Lowestoft Corpn.* (1901), 65 J.P. 326; *Hawthorn Corpn. v. Kannuluik* (1906), 93 L.T. 644; *Smeaton v. Ilford Corpn.*, [1954] 1 All E.R. 923.

[6] *Glossop v. Heston & Isleworth L.B.* (1879), 44 J.P. 36; *A.-G. v. Dorking Union* (1882), 46 J.P. 573; *Robinson v. Workington Corpn.* (1897), 61 J.P. 164; *Pride of Derby Angling Assocn. Ltd v. British Celanese Ltd*, [1953] 1 All E.R. 174.

[7] *Vide* s. 278 of the Public Health Act, 1936, *see also Stainton v. Woolrych* (1857), 21 J.P. 180; *R. v. Darlington L.B.* (1865), 29 J.P. 419; *London General Omnibus Co. Ltd. v. Tilbury Contracting Co.* (1907), 71 J.P. 534.

Act, 1936.[1] A local authority who discharge sewage matter into a stream by means of a sewer constructed by and vested in them are under the same liability as a private person for allowing the stream to become polluted by the escape of sewage and will be restrained by injunction from discharging sewage and liable to damages.[2]

---

[1] *Hesketh v. Birmingham Corpn.* (1924), 88 J.P. 77; *Dent v. Bournemouth Corpn.* (1897) 66 L.J.Q.B. 395.

[2] *Haigh v. Deudraeth R.D.C.*, [1945] 2 All E.R. 661; *Jones v. Llanrwst U.D.C.*, [1911] 1 Ch. 393.

INDEX

A

C

M

N

O

P

T

U

V

W